TARGET
HONG KONG

OPERATION GRATITUDE

OSPREY
PUBLISHING

TARGET
HONG KONG

A TRUE STORY OF U.S. NAVY PILOTS AT WAR

OPERATION GRATITUDE

STEVEN K. BAILEY

OSPREY PUBLISHING
Bloomsbury Publishing Plc
Kemp House, Chawley Park, Cumnor Hill, Oxford OX2 9PH, UK
29 Earlsfort Terrace, Dublin 2, Ireland
1385 Broadway, 5th Floor, New York, NY 10018, USA
E-mail: info@ospreypublishing.com
www.ospreypublishing.com

OSPREY is a trademark of Osprey Publishing Ltd

First published in Great Britain in 2024

ISBN: HB 9781472860101; PB 9781472860095; eBook 9781472860088; ePDF 9781472860132;
XML 9781472860125; Audio 9781472860118

24 25 26 27 28   10 9 8 7 6 5 4 3 2 1

Image captions and credit lines are given in full in the List of Illustrations (pp. 10–11).

Maps by www.bounford.com
Index by Alan Rutter

Typeset by Deanta Global Publishing Services, Chennai, India
Printed and bound in Great Britain by CPI (Group) UK Ltd, Croydon CR0 4YY

Contents

Acronyms

ACA – aircraft action report
ACI – air combat intelligence
AGAS – Air Ground Aid Section
AGRS – American Graves Registration Service
AGRS-CZ – American Graves Registration Service-China Zone
AMM3c – aviation machinist's mate third class
AOM1c – aviation ordnance man first class
AOM2c – aviation ordnance man second class
AOs – fast oilers
ARM3c – aviation radio man third class
BAAG – British Army Aid Group
BMA – British Military Administration
CAP – combat air patrol
CAVU – clear and visibility unlimited
CQTU – carrier qualification training unit
CTSD – China Theater Search Detachment
CV – aircraft carrier (fleet)
CVG – carrier air group (fleet carrier)
CVGN – carrier air group (night capable, fleet carrier)
CVL – light aircraft carrier
CVLG – carrier air group (light carrier)
CVLGN – carrier air group (night capable, light carrier)
FAW – fleet air wing
FDO – fighter director officer
FS – fighter squadron (USAAF)
GP – general purpose (bomb)

HKKIB – Hong Kong and Kowloon Independent Brigade
HKVDC – Hong Kong Volunteer Defense Corps
IJA – Imperial Japanese Army
IJN – Imperial Japanese Navy
IJNS – Imperial Japanese Navy ship
JAAF – Japanese Army Air Force
j.g. – junior grade (rank)
LST – landing ship tank
MIA – missing in action
M¥ – military yen
NAS – naval air station
NATC – naval air training center
ONI – Office of Naval Intelligence
OQMG – Office of the Quartermaster General
OSS – Office of Strategic Services
PPC – patrol plane commander
PSP – pierced-steel planks
RAF – Royal Air Force
RAMP – recovered Allied military personnel
S2c – seaman second class
TF – task force
TG – task group
TRS – tactical reconnaissance squadron
USAAF – United States Army Air Forces
USS – United States ship
VB – dive-bombing squadron
VBF – fighter-bomber squadron
VC – composite air squadron
VF – fighter squadron
VH – rescue squadron
VMF – fighter squadron (U.S. Marine Corps)
VPB – patrol-bombing squadron
VSB – scount-bombing squadron
VT – torpedo-bomber squadron
VT – variable time (bomb fuze)

Place Names

This book refers to cities, provinces, and other geographical landmarks by the placenames commonly used by U.S. Navy personnel in 1945. Present-day placenames are provided here in parentheses.

Amoy (Xiamen)
Canton (Guangzhou)
Cap St. Jacques (Vũng Tàu)
Chungking (Chongqing)
Chungshan (Zhongshan)
Chusan Archipelago (Zhoushan Archipelago)
Formosa (Taiwan)
Kiirun (Keelung)
Kwangtung (Guangdong)
Nanking (Nanjing)
Peking (Beijing)
Pescadores (Penghu Islands)
Sanchau (Shang Chuan)
Shum Chum River (Shenzhen River)
Suchow (Xuzhou)
Swatow (Shantou)
Takao (Kaohsiung)
Tientsin (Tianjin)
Tourane Bay (Đà Nẵng)

List of Illustrations

F4U-1D Corsairs and TBM Avengers on the flight deck of the USS *Essex* during Operation *Gratitude*. (Naval History and Heritage Command)

U.S. Navy PB4Y-1 patrol bomber similar to the aircraft flown by Lt. Paul F. Stevens over Hong Kong and Macau. (Naval History and Heritage Command)

1st Lt. John F. Egan (back row, sixth from right) with fellow pilots of the 118th Tactical Reconnaissance Squadron in October 1944, some two months before he was shot down over Hong Kong. (USAAF)

1st Lt. Egan flew a P-51B-7 nicknamed *Lady Jane* on the day he had to bail out over Hong Kong. *Lady Jane* had been transferred to the 118th Tactical Reconnaissance Squadron at the very end of 1944, but still wore the markings of the 26th Fighter Squadron when it was shot down. (Shirley Moyle, courtesy of Chris Davis)

Pilots in their ready room aboard the USS *Hornet* study chalkboard map of targets at Hong Kong in preparation for airstrikes flown on January 16, 1945. The white square on the map (above the pointed finger of the pilot on the left) marks the Sham Shui Po POW camp. Pilots on the right are wearing the China-Burma-India shoulder patches issued to naval aviators for Operation *Gratitude*. (Naval History and Heritage Command)

Carrier planes from TF 38 bomb and strafe the Tai Koo dockyards on Hong Kong Island, January 16, 1945. (Photo by US Navy/Interim Archives/Getty Images)

Photo taken by the rear-facing radioman-gunner in a Helldiver shows near misses exploding in the water off the Tai Koo dockyard, with the aircraft's right horizontal stabilizer in the foreground. (Photo © CORBIS via Getty Images)

Japanese tankers and escort vessels under attack in Victoria Harbor on January 16, 1945. Kennedy Town on Hong Kong Island can be seen in the background. (Photo by US Navy/Interim Archives/Getty Images)

Ray Jones raises the Union Jack during the flag-raising ceremony at the Stanley camp that marked the liberation of Hong Kong in September 1945. (Photo by: Pictures From History/Universal Images Group via Getty Images)

A bomb – likely a 1,000-pounder dropped by a Helldiver – explodes alongside the *Kamoi* in Victoria Harbor. The warship in the foreground is possibly the *Hasu*, which sustained significant damage during the raids on Hong Kong. (Photo by US Navy/Interim Archives/Getty Images)

The Pan American Airways station at Macau, which was strafed by U.S. Navy fighter aircraft on January 16, 1945. (Pan American World Airways Records, Special Collections, University of Miami Libraries)

The author at the wreck site of Lt. Hunt's TBM Avenger in 2019, holding a fragment of the aircraft wing or fuselage. (Author)

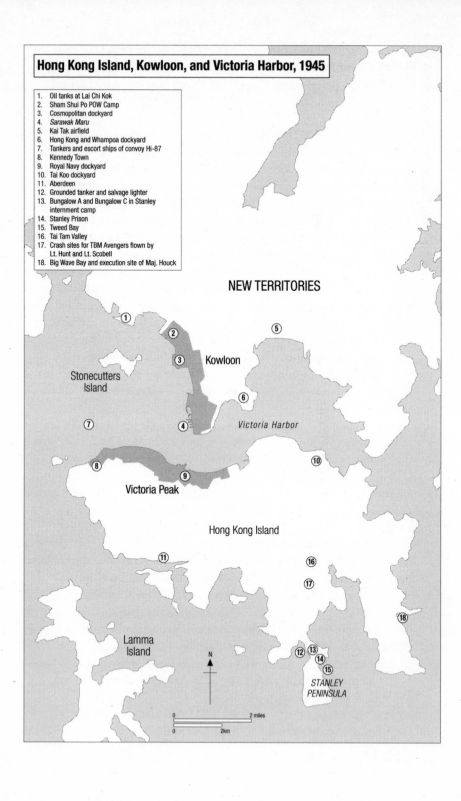

Hong Kong Island, Kowloon, and Victoria Harbor, 1945

1. Oil tanks at Lai Chi Kok
2. Sham Shui Po POW Camp
3. Cosmopolitan dockyard
4. *Sarawak Maru*
5. Kai Tak airfield
6. Hong Kong and Whampoa dockyard
7. Tankers and escort ships of convoy Hi-87
8. Kennedy Town
9. Royal Navy dockyard
10. Tai Koo dockyard
11. Aberdeen
12. Grounded tanker and salvage lighter
13. Bungalow A and Bungalow C in Stanley
    internment camp
14. Stanley Prison
15. Tweed Bay
16. Tai Tam Valley
17. Crash sites for TBM Avengers flown by
    Lt. Hunt and Lt. Scobell
18. Big Wave Bay and execution site of Maj. Houck

NEW TERRITORIES

Kowloon

Stonecutters
Island

Victoria Harbor

Victoria Peak

Hong Kong Island

Lamma
Island

N

STANLEY
PENINSULA

0   2 miles

0   2km

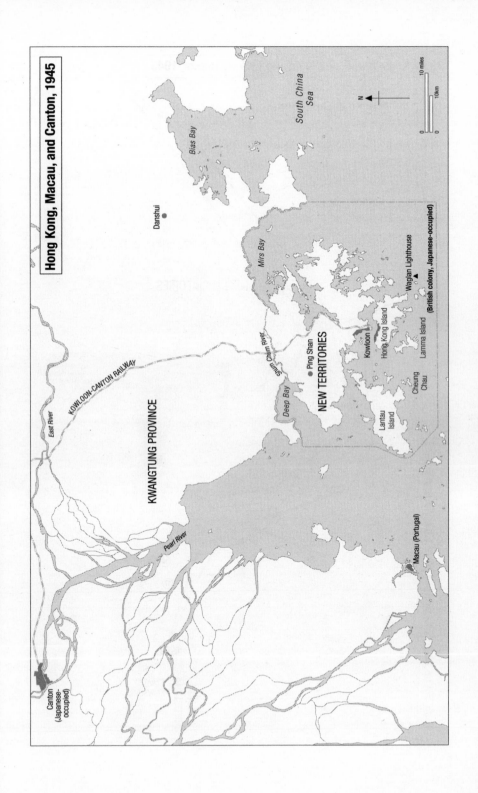

Hong Kong, Macau, and Canton, 1945

KWANGTUNG PROVINCE

East River

KOWLOON-CANTON RAILWAY

Canton (Japanese-occupied)

Pearl River

Shum Chun River

Deep Bay

Danshui

Mirs Bay

Bias Bay

South China Sea

Ping Shan

NEW TERRITORIES

Lantau Island

Cheung Chau

Kowloon

Hong Kong Island

Lamma Island

Waglan Lighthouse

(British colony, Japanese-occupied)

Macau (Portugal)

N

0   10 miles
0   10km

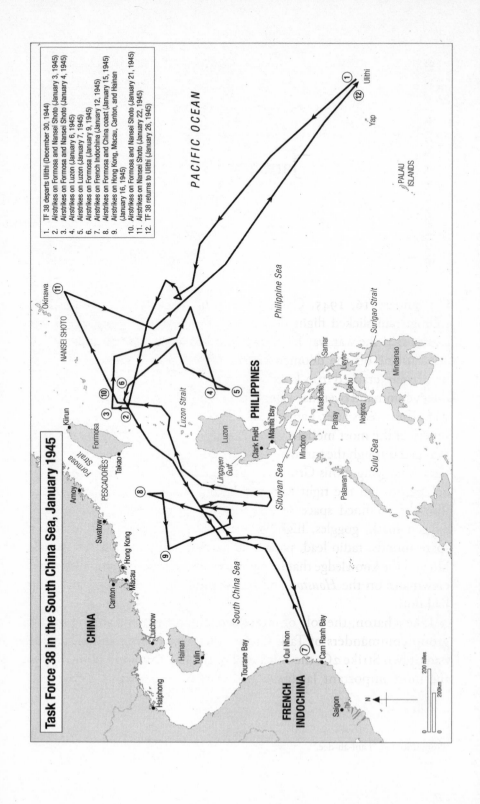

Task Force 38 in the South China Sea, January 1945

1. TF 38 departs Ulithi (December 30, 1944)
2. Airstrikes on Formosa and Nansei Shoto (January 3, 1945)
3. Airstrikes on Formosa and Nansei Shoto (January 4, 1945)
4. Airstrikes on Luzon (January 6, 1945)
5. Airstrikes on Luzon (January 7, 1945)
6. Airstrikes on Formosa (January 9, 1945)
7. Airstrikes on French Indochina (January 12, 1945)
8. Airstrikes on Formosa and China coast (January 15, 1945)
9. Airstrikes on Hong Kong, Macau, Canton, and Hainan (January 16, 1945)
10. Airstrikes on Formosa and Nansei Shoto (January 21, 1945)
11. Airstrikes on Nansei Shoto (January 22, 1945)
12. TF 38 returns to Ulithi (January 26, 1945)

PACIFIC OCEAN

Ulithi

Yap

PALAU ISLANDS

Philippine Sea

Surigao Strait

Samar

Leyte

Mindanao

Okinawa

NANSEI SHOTO

Cebu

Masbate

Panay

Negros

PHILIPPINES

Luzon Strait

Luzon

Manila Bay

Clark Field

Mindoro

Sibuyan Sea

Palawan

Sulu Sea

Kiirun

Formosa

PESCADORES

Takao

Formosa Strait

Lingayen Gulf

Amoy

Swatow

Canton

Hong Kong

Macau

Luichow

CHINA

Hainan

Yulin

Haiphong

Tourane Bay

Qui Nhon

Cam Ranh Bay

South China Sea

FRENCH INDOCHINA

Saigon

N

200 miles

200km

I

January 1945

On January 16, 1945, Commander John D. Lamade* stood on the rolling, rain-slicked flight deck of the fleet carrier USS *Hancock*. He had started the war way back in December 1941 as a lieutenant flying a floatplane off the doomed cruiser USS *Houston*. His little biplane had barely cracked 100 knots (115mph) at full throttle, and he had direct command over just a single man – his observer-gunner in the rear seat. Three years later, Lamade led CVG-7, an air group equipped with ninety of the most modern naval aircraft in the world.[1] As the *Hancock* plunged through the turbulent South China Sea, he clambered onto the navy-blue wing of his Grumman F6F-5 Hellcat, which bore the name "T. Benny" on the right engine cowling.[2] Lamade shimmied himself into the confined space of the cockpit, burdened with chartboard, oxygen mask, goggles, flight helmet, flashlight, Mae West, revolver, spare rounds, radio lead, parachute harness and pack, life raft, jungle kit, and the knowledge that he had survived when so many of his former crewmates on the *Houston* and fellow pilots in the *Hancock* air group had not.

Like a baton, the role of target coordinator rotated among the air group commanders of Task Group 38.2, and Commander Lamade had drawn Strike 2C, the third raid of the day to pound Hong Kong, the most important Japanese-held port on the south China coast.

---

*Pronounced as "Lam-ah-dee."

As target coordinator, he would lead some eighty aircraft from the air groups of TG 38.2, which included the *Hancock* as well as the carriers *Hornet* and *Lexington*. A full deck load – navy speak for the maximum number of combat-loaded aircraft that could be arranged on deck for launch at any one time – had been assembled on the stern of the *Hancock* in preparation for Strike 2C. Packed together with wings folded to save space, the dense tangle of aircraft included warplanes from all three of the squadrons that collectively comprised CVG-7.[3]

Strike 2C had been preceded by a morning fighter sweep and Strike 2A and 2B, so named because they were the first and second strike of the day flown by TG 38.2. Strike 2C in turn would be followed by Strike 2D in the late afternoon. In Commander Lamade's opinion, however, sending in a series of smaller strikes throughout the day amounted to tactical incompetence. Strike 2C should have involved the majority of the task group's aircraft, Lamade believed, particularly since pilots who had flown strikes against Hong Kong earlier that day had reported intense antiaircraft fire. Experience had shown him that repeated strikes by understrength formations inflicted less damage on the target while providing the enemy with more opportunities to shoot down planes. Far better to send in one or two all-out strikes, overwhelm the enemy, and sledgehammer the target. Half-strength efforts like Strike 2C could still inflict considerable pain on the enemy, but Lamade believed the cost in aircraft could border on the unsustainable when going up against a heavily defended harbor like Hong Kong.[4]

Commander Lamade and his wingman enjoyed the lead position in the launch order since they would be going to Hong Kong with guns only. Unburdened by the weight of bombs and rockets, Lamade would need less deck space to get his F6 aloft, though the stretch of open deck from the blunt nose of his Hellcat to the bow of the *Hancock* still left little margin for error. Unassisted by the catapult, he would be taking off under his own power from a stubby runway that was rolling and plunging with the waves of the South China Sea. As per standard procedure, the plane handlers had positioned or "spotted" the heaviest and slowest aircraft at the very back of the launch order by the stern, so that by the time the pilots spooled up their engines the more lightly loaded planes would have already launched, and they would have the longest possible stretch of flight deck to get airborne. To assist the launch operations, the "Big John" would steam into the wind to create additional lift while a lifeguard destroyer stood by to retrieve any aviators who went over the bow and into the water.

In the cockpit of number 124, Lieutenant Junior Grade (j.g.) Richard L. Hunt of Kansas City watched as Commander Lamade and the other Hellcat pilots launched at a rapid clip into overcast skies opaque with drizzle. Like every other pilot in Torpedo Squadron Seven (VT-7), the twenty-three-year-old Hunt had endured miserable flying weather ever since the *Hancock* had entered the South China Sea, and what he saw as he waited for launch confirmed what he had heard during the briefing in the ready room. He would have to punch through bands of turbulence and rain during the run to Hong Kong, with poor visibility and clouds pressing down so low they nearly kissed the waves. Hunt anticipated more instrument flying, which made for a particularly fatiguing day in the cockpit even without factoring in the stress of combat. Two weeks of flying strikes against Formosa, Luzon, and Indochina had exhausted everyone in the air group, which had lost a number of men and machines, including the commander of the *Hancock*'s fighter squadron, VF-7. Hunt himself had nearly been downed during a hairy mission to Formosa on January 3 and had returned to the *Hancock* with two bleeding crewmen in the shredded rear section of his TBM-3 Avenger.[5]

Like all aircraft in the three squadrons of CVG-7, the Avenger piloted by Lieutenant Hunt sported a white horseshoe emblem on the vertical stabilizer, painted with the open end up to catch some good luck. In the same way that a ranch's unique brand identified its cattle, the horseshoe functioned as a simple way to identify aircraft from the *Hancock*. Other air groups had their own distinctive tail codes, which ranged from simple triangles to more complex checkerboard patterns, and pilots learned to memorize the symbols so they could instantly discern a plane's air group and carrier. Tail codes became an integral part of a unit's identity, and many pilots based their individual squadron emblems on these simple white-on-blue tail symbols. The patches worn by members of Hunt's squadron displayed a torpedo flying through the ends of an upturned horseshoe, though VT-7 dropped far more eggs than it did fish. In the capacious bomb bay of his TBM, in fact, Hunt carried the heaviest bomb available to naval air groups – the

2,000-pound AN-M66, a weapon too bulky for the Helldiver and too heavy for the Hellcat. In early December, Hunt had scored a direct hit on the *T-106* with one of these blockbusters, which had blown the 950-ton landing ship tank (LST) apart. Hunt hoped to repeat this trick at Hong Kong, and so did his crew.[6]

Unlike the Hellcat pilots, who flew alone, and the dive-bomber pilots, who flew with a gunner, the torpedo pilots could genuinely be said to fly with a crew, as each Avenger carried a turret gunner and a radioman-gunner in addition to the pilot. Hunt's new turret gunner, Louis W. Gahran, Aviation Ordnance Man Second Class (AOM2c), folded himself into a rotating glass bubble with a .50-caliber machine gun and an ammunition can holding 200 rounds of 12.7mm ammunition. Eugene W. Barrow, Aviation Radio Man Third Class (ARM3c), sat below the turret and aft of the bomb bay, ensconced deep in the innards of the aircraft in a compartment known as the "tunnel" with a rearward-facing .30-caliber machine gun and an array of radar and communications gear. Barrow sat on his bulky parachute pack just like Lieutenant Hunt, but Gahran could not wear a parachute in the cramped turret, so his pack hung from a hook on the wall of the tunnel by the side hatch.

With the businesslike precision of men who had been working together for days on end, a team of plane handlers – often referred to as "airedales" – assisted Lieutenant Hunt as he unfolded the wings of his aircraft and locked them into place in preparation for launch. Hunt prepared to start the fourteen-cylinder Wright-Cyclone engine of his TBM-3. Once airborne, he would fly alongside his wingman and close friend Lt. (j.g.) Richard C. Scobell, who also had two crewmen under his command. John F. Gelnaw, AOM1c, occupied the turret on Scobell's TBM-1C and William P. Walton, ARM3c, served as the radioman-gunner. Hunt and Scobell often flew close enough that the men aboard the two aircraft could wave to each other, exchange hand signals, and, if they had removed their oxygen masks, even glean facial expressions. The Avenger might not have been glamorous to fly, as its nickname the "Turkey" implied, but its pilots loved the TBM for its durability, stability, and predictability. Unlike the SB2C dive-bomber, which required an attentive pilot alert to squirrely aerodynamics, the TBM virtually flew itself and seldom surprised an experienced aviator.[7] Scobell and Hunt often tucked themselves on each other's wings and flew so close they almost functioned as a single aircraft. If the weather allowed, they would hold close formation all the way to Hong Kong.

On the flight deck of the USS *Yorktown* – the second incarnation, built to replace the first one sunk by the Japanese in 1942 – Lt. (j.g.) John H. Lavender sat in the pilot's seat of a Curtiss SB2C-4 Helldiver, number 104, and ran through his preflight checklist. Chocks cradled the landing gear of his aircraft and he had not fired up his Wright-Cyclone engine yet, but he could nonetheless feel the plane moving as the ship pitched in the heavy seas. Though nowhere near as bad as the monster typhoon the *Yorktown* had endured the month before, the squally weather was gusting to thirty miles per hour, with a ceiling as low as 800 feet and intermittent rain whipping across the flight deck like buckshot.[8]

In the rear cockpit, Jean F. Balch, ARM3c, sat in the rotating gunner's seat. He wore a bulky parachute pack and the usual array of flight gear, including goggles and a holstered .38-caliber revolver, the standard sidearm issued to naval aviators flying over enemy territory. In his pockets, he carried a navy pocketknife, his wallet, some Chinese currency, and a pair of dice. He had, however, neglected to wear his dog tags.[9] Like all aircrew, he wore a Mae West life jacket with a dye pouch in case he wound up in the water; the former piece of equipment would keep him afloat while the latter would stain the waves and mark his position for rescuers. In addition, an uninflated life raft in a storage tube remained within easy reach in the compartment between the front and rear sections of the cockpit, though Balch hoped he wouldn't have to make use of it again.

Balch and Lavender had already ditched once before during a predawn training flight in May 1944. An engine failure had forced Lavender to descend towards the ocean surface for an emergency water landing just off the coast of Hawaii. He had kept the landing gear tucked snugly into the wings, but he extended the arrestor hook, which hung low under the tail, and used it as an early warning system to alert him when he had just a few feet of altitude left. At the last moment, he had pulled on the stick, which stalled the blunt-nose warplane and slapped it into the waves in a blossom of salt spray near an anchored LST. Uninjured by what had amounted to a controlled crash landing, Balch and Lavender had vaulted from each end of the cockpit in the seconds before the plane gurgled beneath the warm Pacific waters and disappeared. Despite the darkness, the crew of the LST had soon hauled the two aviators aboard. As if to underscore the inherent dangers of training operations as well as the unreliability of their well-worn SB2C-1s, a second Helldiver crew from the squadron experienced engine failure and went into the drink later that day. Once again, the pilot and rearseatman avoided injury and soon found themselves back on dry land.[10]

Lavender and Balch had flown their first bombing mission together on November 13, 1944, when the *Yorktown* air group had struck Japanese shipping near Cavite in Manila Bay. The pair had flown seven additional bombing missions since then, hitting targets in the Philippines, Formosa, and French Indochina. In a matter of minutes, Balch knew, they would take off to fly their ninth airstrike, this one against the port of Hong Kong. Once airborne Balch would unlimber a pair of rear-facing .30-caliber Browning machine guns. At this late stage of the war, the U.S. Navy had gained near-total air superiority, but in the unlikely event that an enemy fighter pilot penetrated the escorting posse of Hellcats and swept in behind his Helldiver, Balch would use the twin thirties to send him packing. Or that was the theory, anyway. Even when bundled into a twin-barrel configuration, the baby Brownings left the man in the rear seat badly outgunned in a shootout with an Oscar, Tojo, or Tony.[11]

Including the machine crewed by Lavender and Balch, a dozen rain-glossed Helldivers crouched on the flight deck of the *Yorktown* in preparation for the launch of Strike 1C. The Helldivers collectively constituted Bombing Squadron Three (VB-3), one of the three squadrons that comprised CVG-3, the *Yorktown*'s air group. The *Yorktown* in turn belonged to Task Group 38.1, one of the three task groups in Task Force 38 (TF 38), an armada of thirteen aircraft carriers under the command of Admiral William F. "Bull" Halsey. Strikes 1A and 1B had gone in that morning with minimal loss of aircraft and left Hong Kong's harbor wreathed in a halo of smoke from its burning dockyards. Strike 1C – the third strike of the day flown by TG 38.1 – would constitute the next wave and reach Hong Kong at roughly the same time that Commander Lamade arrived with the planes from TG 38.2 assigned to Strike 2C.

At 1400 hours – or 2:00 p.m. on the civilian clock – the Hellcat pilots of VF-3 left the *Yorktown* in rapid succession, followed by the Avenger crews of VT-3. The Helldivers of VB-3, laden with a single 250-pound bomb, a pair of 500-pound bombs, 400 rounds of 20mm ammunition, 2,000 rounds of .30-caliber ammunition, and 378 gallons of aviation gasoline, began rolling forward from the aft end of the flight deck.[12] As each Helldiver sped down the deck and lifted into the air, the next pilot in the launch order ran up his engine, listening for any telltale coughs, rattles, or unfamiliar vibrations that might signal an impending engine failure at the critical moment when the plane hurtled off the bow of the *Yorktown*. By the time he reached the lead position and found himself peering down the expanse of the wooden flight deck that would serve as his runway, Lavender felt satisfied that his SB2C or "Son of a Bitch Second Class" would make it to Hong Kong and back.

Lavender throttled up and released the brakes when he got the signal from the flight deck officer. In the rear seat, Balch had double-checked the straps and buckles of his flight gear and pulled down his goggles. Vibrating with raw horsepower, the Helldiver accelerated down the flight deck, gathered momentum, and plunged off the forward end of the ship. For a moment, the plane wallowed, as if it might concede the contest with gravity and fall with a fatalistic smack of spray into the waves, but then the four-bladed propeller bit into the humid salt air and the *Yorktown* began to fall away behind. Balch could see the *Wasp* and the *Cabot*, and the circle of battleships, cruisers, and destroyers that ringed the carriers in concentric circles known as the "screen." Soon the fleet vanished beneath the low-hanging scud. Once the forty-two planes assigned to Strike 1C had launched and formed up as best they could in the poor flying conditions, the pilots commenced the 170-mile run to Hong Kong. For Balch and Lavender, fellow Texans who had survived eight hairy missions through flak-rippled skies, the flight would prove to be a one-way ride that only one of them would survive.

December 1941

By January 1945, thirty-nine-year-old Ray Jones had celebrated – if such a term could be used under the circumstances – three birthdays behind the barbed-wire fencing of the Stanley Military Internment Camp. Like a sort of giant human junk drawer, the makeshift compound warehoused the Allied civilians – British primarily, but also Australians, Dutch, Russians, Poles, Greeks, Belgians, and Norwegians – that the Japanese had not known what else to do with after the fall of the colony to the Imperial Japanese Army (IJA) in December 1941. More than 2,500 men, women, and children had been forced into the camp athwart the picturesque Stanley Peninsula, a boulder-strewn finger of land jutting from the southeast coast of Hong Kong Island, the mountainous heart of what the Japanese called the Conquered Territory of Hong Kong.[1]

The Union Jack, of course, had rippled proudly over Hong Kong in prewar days. The British imperial project in Hong Kong had lasted for a century and been punctuated by acquisitions of Chinese real estate that steadily increased the size of the colony. Hong Kong Island had been a war trophy ceded to the British in perpetuity after the Opium War of 1841, which had gone poorly for the Chinese emperor and rather well for the British. In 1860, the British enlarged their nascent colony when an Anglo-French expeditionary force bullied the Chinese emperor into the Treaty of Tianjin, which ceded in perpetuity the Kowloon Peninsula and Stonecutters Island as well. Ultimately, the greatest prize was neither Hong Kong Island – famously dismissed by British Foreign Secretary Lord Palmerston as a "barren island with hardly a house upon it" – nor the Kowloon Peninsula; rather, the greatest prize was the deep-water harbor that rested between them.[2] Like other prominent locales in Hong Kong – Victoria Peak, Victoria Park, Victoria City – this protected anchorage would be named after a queen enthroned on the opposite side of the globe. Warships and merchant vessels from all over the world sailed and steamed into Victoria Harbor, which soon grew a fringe of wharves, warehouses, and dockyards along its irregular shoreline.

In 1898, the British acquired a large piece of Chinese hinterland north of Kowloon on a ninety-nine-year lease that became known as the New Territories. This 365-square-mile parcel – more than twelve times the size of Hong Kong Island – stretched from the edge of Victoria Harbor to the Shum Chum River far inland, which became the new frontier with China.[3] A sizeable population of local Chinese living in isolated walled villages suddenly found themselves subject to a distant royal family rather than a remote emperor. So did the boat people scattered among the 230 islands of the newly acquired territory. The smallest islands amounted to low-tide reefs capable of slicing a ship's keel like a fillet knife through a carp. Lantau, the largest of the islands, loomed to the west of the harbor, a brooding beauty serrated with mountains that often disappeared with ethereal majesty into cloud and mist.

Britain still reigned as the dominant world power when it acquired the New Territories at the end of the nineteenth century, but in the opening decades of the twentieth century Japan emerged as a new imperial rival with a prodigious appetite for Chinese land. Britain, the United States, and other Western nations had been content with small colonial footholds like Hong Kong and unfettered access to the China trade on terms they dictated. In contrast, Japan had sought to conquer entire regions of China, starting with the northeastern province of Manchuria in 1931. A year later Japan provoked a short mini-war at Shanghai, and after vicious street fighting Japanese troops eventually gained the upper hand. Chiang Kai-shek, the leader of Nationalist China, knew that his country was not yet ready for war and concluded that he had no choice but to negotiate a truce on terms favorable to Japan. Manchuria became the grandly titled nation of Manchukuo ("Country of the Manchus"), a puppet state and effectively Japanese territory.[4]

In 1937, full-scale war broke out between China, which still lacked the armed forces to repel Japanese aggression, and an increasingly bellicose Japan. China thus became the first nation to face an Axis power, some two years before the German *blitzkrieg* swept aside the Polish army and more than four years before Japanese carrier aircraft devastated Battleship Row at Pearl Harbor. In the first year of the war, Japanese troops easily took Peking and Tientsin. After sustained and bloody fighting, Shanghai also fell. The IJA then advanced inland and took the Nationalist capital of Nanking in the face of stubborn resistance from the Nationalist army, which set much of the city ablaze as it fell back. Japanese troops entered the city and ran amok, raping, torturing, and beheading much of the civilian population as well as captured Chinese soldiers. By the end of 1937, Chiang Kai-shek had shifted his wartime capital to Chungking. Famously known as a *shancheng* or "mountain city," Chungking was lodged like a national redoubt deep in the heart of Sichuan Province above the Yangtze River gorges, where it could be more easily defended against Japanese advances.

In January 1938, the IJA launched a two-pronged offensive designed to take the central Yangtze region. The Japanese encountered considerable resistance from the Chinese army and even suffered a rare defeat at Taierzhuang, an ancient stone-walled town on the outskirts of Suchow. However, the IJA soon regained the initiative and continued its drive towards Hankow, the most important industrial area still under Nationalist control. In desperation, Chiang ordered the breaching of the dykes that channeled the Yellow River, which drowned half a million civilians in an early summer flood that put 21,000 square miles underwater. Millions more found themselves homeless refugees. Despite the biblical scale of the silty inundation unleashed by an unrestrained Yellow River, the flooding merely delayed the Japanese advance towards Hankow.[5]

Hankow lay 650 miles to the north of Hong Kong, but the colony's position became increasingly precarious as the Japanese military turned its attention to southern China and the vexatious presence of the British. The United Kingdom remained a nonbelligerent in the Sino-Japanese war, but the colony nonetheless served as the Nationalist regime's most important supply conduit from the outside world, with some 60 to 70 percent of its imports offloaded in Hong Kong and shipped inland. These imports included vital military supplies that ranged from uniforms to disassembled aircraft.[6] Meanwhile, exports from Nationalist China filled the holds of merchant ships steaming from Victoria Harbor to ports in the United States, the Soviet Union, and elsewhere. The Japanese military calculated that by invading Kwangtung Province they could seal off Hong Kong from interior China, cut Nationalist supply lines, support the offensive to take Hankow, and end the war in China with a Japanese victory – all without provoking a fight with Great Britain.

On October 12, 1938, a Japanese expeditionary force of 30,000 troops made an unopposed landing at Bias Bay just twenty miles north of the Hong Kong border. Ten days later the Japanese force had swollen to 50,000 troops, and it quickly swept aside local Nationalist units and captured the key southern port of Canton, capital of Kwangtung Province.[7] Japanese soldiers also moved up to the Shum Chum River, which marked the border with Hong Kong, though they showed no inclination to cross the frontier. In the north, meanwhile, the IJA finally took Hankow.

Hankow and Canton had fallen, but 1938 ended in military stalemate nonetheless. Chiang's Nationalist government continued to rule China, albeit tenuously and incompletely, from the remote mountain fastness of Chungking. Chiang knew that the Nationalist army could not defeat the IJA in open battle, so he ordered his remaining military forces to avoid head-to-head engagements and withdraw to Sichuan and other remote locations. As a result, the Japanese failed to deliver the knockout blow to Chiang's military that would have forced him into a political settlement.

Faced with what appeared to be an intractable deadlock on the Chinese mainland, the Japanese Imperial Council began looking to Southeast Asia and the Pacific for a larger strategic solution. Geopolitically, the world had shifted with the fury of the German *blitzkrieg*. Belgium, Denmark, France, Luxembourg, the Netherlands, and Norway had all been occupied by the Germans in 1940. Great Britain was fighting for its very survival. In June 1941, German panzer divisions surged into the Soviet Union, which ensured that Japan no longer had to guard against a Russian invasion of Manchuria. All of these factors allowed the Imperial Council to shift its strategic focus to European colonial possessions in Southeast Asia, which were rich with natural resources, but thinly guarded. In the case of French Indochina, there was really no guard at all, and Japanese troops occupied the territory in September 1940. Planning began for an attack on the American Pacific Fleet at Pearl Harbor and a rapid strike to the south that would take the

Philippines, the Dutch East Indies, Malaya, and Singapore. As part of this broader offensive, the IJA would also seize Hong Kong.

———

In Hong Kong, European and Chinese residents had long assumed that the Japanese would eventually make a grab for the colony. Preparations for war had been ongoing for years in Hong Kong, though these preparations had been circumscribed by the Washington Treaty of 1922, which prohibited the Americans and the British from constructing major fortifications any closer to Japan than Pearl Harbor and Singapore, respectively. Attempts to upgrade the defensive posture of the colony within the limitations of the treaty and the British economy tended to be inconsistent and half-hearted due to competing visions about the nature of that defense. Some voices in Hong Kong as well as in Britain argued for defending the colony at all costs. Proponents of this approach clamored for increasing the size of the garrison so that Hong Kong Island could withstand a prolonged siege. Other voices contended that Hong Kong remained indefensible, given its small size, its lack of a full-size airfield and land suitable to build one on, and its isolated location so far from the main British naval base at Singapore. They believed that a symbolic defense would be the wisest move, since any troops and equipment in the city would inevitably be lost in the event of war and therefore be unavailable for better use elsewhere. Some even suggested that the city should be completely demilitarized, arguing that this would spare the city from the death and destruction inflicted upon Nanking and other Chinese cities, and that moreover, the business of Hong Kong was trade and commerce, not geopolitics and military adventure.[8] An imperfect compromise resulted. Fortification of the colony proceeded, albeit on a relatively modest scale, and by 1941 the colony had acquired an accretion of military barracks, bunkers, parade grounds, hospitals, depots, magazines, and dockyards.

In 1941, Maj. Gen. Christopher M. Maltby arrived to take command of the garrison. His order of battle included four infantry battalions, plus assorted support units and a generous complement of artillery batteries that included massive 9.2-inch coastal artillery guns at Fort Stanley. However, the garrison could field relatively few antiaircraft guns and lacked radar sets for early warning of incoming air raids. Moreover, the garrison could not muster a single tank. On the plus side, the Hong Kong Volunteer Defense Corps (HKVDC) – an enthusiastic and heavily armed militia complete with automatic weapons, armored cars, and artillery pieces – augmented the regular troops. Nobody knew Hong Kong better than the men of the HKVDC, who provided invaluable cultural, linguistic, and geographical knowledge of the local terrain.

The Royal Air Force (RAF) presence in Hong Kong had never been a large one, and by 1941 it had dwindled to an expendable token force with little combat power. The RAF base at Kai Tak airfield could send just three Vickers Vildebeest torpedo bombers aloft, though this trio of obsolete biplanes had arrived in Hong Kong without any torpedo-launching equipment.[9] The Fleet Air Arm of the Royal Navy berthed two Supermarine Walrus seaplanes at Kai Tak, but like the Vildebeest these slow-moving aircraft could do little more than fly reconnaissance missions. Vildebeest pilots liked to joke that the only way their lumbering biplanes would ever be able to kill the enemy would be if the Japanese got a good look at the old open-cockpit crates and died laughing.[10]

Hong Kong had always served as an important base for the Royal Navy, which maintained extensive support facilities in Victoria Harbor. With its 100-ton crane and massive dry dock, the Royal Navy dockyard dominated the northern shore of Hong Kong Island. The white-hulled HMS *Tamar*, an old troopship stripped of engines and armament that served as a stationary headquarters and barracks vessel, remained a permanent fixture of the harbor front. Despite the reassuring presence of the *Tamar*, however, the navy had drawn down its assets in the colony in favor of Singapore, which hosted the largest British naval base in Asia. By late 1941, the Royal Navy flotilla in Hong Kong had shrunk to a handful of motor torpedo boats, four river gunboats, and a trio of elderly destroyers.

The colonial government had begun preparations for war in the late 1930s and placed considerable emphasis on protecting the population from air attack. In September 1938, blackout exercises became a regular feature of Hong Kong life and regularly plunged the city into an unfamiliar darkness policed by Air Raid Precautions (ARP) wardens. Contractors hired by the government began work in 1940 on an extensive network of air-raid tunnels in the urban areas along the northern coast of Hong Kong Island and in Aberdeen on the southern coast. Work commenced on a smaller number of tunnels across the harbor in Kowloon as well. Various forms of above-ground shelters supplemented the tunnels, and workers bricked up the arcades of the Supreme Court and many other buildings to provide pedestrians with emergency street-side cover from falling bombs. Meanwhile, the local newspapers featured advertisements from C.E. Warren & Company that touted the firm's ability to construct custom-built air-raid shelters that could withstand bombing as well as poison gas.[11]

At London's urging, the colonial administration issued a mandatory evacuation order for European women and children at government expense. The Eurasian and Chinese communities responded with considerable outrage to the evacuation scheme, which had been constructed along racial lines and applied only to white civilians. In any case, many European families refused to be split apart and dodged the order through both official means – exemptions for women with essential wartime duties that may not, in fact, have been all that essential – and simple refusal to comply. In the end more than 3,500 European women and children boarded ocean liners bound for Australia in summer 1940, but many more remained in the colony.[12]

Meanwhile, most of the European men residing in Hong Kong found themselves subject to a Compulsory Service Ordinance instituted in 1939. The ordinance required all male British subjects of European ancestry between the ages of eighteen and fifty-five to perform some form of mandatory service. For many men, this meant joining the HKVDC. Prison warden Raymond Eric Jones, known as "Ray" to many acquaintances, had worked for the Prisons Department since 1935 and enlisted as a private in the Stanley Platoon, a special unit of the HKVDC comprised of prison guards and other staff at Stanley Prison. If war broke out between Britain and Japan, the Stanley Platoon would mobilize for the defense of Hong Kong.

Jones and Dorothy Marjorie Cumming had been married for less than a year before the government evacuation order intervened. Their courtship had been a long-distance affair, with Jones working in Hong Kong and Marjorie living in their shared hometown of Skegness, a seaside holiday community on the coast of England. Marjorie lived with and looked after her widowed father, a retired sea captain, and had been reluctant to leave him.[13] She had resisted Jones's marriage proposals for this reason, though caution and practicality may have factored into her initial reluctance as well. Marjorie needed to be sure that Raymond Eric Jones was the man she wanted to marry and that she could trust his plans to sweep her off to expatriate life in Hong Kong. In the end, she agreed to take Jones's hand and they swapped wedding rings in England in 1939, the same year that war erupted on the European continent.

Jones called his new wife "Marj," while she often referred to her husband as "Joney." He had brown eyes, dark curly hair, and the muscular physique of a man used to handling unruly inmates. Though slim of stature, Marj could nearly match her husband's five-foot ten-inch height. She also had brown eyes, complemented by dark brown hair that fell to just above her shoulders. Marj was twenty-eight years old and six years younger than Jones, who loved her sense of fun, but appreciated her pragmatism. An avid reader, she had an inquisitive mind fortified by a steady diet of books and tempered by a ready supply of common sense. Marj could be fierce when riled, and had once thrown a clock at Jones when he came home unreasonably late, but such flashes of temper faded as quickly as a summer lightning storm.[14] By nature generous of spirit, she leaned towards forgiveness like a flower tilting towards the sun. As for Jones, he brought good humor and an appreciation for music acquired from his father, a pianist and organist. He provided strength, sturdiness, and the opportunities that came with living abroad as a servant of the British Empire.[15]

After arranging for the welfare of Marj's father, the newlyweds boarded an ocean liner bound for Hong Kong. The long sea journey doubled as their honeymoon, though things went awry mid-voyage when the Admiralty requisitioned their ship for the war effort. The two of them spent a month stranded in Ceylon until they secured passage aboard a French steamship heading for Indochina. Though the austere conditions of the ship would have been familiar to Jones, a Royal Navy veteran who had served in the spartan confines of O-class submarines, the no-frills functionality of the steamer left Marj eager to disembark when they finally reached Saigon. Like a dreamscape, the French colonial city shimmered in the heat, prostrate on the banks of a muscular river and hemmed in on all quarters by surging brown waters, undulating curtains of jungle, and glistening rice paddies of luminescent green. Along the boulevards and back alleys, the smell of fish sauce and joss smoke hung in the humidity, while overhead lightning veined across the night sky. Marj loved the city from the moment she first laid eyes on it.[16]

Hong Kong made a rather different impression, with its bustling harbor ringed by mountain peaks so high they disappeared into the clouds. Upon arrival in the colony, Jones and Marj moved into one of the flats that the Prisons Department provided to wardens who worked at Stanley Prison on the Stanley Peninsula. The short walk to work offered Jones, a heavy smoker, just enough time to enjoy a Chesterfield, his preferred form of tobacco. The couple furnished their new apartment with a refrigerator, stove, and other trappings of domestic life, and since they both loved dogs, they adopted a retriever named Blackie. No doubt they talked of children as well. Like most European residents in Hong Kong, they could afford to hire an *amah** to do the household chores and help with shopping in the market. They settled into the privileged routines of colonial life, with its bathing beaches, tennis courts, cricket pitches, and dinner dances. In the end, however, the threat of war between Britain and Japan cut short their time together as a married couple.[17]

In July 1940, Marj joined the exodus of evacuees and departed for Sydney, where she gave birth to a daughter, Rae, in early 1941. She found lodgings on Beach Road not far from the famous sands of Bondi, while Ray and Blackie continued to live in their flat in Hong Kong. He sent his wife and daughter numbered letters – sometimes several in one week and often mailed from the Stanley Prison pillar-box – so that Marj would know if they arrived out of sequence or if one went missing. He had posted his seventy-second letter by the start of August 1941.[18]

Though letters to Marj demanded most of his scribal energy, Jones had started keeping a journal at the very end of 1940. As a diarist, he was terse but diligent, indifferent to punctuation, and prone to idiosyncratic abbreviations. He rarely wrote an entry more than a few sentences long, but nonetheless felt compelled to write an entry every day. In the same matter-of-fact tone, he jotted down in minimalist fashion descriptions of the social events he attended – "Dinner at Grindleys" – and incidents from work at the prison: "Hung Shau Kei Wan boatyard killer 7am." He had a meteorological streak and often took notes on the weather. "Very hot and sticky," he penciled in his

---

*An *amah* was a domestic servant who cared for her employer's children and performed other household chores.

diary on August 21. On September 6, he recorded weekend maneuvers with the Stanley Platoon. "Manned trench all evening to past midn't," he wrote with his usual brevity, then noted that he had posted letter number seventy-eight to Marj in Australia.[19]

Sir Mark Aitchison Young assumed the colonial governorship in September 1941 and continued Hong Kong's increasingly urgent preparations for war. In November, two Canadian infantry battalions disembarked at Kowloon, albeit without their heavy equipment, bringing the garrison's total strength to 14,000 men. The Hong Kong government held more mandatory blackout exercises and distributed pamphlets that gave advice for civilians to follow should hostilities break out.[20] Jones and the Stanley Platoon continued to drill, as did the rest of the HKVDC. Units of the Royal Engineers wired bridges in the New Territories for demolition, and work crews rushed to complete the Gin Drinkers Line, a fortified web of blockhouses and trenches in the hills north of Kowloon that drew ominous comparisons with the Maginot Line. Barbed wire sprouted like metal thickets along the shoreline of Hong Kong Island, where an extensive network of coastal pillboxes concealed the snouts of belt-fed .303 machine guns.

Meanwhile, the Asiatic Fleet of the U.S. Navy evacuated its forces from China, which included the gunboats of the Yangtze Patrol and a garrison of Marines concentrated in Shanghai. In preparation for war and in accordance with a directive from the Navy Department, the commander of the Asiatic Fleet, Admiral Thomas C. Hart, ordered the China Marines to embark on fast passenger liners to Manila and the gunboats to cross the South China Sea to the Philippines. The USS *Mindanao*, which had served as the south China gunboat for the Yangtze Patrol for over a decade, departed Victoria Harbor on December 3. The civilian tugboat *Ranger* of the Luzon Stevedore Company left Victoria Harbor as well, laden with war supplies for the *Mindanao* that included 800 rounds of 3-inch shells and 125,000 rounds of .30-caliber machine-gun ammunition, all pulled from where they had been stored in British magazines at Hong Kong. With the unceremonious withdrawal of the *Mindanao*, the U.S. Navy had ended its long-standing presence in south China and signaled its assumption of an imminent shooting war in the western Pacific.[21]

Though just as aware as Admiral Hart that war with Japan remained likely, Major General Maltby nonetheless misinterpreted Japanese troop movements during the first week of December 1941 and failed to recognize the scale and immediacy of the impending Japanese assault. However, he exercised an abundance of caution and put the garrison on a war footing. On December 5, Maltby mobilized both the HKVDC and the police force. The next day the colony's meager assortment of antiaircraft guns had their barrels raised skywards with ready ammunition stocked nearby and crews on duty. On December 7, Governor Young declared a state of emergency and Maltby ordered all military personnel to report for duty. By nightfall, the garrison had been fully alerted and deployed.[22]

On the morning of Monday, December 8, 1941, Ray Jones – prison warden and rifleman – heard the first distant explosions not long after sunrise. Japanese bombs, he reckoned, and some antiaircraft fire, too. Jones had just turned thirty-six and prepared to celebrate his birthday by going to war.

3

We Are Now Prisoners of War

By Christmas Eve the contest for Hong Kong had entered its endgame and Ray Jones was preparing for the last stand. Just seventeen days had elapsed since his birthday and the air raids that had kicked off the war. The British garrison had not been taken by surprise like the American fleet at Pearl Harbor, but the battle for Hong Kong had nonetheless gone poorly for the defenders. There was little comfort in recognizing that this military reversal had more to do with the overwhelming strength of the Japanese invaders and the isolated position of Hong Kong than any failures on the part of General Maltby and the men under his command. Maltby had understood that any Japanese invasion would include a crossing of the Shum Chum River followed by a thrust down the length of the New Territories towards Kowloon. However, Maltby also knew that the Japanese warships of the 2nd China Expeditionary Fleet (2nd CEF) might support a simultaneous amphibious landing on Hong Kong Island as well. The 2nd CEF had blockaded Hong Kong on the morning of December 8, but its ships kept prudently out of range of Hong Kong's powerful coastal defense artillery. Maltby nonetheless had to guard against the possibility of a Japanese amphibious assault on the southern coast of Hong Kong Island. To meet these dual threats by land from the north and by sea from the south, Maltby chose to divide his forces into two brigades – the Island Brigade and the Mainland Brigade, each with three infantry battalions. The former would defend Hong Kong Island, while the latter would delay the Japanese advance through the New Territories for as long as possible at the Gin Drinkers Line – named not for inebriated soldiers but because the western end of the line terminated at Gin Drinkers Bay – and then withdraw to Hong Kong Island. The two brigades would then hunker down for an extended siege.

With just three battalions, however, the Island Brigade could not field enough men to significantly delay, much less halt, the Japanese advance towards Kowloon. Even the Shing Mun redoubt – the most strongly fortified portion of the Gin Drinkers Line – could not be adequately manned. As a result, the thinly defended network of tunnels and bunkers at Shing Mun fell just thirty-six hours after the 38th Division of the IJA crossed the Shum Chum River. With the loss of Shing Mun and the penetration of the Gin Drinkers Line by the IJA, the badly outnumbered men of the Island Brigade had no choice but to fall back towards Kowloon.

In the meantime, Jones had remained on duty at Stanley Prison, which caged more than a thousand prisoners, and listened to the ferocious blast of the 9.2-inch coastal defense guns, which had been swiveled around to lob shells at the advancing Japanese in the New Territories. Only battleships mounted heavier guns, and each salvo from the 9.2-inch cannons terrified Blackie and presumably did the same to the Japanese soldiers on the receiving end of the barrage. Despite the obvious proximity of the enemy, however, Jones remained optimistic. On December 12, he wrote in his journal that "Jap. position not so good. They are in Kowloon being smashed up by our heavy guns & the Chinese army are advancing through the New Territories."[1]

In fact, the Nationalist Chinese would never reach Hong Kong, and General Maltby had already ordered the Mainland Brigade to withdraw to Hong Kong Island. The brigade had only managed to stave off the Japanese advance for four days, but it had also avoided a complete rout when it executed the tactically perilous feat of withdrawing across Victoria Harbor while under fire. Moreover, the retreat had largely been an orderly one, with tracked Bren gun carriers, armored cars, and other heavy equipment ferried over to Hong Kong Island. The Indian soldiers of the Mule Corps had even managed to evacuate fifty of their braying beasts of burden.[2] Though the Mainland Brigade had escaped the invaders, however, the fact remained that the New Territories and Kowloon now belonged to the IJA.

Maltby reorganized his forces on Hong Kong Island into the East Brigade and West Brigade, each of which defended half of the island. Meanwhile, Governor Young spurned two different Japanese demands that he surrender the colony unconditionally. As Jones recorded in his journal on December 17, "Japs truce 11AM to 4.15PM to give us time to give in. Gov. told them where to step off."[3] The island's northern coast came under heavy bombardment in the wake of the governor's refusal, and on the night of December 18, a Japanese landing force crossed Victoria Harbor and struggled ashore at North Point, Tai Koo, and Shau Kei Wan. Though badly shot up, Japanese units quickly gained a foothold and pressed their attack inland.

December 19 proved to be the single bloodiest day of the entire invasion when Japanese infantry drove a wedge between the two defending brigades by forcing their way through Wong Nai Chung Gap, a strategic pass that cut through the mountainous spine of Hong Kong Island. The Japanese assault split the island in two, with the West Brigade defending the western half of the island in a line that ran roughly from Aberdeen to the Wan Chai district of Victoria City. The East Brigade, meanwhile, pulled back towards the Stanley Peninsula, a natural defensive position but also a tactical cul-de-sac.

Ray Jones and the Stanley Platoon never needed to move up to the front lines. Instead, the front lines came to them. On December 19, they took up position on the edge of Stanley Village. Though comprised entirely of prison staff, the unit did not lack in military experience. Most of the men in the platoon had served in the armed forces before joining the Prisons Department, and Jones himself had enlisted in the Royal Navy at age sixteen. As a leading seaman aboard the submarine HMS *Oswald*, he had cruised to the Far East in the early 1930s and enjoyed port calls in Singapore and Hong Kong.[4] Back in England, Jones had appeared in a photo printed in the local newspaper, the *Skegness Standard*. The photo showed Jones and his crewmates reading a copy of the *Standard* that his mother had apparently mailed to him in Singapore. Eager to claim Jones as a native Skegnessian, the article reported on his adventures in the Far East and ended with the jocular approbation, "We do get about!"[5] Jones had indeed journeyed far from the coast of England, but he showed no inclination to return. After fourteen years in the navy, he had mustered out and begun working as a prison warden in Hong Kong in 1935. In 1940, Jones had learned from newspaper reports that the Italians had sunk the *Oswald* in the Mediterranean.

In addition to their military backgrounds, the men of the Stanley Platoon possessed detailed knowledge of the Stanley Peninsula, where they both lived and worked. This gave the platoon a home-court advantage, and Jones knew that his unit would need every advantage it could get in the battle to come. Their automatic weaponry would provide them with an additional edge, as the Stanley Platoon had been equipped with Vickers machine guns. Other units had dug in nearby with additional tripod-mounted machine guns and 2-pounder antitank guns. By December 24, the Japanese had pushed the East Brigade back to the neck of the Stanley Peninsula, and the village of the same name had become the front line. The Stanley Platoon and the other units holding this line prepared to block the inevitable Japanese attempt to take Stanley Village. If the Japanese successfully stormed the village, they could then start pushing the defenders southwards down the peninsula until the soldiers of the East Brigade had their backs to the sea.

On the night of December 24, Jones and his comrades heard an ominous clanking sound in the darkness. Three Japanese light tanks soon came trundling down Stanley Village Road. The 2-pounder antitank guns opened fire at close range, destroying the first two tanks and convincing the crew of the third to retreat. Jones soon heard Japanese officers hollering at their men, no doubt to urge them forward, and then his position came under full-scale attack from the seasoned regulars of the 38th Infantry Division. As lines of tracer fire crisscrossed between the shifting battle lines, Jones and his men repelled repeated assaults, some of them at nearly pointblank range.

When their position became untenable at midnight, Jones and his comrades fell back towards the junction at the south end of Stanley Village. Along the way, they came under fire from friendly units unable to tell friend from foe in the darkness. Two men went down and Jones saw bullets gouging the road just three feet from where he stood, but the platoon successfully reached the crossroads. Taking whatever cover they could find, the members of the platoon then supported the machine-gun position at the junction until the Japanese knocked it out with grenades. Since Jones and almost everyone else had run out of rifle ammunition, the platoon then made a perilous withdrawal under fire down Fort Road to the grounds of the military base known as Stanley Fort.*

Jones and his comrades secured 300 rounds of .303 ammunition for their Lee Enfield rifles when they reached the base. By this point, the Japanese had pushed past the first line of defense, and East Brigade headquarters sent Jones and the survivors of the Stanley Platoon to reinforce the second defensive line on the grounds of St. Stephen's College Preparatory School. Jones believed at least nine men from the platoon had been killed outright or gone missing during the attempt to hold the first line, including his good friend Ernest J. Stevens, and several others had been wounded.[6] Though much reduced in strength, the platoon continued to fight in the strange half-light produced by burning buildings, the flash of exploding grenades, and the brilliant trajectories of tracer rounds. Working the bolts of their Lee Enfields, the men of the Stanley Platoon fired at muzzle flashes and shadowy figures as incoming rounds cracked past or struck men with a sound like an oar slapping a wet sack of rice.

Jones and the Stanley Platoon feared they would be overrun, but their position never deteriorated to the point where they had to resort to the bayonet. However, many of their comrades in the East Brigade found themselves pulling triggers and grenade pins at pointblank range. Some of the most vicious close-quarters combat occurred during an all-night contest for three residential buildings on the St. Stephen's campus known as Bungalow A, B, and C. Defended by an ad hoc force of British machine gunners and artillerymen from the HKVDC, the bungalows sat athwart the second defensive line. The battle for possession of the homes raged all night until a Japanese flamethrower team settled the matter just before dawn.

By sunrise on Christmas Day, the second defensive line had been shattered and St. Stephen's College belonged to the Japanese. The Stanley Platoon fell back with the remnants of other units to the third and final defensive line on the edge of Stanley Fort. Facing long odds of success and firing from the hip, a Canadian infantry company assaulted Bungalow C in the afternoon. After some initial success, and considerable carnage in and around the one-story dwelling, the

---

*Fort Road is now named Wong Ma Kok Road.

counterattack stalled and the surviving Canadian riflemen fell back. In what had amounted to a *banzai* charge, 84 percent of the men in the company had been killed or wounded.[7] The battered shell of Bungalow C remained in Japanese hands with dead soldiers and their kit fanned out on the lawn.

The IJA held back from a daylight assault on the third line, which bisected the Stanley Peninsula about halfway down the nearly two-mile-long isthmus. Since the IJA would have to cross a narrow stretch of the peninsula while under fire from units positioned on higher ground in Stanley Fort, the officers of East Brigade headquarters assumed the Japanese would wait until darkness to launch their final attack. At 7:00 p.m. that evening, Jones and his exhausted platoon moved back into Stanley Fort to provide security for brigade headquarters. Heavy firing continued into the night, but the expected Japanese infantry assault never came. Instead, East Brigade headquarters received word that Governor Young had surrendered Hong Kong to the Japanese.

"Posted as B.H.Q. [brigade headquarters] guard for the final stand but it never materialized. Terms of surrender discussed & all was over for us about 11PM," Jones penciled in his hardback diary that night. "We are now prisoners of war."[8]

4

Boxing Day, 1941

On Boxing Day 1941, Jones and the surviving members of the Stanley Platoon scrounged up some warm beer and rum, which calmed their jangled nerves and their fear of captivity. They stacked their rifles and ammunition as ordered and waited for further directives from the Japanese. To Jones's relief, some of the men from the unit that he presumed to be dead turned up alive, including his friend Ernest Stevens. Still, the platoon had lost seven members – a quarter of the unit – and at least two more men had been wounded, including Stevens. One had lost his entire hand.[1] All things considered, Jones counted himself very fortunate to be alive and unscathed.

"Although capitulation is not so good," Jones wrote, "it feels nice to know that the likelihood of being shot or blown apart is gone."[2]

Hong Kong had held out for just eighteen days, far less than had been hoped for, though entire European nations had fallen in less time to the Axis powers. Luxembourg had resisted the German *blitzkrieg* for only a single day, while the Netherlands surrendered to Germany after just five days. Belgium held out for about the same length as the Hong Kong garrison, which had lost over 1,500 men during the battle. Japanese casualties had been heavy as well, with particularly grievous losses among the officers of the 38th Infantry Division.[3]

As for the local Chinese, they found themselves caught in the crossfire between two foreign armies, each with its own imperial agenda for China. As many as 4,000 civilians died, killed by ordnance fired by both sides, with many more injured.[4] Japanese troops looted and raped as well, though not on the wholesale scale seen in other captured Chinese cities. Still, some estimates suggested that IJA troops murdered several hundred Cantonese civilians and sexually assaulted more than 10,000 women in the immediate aftermath of the British defeat.[5]

Hong Kong and its capacious harbor became an outpost of the expanding Japanese Empire, albeit one still littered with the colonial detritus of its former British masters, from cricket pitches to statues of Queen Victoria. The newly conquered territory came with its share of logistical challenges, including the question of where to confine 12,000 captured British, Canadian, and Indian soldiers. In the aftermath of the capitulation, these troops gradually entered makeshift POW camps, though civilians of all nationalities remained free in the first weeks after the surrender. The Japanese soon thought better of allowing British and American civilians to remain at large, however, and by the end of January 1942 the Japanese had transported most citizens of Allied nations to the Stanley Civilian Internment Camp.

The camp sat between Stanley Village and Stanley Fort on the Stanley Peninsula, all named for Edward Stanley, secretary of state for war and the colonies in 1841, the year Britain had first claimed Hong Kong. Placing the camp on the relatively isolated isthmus reduced the likelihood of successful escape attempts, but it also offered healthy conditions for the internees, since the rocky topography and sea breezes reduced the threat of malarial mosquitoes. The grounds of the camp incorporated the old Stanley cemetery, the campus of St. Stephen's College, and the outbuildings of Stanley Prison. However, while the prison abutted the camp, it remained a separate facility incarcerating common criminals as well as anyone who ran afoul of the Japanese administration. In an odd juxtaposition, a crescent of sand below the prison bluff fronted Tweed Bay and offered such fine swimming opportunities that it had been reserved for the colonial governor's use in prewar days. An assortment of buildings fell within the camp perimeter, including the housing blocks for the European and Indian staff of Stanley Prison, houses for the Prison Commissioner and his assistant, the H-Block main hall for St. Stephen's, the school's Science Block, and the six residential bungalows lettered A to F that had been built for college staff and faculty.[6]

In total, 2,500 to 2,800 Allied civilians entered the Stanley Civilian Internment Camp in January 1942. The process of rounding up enemy noncombatants played out repeatedly in the newly conquered lands of the Japanese Empire, though in Hong Kong the Japanese chose not to separate internees by gender. As a result of this policy, the camp held roughly 900 adult women and 1,300 adult men. Extended families often trudged through the gates together, suitcases and cooking pots in hand, and just over 300 internees were children aged sixteen or younger, making them a significant presence in the camp population. The internees consisted primarily of British civilians, a classification that included Australians and Canadians. However, the multinational camp population also included about 300 Americans, smaller numbers of Dutch and Norwegian citizens, a handful of White Russians, and a few internees from Poland, Greece, and Belgium. Race and nationality did not always align in ways that the Japanese overseers expected, and while most prisoners were white, the camp population also included Chinese or mixed-race citizens of Allied nations.[7]

Though the European police and prison officers had fought as armed militia during the battle for Hong Kong, the Japanese classified them as civilians and sent them to Stanley rather than a POW compound. As a result, Ray Jones ended up in the Stanley camp with Ernest Stevens, whose battlefield injuries did not prove to be life threatening. Jones soon learned that the Japanese would occupy his flat, even though it fell within the boundaries of the camp, but he managed to salvage some of his belongings and bring them with him into captivity, including a guitar, his wedding suit, photos of Marj and Rae, a pair of binoculars, and a mattress. The fate of his dog Blackie, however, remained unclear. Ruefully, he wrote in his diary, "Had we known that we were to be interned here we could have buried & hidden quite a lot of useful stuff from the Prison."[8] Jones did manage to hide a Union Jack, which he sewed inside his mattress to conceal from his Japanese captors. He anticipated raising the flag above the camp when the Allies retook Hong Kong.

"Well darling," he penciled into his journal on January 22, "our Rae is 12 months old & I sincerely hope & pray that this her first birthday will be the first & last that we are parted until she leaves us to start a home of her own. I hope you had a nice little party sweetheart with one candle on the cake. God Bless you both."[9]

Jones continued to keep his daily journal during the interminable and increasingly hungry months of incarceration that followed the surrender of the British garrison. He longed desperately for Marj – whom he referred to as "pal" in his journal – and occasionally waxed nostalgically about their married life. On March 15, he wrote, "Two years ago tonight sweetheart you threw the clock at me for being late. I wish you were here to do it again pal. I'd catch it this time though." Many of his entries recorded the latest news about the progress of the war and the likelihood that the internees would be repatriated in exchange for Japanese civilians held in Allied countries. Jones did his best to sort through the military gossip that circulated through the camp, some of it sheer fantasy – Allied armored divisions had landed in Belgium and captured Liege, and Russian troops had reached Danzig and Warsaw – and some of it almost certainly true, such as the fall of Singapore and the Dutch East Indies. Evidence of impending repatriation, however, proved as hard to find as fresh eggs or new shoes. On a day of heavy rain in June, Jones opened his journal, the pages damp as a washcloth with humidity, and penciled in frustration, "No news – much talk re repatriation." Not surprisingly, given his open-ended prison sentence, Jones experienced periods of utter demoralization. In early summer, he wrote, "Feel awfully sad & lonely today Marj darling, hungry too."[10]

The rumors of repatriation proved to be true, but only for the American internees. In June 1942, the International Red Cross brokered a prisoner swap between Japan and the United States. Under the terms of the deal, the Japanese released several hundred American civilians from the Stanley camp, including an evangelical Christian missionary named Merrill Steele Ady, who would later return to China and play a role in the escape of U.S. Navy aviators shot down over Hong Kong. Watched with envy by the British internees who would be left behind at Stanley, the Americans boarded the passenger ship *Asama Maru*, which already carried more than 400 U.S. citizens repatriated from camps in Japan. After picking up additional civilian internees at Saigon, the *Asama Maru* steamed for the neutral Portuguese colonial city of Lourenço Marques on the eastern coast of Africa. In a carefully orchestrated exchange refereed by the Red Cross, Japanese and American internees swapped ships, with the Americans boarding the Swedish liner *Gripsholm* bound for New York and the Japanese boarding the *Asama Maru* bound for Yokohama.[11]

At the Sham Shui Po POW camp in Kowloon, meanwhile, the Japanese ordered the senior officers among the POWs to identify the healthiest men for transport to Japan. The soldiers selected for the journey had been preceded by high-value prisoners like Major General Maltby and Governor Young, who had been spirited out of the colony to special prisons elsewhere in the Japanese Empire. In September 1942, Japanese guards herded 2,452 POWs from Sham Shui Po into the cavernous cargo holds of the merchant vessels *Shi Maru* and *Lisbon Maru*, which would carry them to Japan to work as slave labor. The war had stripped the home islands of manpower, so the women, maimed ex-soldiers, and grandfathers toiling in the factories, shipyards, and coalmines would be supplemented with Allied POWs, who would have to work if they wanted to eat. The *Shi Maru* sailed first with 618 POWs locked in its holds, followed by the *Lisbon Maru* with 1,834 prisoners aboard.[12] The men crowded into the holds faced every deprivation possible – darkness, heat, starvation, thirst, disease, and seasickness, all compounded by a lack of ventilation and sanitary facilities in a crowded and confined space. A glaze of urine, feces, and vomit slicked the rolling floor of the hold, where men slouched together in their shared misery.

Like the Imperial Japanese Navy (IJN), the Royal Navy, and the Kriegsmarine, the U.S. Navy had adopted a policy of unrestricted submarine warfare. Anything flying the Japanese flag therefore qualified as a legitimate target for American submarines, whether civilian or military. Hospital ships remained an exception, as did any vessel with prisoners of war or civilian internees aboard. However, the *Shi Maru* and *Lisbon Maru* sailed without any of the usual symbols that might have prevented a submarine attack – white, red, or green crosses on the hull, for example, or running with deck lights switched on throughout the night. Consequently, U.S. Navy submarine captains would assume that the *Shi Maru* and *Lisbon Maru* carried tin, rubber, tungsten, or iron ore, not Allied prisoners of war.

The *Shi Maru* made it to Japan, but on the first day of October the USS *Grouper* torpedoed the *Lisbon Maru* in the waters of the Chusan Archipelago near Shanghai. The crew of the *Lisbon Maru* left the POWs locked in the holds and took to the lifeboats when it became clear that the torpedoes had inflicted mortal damage. Before the ship foundered, many of the Allied soldiers broke free, but 828 of the POWs went down with the ship.[13] However unintentionally, the U.S.

Navy had substantially increased the casualties suffered by the Hong Kong garrison. The surviving POWs as well as the British government held the U.S. Navy blameless for the incident and found the Japanese to be culpable, since the ship had been conveying POWs in locked holds aboard an armed merchant vessel that, unlike the *Asama Maru*, had not been marked with white crosses or any other symbol that might have alerted submarine skippers that the *Lisbon Maru* carried Allied prisoners.

News of the sinking soon reached the Stanley camp. On October 12, Jones wrote, "Camp women much upset by paper report of sinking of Lisbon Maru with loss of 900 HK prisoners of war." Some of the internees had relatives aboard the *Lisbon Maru*, spouses mostly, but also fathers and sons. They had to endure the agony of not knowing whether their loved ones aboard the *Lisbon Maru* had survived, and if they had, where they might be or when they might return.[14] The sinking had no direct impact on Jones, though like all the internees, he had experienced multiple traumas since the start of the war. He had endured combat, the complete erasure of his comfortable prewar life, separation from his wife and daughter, continuous hunger, and captivity with no immediate prospect of release. He and his fellow prisoners had to face the tentative nature of their own continuing survival, too. They understood that they might not live through the war. Everything Jones knew had been upended, and like so many in the camp, he found himself bonding with those facing the same privations and fears as he did. By the end of 1942, the entries in his journal had become increasingly cryptic, as he had entered into a wartime affair with a woman he identified only as "G" in his journal. He referred to Marj and Rae with decreasing frequency, but they remained very much in his thoughts. In November, apparently in reference to his secretive love affair with G, who was also married, he scrawled, "Life is an awful mess in some ways."[15] Still, most of his journal entries consisted of war news interspersed with references to G, descriptions of camp food or lack thereof, and time spent with his close friend and fellow veteran of the Stanley Platoon, Ernest Stevens, whom he invariably referred to as "Steve." War functioned like moral vertigo, and Jones's affair with G as well as his friendship with Steve served as a kind of psychological shock absorber and a mechanism for survival in a wire enclosure where people largely lived day-to-day, wondering if tomorrow the Japanese would march them into the bowels of a Japan-bound freighter or simply bind them to a pole and use them for bayonet practice.

On December 8, 1942, Jones celebrated his thirty-seventh birthday. By necessity, gifts in the camp tended to be makeshift and modest, but Steve still managed to give his friend some cigarettes and a pair of shoes – used, of course. G gave him a bookmark, presumably handmade, that he could put to use while reading the eclectic assortment of frayed books in the camp library.[16] The fact that the camp now had its own library complete with codified rules for borrowers reflected the resignation of the camp population, who had come to accept they were in for the long haul. Faced with this reality, they recreated their prewar lives as best they could, complete with a camp government, a hospital, a school, places of worship, and communal kitchens. They did not lack for pertinent expertise, since the internees represented a remarkable array of vocations, including doctors, dentists, pharmacists, electrical engineers, police officers, government administrators, linguists, mechanics, clergy, educators, and merchant mariners. The camp population also included a fair share of men and a few women with experience in commerce and trade, often gained as employees of prominent prewar firms like Jardine Matheson or Butterfield and Swire. Collectively, the internees had proven to be resourceful and resilient, if at times querulous and factional.

Though Jones and Steve had days when they both felt "fed up" – a term that Jones used frequently in his journal – the two veterans of the Stanley Platoon continued to remain loyal friends. Jones's romance with G, however, proved to be short lived. G received a letter from her husband on Boxing Day, and in an apparent spasm of remorse ended the affair with Jones shortly thereafter. Jones worked to patch things up, and his journal entries often recorded his progress in this regard. On some days, he noted G had been amiable and chatty; on other days, he wrote she had been testy and aloof. "G very fed up & moody," he noted on January 4, and two days later added that their affair "seems all over except for frdship."[17]

While G absorbed much of Jones's emotional energy, the war absorbed his analytical skills. He frequently summarized in his journal what he had learned about the various fronts and theaters, primarily from the contradictory rumors filtering into the camp and the *Hongkong News*, the pro-Japanese newspaper delivered to the internees each day like a daily ration of propaganda. Though Jones could speak and read

Cantonese, he had no access to local news sources and had to rely on the English-language *Hongkong News*, which served up a strange stir-fry of lucid fact and total fantasy. A shrewd reader like Jones could still glean a sense of the war by reading between the lines, however. "Paper contains much good news for us indirectly," he wrote in one entry.[18] He also chronicled his own direct observations of the conflict. On one particularly memorable afternoon, Jones and the other internees craned their necks as American fighter planes from the China-based 14th Air Force made low-altitude runs over the rooftops of the camp buildings.

"About 12 P.40s* did aerobatics & low flying at 4.30pm a sight for sore eyes," Jones recorded on September 12. "One pilot acknowledged us with a wave, another machine gunned the Gendarmerie station in Stanley village. No opposition. Everyone happier."[19]

For a select few internees, that happiness soon turned to jubilation when the International Red Cross finally arranged a second prisoner swap. The few American passport holders left in Hong Kong would be repatriated along with a handful of stray citizens from South American countries and most of the remaining Canadian nationals, G among them. That spring she had received word that her husband was dead, but in the absence of official proof she held out hope he might still be alive. Repatriation offered escape from the camp as well as a chance to learn the fate of her husband and, if necessary, start over in Canada.

The carefully negotiated agreement stipulated that Japanese diplomats and other civilians detained in North America would be swapped for American and Canadian civilians held at various locales in Asia. One ocean liner from Asia would convey the Allied internees to Goa, a neutral Portuguese colonial enclave on the west coast of India, where it would meet a second ocean liner carrying Japanese internees from New York. Under the watchful supervision of Red Cross officials, the Japanese and the American and Canadian passengers would disembark from one ship and immediately board the other, at which point they would be free to return home to their respective countries.

On September 22, 1943, the *Teia Maru* anchored in Stanley Bay, where it swung with the tide in full view of Ray Jones and everyone

---

*Though Jones identified the aircraft as P-40s, wartime records suggest they were P-38 Lightnings from the 449th Fighter Squadron, 23rd Fighter Group.

else who would be left behind. The ship already carried hundreds of American civilians from internment camps in Tokyo and Shanghai, and they thronged the railings, scrutinizing what they could see of the Stanley camp and comparing it to the compounds where they had been held since the start of the war.

As for the 2,400 primarily British internees in the Stanley camp, they faced the prospect of spending the entire war behind the wire. There had been rumors of prisoner exchanges between the British and Japanese governments, but as the war dragged on these tales of imminent release had become harder and harder to believe. All that Jones and the other British internees could do was say their goodbyes on September 23 and then walk up to the cemetery on the western edge of the camp, their steps slowed by hunger and burdened with the bitter resignation of continued imprisonment. They sat on the stone wall or leaned against the hand-chiseled gravestones scattered beneath the casuarina trees. From their hillside vantage point, the internees had an unobstructed view of Stanley Bay. They watched as launches shuttled two dozen Americans and about seventy-five Canadians out to the *Teia Maru*, which took some time in the whitecap swells and rainsqualls.

At 9:30 that evening the *Teia Maru* hauled anchor and departed for Manila, where it would take aboard the last of the 1,500 internees – fully half of them missionaries – who would be repatriated. Three giant white crosses painted on the hull of the ship identified the *Teia Maru* as a noncombatant vessel to any American submarines that might be hunting in the South China Sea, as did the fact that the liner sailed with all deck and mast lights switched on. Once at sea the ship would hold to a steady bearing instead of running in the zigzag pattern that merchant ships used to foil torpedo attacks.

Jones and the rest of the British internees watched in silence as the brightly illuminated passenger liner eased out of Stanley Bay. The drizzle matched their somber mood. As the wind sighed in the casuarinas, the ship slowly melted into the haze until they could see nothing but gray. That night Jones opened his journal and wrote, "G going has left a big blank in the Camp for me now." Then he put away his pencil and journal and never wrote about her again.[20]

By late 1943, Jones could see that the air war overhead had reached a new level of intensity as the 14th Air Force ramped up the tempo of its operations. Commanded by Brigadier General Claire Lee Chennault of Flying Tigers fame, the 14th Air Force sought to support the government of Chiang Kai-shek by degrading Japanese air assets in China; providing air support for Nationalist Chinese troops; interdicting Japanese road, rail, and river traffic; sinking shipping in the South China Sea; and wrecking port facilities along the south China coast. As part of this air campaign, the 14th Air Force struck Hong Kong on a regular basis with P-38, P-40, and P-51 fighters, B-25 medium bombers, and B-24 heavy bombers. Often incoming American squadrons faced determined resistance from Japanese Army Air Force (JAAF) fighter pilots based at Canton and Kai Tak. Despite the robust defenses that had claimed more than a few of his pilots, Chennault viewed Hong Kong as a friendly city under enemy occupation. Rather than seek the wholesale destruction of Hong Kong, the units under his command instead waged a discriminate bombing campaign against dockyards, fuel storage facilities, shipping, Kai Tak airfield, and other militarily significant targets. Most air raids targeted Victoria Harbor, which remained out of view of the internees in the Stanley camp, though well within earshot.

From his position on the southern coast of Hong Kong Island, Jones could hear the rumble of the bomb trains rolling in like distant thunder. Sometimes he spotted flak bursts fired by the defending antiaircraft batteries or caught glimpses of aircraft that might have been American or might have been Japanese, but the mountainous spine of the island blocked his view of the bombing itself and he had no way to directly observe the action. Jones and the rest of the camp population remained entirely unaffected, in fact, and the daily routine of the compound continued largely as normal despite the distant thunder of exploding American ordnance. Work parties cut wood, weeded vegetable plots, boiled cauldrons of watery soup, ground rice, and performed all the other mundane tasks necessary to ensure their survival. They kept a wary eye on the "turnip heads" – the name many used to refer to their Japanese captors – and tried to divine their final intentions. Many internees predicted their own massacre should the war turn decisively against the Land of the Rising Sun.

Fear of the Japanese never really went away, but the internees shoved their fear to the fringe of conscious thought and lived their days as best they could. Jones found the energy to play softball and sing in the camp choir. He wrote music and played his guitar. He took German lessons and occasionally wrote his journal entries in Deutsch. He repaired shoes, suitcases, and beds for his friends. He had a tooth extracted by one of the camp's two dentists in early December, an experience he recorded with pained understatement as "tough." On December 8, he marked his thirty-eighth birthday with Steve and his wife Mary, who prepared a modest celebratory repast of rice-flour pancakes. The weather turned clear and cold, but warmed in time for Christmas. Everyone broke out their food reserves, the hoarded canned goods and stashes of brown sugar, salt, curry powder, and cooking oil. Jones sang carols and feasted on peanuts, soybean biscuits, rice pancakes, and sweetened white coffee and tea. "Had to ease top button by 5pm," he wrote before turning in. "To bed with full tummy for once."[21]

Jones ended his final journal entry of 1943 with an address to his wife and daughter. "Best wishes Marj darling & baby Rae," he penciled, "may all our desires be realized next year. Goodnight & God Bless you both."[22]

Like the sodden laundry that weighed down the camp's improvised clotheslines, the prospect of another year in captivity pressed down on everyone in the compound. Optimism faded, replaced by the bone-deep chill of winter and the gnawing enervation of empty stomachs. Jones had not ventured far into 1944 before he wrote of his own despair. "Hopelessness creeping in, thinking of how old M & I are getting with no hopes of meeting again for sometime to come," he confided in his journal. "Marrying seems to have been a mistake."[23]

In February, Jones peddled his wedding ring to raise some extra military yen (M¥) – the occupation currency in Hong Kong – that he could use to purchase food. He had already sold his guitar for M¥50 by this point, and wondered if his dwindling stock of saleable possessions might run out before the end of the war. Food deliveries to the camp had become as erratic as the electric power, and much of what reached the camp Jones would have consigned to the garbage heap in prewar days.[24]

By March 1944, Jones saw internees eating sparrows they had killed with homemade slingshots. He found himself constantly thinking of food, particularly sugar-laden confections like fruitcake and bars of chocolate. Camp life lurched onwards in a haze of malnutrition and starvation warded off with gritty rice and watery stew until, like some kind of strange cosmic joke, an unexpected bounty rattled into the camp in the back of the daily supply truck. The local power grid had seized up like a sclerotic heart, starved of coal and bombed full of holes, and the Japanese had suddenly found themselves with an abundance of rapidly thawing victuals in the city's cold storage lockers. Much of this use-or-lose surplus found its way to the camp, which meant that in August the internees went easy on the sparrows and supped on gourmet cuisine like pheasant and partridge instead. A single fowl had to be split between seventeen people, but Jones had no complaints. "Lovely & succulent," Jones noted approvingly of the birds. He had not tasted meat in eight months.[25]

With so little protein in their diets, the internees found the continual toil of camp life thoroughly exhausting. The labor was hard, but necessary, and it kept otherwise idle internees busy. Work offered dignity, comradery, and a sense of purpose. Jones and a work detail built a water boiler during the summer, which required demolishing a wall for bricks. He chopped wood to fuel the boiler, and when deliveries of firewood ended, he cut grass to burn instead. He planted sweet potatoes and turnips. He constructed a cookhouse in October; he cleared rubble and cleaned bricks in November. In late autumn, a pending water shortage meant that Jones and the work teams had to start digging wells and outdoor latrines. Malnourishment ensured that none of these jobs moved quickly, but the slow pace of progress hardly mattered because if the internees lacked energy, they did not lack for time.

By the autumn of 1944, the internees saw the specter of starvation staring back at them when they greeted each other in the kitchen queues, which often offered the barest of sustenance for the increasingly gaunt men and women who stood in line. "All war news good but our position here is deteriorating due to Jap inability to procure supplies," Jones wrote on October 3. Of those supplies, tobacco ranked as one of the most important. Most of the men in the camp smoked, including Jones, and he often noted shortages of tobacco as well as of matches. With a dearth of tobacco and an abundance of nicotine addictions, cigarettes acquired enough value to function as a de facto camp currency. In a compound where the inmates could go for months without eating meat, Jones discovered a tin of corned beef could be bartered for just four cigarettes.[26]

Jones monitored the camp's black market with the same dedication that he analyzed the progress of the war. Internees often sold their possessions to traders within the camp, who were typically fellow internees who had the hustle, tolerance for risk, business acumen, and ready supply of cash to jumpstart and maintain a black-market enterprise. When it came to illicit transactions, however, the perimeter fence remained as porous as the colanders in the camp kitchens, so many internees flogged their valuables to buyers outside the camp, often with the furtive assistance of the Formosan camp guards. Jones noted in November that jewelry – the last of the rings, necklaces, bracelets, and wristwatches that many internees had brought into the camp with them nearly three years ago – now fetched astonishing prices as those with wealth in Hong Kong converted their increasingly worthless military yen into anything that could hold its value. Not surprisingly, gems and gold remained in high demand on the black market, and some internees even resorted to selling their gold teeth fillings.[27]

On December 8, 1944, Jones – now designated as internee number 985 – faced another birthday in captivity. He wrote, "39 today & cold & miserable it is." The mercury held steady at fifty degrees, a temperature sufficient to chill the poorly clad and malnourished internees, who huddled in buildings with no heat, swaddled in every scrap of clothing they owned. His circle of close friends, now expanded by the inclusion of a British nurse named Gwen Flower, gave Jones gifts and offered their birthday best wishes.[28] The thirty-four-year-old Flower, whom Jones had begun to spend a great deal of time with, presented him with some precious tobacco.[29] The Yanks, meanwhile, obliged him with not one but two air raids by silver P-51s that flashed liked drawn swords in the sun.

Four days later a small Japanese tanker struck some shoals near Beaufort Island, a lonely jumble of granite that the Cantonese called Lo Chau. When viewed through the windows of the camp hospital, Lo Chau floated in the haze some four miles from shore with its larger sibling, the rocky isle of Po Toi. In an operation witnessed by any internee with both the time and the interest – most internees had plenty of the former, but relatively few possessed the latter, though Jones would certainly have been among them – two salvage vessels yanked the wayward ship free of the rocks like a dentist pulling a stubborn tooth. In an apparent attempt to keep the single-stack vessel from sinking, the salvers towed the tanker into Stanley Bay and beached it along the shore below the camp gardens. This prompted the suspicion that the Japanese had purposefully stranded the ship near the main hall of St. Stephen's as well as the six staff bungalows, which collectively housed a substantial number of internees. The Americans would never bomb targets close to the Stanley camp, went the logic, even one as tempting as an immobile tanker.[30]

In a repeat of the previous December, the frigid weather turned balmy with the approach of Christmas, 1944. With culinary ingenuity and the help of the black market, the internees managed to scrape together another holiday feast – the third Christmas in captivity for most people in the camp, but the fourth for Jones, who had surrendered and been taken prisoner on December 25, 1941. In the evening Jones dined on rice, baked sweet potato, stew, and pasties. He even had some tobacco. The day ended with an air-raid alarm, and then Jones cracked open his journal before going to bed. His thoughts traveled to Australia, and the hope that 1945 would be his last year of incarceration. He penciled, "I hope you are having a happy time Marj dearest & Baby Rae & am convinced that our next Xmas will be together."[31]

5

Training Days

On January 21, 1943, first lady Eleanor Roosevelt arrived at the Newport News Shipbuilding and Dry Dock Company in Virginia to serve as the guest of honor for the launching of a brand-new Essex-class aircraft carrier, hull number CV-10. In what its crew would later claim was a portent of the ship's aggressive nature, the partially complete carrier rumbled down the slipway and plunged into the James River several minutes ahead of the scheduled launch time. Understanding that she had a moving target on her hands, Roosevelt quickly swung her champagne bottle against the hull as it slid past and christened the ship with a fizzy spray of alcohol.[1] Though the navy had originally planned to name CV-10 the USS *Bonhomme Richard*, the newest addition to the carrier fleet had instead been named the USS *Yorktown* in honor of CV-5, the warship of the same name that had also been built by Newport News Shipbuilding, but lost during the Battle of Midway in 1942.

Newport News Shipbuilding specialized in carrier construction, with 31,000 employees on the payroll in spring 1943, and work continued at a rapid pace on the second incarnation of the *Yorktown*.[2] Commissioned on April 15, 1943, the 856-foot *Yorktown* soon joined the Pacific Fleet with the planes of air group CVG-5 stowed in the hangar deck like wasps in a nest. In the months that followed, the crew of the *Yorktown* and the fliers of CVG-5 participated in a string of bloody engagements at locales with incongruously exotic names suggestive of South Pacific paradises – Kwajalein, Wotje, Truk, Saipan, Tinian, Palau, Woleai, and Hollandia. Like a saber or sword, however, CVG-5 grew dull from repeated use, with thirty-three airmen and thirty-nine aircraft lost to enemy action and operational mishaps.[3]

In June 1944, CVG-1 replaced CVG-5 aboard the *Yorktown*, which went on to participate in the invasion of the Marianas and the Battle of the Philippine Sea, the largest carrier action of the war. The lopsided American victory cost the IJN three flattops and hundreds of naval aviators and planes. American pilots soon began referring to the battle as the Marianas Turkey Shoot because so many Japanese aircraft had been swatted from the sky and fallen into the waves, leaving blots of aviation fuel to roil on the crenelated swells. Though American naval intelligence did not fully comprehend the decisive scale of the Japanese defeat and would continue to view the surviving Japanese aircraft carriers as a significant threat, in actuality the IJN carrier air groups had been so thoroughly decimated that they no longer existed as an effective fighting force.[4] Those Japanese carriers that remained afloat were, quite literally, empty vessels. No U.S. Navy flattops had been lost during the battle, but the elimination of Japanese carrier-based airpower had not been without cost for the American air groups. CVG-1 of the *Yorktown* alone listed forty-eight aviators killed or missing and forty-two aircraft as crashed, ditched, or shot down during missions to attack the Japanese fleet or support the landings in the Marianas.[5]

The exhausted airmen of CVG-1 rotated off the *Yorktown*, and in August 1944, the ship returned to the West Coast for refitting, equipment upgrades, and some much-earned shore leave. In October 1944, the *Yorktown* steamed to Hawaii to pick up the planes and personnel of CVG-3, its new air group. In U.S. Navy nomenclature, an air group aboard a fleet carrier like the *Yorktown* was referred to as a "CVG," which typically consisted of a fighter squadron, known as a "VF," a dive-bomber squadron, known as a "VB," and a torpedo-bomber squadron, known as a "VT." The "F," "B," and "T" squadron designators stood for "fighter," "bomber," and "torpedo," while the "V" indicated heavier-than-air, a designation that harkened back to the days when lighter-than-air ("ZP") dirigibles had represented a substantial portion of naval airpower. In naval-speak, the designation "CVG" literally translated as "Fleet Carrier Heavier-than-Air Group," though fliers and non-fliers alike used the simpler "Carrier Air Group."

This explained why the acronyms "CAG" and "AG" also remained in widespread use throughout the navy.

The original CVG-3 had been stationed aboard the first *Yorktown* at Midway in 1942, so a reunion with the second *Yorktown* in 1944 brought things to full circle. However, the latest iteration of CVG-3 had little in common with the earlier version of the air group other than its name and function, since the unit had been recommissioned with fresh pilots and aircrew as well as the next generation of carrier warplanes – the Grumman F6F Hellcat, the Curtiss SB2C Helldiver, and the Grumman TBM Avenger. Lt. John Lavender and Jean Balch, ARM3c, numbered among the new aviators of CVG-3. As members of VB-3, the air group's dive-bomber squadron, they had racked up plenty of logbook hours and even survived an emergency water landing together during a training flight, but they had never flown a combat mission.

Lt. John Homer Lavender Jr. – "Lav" to his fellow pilots in VB-3 – had been born in Texarkana on November 28, 1920. Brown-haired and blue-eyed, he grew up in the city of his birth and stood six feet tall when he graduated from Texarkana High School in 1939. From summer 1939 to spring 1940, he served as a private in the 112th Cavalry of the Texas National Guard. In the autumn of 1940, he began working at Wommack's Men's and Boys' Wear, a Texarkana clothing store known for its slogan, "Exclusive but not Expensive." He applied for flight training in the U.S. Naval Reserve in May 1942, an application supported by a letter of recommendation from his employer, Herman H. Wommack. George W. Coffman, the owner of Highland Park Grocery where Lavender had worked for two years, provided a second letter. The president of the Texarkana Junior Chamber of Commerce, who resided on Hazel Street across the road from the Lavender family, provided the third letter. He wrote, "I have no hesitancy in recommending this young man for anything for which he might make application."[6]

No doubt due in part to his sterling letters of recommendation, not to mention a medical examination that found him to be in good physical and psychological health, the Naval Aviation Cadet Selection Board in New Orleans recommended Lavender for flight training in the U.S. Naval Reserve. He enlisted for four years on May 23, 1942, as a seaman second class (S2c) and just two days later entered Naval Pre-Flight School at Athens, Georgia. Upon completion of preflight training on August 7, 1942, his rating changed from S2c to aviation cadet, and he reported to the Naval Air Training Center (NATC) in Corpus Christi, Texas. At the NATC, Lavender completed intermediate flight training, at which point the navy terminated his enlisted status and appointed him as an officer at the rank of ensign on May 5, 1943. He specialized in VSB, which meant his NATC training had prepared him to fly aircraft that operated in both a scouting and bombing role, such as the rugged and dependable Douglas SBD Dauntless that had served naval pilots faithfully since the start of the war. Lavender then received orders for the naval air station (NAS) at Vero Beach, Florida, where he completed operational training in August 1943.[7]

Though Lavender had earned his wings, he still had to qualify as a carrier pilot before the navy would assign him to a carrier air group. For this reason, he received orders in August to report to the Carrier Qualification Training Unit (CQTU) at NAS Glenview in Illinois. A uniquely equipped naval unit, the CQTU operated a pair of unarmed, coal-burning aircraft carriers. In 1942, the navy had purchased the paddle-wheeled cruise ships SS *Seeandbee* and SS *Greater Buffalo*. Dockyard workers had then removed the superstructure of these luxurious Great Lakes excursion vessels and replaced them with 550-foot flight decks. Renamed as the USS *Sable* and USS *Wolverine*, the improvised carriers served as training vessels in Lake Michigan, a freshwater body so large it provided a convincing stand-in for the ocean, complete with gale-force winds, thirty-foot swells, zero-visibility fog, and subzero temperatures. The lake also proved advantageous for training operations because the *Wolverine* and *Sable* could operate without fear of enemy submarines, and the ship's crew and trainee pilots did not have to observe radio silence. From August 21 to 28, Lavender trained at the CQTU and successfully executed repeated landings and takeoffs from the makeshift flattops, thereby qualifying for duty in a carrier air group. Numerous other pilots rotated through the CQTU during this same seven-day period, including an unusually young aviator named George Herbert Walker Bush, who qualified for carrier duty at just eighteen years of age and would eventually become the forty-first president of the United States. After a fifteen-day leave that marked the liminal point between training and combat, Lavender traveled to the West Coast for active duty with VB-3, which he joined on September 26, 1943.[8]

Jean Felton Balch also received orders for VB-3, where he wound up flying as Lavender's rear-seat radio-gunner. The two aviators both had roots in Texas, as Balch had been born in Abilene in 1923, and both men came from Baptist religious backgrounds. Before the war, Balch had worked at Meads Bakery in Abilene and completed three semesters of college at Hardin-Simmons University in pursuit of an A.B. in Business Administration. Then the war had upended his plans like a Texas twister, and like so many young men, the eighteen-year-old Balch decided to enlist in the military. This involved a substantial amount of paperwork. His father, Donald Newman Balch, had to sign a form titled "Consent and Declaration of Parent or Guardian in the Enlistment in the Naval Reserve of a Minor Under Twenty-One Years of Age." On his "Application for Enlistment," Balch filled in the blanks in response to a menu of questions that asked him to list his language qualifications ("English"), race ("White"), and civilian trade ("baker"). He indicated that he was unmarried, that his parents were still alive, that he was a U.S. citizen, and that he had never served in any branch of the military. He responded "no" to the questions that asked, "Do you drink intoxicating liquors?" and "Have you ever been arrested or in the custody of police?" When asked to state his reason for enlisting, he went for brevity and wrote, "Service to U.S." He indicated that he had traveled no further than Mexico, and that he had never once been to sea. Still, Balch was in good health, had 20/20 vision, and reported nothing more serious in his health history than a childhood tonsillectomy and a bout of pneumonia.[9]

Balch enlisted in Dallas on August 5, 1942, for a three-year hitch in the naval reserves. Like all new recruits, he started as a lowly apprentice seaman. He completed recruit training at the U.S. Naval Training School in San Diego, advanced to S2c, and then went through radio school. In early 1943, Balch received orders to report to the U.S. Naval Air Technical Training Center in Memphis, Tennessee. His ten-week course focused on radio communications, but included two weeks of training in radar operation that qualified him as an airborne radar operator. Balch placed 154 out of 154 in his class, though despite this last-place ranking he still scored a respectable 80.3 out of 100 and earned his ARM3c rating on April 3, 1943. He spent April and May of 1943 at Naval Air Gunners School in Jacksonville, Florida, and then trained as a torpedo-bomber crewman in VTB Operational Training Unit 2.

In July, Balch was designated a combat aircrewman, specialty VTB, and assigned to Carrier Aircraft Service Unit 7 (CASU 7) at the Seattle Naval Air Station. On October 5, 1943, he transferred into VB-3, a dive-bomber squadron, even though he had been trained to fly as a radio-gunner in torpedo bombers.[10]

In April 1944, VB-3 deployed to Hawaii, and by this time Balch had been designated a combat aircrewman qualified in VSB-type aircraft for the twin duties of radioman-gunner. Ensign Lavender, meanwhile, earned a promotion to lieutenant junior grade. Balch served as his gunner and flew with him on every mission. Like the other Helldiver crews in VB-3, Lavender and Balch trained extensively in Hawaii in preparation for combat in the Pacific, with particular emphasis on dive-bombing, the presumed primary role of the squadron, and little practice in shallow-angle glide-bombing or low-level skip-bombing. Nocturnal flight operations also featured prominently on the syllabus, which continually tested both plane and pilot. During one predawn mission, for example, the engine on Lavender's Helldiver seized up and left him with a white-knuckle grip on a dead stick. He told Balch to prepare to ditch and then executed a flawless water landing in the darkness. After a brief interval of bobbing about in a life raft like a pair of castaways, the crew of a nearby LST plucked the two aviators from the sea. Lavender's feat of airmanship had impressed his rear-seat gunner, who needed no further convincing that he would be flying with a pro.

In October, Lavender and Balch heard the scuttlebutt about the squadron embarking aboard the *Yorktown* with the rest of CVG-3. On October 18, the *Yorktown* arrived at Pearl Harbor from the West Coast, which verified the rumors. On the morning of October 24, the carrier departed from the sprawling naval base and steamed into the open Pacific, at which point the ninety-seven aircraft of CVG-3 flew out from Hawaii and landed aboard the flattop without incident. Escorted by three destroyers, the *Yorktown* set course for Ulithi, the coral atoll east of the Philippines that had become the advance staging area for the U.S. Pacific Fleet. Lavender and Balch would soon be in the war.[11]

6

Little Jack and the Big John

Commander John D. Lamade had been in the war since Pearl Harbor. Like all good air group commanders, he led from the cockpit, in this case the cockpit of an F6F-5 Hellcat with "T. Benny" painted on the engine cowling. A native of Williamsport, Pennsylvania, Lamade had graduated from the U.S. Naval Academy in 1932, earned his commission as a naval aviator in 1934, and served on four of the navy's prewar carriers, the *Langley*, *Lexington*, *Ranger*, and *Saratoga*. In 1937, while stationed aboard the *Lexington*, he had participated in the unsuccessful search for Amelia Earhart, who had gone missing over the Pacific while trying to circumnavigate the globe. In 1939, after a one-year stint as a flight instructor at NAS Pensacola, the navy posted Lamade to the cruiser USS *Augusta*, flagship of the Asiatic Fleet commanded by Admiral Thomas C. Hart. The *Augusta* returned to the States in late 1940, but Lamade remained with the Asiatic Fleet and reported aboard Admiral Hart's new flagship, the USS *Houston*.

Lt. Thomas Benjamin Payne ranked as the senior aviator aboard the *Houston*, a Northampton-class cruiser armed with a main battery of nine 8-inch guns that could lob shells out to eighteen miles. Long-range gunfire often called for a forward observer in an aircraft, so the *Houston* carried four catapult-launched Curtiss SOC-3 Seagulls and, with the addition of Lieutenant Lamade, five pilots. Payne dubbed his little squadron of underpowered biplanes the "Flying Wombats" and showed similar creativity when referring to his newest and most diminutive pilot. When flying a Seagull, every pound of weight counted, and Lamade registered a trim 155 pounds on the scale. This made him the lightest and shortest of the five pilots, which earned him the sobriquet "Jack Sprat" or "Little Jack" from a gleeful Tommy Payne. The two aviators soon became close friends and partied hard when on liberty, particularly at the Army-Navy Club on Manila Bay. Both men had a penchant for gags, pranks, tall tales, and bottles of San Miguel beer. After one alcohol-soaked night out on the town, the two pilots purloined an antique cannon dating to the Spanish–American War from the lawn of the club and mounted it on the launch conveying them back to the *Houston*. Upon arrival at the *Houston*, Payne lost interest in the pilfered artillery piece and instructed the coxswain, "Do something about that thing." In the morning, the skipper of the cruiser, Captain Albert H. Rooks, roused Payne from his bunk and said, "You wouldn't know anything about a cannon that's disappeared from the lawn of the club, would you, Tommy?"

When war broke out on December 8, 1941, the *Houston* was riding at anchor at Iloilo, a town on the island of Panay some 200 miles south of Manila Bay. Lieutenant Lamade was drinking coffee in the wardroom and preparing to take over his morning watch topside. Knowing that Lamade would soon have the deck, the communications officer brought the lieutenant the same no-nonsense war order from Admiral Hart that the radio room had just delivered to Captain Rooks. "Japan has started hostilities," stated the terse seven-word message. "Govern yourselves accordingly." Hart had prepared his fleet so thoroughly that neither Rooks nor Lamade needed further instructions.[1] Lamade immediately sprinted up to the bridge, where Rooks issued the directive everyone aboard the *Houston* had long expected, but dreaded hearing nonetheless: "Prepare the ship for war."

In a tactical maneuver that had been planned before the outset of hostilities, the *Houston* and major elements of the Asiatic Fleet withdrew from their exposed positions in the Philippines and steamed southwards to the Dutch East Indies. A naval rearguard of PT boats, river gunboats, tugs, minesweepers, and other auxiliaries remained behind in Manila Bay to support the land forces of General Douglas MacArthur. However, Manila fell in the opening days of 1942, and the U.S. Army's defense of the Philippine archipelago devolved into a desperate holding action on the Bataan Peninsula and the fortress island of Corregidor in Manila Bay. Having abandoned the Philippines, the U.S. Navy reluctantly concluded that the defense of the Dutch East Indies by the combined American, British, Dutch, and Australian (ABDA) forces would likely amount to a holding action as well.[2] ABDA naval forces under Admiral Hart would be forced to retreat from the Indies and fall back to northern Australia, went the grim calculus, and consequently by mid-February the navy had dissolved the Asiatic Fleet and created a new command – U.S. Naval Forces, Southwest Pacific – that reflected the shifting strategic realities faced by the American military. Admiral Hart would no longer command naval forces in the region, due to pressure from the White House as well as the British and the Dutch, who had lost confidence in Hart despite his adroitly executed withdrawal of the Asiatic Fleet from the Philippines.[3]

The *Houston* spent much of February 1942 escorting ABDA convoys running between Darwin and the Dutch East Indies. On February 16, Captain Rooks ordered Lieutenant Lamade to fly his SOC-3 to Australia to deliver the most recent ship's roster and deck logs. Rooks may also have wished to get the fragile and highly combustible Seagull – his last operable floatplane – safely off his ship before an anticipated Japanese air attack. A few of the senior officers penned brief notes for their families and gave them to Lamade before the *Houston*'s catapult hurled him aloft. Aided by a *National Geographic* map unpinned from a bulletin board in the officer's wardroom, Lamade and his radioman made the 500-mile flight to Roebuck Bay in northwestern Australia with no fuel to spare. As per his orders, he delivered the ship's papers and monitored the floatplane's radio in anticipation of receiving instructions from the *Houston* about when and where to rendezvous with the cruiser. On February 18, the *Houston* returned to Darwin, some 700 miles to the east of Roebuck Bay, but remained in port just long enough to refuel. As a result, Lamade did not receive the order to rejoin the ship until after the cruiser had returned to sea and he had missed his window for a rendezvous. Shortly thereafter, the *Houston* survived the disastrous Battle of the Java Sea on February 27 – a decisive defeat for the Dutch-led ABDA naval forces – only to go down during a confused night engagement in the Sunda Strait a few days later, taking the shrapnel-riddled body of Captain Rooks with it.

The fortunes of war, however, had spared Lt. Lamade and his gunner, Robert L. Tubbs, ARM2c, who found themselves stranded in Australia with the sole surviving SOC-3 from the *Houston*. The lieutenant's orphan status soon ended, however, and he received orders to fly to Darwin to join the remnants of Patrol Wing 10, originally based in the Philippines with the Asiatic Fleet, but now operating out of northern Australia. In March, the Japanese completed their conquest of the Dutch East Indies. General MacArthur escaped to Australia the same month; Bataan fell in April, and Corregidor in May, ending American resistance in the Philippines. Meanwhile, Lamade flew antisubmarine missions in his SOC-3 until May 1942, when the wake of a PBY Catalina coming in for a landing overturned the little biplane as it bobbed at a saltwater mooring in the Swan River.

Shipped home to the States, Lieutenant Lamade served in an operational training unit at NAS Jacksonville, where he transitioned from floatplanes to fighter aircraft and served as a flight instructor. Promoted to the rank of commander, Lamade took command of CVG-7 in November 1943, though his carrier air group remained a land-based operation until August 1944, when it embarked aboard the newly commissioned fleet carrier USS *Hancock*. Lamade painted "T. Benny" on the nose of his F6F Hellcat in honor of his good friend Tommy Payne, who had survived the sinking of the USS *Houston* and been taken captive by the Japanese along with several hundred members of the crew.[4]

On August 3, the *Hancock* and CVG-7 began the long steam from Hampton Roads to San Diego via the Panama Canal. As the cruise to California demonstrated most painfully, carrier aviation remained an inherently hazardous undertaking, particularly for a newly formed air group on its inaugural deployment. Three of the dive-bombers in Commander Lamade's air group crashed into the sea during launch and recovery operations, and two Hellcats cracked up on the flight deck. A pilot and a gunner as well as three sailors from the *Hancock* died in these mishaps, with eleven more seamen stretchered down to sickbay.

Upon arrival in San Diego, the *Hancock* ceased flight operations, and the plane handlers stowed the carrier's complement of ninety aircraft down in the hangar deck with the careful precision of master craftsmen storing valuable implements in the drawers of their tool chest. Like most carriers bound for the Territory of Hawaii, the *Hancock* would be ferrying military personnel and oversized cargo to Pearl Harbor. Exactly 998 military passengers boarded the carrier as wharf-side cranes hoisted twin-engine transport planes up on to the flight deck, where the deck crew lashed them down like unruly patients on a gurney. With the flight deck clogged by an interlocking jumble of transport planes and their own aircraft cached in the hangar deck, Commander Lamade and his pilots would be taking a break from flying during the cruise to Pearl Harbor.

The *Hancock* left San Diego on August 23, and seven days later the carrier threaded the channel into Pearl Harbor and moored on the starboard side of Pier F-12 on Ford Island. The transit from the West Coast to Hawaii had unfolded without mishap, but this brief respite ended once the transport planes had been offloaded and flight operations resumed. On September 21, an Avenger piloted by the squadron commander of VT-7 crashed off the port bow of the *Hancock* during a training exercise. None of the three men aboard the aircraft survived, and Commander Lamade had to appoint a new squadron commander. To further underscore the perils of naval aviation, five aircraft suffered severe damage during landing accidents aboard the *Hancock* in September.[5]

On September 24, the *Hancock* departed Pearl Harbor for Manus in the Southwest Pacific. Three destroyers accompanied the flattop, as did the reincarnated battleship *West Virginia*. Salvaged from the wreckage of Pearl Harbor, the dreadnought had been refloated, repaired in a West Coast shipyard, retrofitted with modern weaponry, and returned to service for its inaugural combat cruise. As the task group steamed through the vast Central Pacific, the *Hancock* received new orders to proceed to Ulithi with two of the destroyers, while the third destroyer proceeded to Manus with the *West Virginia* to join the 7th Fleet. After an uneventful crossing of the Pacific, the *Hancock* reached Ulithi on October 5 and anchored at Berth 10 in the atoll's capacious lagoon. Warships of every shape and size surrounded the *Hancock*, from landing craft to the battleship *New Jersey*, flagship of Admiral Halsey, the commander of the 3rd Fleet. As expected, Halsey assigned the "Big John" to TF 38, the armada of fast carriers that had spearheaded the American counterattack across the Pacific.[6]

In the years following Pearl Harbor, the American offensive against Japan had followed two broad routes of advance, the first led by Fleet

Admiral Chester W. Nimitz, who had overall command of American forces in the Central Pacific, and the second by General MacArthur, who had overall command of American forces in the Southwest Pacific. Nimitz and MacArthur both sought to destroy the Japanese army and navy, but beyond this immediate goal the two commanders shared a pair of objectives that collectively represented the desired strategic outcome of the war for the United States. Blocking the Japanese maritime supply lines that stretched from Southeast Asia to the home islands remained the first objective. The obvious place to do this would be in the relatively narrow straits that ran between the Chinese mainland and Formosa and Luzon. Once this passage had been denied to the Japanese merchant marine – a move that the Americans called "corking the bottle" – the home islands would no longer be able to import Southeast Asian oil, rubber, and other raw materials vital to modern warfare, and the Japanese military would be crippled. At this point, long-range strategic bombers, shorter-ranged tactical aircraft based on newly captured offshore islands like Okinawa, and warplanes from U.S. Navy carriers could begin softening up targets on the home islands in preparation for the second and final strategic objective: the invasion and occupation of Japan.

Primarily though not exclusively a naval operation, the first American route of advance under Admiral Nimitz had punched east to west through the scattered atolls of the Central Pacific that constituted the outer ramparts of the Japanese Empire. Amphibious assaults spearheaded by the U.S. Marine Corps had stormed the Gilbert Islands in the late autumn of 1943, the Marshall Islands in early 1944, and the Marianas Islands with their strategically valuable airfields in summer 1944, which precipitated the Battle of the Philippine Sea and the decisive American victory over the carriers of the IJN. From newly constructed airbases on the Marianas, B-29 heavy bombers would be able to fly long-range strikes against Tokyo. The second route of attack under General MacArthur had started below the equator in Australia, ground zero for Allied forces in the Southwest Pacific, and then moved on to Guadalcanal and the Solomon Islands while also wresting control of New Guinea from the Japanese. In some cases, Nimitz and MacArthur chose to dodge well-defended islands with sizeable enemy garrisons – the former bypassed Truk, for example, while the latter leapfrogged over Rabaul – after first neutralizing their offensive potential. This tactic came to be known as leaving the enemy to "wither on the vine," and it avoided costly assaults on fortified islands with no strategic value.

MacArthur believed that the two arms of the American advance should converge at the Philippines. In contrast, Fleet Admiral Ernest J. King, Commander in Chief of the U.S. Navy and Nimitz's direct superior, felt that the Philippines – an archipelago of 7,000 islands stretching for 750 miles – would be fiercely defended by the large Japanese occupying force. While supportive of invading the southern and central Philippines, he advocated bypassing the main island of Luzon, which would entail fighting the Japanese in the urban areas of Manila as well as the jungle-clad mountains that studded the island like natural redoubts. Instead, King called for invading Formosa, an action that would definitively cork the bottle and pave the way for linking up with Nationalist Chinese forces on the mainland. Once Formosa had been secured and landings made on the China coast, airbases for the B-29s would be constructed to augment those seized in the Marianas. The stage would then be set for the next sequence of major operations: the invasions of Iwo Jima and Okinawa. In King's opinion, a wholesale invasion of the Philippines would slow the American advance and prolong the war. In contrast, MacArthur argued that the United States had a moral obligation to liberate the Philippines, an American commonwealth whose people it had sworn to protect, and that retaking the Philippines would erase the ignominy of its fall to the Japanese in 1942. In addition, controlling Luzon would work for corking the bottle just as easily as Formosa. Nimitz himself recognized that an invasion of Formosa would first require the neutralization of Japanese forces on Luzon. Furthermore, invading an island as large as Formosa would require a staging ground, and Luzon remained the obvious choice. MacArthur's argument ultimately proved persuasive to President Franklin D. Roosevelt, who chose the Philippines over Formosa. American forces would start by taking Leyte, a large island in the central region of the archipelago. Luzon would be the next objective. American forces would then surge north to seize the volcanic islands of Iwo Jima and Okinawa, which would play pivotal roles in the American air campaign against the home islands.[7]

Scheduled for late 1944, the invasion of Leyte would be a massive undertaking supported by not one but *two* fleets of the U.S. Navy. Admiral Halsey's 3rd Fleet would take on an offensive role with its

Fast Carrier Task Force, which had been codenamed Task Force 38 and included the *Hancock*. Under the tactical command of Vice Admiral Marc A. "Pete" Mitscher, TF 38 would surge forward to engage the Japanese fleet if and when it sortied for the Philippines from Singapore, the home islands, or both simultaneously. TF 38 would also destroy Japanese airpower by launching proactive airstrikes on Japanese airbases on Formosa, throughout the Philippines, and in the Nansei Shoto chain of islands that dangled from the southern end of the Japanese home islands like stepping-stones to Tokyo. Vice Admiral Thomas C. Kinkaid's 7th Fleet, in contrast, would take on a defensive role. His fleet consisted of destroyers and destroyer escorts, diminutive escort carriers, and older, slower battleships – some resurrected from Pearl Harbor – that would shepherd the transports and landing ships to the beachhead at Leyte Gulf, conduct a pre-invasion shore bombardment, protect the assault force as it stormed ashore, and cover the empty transports as they withdrew once the troops had landed. The 3rd Fleet and the 7th Fleet had been tasked with fundamentally different missions, and they answered to different masters as well. Halsey and the 3rd Fleet reported directly to Admiral Nimitz, whereas Kinkaid and the 7th Fleet had been loaned to General MacArthur and fell under his immediate command.

In late October, American troops landed at Leyte Gulf with both the 3rd Fleet and 7th Fleet in attendance. As the IJA fought hard in the jungles and special air units launched *kamikaze* raids against U.S. Navy ships for the first time, the IJN initiated an ambitious surface action involving three separate task forces. If the complex operation went according to plan, one column with the IJN's remaining flattops would lure Admiral Halsey and the fast carriers away from their position offshore from the beachhead at Leyte. IJN carrier air groups had been largely exterminated by this stage of the war, which meant that the Japanese carriers could not maintain a viable combat air patrol (CAP), much less mount a solid counterstrike against the American carriers. If Halsey took the bait, the IJN would likely lose the thinly defended flattops. However, the other two columns, consisting of destroyers, cruisers, and battleships, would then be free to sweep aside Vice Admiral Kinkaid's 7th Fleet and make a classic pincer attack on the American transport ships as they unloaded men and materiel onto the invasion beaches at Leyte Gulf. The multipronged assault involved nearly every major IJN warship and almost succeeded in accomplishing its objective due in part to tactical lapses on the part of Admiral Halsey, who had been decoyed away from the invasion beaches in his eagerness to destroy the IJN carrier fleet, but in the end what came to be known as the Battle of Leyte Gulf proved to be a decisive victory for the Americans.

Casualties among American sailors and aviators had been grievous, if militarily insignificant, and the same steely calculus held true for the destruction of U.S. Navy warships. TF 38 lost the light carrier USS *Princeton*, and the 7th Fleet lost two escort carriers, two destroyers, and a destroyer escort, but these sinkings had little impact on the total combat power of the U.S. Navy. In contrast, all three Japanese task forces suffered catastrophic losses, with more than two dozen irreplaceable IJN warships sent to the bottom, including one heavy carrier, three light carriers, three battleships, six cruisers, four light cruisers, and twelve destroyers.[8] Just a single warship survived from the southernmost column – the charmed destroyer *Shigure*, which defied all odds and eventually made it back to the home islands.

The *Hancock* had sortied from Ulithi some three weeks before the Battle of Leyte Gulf with elements of TF 38 that included the carriers *Intrepid* and *Lexington* and Admiral Halsey's flagship, the battleship *New Jersey*. Combat operations commenced on October 10 when the fast carriers pounded targets on Okinawa, the largest of the islands in the Nansei Shoto chain. Commander Lamade and the pilots of CVG-7 launched from the *Hancock* to fly a series of airstrikes against the island, and in the weeks that followed, the air group shed aviators and aircraft at a steady rate. Some planes spun in while clawing for altitude during launch operations, while others went into the water while approaching the stern of the *Hancock* for landing. Other pilots managed to touch down but then mashed into the crash barrier, the net-like device of woven steel cable that caught out-of-control planes before they could careen into forward-spotted aircraft. Over enemy-held islands or above enemy warships, navy-blue planes belched flame and dove into the dirt or the equally hard sea. Others ditched halfway home, out of gas or shredded to the point of mechanical failure. Most of the flight personnel aboard shot-down or ditched aircraft never returned, but sometimes men from CVG-7 came back from the dead. After bombing a Japanese dreadnought during the Battle of Leyte Gulf on October 25, Lt. (j.g.) Richard C. Scobell of VT-7 had ditched his shot-up torpedo bomber in the Philippine Sea. He disappeared and joined the ranks of the missing in action (MIA), only to board the *Hancock* days later to reunite with his squadron.

Lieutenant Scobell had been born and raised in Rochester, a city bisected by the Genesee River in western New York. He left home to enroll in the University of Connecticut, where he worked his way through college as an apprentice pipefitter, electrician, and draftsman. For extra cash, Scobell worked odd jobs as a golf caddy, hospital worker, student cashier, and waiter in the faculty dining room. He graduated with a BS in Architecture, and went on to work for the Eastman Kodak Company, a major employer in Rochester, as an architectural designer. The war and the prospect of the draft interrupted his career, however, and Scobell enlisted in May 1942. He soon entered flight school as an aviation cadet, and in April 1943, he earned his wings and his commission as an ensign in the United States Naval Reserve. Scobell went on to complete his operational training in torpedo bombers and joined torpedo squadron VT-305 in November 1943.[9]

Ensign Scobell first saw combat in the Southwest Pacific with VT-305, which operated from a forward airbase instead of an aircraft carrier. In the spring and early summer of 1944, he flew twenty-five combat missions against targets in the Solomon Islands and Bismarck Archipelago. As a jack-of-all-trades squadron equipped with the multipurpose TBM Avenger, Scobell and his comrades flew bombing raids against airfields, antisubmarine patrols, night minelaying runs, and improvised crop defoliation missions involving seventy-five-gallon spray tanks filled with diesel oil and mounted in the bomb bays. Scobell never had to ditch or pull his ripcord, but on three separate occasions he returned to base with a battle-damaged TBM and a deep appreciation for the ruggedness of American aircraft designs. When VT-305 disbanded on August 1, 1944, the newly promoted Lieutenant (j.g.) Scobell received orders transferring him to Commander Air Force, Pacific Fleet, for reassignment.[10]

After temporary duty with several different squadrons, Lieutenant Scobell had reported aboard the escort carrier USS *Nassau* of TG 30.8, a service group under the command of Capt. Jasper T. Acuff that provided at-sea logistical support to the fast carriers. Like a floating delivery truck, the *Nassau* served as a "transport carrier" conveying spare pilots and planes to TF 38 during combat operations, when attrition rapidly burned through aviators and airplanes alike. On October 16, 1944, the *Nassau* had rendezvoused with elements of TF 38 and transferred fresh aircraft and aviators to the fast carriers, while receiving "flyable duds" in exchange from air groups that wanted to offload war-weary aircraft.[11] Experienced combat pilots from the fleet carriers flew the castoff planes over to the transport carriers and then returned with new aircraft. The air groups did not trust replacement pilots to do the job, since some had gone long periods without making a carrier landing or undergoing refresher training. In addition, many replacement pilots lacked combat experience, and more than a few had been moldering for weeks or even months in the replacement pools on Ulithi, Guam, and other forward operating bases of the U.S. Navy.[12] Consequently, replacement pilots rarely flew their own plane to their next assignment and usually made the transfer by breeches buoy instead.

In what amounted to a nautical high-wire act, a breeches buoy transfer used a cable strung between two warships and a highline chair, which was suspended from the cable and pulled across the gap between the ships from one deck to the other. In rough seas, a replacement pilot strapped into a highline chair faced the prospect of a salt-water dunking. Sometimes the ships rolled in such a way that the cable went slack mid-transfer, dropping the chair into the surf, and sometimes a wave surged high enough to momentarily submerge the chair and its occupant. Either way, the pilot arrived on his new ship sopping wet. Lieutenant Scobell had more hours in the cockpit than many replacement pilots and had already completed one tour of duty, but this made no difference. Rather than fly a TBM over to his new billet, he was ordered to transfer by highline chair from the *Nassau* to a destroyer, which then used the same mechanism to deliver him to the *Hancock*, where he reported for duty with VT-7 as a replacement pilot.

Lieutenant Scobell had arrived aboard the carrier during its first combat cruise, which had opened with strikes against targets on Okinawa and Formosa. After a round of strikes in the Philippines, the cruise culminated in the Battle of Leyte Gulf, when Scobell glide-bombed a Japanese battleship – possibly the *Nagato* – and likely scored a hit with a 1,000-pound bomb, though the armored behemoth absorbed the blow like a prizefighter shrugging off a right hook. In the process, his TBM-1C flew through a barrage of multicolored flak bursts and absorbed a fatal dose of shrapnel, leaving Scobell with no choice but to ditch in rough seas. Scobell and his gunner swam free of the cockpit and turret before the Avenger slid beneath the waves, but the radioman-gunner failed to emerge from the belly compartment, which could be difficult to escape from during a water landing.* After nearly forty-eight hours of riding the rollercoaster swells in a pair of inflatable life rafts, the destroyer USS *Preston* rescued the two waterlogged aviators and brought them to Ulithi. Scobell and his gunner eventually returned to the *Hancock*, and if the standard transaction occurred, the *Hancock* would have first paid a ransom in ice cream before the destroyer's crew handed over the two naval aviators. As a reward for his resurrection, Scobell received a new TBM-1C, a replacement radioman-gunner, and orders from Commander Lamade to man his plane. November would be another busy month for the *Hancock* and its air group.[13]

---

*Lieutenant Scobell's crew included C.D. Boyer, AMM1c, who survived the ditching, and Wallace "Wally" A. Barney, ARM3c, who never emerged from the plane.

Manila Bay

On November 3, 1944, after eleven days at sea broken by just a single night's anchorage at Eniwetok in the Marshall Islands, Lieutenant John Lavender and his gunner, Jean Balch, arrived at Ulithi atoll aboard the USS *Yorktown*, one week too late to join the Battle of Leyte Gulf. Strategically located 850 miles to the east of the Philippines, Ulithi served as the forward base for the U.S. Navy's thrust across the Central Pacific. With a lagoon that totaled more than 200 square miles, Ulithi could harbor the entire 3rd Fleet as well as a substantial logistical force equipped with everything from floating dry docks to cold-storage ships. Assisted by Service Squadron 10, the *Yorktown* dropped the hook and began taking on bunker fuel, aviation gasoline, ammunition, and other stores in preparation for joining one of the four task groups that collectively comprised Task Force 38. Each of the task groups – codenamed sequentially as TG 38.1, TG 38.2, TG 38.3, and TG 38.4 – contained a nucleus of fast carriers screened by destroyers, cruisers, and battleships. Depending on the tactical requirements, the four task groups could operate independently, often separated by hundreds of miles of open ocean, or they could operate in close proximity and combine their combat potential into the most powerful armada ever assembled in the history of naval warfare. Though formidable, however, the fast carriers were far from invulnerable, and the task force had sustained serious damage during operations offshore from the Philippines in late October. Japanese *kamikaze* pilots had slammed their planes into the fleet carriers *Intrepid* and *Franklin* as well as the light carrier *Belleau Wood*, and while all three ships remained afloat, the *Franklin* and *Belleau Wood* would have to return to the shipyards of the West Coast for repairs. With two flattops out of commission, the *Yorktown* and its fresh complement of aviators made for a welcome addition to the task force.[1]

Vice Admiral John S. McCain had relieved Vice Admiral Mitscher as the commander of TF 38 just before the *Yorktown* had arrived at Ulithi. In accordance with his obligation to cover the ongoing invasion of Leyte by General MacArthur's Sixth Army, McCain ordered TF 38 to take up station east of Samar and go hunting for enemy ships and planes. On November 11, the *Yorktown*, now assigned to TG 38.1, assembled a full deck-load strike of fifty-five aircraft involving all three of the squadrons – VF-3, VB-3, and VT-3 – that collectively comprised CVG-3. Led by Commander John T. Lowe, VB-3 went into combat for the first time since recommissioning, flying all twenty-three of its Helldivers on a bombing mission against Japanese warships and transports attempting to convoy reinforcements to Ormoc Bay on the western coast of Leyte. Lavender and Balch, however, sat out their squadron's inaugural combat mission, no doubt anxiously awaiting the return of their comrades in their respective ready rooms, playing acey-deucy or throwing dice, as the acrid cigarette smoke spiraled upwards into the wiring and ductwork overhead and the floor vibrated with the throb of the ship's colossal propulsion system. All planes from VB-3 returned from the strike, though antiaircraft fire forced one F6F-5 pilot from the squadron to ditch. In total, some 300 carrier planes from multiple air groups struck targets at Ormoc, leaving the bay strewn with burning hulks and the wreckage of sunken ships.[2]

After blunting Japanese attempts to reinforce Leyte, TF 38 and the *Yorktown* proceeded north to a position east of Luzon to strike airfields, shipping, and IJN warships. On the morning of November 13, VB-3 drew Manila Bay as a target. During the preflight briefing, Lieutenant Lavender and ten other pilots learned from the squadron's air combat intelligence (ACI) officer that they would fly Strike 1C, the third strike of the day. Jean Balch received a similar briefing in the gunner's ready room. As Lavender and Balch would both have realized, Strike 1A and Strike 1B would thoroughly rile up the Japanese gun crews. By the third strike, any element of tactical surprise would be lost, and the enemy gunners would be fully alerted and ready to swat the incoming planes of Strike 1C from the sky. Their first bombing mission was going to be a hot one.

At a quarter to noon, Lavender and the other ten pilots scheduled to fly Strike 1C began taking off from the *Yorktown* in quick succession. VF-3 contributed thirteen F6F-5s and VT-3 brought seven TBM Avengers to the mission, respectively hauling napalm and 500-pound bombs. The eleven Helldivers of VB-3 flew in two divisions, with Lavender and Balch assigned to the second division of five aircraft, and all planes toting a thousand-pounder in the bomb bay supplemented by a 250-pound bomb under each wing.[3] All of the VB-3 pilots flew the Curtiss SB2C-4, the most recent variant of the Helldiver. When first introduced in late 1943, the SB2C-1 had been unpopular with VB pilots, who swore by the trusty SBD Dauntless, otherwise known as the "Slow but Deadly." It remained an apt moniker, for the Dauntless had vanquished the Japanese carrier fleet at Midway. However, the navy had wanted a dive-bomber that could fly further, faster, and with a heavier payload, and chose the SB2C from the Curtiss Wright Company to replace the SBD-5. Design flaws and technical problems riddled early models of the Helldiver, including aerodynamic instabilities, unreliable electrical systems, and potentially catastrophic structural weaknesses. One executive officer in a training squadron had spun up his 1,900-horsepower engine on the tarmac, at which point the tail of his Helldiver snapped free from the rest of the airplane and blew across the mat in the prop wash like a loose feather from the back end of a goose. Other pilots reported problems with crossed circuits so that when they flipped a switch to turn on their bombsight, for example, the electrical system would drop the landing gear instead. "We were all afraid of the SB2Cs," one trainee pilot would later write, "and we flew them as though they were booby-trapped." By February 1944, the Bureau of Aeronautics had demanded that Curtiss make more than 880 design changes to the Helldiver, and by July 1944, the modified and much-improved dive-bomber had completely replaced the Dauntless aboard the fast carriers. In subsequent naval operations the "2C" had proven to be a reliable, if unglamorous, combat aircraft. Still, like all VB pilots, Lavender understood that the Helldiver demanded a pilot's full attention and, in comparison to the steady TBM, could be unforgiving to a less than vigilant aviator. Pilots called it "the Big-Tailed Beast" or simply "the Beast," and this too remained an apt moniker.[4]

Lieutenant Lavender's flight path took him westwards over the mountains of Luzon to Manila, where he and his fellow pilots discovered that a bandage of clouds shielded the Japanese ships docked along the waterfront or anchored inside the breakwater of the city's port area. However, VB-3 found clearer conditions over Cavite, a peninsula on the southern coast of Manila Bay tipped with the wharves and warehouses of a naval base that had once serviced the U.S. Navy's ill-fated Asiatic Fleet. Most of the squadron went after a medium-sized freighter, while Lavender and two other pilots lined up on what they believed to be two destroyers and a small tanker moored close together near the tip of Cavite. One after the other, the three pilots dropped their planes into the signature nosedive of the 2C.

Helldivers, of course, had been purpose-built for dive-bombing, but the same could not be said of the human body or the human psyche. Executing a dive-bombing run went against a pilot's natural instincts, in fact, since the maneuver put the plane in a near-vertical plunge towards the ground or the sea. Though not particularly difficult in comparison to loops and rolls, a dive-bombing run taxed the physical and mental stamina of pilot and gunner alike. The rapid descent could burst eardrums like a popped balloon, though screaming helped to relieve the pressure as well as the tension, and the high-G pullout could trigger gray-outs that pushed the pilot against the dark threshold of unconsciousness. If he stumbled through that doorway, a fiery handshake with land or water would soon follow in a spray of radial-engine cylinders, crumpled scraps of wing and fuselage, and random pieces of human anatomy. When a plummeting dive-bomber came under fire – and it invariably did, since not many targets worth bombing failed to shoot back – all the pilot could do was rely on the dive brakes to keep the airspeed under the 400mph threshold, kick the plane back onto the target as he peered through his bombsight, and keep glancing at the unwinding altimeter dial as it cranked away like some kind of manic wind-up toy. At the bottom of the dive, when the dial unspooled to 2,000 feet, he pushed the button on the stick, dropped the eggs, closed the dive brakes, and pulled out in a full-throttle bank in the hope of glimpsing a direct hit while avoiding taking one in return.[5]

Lieutenant Lavender's falcon-like pounce on the ships off Cavite proved frustratingly inconclusive, as he failed to ascertain whether his bombs had struck home. His aircraft remained unscathed, however, and he felt reasonably certain that at least one of the three pilots in his division had scored a hit on the tanker with a 1,000-pound bomb. In the rear seat, Balch had kept his twin Brownings chambered up and ready to fire throughout the dive and pullout. With no enemy fighters in evidence, Balch and the other gunners opted to engage in some opportunistic strafing of the many ships and small craft spread across Manila Bay. Lavender and the other pilots certainly made liberal use of their 20mm wing cannons, since by day's end VB-3 had hammered nearly 5,000 rounds into ships of all shapes and sizes in Manila Bay, including freighters, tankers, self-propelled barges, and a floating dry dock. As anticipated, however, the gunfight had been a two-way affair. Japanese antiaircraft gunners painted the sky with black smoke puffs and streaks of tracer fire that glowed with a heat reminiscent of molten lava. After taking hits in the cowling and briefly catching fire, one Helldiver pilot headed back for the *Yorktown* with an oil leak that eventually forced him to make a water landing short of the fleet, though the picket destroyer USS *Maddox* rescued both the pilot and the gunner. Meanwhile, automatic antiaircraft fire shot down one Hellcat from VF-3 and peppered two more as the pilots flat-hatted down the Pasig River to splatter napalm along the Manila waterfront.[6]

Like a clock face masking the tightly wound assemblage of springs and gears needed to keep accurate time, the simplicity of the system for codenaming the strikes flown each day by the flattops of TF 38 belied the complexity of launching, executing, and recovering a naval airstrike. Each of the subordinate task groups designated their strikes in alphabetical order – Strike A, Strike B, Strike C, Strike D, and on days with a particularly frenetic tempo of air operations, Strike E and Strike F. Task groups placed their task-group number before the alphabetic designators. For example, TG 38.1 designated its strikes as 1A, 1B, 1C, and 1D, while TG 38.2 designated them as 2A, 2B, 2C, and 2D. Strikes flown by different task groups often overlapped, which meant, for example, that Strike 1A flown by the air groups of TG 38.1 might arrive over the same target at the same time as the Strike 2A aircraft from TG 38.2. At their best, coordinated attacks allowed the task groups to mass their combat power and overwhelm enemy defenses, but at their worst, they degenerated into a confused melee that pilots derisively referred to as a "rat race."

John Lavender and Jean Balch returned to Manila Bay the next morning when they drew Strike 1A, their second bombing mission and the lead strike of the day, which launched from the *Yorktown* and the other carriers of the task group before sunrise. Led by Commander Lowe, VB-3 contributed a dozen Helldivers for Strike 1A, while VF-3 provided fourteen Hellcats. VT-3 rounded out the formation with eight Avengers hauling 500-pound general-purpose (GP) bombs rather than torpedoes. The cloudy weather had dissipated during the night, and dawn brought the clear skies ideal for dive-bombing work. When VB-3 reached the target zone at 8:00 a.m., taking care to avoid overflying the flak batteries emplaced on the island of Corregidor at the mouth of Manila Bay, all twelve Helldiver pilots tipped over into their dives at 12,000 feet and hurtled downwards towards a transport ship just outside the Manila harbor breakwater. Antiaircraft fire chased the plummeting American planes, and VB-3 gunners spotted Japanese fighter aircraft wheeling in the distance. All this made for a particularly tense dive, perhaps with a generous dose of screaming to help release the stress and the pressure, though in the end the enemy pilots never closed within firing range, the flak proved as harmless as a holiday fireworks display, and the freighter swallowed a lethal cocktail of 250- and 1,000-pound bombs. Burning, the ship started to settle at the stern like an unbalanced teeter-totter. A second airstrike later in the day by VB-3 and the rest of the air group inflicted still more maritime carnage and set the naval base at Cavite ablaze for good measure. Flak punched a sizeable hole in the wing of one Helldiver, but everyone from VB-3 made it back to the *Yorktown* that day, Lavender and Balch included. VF-3, however, lost two more Hellcats to Japanese gun crews braced with just as much fortitude as the American pilots trying to kill them. Commander Macpherson B. Williams, who led the *Yorktown* air group, had come to respect the prowess of Japanese antiaircraft gunners. "It was observed," he wrote with implicit admiration in his post-strike report, "that even under the most intense strafing attacks, the Japs stayed at their guns and continued firing."[7]

***

After moving out to sea to refuel from the fast oilers, TF 38 and the *Yorktown* steamed to the north. On November 19, the task force launched a series of strikes against Japanese air assets on Luzon. VB-3 targeted two airfields at Mabalacat, not far north of the former American airbase at Clark Field. Lavender and Balch, however, sat the missions out, which failed to do much damage because the Japanese had dispersed their aircraft into the surrounding jungle beneath canopies of artfully constructed camouflage. At the conclusion of the raids against the many airfields on Luzon, the *Yorktown* and TG 38.1 parted from TF 38 and returned to Ulithi, that sandy home-away-from-home with its warm beer, rapidly dwindling supply of coconuts, and the spectacle of hundreds of American warships riding together at anchor.[8]

On November 24, the *Yorktown* anchored in berth number 29 in the Ulithi lagoon. Rather than raise the morale of VB-3, however, the respite from combat operations undermined it. Orders arrived to cut the squadron's complement of Helldivers by half in order to make room for an expanding VF-3, which flew the more versatile F6F-5 Hellcat. Though a superb fighter aircraft, the "F6" could also serve as a fighter-bomber equipped with bombs and rockets. Commander Lowe faced the difficult decision of deciding who would remain with the downsized VB-3 aboard the *Yorktown* and who would be reassigned. Lavender and Balch made the cut, but fully half the squadron did not. On November 29, twelve of the squadron's twenty-four Helldivers took off from the *Yorktown*, an operation that required the use of the catapults since the ship rode at anchor and could not steam into the wind. Flying in formation, the twenty-four pilots and gunners deployed to Naval Air Base Guam for further assignment. Some of the men had been with VB-3 since early 1943, but four had served just a single day in the squadron. They had arrived aboard the *Yorktown* on November 23 to report for duty with VB-3 and then flown off the ship twenty-four hours later for reassignment.[9]

A later revision of orders upped the complement of Helldivers aboard the *Yorktown* to fifteen. However, this adjustment had little impact on squadron morale, which took an additional beating in mid-December when the fast carriers sortied from Ulithi to support American landings on Mindoro, an island midway up the Philippine chain. The *Yorktown* air group participated in strikes against airfields in the Manila area during the Mindoro operation, but relied exclusively on its Hellcats. Squadron ACI officers briefed the pilots and gunners of VF-3, VB-3, and VT-3 as they sat in their ready rooms, suited up in their flight gear and tense with pre-combat jitters, but only the pilots of VF-3 received the order to man their planes. In the end, neither the dive-bomber pilots nor the torpedo pilots participated in any bombing missions, but on December 18 they had to ride through a typhoon so violent it sank three destroyers and badly damaged nine additional ships, including three fleet carriers. Though rattled by twenty-degree rolls, the *Yorktown* came through the storm with minor damage, and VB-3 pilots searched for survivors from the capsized destroyers. Rescuers plucked some men from the sea, but in total, nearly 800 officers and sailors perished.[10]

When the *Yorktown* returned to Ulithi, Lieutenant Lavender heard the scuttlebutt circulating among the pilots of VB-3 that claimed all remaining bombers aboard ship – both VB *and* VT – would be swapped out for Hellcats. Talking with his fellow gunners, Jean Balch heard the same rumors. However, though Vice Admiral McCain had advocated for replacing Helldivers aboard TF 38 carriers with additional Hellcats, which he argued could operate as multipurpose fighter-bombers, the decision about carrier air group complements rested further up the chain of command. For the time being, the fast carriers would continue to carry the standard trio of aircraft types – Hellcat, Helldiver, and Avenger. VB-3 remained aboard the *Yorktown*, albeit at a lean 60 percent of its former size, and its skipper, Commander Lowe, moved up to take the helm of the entire air group to replace Commander Williams, who had been shot down over Luzon by the Japanese antiaircraft gunners whose fighting spirit he had come to respect. After flying multiple missions over the previous two days, Commander Williams – known as "Mac" to his fellow aviators – had said, "I'm going on only one hop today." As the *Yorktown* pilots later noted, his words had proven to be prophetic.[11]

On Mindoro, meanwhile, a U.S. Army brigade secured a perimeter around San Jose, the principal city on the island, and construction battalions began bulldozing airfields for land-based aircraft of the 5th Air Force. From San Jose, the army pilot of a P-38 Lightning or the crew of a B-25 Mitchell only had to log 150 air miles to hit targets around Manila Bay. Mindoro would serve as a forward base camp for the impending American assault on Luzon, which would kick off with amphibious landings on the beaches of Lingayen Gulf in early January 1945. The 5th Air Force and the fast carriers would provide the necessary air umbrella, supplemented by the escort carriers of the 7th Fleet. The *Yorktown* and the fast carriers departed Ulithi on December 30 to support the upcoming invasion of Luzon, the endgame of the Philippines campaign that would ram the cork in the bottleneck so firmly that no Japanese corkscrew – *kamikaze* or otherwise – would ever be able to twist it back out.

8

Convoy Hi-87

The ships gathered at Moji, their dimpled hulls as gray as the overcast. Some arrived singly, others in groups. By the end of December 1944, nearly twenty warships and merchant vessels had reached the port city, which sat on the narrow Straits of Shimonoseki. Situated on the southernmost home island of Kyushu, Moji had long served as the jumping-off point for voyages to the outer reaches of the Japanese Empire, and the captains of the rust-stained ships gathering there in the final days of 1944 knew they would soon depart with the next southbound convoy, codenamed Hi-87.[1]

Starting in mid-1943, the Japanese high command had given the designation "Hi" to all high-speed convoys moving between Japan and Singapore. Odd numbers signified southbound convoys, while even numbers indicated northbound convoys.[2] Convoy Hi-87 was thus the eighty-seventh southbound convoy to Singapore, and was scheduled to depart from Moji on the last day of 1944, a year that had marked the near-total destruction of the Japanese navy and merchant marine.[*] Despite the wartime construction of new freighters and tankers, the merchant fleet had been reduced to just 40 percent of the cargo capacity available before the attack on Pearl Harbor in 1941.[3] Combat losses among the IJN, which no longer possessed any carrier battle groups,

---

[*]The Romanized transliteration of the Japanese character "ヒ" is "*hi.*" In Japanese characters, therefore, convoy Hi-87 is ヒ 87.

had been just as grievous. Convoy Hi-87 had been cobbled together from the remnants that still remained afloat and included seven precious civilian tankers and the navy oiler *Kamoi*, which had been built in 1921 in Camden, New Jersey.

The *Sarawak Maru*, the smallest of the merchant tankers, had already made the hazardous Moji to Singapore run three times. A Type 1TM design, the aft-stack *Sarawak* had been constructed in Yokohama by Mitsubishi, launched in October 1943, and gone on to incur some substantial battle scars while hauling crude oil from Southeast Asia to the home islands. An American submarine torpedoed the 5,136-ton tanker in December 1943, but the ship had stubbornly refused to sink. Welders and machinists of the 101st Repair Unit in Singapore had patched up the mangled hull and sent the *Sarawak* back to sea. Six months later another submarine put a torpedo into the *Sarawak*, and this time the IJN repair unit in Manila stitched the tanker back together. The *Sarawak* had then steamed north to Japan for additional repairs in Yokohama before proceeding to Moji to form up with convoy Hi-87.

Slow-moving freighters had been excluded from the convoy, though the cargo-passenger liner *Tatsuwa Maru* joined the lineup since it could match the pace of the relatively speedy tankers. None of the tankers carried any cargo, though the *Kaiho Maru* embarked some 600 men from the 30th Shipping Engineer Regiment, which was deploying overseas. The convoy commander, meanwhile, sailed aboard the *Kamoi*. All the merchant vessels mounted an assortment of antiaircraft weapons and deck guns, though a chronic shortage of armaments and ordnance meant the tankers would leave port with too few gun tubes.[4] On the night before departure, the blackness sparked with acetylene torches as workers from the naval arsenals welded additional antiaircraft weapons, new radar arrays, extra racks for life rafts, and other last-minute upgrades to the tankers and their screen of warships.

Hi-87 included four small escort vessels – *CD-13*, *Kurahashi*, *Mikura*, and *Yashiro* – and the light carrier *Ryuho*. Most significantly, five of the IJN's remaining destroyers had been assigned to the convoy, and the inclusion of these precious naval assets reflected the importance of Hi-87. The destroyers included *Hamakaze*, *Hatakaze*, *Isokaze*, *Yukikaze*, and *Shigure*.[5] Nicknamed "Indestructible," the *Shigure* had survived multiple engagements with the U.S. Navy under the command of Capt. Hara Tameichi, one of the most talented destroyer commanders in the IJN. Hara had been reassigned at the end of 1943, but the epic of the unsinkable *Shigure* continued even without his presence on the bridge. In October 1944, Commander Nishino Shigeru took the destroyer into the Surigao Strait with an IJN task force during the Battle of Leyte Gulf, where the U.S. Navy sank every ship in the formation except the *Shigure*. Of all the commanding officers in the task force, only Nishino survived the engagement.[6]

Lt. Cdr. Hagiwara Manubu, the current captain of the *Shigure*, would have understood the strategic rationale for convoy Hi-87. He would have known that the eight tankers assigned to the convoy represented a substantial percentage of Japan's remaining tanker fleet, which had been relentlessly hunted by American submarines. Japan's war machine relied on oil imports from Southeast Asia, and the whittling down of its tanker fleet had led to a critical fuel shortage in the home islands. In 1944 alone, 132 tankers had been lost.[7] The surviving tankers and whatever escort vessels could be spared would have to chance a run south through the American blockade, decided the high command. Laden with nothing but ballast, the tankers and their escorts would ghost south past the American submarines and aircraft to Japanese-occupied Singapore, now renamed as Syonan-to or "Light of the South Island." There they would belly up to the dockside depots and take on the crude oil, bunker fuel, gasoline, and other petroleum products needed in the fuel-starved home islands. Then they would run the blockade back to Moji. Or so went the plan.

In truth, the odds did not favor the tanker crews, many of them nursing hangovers from a final night of raucous, tomorrow-we-die carousing in Moji, where they had downed cup after cup of *sake* to dull the fear of their morning departure. They knew full well that they would need more than a little of the *Shigure*'s famed luck to survive the 3,500-mile voyage down to Singapore and back. However, no vessel epitomized the endgame desperation of the Japanese military more than the *Ryuho*, which sailed without an air group because the IJN had lost nearly all of its naval aviators and airplanes. Rather than conventional aircraft, the *Ryuho* carried fifty-eight *Ohka* rocket-powered *kamikaze* planes instead. These human-guided flying bombs could not take off from the carrier, which served as a glorified cargo ship; instead, the

Ohka would be unloaded at the port of Kiirun on Formosa, the convoy's first port of call, where they would be slung beneath the belly of a twin-engine bomber and hauled aloft. Once within range of American ships, the *Ohka* would be dropped from the bomber, the pilot would ignite the rocket engine, and the stubby-winged plane would begin its death dive into the nearest warship of the U.S. Navy. Perhaps no other aircraft in the entire conflict bore a name of such tragic beauty, for the name "*Ohka*" ("Cherry Blossom") served as a metaphor for the short lives of their young pilots.

Convoy Hi-87 departed Moji at 8:20 a.m. on December 31 with nineteen ships, but this number soon fell to eighteen when a ruptured steam pipe forced the destroyer *Yukikaze* to return to port. As the convoy left Kyushu behind and ventured out into the open ocean, the tanker captains paced their bridges and kept their ungainly vessels on station while watching the swells for the telltale wakes of incoming torpedoes. Steaming on a westerly bearing, the convoy crossed the straits that separated Kyushu from the Korean peninsula and then traced the coast of the Japanese colony. Despite the loss of the *Yukikaze*, good fortune seemed to favor the convoy, which avoided contact with the American submarines that rumor said ran in wolf packs so large that a man could walk from Moji to Singapore on the tops of their periscopes.[8]

Once the convoy had pushed deep into the pocket of the Yellow Sea, the convoy commander gave the order to head for the Chinese mainland. On the morning of January 3, as the convoy moved south along the China coast, the ships received a radioed warning that ports and airfields at Formosa had been struck by American carrier-based aircraft. Since continuing on to Formosa would invite attack by U.S. Navy warplanes, the convoy took refuge in the Chusan Islands to the south of Shanghai, which the convoy commander assumed to lie beyond the range of the American carrier planes. However, U.S. Navy submarines posed a significant threat in the Chusan Islands, where the *Lisbon Maru* had been torpedoed in late 1942, killing more than 800 POWs from Hong Kong. In these dangerous waters on the edge of an even more perilous sea, the eighteen ships dropped anchor and waited for the all-clear signal to proceed to Formosa.

At dawn on January 3, the three task groups of TF 38 took up station east of Formosa in rough seas dominated by six- to eight-foot swells. All of the groups launched a series of airstrikes on the mountainous island, which sat between Luzon and Kyushu and had long been a Japanese colony. Most of the raids focused on the airfields that could send both conventional and *kamikaze* aircraft against the invasion force bound for Lingayen, though some air groups targeted harbors and merchant vessels. TG 38.1, which included the *Yorktown*, dispatched its fighters on multiple sweeps over enemy air installations in northern Formosa. In addition, the VB and VT squadrons of TG 38.1 attacked shipping and port facilities. As part of this effort, John Lavender and Jean Balch joined ten other Helldiver crews from VB-3 on Strike 1B against the port of Kiirun on the northeast tip of Formosa. Twenty-two Hellcats and eleven Avengers brought the total formation up to forty-four aircraft, which left the *Yorktown* at 7:00 a.m.

Forced down onto the deck by a low ceiling, the squadron flew the first 200 miles at altitudes ranging from 100 to 500 feet. Fifty miles out from the Formosan coast the overcast broke up, allowing the VB-3 pilots to ascend to a higher altitude in preparation for pouncing on ships in Kiirun harbor. A dive-bombing run required clear skies up to 12,000 feet, the preferred push-over altitude, but when VB-3 arrived over Kiirun they found a layer of overcast at 10,000 feet and a second blanket of clouds hanging over the target from 5,000 to 8,000 feet. Diving blind through the soup would have likely amounted to a *kamikaze* run, so the squadron scouted for holes in the overcast to dive through instead. Eventually, the Helldiver pilots settled for ducking below 5,000 feet and executing glide-bombing runs that, in comparison to dive-bombing, unfolded at relatively sedate speeds and angles of attack. VB-3 pilots had little training in the tactics of glide-bombing, however, and the low ceiling meant that pilots had just a few seconds to acquire targets before bomb release. When they popped out of the clouds and dropped to 1,500 feet moments later, each pilot salvoed a mix of 250- and 500-pound bombs on freighters in the outer harbor and the dockyard on Sharyo-to Island.* Four pilots

---

*Sharyo-to Island is known today as Heping Island, also spelled as Hoping or Ho Ping.

placed their bombs within the perimeter of the shipyard, but just two pilots managed to score hits on merchant ships, which had been the primary objective of the strike. Japanese guns crews defending the harbor likely felt equally disappointed, as they failed to bring down any of the American planes.

All eleven Helldivers then flew down the coast to the prearranged rendezvous point with VT-3, which had flown inland to raid an airfield. On the way to the meeting point, the Helldiver pilots spotted three Sugar Charlies – the Office of Naval Intelligence (ONI) codename for small, single-stack merchant vessels with an aft bridge – hugging the shoreline. Since the VB pilots still had sufficient fuel and ammunition, they banked around to strafe the luckless trio of ships.

VB-3 pilots might have needed to brush up on their glide-bombing skills, but they all knew how to strafe a ship, and they flew a plane that had been designed for just this kind of work. Each Helldiver toted two 20mm cannons – one per wing – with 200 rounds per tube, making them potent gun platforms. A fully automatic weapon, the 20mm functioned much like a machine gun, but fired an explosive round. For this reason, the navy classified it as a cannon. Virtually every ship in the navy carried 20mm Oerlikons for antiaircraft defense, but in naval aviation only the Helldiver and some variants of the F4U Corsair packed the 20mm. By 1945, a degree of ordnance envy had set in among the Hellcat pilots, who had begun to clamor for a new generation of fighter equipped with the 20mm instead of the .50-caliber machine gun that had long been the mainstay of American warplanes. A VB squadron down on the deck could unleash a devastating barrage, since 20mm rounds could penetrate the sides of a metal-hulled merchant ship and rip up its superstructure like a ten-penny nail punched through a tinfoil wrapper. Against wooden vessels, the 20mm worked like a combination buzz saw and Zippo lighter, shattering hull planks with explosive rounds and igniting the splintered boards and beams with tracer rounds.

In total, Lieutenant Lavender and the other ten Helldiver pilots of VB-3 fired 2,900 rounds of 20mm into the Sugar Charlies, plus another thousand rounds from the twin .30-calibers fired by Balch and the other gunners, who snapped off quick bursts when their pilots banked around at the end of their gun run. When the imperatives of fuel consumption as well as ammunition expenditure necessitated that VB-3 head back out to sea for the 200-mile run back to the *Yorktown*, they left behind three columns of smoke, each with a burning ship at its base.[9]

On the same day that TG 38.1 had sent John Lavender and Jean Balch to Kiirun in northern Formosa, TG 38.2 under Rear Admiral Gerald F. Bogan had executed strikes against targets in southern Formosa. Each of the three carriers in Bogan's task group – the *Hancock*, *Hornet*, and *Lexington* – launched a full deck-load strike against the port of Takao. Commander Lamade's air group contributed fourteen Hellcats from VF-7, a squadron so large it consisted of two administrative units, one for fighter pilots and one for fighter-bomber pilots. The designation VF-7 applied to the former, while the designation VBF-7 applied to the latter. Somewhat confusingly, *all* of the pilots belonged to the squadron VF-7, which had a single commander. On this strike, eight Hellcat pilots came from VF-7 and six pilots came from VBF-7.

Dive-bombers and torpedo planes rounded out the strike package from the *Hancock*. VB-7 contributed six Helldivers, and VT-7 provided six TBM Avengers, including one piloted by Lt. (j.g.) Richard L. Hunt. The Missouri native flew a TBM-3 with the number 124 and the squadron's horseshoe emblem painted on the vertical stabilizer. Born in the small town of Keytesville, Missouri, but raised in the sprawling stockyard metropole of Kansas City, Hunt had won the Missouri State Golf Championship in 1937 while a student at Paseo High School. The war had intervened during his senior year at the University of Missouri-Kansas City, and he had abandoned his studies and joined the navy in February 1942, motivated no doubt by patriotism but perhaps as well by a desire to preempt the draft board and enter the military branch of his choice.[10]

Hunt went through flight training, received his commission as an ensign, and went on to specialize in torpedo bombers. He shipped out with VC-39, the composite air squadron equipped with FM-1 and F4F Wildcats and TBM Avengers aboard the escort carrier USS *Liscome Bay*.[11] In November 1943, the *Liscome Bay* joined the armada supporting the invasion of Makin atoll in the Gilbert Islands.

Just before dawn on November 24, as thirteen pilots of VC-39 prepared for launch, a Japanese submarine torpedoed the *Liscome Bay* and triggered a catastrophic secondary explosion in the main magazine that disintegrated the aft end of the ship. Torn open and ablaze, the ship sank in just twenty-three minutes, taking with it three-fourths of the crew. VC-39 lost fourteen of its twenty-nine pilots. Those pilots who survived the sinking had drawn missions scheduled for later in the day, which meant they were in their bunks in a forward section of the ship when the torpedo hit instead of up on the flight deck with the fully fueled and armed aircraft. Presumably, this explained why Hunt survived when so many other members of VC-39 and the ship's complement did not. His abbreviated first combat tour earned him a Purple Heart and a trip back to the States to recuperate from his wounds. He redeployed in the autumn of 1944 and joined VT-7 just in time for the inaugural combat cruise of the *Hancock*.[12]

In addition to flying his customary aircraft, Hunt carried his usual crew for the strike against Takao. Alfred Dejesus, AOM2c, sat in the rear turret with the .50-caliber, and when he peered down between his legs, he could see his friend Gene Barrow sequestered deep in the bowels of the TBM. Barrow shared the tunnel compartment with an array of electronic gear and his .30-caliber "stinger" that he kept charged and ready to fire at enemy bandits coming in at six o'clock low. An extra ammunition can with 200 rounds for Dejesus's machine gun hung on one wall while the gunner's parachute pack hung on the other, which further reduced the available space in the cramped compartment.

Through a small square window in the forward bulkhead next to the relief tube, Barrow could peer into the bomb bay and see the hind end of a Mark 18 torpedo primed with a Torpex warhead that could rip out the guts of a heavy cruiser. Lieutenant Hunt may well have doubted the wisdom of a torpedo attack against ships at Takao, where naval charts indicated the outer anchorage rarely hit fifty feet in depth. Given the tendency of the Mark 18 to dive deep when first dropped into the waves, any torpedoes launched at ships in the outer anchorage ran the risk of burrowing into the seabed. Torpedo runs against ships in the shallower and stoutly defended inner harbor remained even more problematic. Hunt would likely have approved when the target coordinator – the commander of the *Lexington* air group – changed the strike plan during the run into Formosa beneath a ceiling of just 300 feet. Rather than the harbor at Takao, the target coordinator opted to hit a convoy reported offshore from the port instead.

"Torpecker" pilots like Lieutenant Hunt operated the largest and most versatile of the three aircraft types embarked aboard the fast carriers, so they had grown used to carrying diverse ordnance types for a wide variety of mission profiles. A veritable flying Swiss army knife, the Avenger could operate as a torpedo bomber, provide close air support to troops onshore with bombs and wing-mounted rockets, strafe with a pair of .50-caliber wing guns, make glide-bombing or level-bombing runs against targets on land or at sea, patrol for submarines and drop depth charges, execute search missions, act as a radar picket aircraft, block harbor channels with air-dropped mines, and serve in an air-sea rescue role by dropping extra life rafts to downed airmen. VT pilots referred to their TBMs as "Turkeys," an affectionate nickname that stemmed from the Avenger's ungainly earthbound appearance. Like any aircraft, a TBM's wings and vertical stabilizer suggested the feathers and bone structure of a bird. However, the Avenger bore more than a passing resemblance to a *specific* bird, and that bird was the turkey, or more accurately, a pregnant turkey.[13] On the flight deck or the tarmac, for example, a TBM sat on wheels mounted on extended landing gear struts reminiscent of bird legs. The low-hanging sag of the bomb bay, which necessitated the long landing gear struts, connoted the belly of a gobbler, while the cockpit riding high up on a tilted-back fuselage suggested an avian head. Like a turkey standing in the stubble rows of a winter cornfield, the Avenger looked reluctant to take flight when powered down on the hardstand or flight deck, but once airborne the TBM flew with straightforward purpose and power, much like a tom turkey on the wing.

As might be expected, given the versatility of his airframe, Lieutenant Hunt had performed a wide variety of missions since joining VT-7. He remained particularly adept at disassembling Japanese naval architecture, however. During the Battle of Leyte Gulf, Hunt had avenged the loss of the *Liscome Bay* when he torpedoed the light cruiser *Noshiro*, which sank thirty minutes after the warhead of his Mark 18 tore open the hull beneath the number two turret. At least eighty sailors perished, smashed to paste by the blast concussion or pinned by the torrent surging into compromised compartments below the waterline. On December 15, Hunt proved he could drop a bomb with the skill with which he had once dropped golf balls when he used a 2,000-pounder to score a hole-in-one on the *T-106* during a masthead bombing run off the west coast of Luzon, blowing the LST to pieces and drowning or dismembering still more Japanese sailors.[14] Hunt's prowess at sinking enemy ships represented just a tiny fraction of the killing power of TF 38, which could launch hundreds of equally skilled pilots at any given time, each hauling a lethal loading of airborne weaponry that ranged from fragmentation cluster bombs to 5-inch rockets.[15]

Like a typhoon propelled by a blend of vengeance and avgas, the air groups from TG 38.2 descended upon the convoy steaming offshore from Takao. After assessing the battle space, the target coordinator assigned different ships to the three air groups under his tactical control. Hellcats strafed and rocketed a destroyer and five smaller escort vessels as the Helldivers went after two freighters and an LST. Then the torpedo planes went in. Lieutenant Hunt and his five squadron mates had been assigned a freighter, and they executed a classic hammer and anvil attack, with one three-plane division attacking from port and the other from starboard. The Japanese, of course, wanted to kill Lieutenant Hunt just as much as he wanted to kill them, and they certainly had the means. As Hunt made his torpedo run, a flak shell fired from one of the ships exploded in the rear compartment of his plane, riddling Dejesus's right leg with shrapnel and badly lacerating Barrow in the buttocks. To complicate matters further, the torpedo release mechanism malfunctioned, and as Barrow could confirm by peering into the bomb bay, the Mark 18 had refused to drop from its shackles. Hunt found himself nursing a damaged Turkey while hauling a one-ton fish back to the fleet, where he brought plane, torpedo, and crew back aboard the *Hancock* in a virtuoso feat of airmanship.

Though bloody, the experience of Lieutenant Hunt and his crew hardly counted as unique, since shrapnel-spattered TBMs often wobbled back to the fleet with dead or wounded men in the rear compartment. The tunnel gunner remained particularly vulnerable due to his position in the belly of the aircraft, which lacked the armor shielding enjoyed by the pilot and turret gunner. Though some air groups found that wearing cumbersome armored vests known as flak suits could reduce the risk, CVG-4 of the *Essex* ultimately concluded that the casualty rate for their tunnel gunners outweighed the usefulness of having a third man aboard an Avenger. By this stage of the war Japanese fighter pilots rarely intercepted torpedo bombers, went the calculation, and even when they did they seldom made underside gun runs from behind, so the tunnel gunner would probably never fire his stinger in an air-defense role. The increasing sophistication of the communication gear mounted in the TBM meant that the plane's radio no longer required a dedicated crewman. Moreover, arming the bombs, setting the intervelometer, and other functions normally performed by the radioman-gunner could become the duties of the turret gunner, who could drop down into the tunnel compartment as needed, and whose role in defending the aircraft from pursuing enemy zeroes had largely become redundant in any case.[16] After January 3, the very same day that Lieutenant Hunt's TBM had absorbed a blast of shrapnel in its backside, the commander of CVG-4 aboard the *Essex* signed off on VT-4 Avengers launching without a radioman-gunner in the tunnel position. Unlike VT-4 of the *Essex*, however, VT-7 of the *Hancock* made no change to the crew rosters of its Avengers. In the case of Lieutenant Hunt's crew, Dejesus had been injured badly enough to be taken off flight duty for an extended period, but a patched-up Barrow soon returned to duty in the equally patched-up number 124 with a new turret gunner, Louis W. Gahran, AOM2c. Hunt would continue to fly with two men in the rear compartment.[17]

Despite the lack of improvement in flying conditions the next morning, air groups from TF 38 began pounding Formosa for a second day. Lavender and Balch once again drew Strike 1B, which consisted of twelve Helldivers backed by thirteen Avengers and a dozen Hellcats. Upon arrival over Kiirun, the formation circled for thirty minutes in search of a break in the cloud cover that boiled up from the deck to 10,000 feet. A hole in the two-mile-deep bank of clouds would have given the formation a path downstairs, where they could have then executed low-level bomb runs, but no such hole ever appeared. With fuel levels dropping, the strike leader opted to utilize radar and bomb blind through the clouds like a squadron of B-24s over a socked-in target. In a jury-rigged operation, the radar operator in the belly of the lead Avenger peered into his radarscope and attempted to discern the coastline below. When the operator thought he had pinpointed

Kiirun harbor and reached an optimal bomb-release point, he used the interphone to inform his pilot, who then gave the Helldivers on his tail the drop signal. Lavender, Balch, and the other VB pilots watched the squadron's thirty-six bombs melt into the clouds below, perhaps to score a lucky hit on a Sugar Charlie or the dry dock on Sharyo-to, but more likely to kill fish in the harbor or crater the rice paddy of some luckless farmer. Even the Hellcat pilots pickled their bombs in what likely proved to be the only horizontal bombing run of their entire flying career. Still, everyone reckoned that blind bombing of dubious accuracy beat the alternative option of jettisoning their bombs at sea. All planes returned to the *Yorktown* by noon after four hours in the air, at which point deteriorating weather forced Vice Admiral McCain to curtail further strikes against Formosa.[18]

On January 5, the task force repositioned for strikes against airfields on Luzon, the source of many of the *kamikaze* strikes against the armada of ships assembled for the Lingayen landings. *Kamikaze* pilots had already crashed their planes into a number of warships, sinking an escort carrier and an ammunition-laden freighter that had detonated in a cataclysmic explosion that killed the entire crew. In response to this threat, the task force began hitting airfields on Luzon on January 6, and early the next morning John Lavender and Jean Balch suited up to fly another bombing mission. Poor flying weather delayed the launch, however.

When Lieutenant Lavender finally spun up his 1,900-horsepower Double Cyclone and started rolling down the flight deck at 10:45 a.m., the gray sky hung so low that it seemed to scrape the radar masts of the *Yorktown*. In company with seven other Helldivers from VB-3 as well as ten Hellcats and seven Avengers from VF-3 and VT-3, Lavender flew between 200 and 500 feet until the clouds started pulling apart near the coast like smoke in a sudden breeze. As the visibility improved, the VF pilots caught sight of a lone Nakajima B6N torpedo bomber sprinting towards the fleet at 4,000 feet. Though the crew of a B6N normally included two gunners in the rear of the plane, who occupied positions very similar to those in an Avenger, this particular aircraft carried only the pilot, which suggested a *kamikaze* mission rather than a torpedo attack or reconnaissance flight. With no gunners to defend his six o'clock, the pilot played his only card and dropped the landing gear to cut his speed in the hopes the pursuing Hellcats would overshoot.

This gambit failed, however, and two Hellcat pilots started shooting the greenish-brown aircraft to pieces until the engine quit. Shedding wreckage into the slipstream, the bullet-clawed B6N rapidly lost altitude until it caught a wave with its wingtip, splashed to a halt, and sank with its lone aviator, who, as the Hellcat pilots had flown close enough to observe, had never even donned his flight goggles.

Lieutenant Lavender and VB-3 crossed over the coastline at Dingalan Bay and overflew the rugged green topography of Luzon. Visibility rapidly improved as the cloud cover broke up, and soon Lavender could make out the bulk of Mount Arayat, which shouldered up from the surrounding rice paddies to the north of Clark Field. Like the naval base at Cavite, Clark had been an American installation in prewar days, but it now served the needs of the JAAF. VB-3 pilots and gunners spotted numerous planes sitting in the open at Clark, but the fact these aircraft had not been concealed suggested that previous raids had already rendered them nonoperational. Experience had shown the navy aviators that the Japanese hid their flyable aircraft in expertly camouflaged dispersal areas set back from the runway. In the face of sporadic and inaccurate antiaircraft fire, Lavender and the other pilots of VB-3 dropped the usual mix of 250- and 500-pound bombs, strafed with their 20mm cannons, and then rendezvoused at Mount Arayat before winging eastwards back to the fleet. None of the eight pilots reported so much as a single bullet strike on their aircraft, which rarely happened on a bombing mission.

By the end of the day, Lavender and Balch had flown a 500-mile roundtrip, chalked up their fifth airstrike, worked over at least one enemy aircraft on the ground at Clark, and generally given the navy its money's worth. Lavender earned $296.00 a month, including $91.66 for supplemental aviation pay, $16.67 for sea and foreign shore duty pay, and $21.00 for his subsistence allowance. As an enlisted man, Balch drew a more modest pay packet of $140.40 a month, including his supplemental flight pay and overseas duty pay. VB-3 pilots and crewmen had little use for cash on the Yorktown, so they shunted most of their pay into savings, sent it home to their families, or converted it into war bonds. They also kept their pink beneficiary slips up to date, just in case. Lavender designated his mother as his beneficiary. So did Balch. In the event that a mission went bad and they never returned, their mothers would be entitled to six months of their son's navy pay.[19] Pilots talked about flying – always about flying – but tended to avoid talking about beneficiary slips and other portents of death, though its specter haunted the cabins, passageways, and ready rooms, an unwelcome but ever-present member of the squadron.[20] During a follow-up strike on Clark later that day by five VB-3 Helldivers, an SB2C-4 had burst into flame, spun out of control, and drilled into the Philippine dirt like a giant flaming arrow. Fellow pilots had seen just one parachute, so either the pilot or gunner had rode the plane down and become the unit's first combat fatality since joining the *Yorktown* at Pearl Harbor. Officially, and as typed on their Report of Casualty forms, both men aboard the lost plane remained missing in action (MIA). Though their squadron mates could hope the man who bailed out might make it through the war as a POW, everyone had heard the rumors about how the Japanese treated captured American airmen, the dark tales of torture and beheading by samurai sword, and everyone understood that MIA all too often functioned as a placeholder acronym for the starkly permanent designation of killed in action (KIA).[21]

9

Crew Two

On the morning of January 6, 1945, as the carrier pilots of TF 38 pounded targets in the northern Philippines, Lt. Paul F. Stevens taxied his patrol bomber out to the end of the sandy runway at Tacloban, said to be the busiest airbase in the world despite its obscure location in the southern Philippines. He throttled up all four engines, released the brakes, and felt the landing gear shuddering over the carapace of pierced-steel planks (PSP) that lined the runway in lieu of pavement. When Stevens reached takeoff speed, he brought up the nose and eased the 60,000-pound plane into the air. As the hydraulics retracted the tricycle landing gear, he banked out over open water, and Leyte Island receded in the prop wash like a leaf blown loose from a tree.[1]

Lieutenant Stevens settled in for a fourteen-hour mission, which amounted to business as usual in a squadron that regularly executed 2,200-mile search patterns. Most of the U.S. Navy consisted of reservists called up to beat the Axis, but Stevens had joined before the war and belonged to the relatively small cadre of regular navy men. After completing primary flight training in 1941, he had chosen to specialize in multiengine aircraft because he hoped to work for the airlines once he left the navy, a fateful decision that meant that he had been flying patrol bombers on combat missions since the attack on Pearl Harbor. He had started the war as an ensign, but by 1944, the twenty-three-year-old from Joplin, Missouri, had been promoted to lieutenant and appointed the executive officer of VPB-104, a patrol bomber squadron assigned to Fleet Air Wing 10 (FAW 10) of the

7th Fleet. VPB-104 flew the four-engine PB4Y-1, the navy version of the army's famed B-24 Liberator. Stevens had grown to love the slender-winged patrol bomber, which remained identical to the B-24 in most respects.[2] However, the PB4Y-1 differed in one visually obvious way: the nose featured an oversized gun turret plated with armor and equipped with a pair of .50-caliber machine guns. The most important distinction between the two aircraft types had to do with the pilots, who wore naval uniforms, and the nature of their missions, which focused on such nautical functions as maritime reconnaissance and antishipping patrols.

Lieutenant Stevens had departed Tacloban airbase that day with a ten-man crew and 3,400 gallons of aviation gasoline, but he did not have a single ounce of high explosive cached in his bomb bay. A recent directive from higher up had curbed all offensive operations by patrol bombers operating over the South China Sea, much to the frustration of aggressive patrol plane commanders (PPCs) like Stevens. VPB-104 would refrain from arming its aircraft with bombs, went the order, and the battery of machine guns carried by each PB4Y-1 would be used for defensive purposes only. Rather than continue to hone their already formidable expertise in low-level attacks on Japanese shipping – sometimes so low that their four propellers left a wake – the VPB-104 crews would focus instead on searching for enemy surface combatants that might interfere with the Lingayen landings. To ensure that no Japanese warship escaped detection, the VPB squadrons would cover the entire South China Sea, which had been divided into search sectors that radiated out like the spokes of a wheel from the hub of Tacloban airfield on Leyte Island to the outer rim of the China coast.[3]

Unlike army B-24s, which flew with two pilots on the flight deck, a navy PB4Y-1 carried three pilots – the PPC, the first pilot, and the copilot. In another divergence from the B-24, the standard complement of crew positions aboard a PB4Y-1 did not include a navigator, but all three pilots aboard had been trained in navigation, one of the traditional naval arts. Before taking off from Tacloban, Stevens would have assigned either his first pilot or his copilot to the navigation table just aft of the cockpit to plot their flight path, which resembled an elongated slice of pizza with the point of the slice starting at the Tacloban runway and the crust pressed against the Chinese seaboard. Stevens and his flight crew would cruise to the west along one edge of the pizza slice, turn north to trace the crust of the China coast for 200 miles, and then fly east back to Tacloban along the other edge of the slice. They would be over the South China Sea – the oceanic equivalent of no-man's land – for the majority of the fourteen-hour mission.

Lieutenant Stevens and the rest of VPB-104 had originally deployed with fifteen aircraft and eighteen flight crews. A nineteenth crew consisted of twelve non-flying administrative and technical specialists, including an ACI officer and two yeoman to type up the aircraft action reports (ACAs), war diaries, and other naval paperwork. The squadron commander, Lt. Cdr. Whitney Wright, commanded Crew One. As executive officer, Lieutenant Stevens commanded Crew Two. He and his men flew the same aircraft – bureau number 38889 – on every mission, except when mechanical problems or combat damage grounded their aircraft and they had to switch to the backup plane kept on standby for just this kind of eventuality.[4]

On the morning of January 6, Lieutenant Stevens and Crew Two were flying in their regular plane, which featured an APS-15 belly radar in place of the ball turret that hung beneath the fuselage of most of the PB4Y-1s in the squadron. As executive officer, Stevens had rated a plane equipped with radar, and while he appreciated the see-in-the-dark clairvoyance of this new technology, he also missed the pair of .50-caliber guns that would have been in the ball turret. Like most PPCs, he wanted as much firepower as his plane could possibly carry, and he always made sure that his crew loaded extra cans of ammunition – four armor-piercing incendiaries alternating with one tracer round comprised the pattern of the basic belt load – and replacement barrels for the fifties. Still, even without the ball turret, five of the eleven men aboard had their own personal machine guns, giving Stevens a total of eight gun tubes in the nose, top turret, waist, and tail positions. All of the gunners had a clear view of the action, unlike the radar operator, who tried to make sense of blips and traces as he huddled over the green glow of his scope in a windowless closet situated over the bomb bay.[5]

As Lieutenant Stevens and Crew Two crossed the South China Sea, the blunt nose of the plane bucked against a 25-knot (29mph) headwind. Looking out to port – naval terminology reigned on patrol bombers – Stevens could see the blur of the two propellers and the slender fifty-five-foot wing flexing up and down in the turbulence. Like all PPCs, Stevens flew regardless of the weather – he had once piloted a PBY Catalina through the eye of a typhoon – and repeated encounters with weather fronts and other violent meteorological conditions had stripped the navy-blue paint from the leading edges of the wing, leaving bare aluminum that gleamed like pewter when it caught a patch of sunlight.[6]

When Lieutenant Stevens and his crew reached the Chinese mainland, they banked to the north to trace the ragged edge of the coastline. Soon Amoy slid past on the port wing, at which point the radar operator reported over the intercommunication system that he had painted multiple contacts on the sweep of his radarscope about fifteen miles out to sea on the starboard side. Lieutenant Stevens wheeled around through the haze and drizzle, dropped down below the 1,000-foot ceiling, and spotted the lead tanker of convoy Hi-87, which had ventured out to sea and resumed its southward journey when TF 38 shifted its attention from Formosa to Luzon. The convoy's course from the Chusan Archipelago to Formosa crossed multiple spokes of the VPB search sectors, making detection by the radar-equipped patrol bombers virtually inevitable. Cursing his empty bomb bay, Stevens soon saw additional ships materializing out of the fog and rain. He and his crew counted an escort carrier, a light cruiser, seven destroyers, three transports, and two more tankers organized into three columns. However, while they had correctly identified the *Ryuho* as an escort carrier, the light cruiser was actually the destroyer *Shigure*, and the seven destroyers were escort vessels roughly analogous to American destroyer escorts. Without realizing it, Stevens and his crew had paid the enemy warships the ultimate naval compliment by promoting them to the next higher class of combatant.

Lieutenant Stevens radioed a contact report back to Tacloban, but also transmitted a report on the VHF frequency reserved for contacting the lifeguard submarines on patrol in the South China Sea. An aviator dialing up a lifeguard submarine was usually a pilot in extremis, his aircraft running on fumes or punched so full of holes he could see daylight through his wings, and perhaps just minutes or even seconds away from a water landing in a very, very big ocean slit by crisscrossing shark fins. While lifeguard submarines in the South China Sea remained at the ready when it came to rescuing downed aviators, however, their primary mission involved torpedoes. Stevens hoped a lifeguard submarine might be near enough to receive his VHF transmission and then go hunting for tankers and other maritime big game.

With an empty bomb bay, the potential for taking fire from eight warships, and a finite amount of fuel, Lieutenant Stevens saw no reason to loiter over the convoy. He resumed his patrol, and on the return leg overflew the Pescadores before cruising down the west coast of Formosa to Takao, where he received a thorough jostling from the port's aggressive antiaircraft batteries. Then he headed back to home plate at Tacloban, where too little space and too many planes meant that a thicket of propellers fenced both sides of the narrow runway. At the usual landing speed of 105 knots (120mph), the margin for error was thinner than the aluminum skin of a PB4Y-1, but Stevens plunked the gear down on the PSP without incident and taxied clear of the runway. Crew Two had completed another combat patrol.[7]

On the afternoon of January 6, the Gato-class fleet submarine USS *Barb* received a contact report from a friendly aircraft that provided the position of a large Japanese convoy in the South China Sea. In all probability, the report had been radioed from the PB4Y-1 flown by Lieutenant Stevens, though the crew of the *Barb* had no way to identify the sending aircrew. To increase the chance of locating the convoy, the *Barb* immediately passed the word to the other submarines in its wolf pack, the *Picuda* and *Queenfish*. On the morning of January 7, the trio of submarines detected enemy ships some thirty miles off the coast of Formosa and began maneuvering for optimum firing solutions. The *Picuda* fired first and torpedoed the *Munakata Maru* in the bow during a midmorning attack with a spread of four Mark 18 torpedoes. Though badly damaged, the tanker remained afloat and able to make steam. Still, the torpedo hit meant that the *Munakata Maru* would have to abort the run to Singapore and head for Kiirun for repairs instead. Convoy Hi-87 had lost its first tanker, and Lieutenant Stevens and Crew Two could perhaps share in the credit.[8]

In dense fog, the convoy anchored off the northwest coast of Formosa, but not before the destroyer *Hamakaze* had collided with the *Kaiho Maru*. While the big tanker shrugged off the collision, the crumpled *Hamakaze* had to divert to Ansan Naval Base in the Pescadores for emergency repairs. This incident cost the convoy not one but two destroyers, since *Isokaze* had to protect the damaged and vulnerable *Hamakaze* from the American submarines that could peer through the fog with their radar. The departure of the *Shigure* and *Ryuho* further depleted the convoy. Both warships made for the harbor at Kiirun, where dockside cranes soon began swinging the *Ryuho's* cargo of *Ohka* rocket planes ashore. Later that evening, the *Munakata Maru* reached Kiirun as well, where the badly holed tanker joined the *Shigure* and *Ryuho*.

Meanwhile, the remaining ships in convoy Hi-87 fired up their boilers and weighed anchor. Rather than head for Kiirun on the northern end of Formosa, as originally ordered, the ships altered course in response to a new set of directives and steamed for Takao on the southwest tip of the island. Each vessel proceeded independently down the socked-in western coast, since the fog precluded maneuvering as a convoy. By midday on January 8, the destroyer *Hatakaze*, the escort vessels *CD-13*, *Kurahashi*, *Mikura*, and *Yashiro*, and all of the tankers except the *Munakata Maru* had safely reached Takao without coming under further attack by the *Picuda*, the *Barb*, and the *Queenfish*.

Some of the ships threaded the gap in the breakwaters that shielded the channel into Takao harbor from the rollers of the South China Sea. Barely raising a wake, each of the inbound vessels steamed down the channel delineated by the low concrete jetties and into the inner harbor. To starboard, the Cihou lighthouse sat atop a rocky bluff riddled with tunnels and fortifications. A matching bluff to port featured a graceful brick home that had once served as the British consulate, though the sailors readying the hawsers for docking neither knew nor cared about such historical details. Assisted by tugboats, the ships docked at the Kigo Naval Yard or the quays along the industrial waterfront with its aluminum smelter, warehouses, railroad yard, gas works, fuel depots, magnesium plant, and other industrial installations.[9] Those vessels that did not enter port – including the *CD-13*, *Mikura*, and *Yashiro* as well as the oiler *Kamoi* and tanker *Kaiho Maru* – dropped anchor in the roadstead outside the harbor. Convoy Hi-87 had completed the first leg of its perilous journey south to Syonan-to, but intercepted American radio traffic warned of another attack on Formosa by carrier-based aircraft. Preparations began immediately to reconstitute Hi-87 and get the convoy back out to sea so that it could steam southbound out of reach of the fast carriers.

———

After striking airbases on Luzon on January 6 and 7, TF 38 linked up with the fast oilers of TG 30.8 on January 8 and refueled at sea while the transport carriers shuttled replacement aircraft over to the fast carriers, including two SB2C-4s for VB-3 of the *Yorktown*. This much-welcomed infusion of new airframes brought Lieutenant Lavender's squadron back up to its full complement of fifteen dive-bombers.[10] Refueled and restocked with fresh aircraft, TF 38 headed northwest towards Formosa. On the morning of January 9, as General MacArthur watched from the cruiser USS *Boise*, the Sixth Army thundered ashore at Lingayen. In support of these landings, TF 38 launched strikes against airfields and ports on Formosa.

At the southern end of the peapod-shaped island, the airstrikes caught convoy Hi-87 at Takao. Anchored in the roadstead offshore, the *Kaiho Maru* presented an easy target and took six hits down the length of the ship – two in the engine room, one in the oil tanks, two on the bridge, and one on the bow. The crew as well as the men of the 30th Shipping Engineer Regiment, who had not yet disembarked, suffered heavy casualties. Burning, the tanker lurched over with a severe list that soon hit a near-terminal forty degrees. All surviving crew and engineers had abandoned ship by midafternoon, leaving some 300 dead aboard. By this time, the tanker *Kuroshio Maru* had already gone under, the tanker *Matsushima Maru* had been bombed and strafed, and a near miss had inflicted superficial damage on the oiler *Kamoi*. Though the escort vessels hammered away with every available gun tube, a close miss caused minor damage to the *CD-13*, while the *Yashiro* fared much worse, with a hit to the bridge that wiped out the commander and a dozen members of the crew. The day had been a costly one for convoy Hi-87, which had lost two more of its precious tankers.[11]

At the northern tip of Formosa, meanwhile, the *Yorktown* sent its air group out to take another crack at Kiirun despite the zero-zero flying conditions. John Lavender and Jean Balch were not assigned to this mission, though the strike included ten Helldivers from VB-3 as well as contingents from Fighting Three and Torpedo Three. The VB-3 planes launched at 7:20 a.m. and ascended through cloud cover that began just above the wave tops. While the ten Helldiver crews eventually popped out into the sunlight at 15,000 feet, they never found the target and ultimately opted to jettison their bombs over the ocean. Radar and radio homing beacons allowed the VB-3 planes to grope their way back to the fleet, at which point the pilots used their instruments to make a blind descent through the clouds. Despite the dicey nature of such an approach, everyone dropped out of the low ceiling, pulled up just above the foam-streaked ocean surface, and brought their 2C in over the familiar gray stern of the *Yorktown* for a regulation landing.

Since the overcast conditions ruled out a dive-bombing attack, the next strike went in on the deck with ten Helldivers, including one machine crewed by Lavender and Balch. Together with twelve Avengers from VT-3 and a muscular contingent of eighteen Hellcats from VF-3, the dive-bombers skimmed the waves all the way to Kiirun, which remained concealed beneath the low-hanging cloud cover. Six of the Avenger pilots and seven of the VB-3 pilots pounced on an unidentified escort vessel – likely the *CD-3* – offshore just to the north of Kiirun. However, lack of training in low-level bombing hampered the performance of the VB pilots, who had never mastered the art of skip-bombing. Consequently, their bombs either hit and failed to explode or sank too deep before detonating. One of the Avenger pilots from VT-3 showed his comrades in VB-3 how things should be done when he scored a direct hit with a 500-pounder, which amputated the entire bow of the *CD-3*. Strafing and rocketing by the Hellcats inflicted further damage, and the truncated vessel soon tipped up its stern and slid beneath the waves.

In company with the other six torpedo bombers and two Helldivers, Lieutenant Lavender made a risky low-level run into the outer harbor, where he counted seven transport ships. Lavender and one squadron mate bombed a freighter without success, while the third VB-3 pilot bombed and strafed the shipyard on Sharyo-to Island. As tracer fire stabbed out of the mist, the three VB-3 pilots throttled up and streaked back out of the harbor, their departure covered by the poor visibility and the bulk of Sharyo-to. None of the Helldivers took any hits, but automatic antiaircraft fire from ships and shore batteries shooting at nearly pointblank range ripped into five of the six TBMs and shredded one so badly that the pilot had to ditch offshore.[12]

Some of the antiaircraft fire that shot up the Avengers likely came from the 25mm batteries aboard the light carrier *Ryuho*. Perhaps due to the poor visibility, which made it difficult for pilots to acquire targets, the raids on Kiirun left the *Ryuho* unscathed. However, the carrier would travel no further with convoy Hi-87. After unloading its cargo of *Ohka* rocket planes, the *Ryuho* departed Formosa and returned to Japan on what would prove to be the last sortie by an IJN aircraft carrier from Japanese home waters.*

Despite the massive losses suffered during the Battle of Leyte Gulf and the destruction of its once-vaunted carrier task groups, the IJN still possessed enough warships to present a very real menace to the invasion of Luzon. American naval intelligence assumed that counterattacks by the remaining IJN cruisers and battleships would be launched against the Lingayen landings. The IJN battle fleet based at Singapore presented a particularly potent threat to the Lingayen operation. Naval intelligence believed that this fleet had deployed into the South China Sea, possibly to Cam Ranh Bay in French Indochina. From this protected harbor, the hybrid battleship-carriers *Ise* and *Hyuga* as well as four heavy cruisers and a posse of destroyers would be positioned to sortie into the South China Sea.[13] With the right combination of skill, bravery, and luck – and the crews of the *Ise* and *Hyuga* had proved that they possessed plenty of all three during the Battle of Leyte Gulf – the two dreadnoughts might be able to dash across the South China Sea and hit the American supply line that ran for 300 miles up the western coast of the Philippines from Leyte via Mindoro to Lingayen. If the IJN battleships managed to intercept a convoy of Liberty ships and LSTs, the slaughter would be catastrophic. A shelling of the Lingayen beachhead, a scenario that worried General MacArthur, would be even worse.[14]

In what amounted to a preemptive strike, Admiral Nimitz had granted Halsey permission to execute his plan to steam into the South China Sea, hunt down the Japanese battleships and cruisers, and sink them before they left port in French Indochina. U.S. submarines based in Manila had commenced operations in the South China Sea just

---

*Though severely damaged by U.S. Navy warplanes at Kure in March 1945, the IJNS *Ryuho* survived the war.

hours after the attack on Pearl Harbor and had been hunting there ever since, but Halsey's sortie would be the first time that U.S. Navy surface vessels would venture into the South China Sea since the USS *Mindanao* had fled Hong Kong for Manila just days before the war had begun. The *Mindanao* and the tugboat *Ranger*, which had accompanied the gunboat on its storm-tossed chug to Manila Bay in December 1941, had both been lost in the opening months of the war along with many other ships of the U.S. Asiatic Fleet. The fortunes of war had changed for the U.S. Navy since the desperate days of early 1942, however, and ships named for American values, victories, founding fathers, cities, and states – *Independence, Yorktown, Hancock, Boston, Wisconsin* – would return to the South China Sea under the command of an aggressive and wrathful admiral who often ended his dispatches with the exhortation, "Keep 'em dying."[15]

Admiral Halsey would obey his own commandment to keep the Japanese dying and accompany TF 38 into the South China Sea aboard his flagship, the battleship USS *New Jersey*. As commander of the 3rd Fleet, Halsey would handle big-picture decisions about where, when, and how to employ the fast carriers. However, tactical command of TF 38 fell to Vice Admiral McCain, who shared Halsey's aggressive spirit and a leadership style that motivated the men of TF 38 to follow them into the searing crucible of naval combat.[16] The composition of the task force continually changed in response to wartime variables, but at the point that Halsey and McCain prepared to take the fleet into the South China Sea it numbered nearly a hundred surface combatants, including six fast battleships and thirteen fast carriers split between four task groups. A rear admiral with extensive experience and proven ability in fast carrier operations commanded each of the four task groups, which typically cruised close enough for mutual protection but far enough apart that they could maneuver without fear of running into each other. In standard cruising formation, the task force covered a stretch of blue water some nine miles wide and forty miles long.[17] Rear Admiral Arthur W. Radford led TG 38.1 with the *Yorktown* and the *Wasp* as well as the light carriers *Cabot* and *Cowpens*. Rear Admiral Bogan commanded TG 38.2, which centered on the fleet carriers *Hancock, Hornet,* and *Lexington*. TG 38.3 belonged to Rear Admiral Frederick C. Sherman, whose task group included the fleet carriers *Essex* and *Ticonderoga*, plus the light carriers *Langley* and *San Jacinto*. Rear Admiral Matthias

B. Gardner had control of the Night Carrier Task Group, designated as TG 38.5 and consisting of the fleet carrier *Enterprise* and the light carrier *Independence*. Formed on January 5 when the *Enterprise* first joined TF 38, the specialized task group had been assigned to Bogan's TG 38.2, but because Gardner's flattops carried air groups trained for night flying, he operated his carriers independently as TG 38.5 during the nocturnal hours when so ordered by McCain.[18] During daylight hours the night carriers reintegrated back into TG 38.2 and operated under Bogan's immediate tactical control.

Task Group 30.8 under the command of Captain Acuff – an Annapolis graduate with nearly a quarter-century of navy service under his belt – would provide at-sea logistical support. Though not as glamorous as the battleships and fleet carriers of TF 38, the fast oilers and transport carriers of Captain Acuff's command remained just as crucial to combat operations. An Essex-class fleet carrier averaged about 170 gallons to the mile and could burn up to three million gallons of bunker fuel during a month of combat operations.[19] Speedier than merchant tankers and configured to refuel ships while under way on the open ocean, the fast oilers (AOs) would periodically rendezvous with TF 38 in the South China Sea and provide the prodigious quantities of bunker fuel and aviation gasoline necessary for extended fast carrier deployments. The transport carriers – escort carriers laden with spare warplanes, but with no air group embarked – would provide replacement aircraft and pilots. Given the rapid pace of the air operations that TF 38 would undertake in the South China Sea, the attrition rate among the air groups would inevitably be a high one. For this reason, the fast carriers would need a steady flow of new planes and fresh aviators to replace the men and machines lost to flying accidents and enemy fire. Escort carriers with air groups and a screen of destroyers would provide the in-house muscle needed to protect the vulnerable oilers and transport carriers.

The frenetic tempo of air operations would be matched by its massive scale, since the thirteen carriers of TF 38 could launch a theoretical maximum of nearly 900 aircraft, the majority of them F6F-5 Hellcats. Additionally, the six battleships and thirteen cruisers could contribute about thirty catapult-launched floatplanes for scouting and air-sea rescue missions. In practice, however, combat losses constrained the number of aircraft the task force could put aloft, as did operational mishaps, mechanical problems, downtime for refueling and rearming, and various other factors. Still, on any given day TF 38 could easily send hundreds of aircraft out to strike multiple targets and still have sufficient planes left over for CAPs over the fleet, antisubmarine work, long-range sweeps in search of enemy surface combatants, and air-sea rescue missions.[20]

Halsey planned to track down and sink the *Ise* and *Hyuga*, which to his frustration had eluded him during the Battle of Leyte Gulf, but his carrier air groups would also continue their campaign to neutralize Japanese aircraft flying out of the fields that ringed the South China Sea, particularly the bases in Formosa that could launch *kamikaze* missions against the transports anchored off the landing beaches at Lingayen. Halsey hoped to strike Japanese convoys and key ports like Saigon and Hong Kong as well. Everything in and around the South China Sea would be fair game, from barges to battleships, and no Japanese sailor, soldier, or airman would be spared. Halsey's foray into the South China Sea would be codenamed, of all things, Operation *Gratitude*.

Hot, Straight, and Normal

Operation *Gratitude* commenced just before midnight on January 9, 1945, when TF 38 threaded the gap between Japanese-held Luzon and Formosa without detection and entered the South China Sea in search of the *Ise* and *Hyuga*. Night fighters from the carrier *Independence* splashed several Japanese planes before dawn on January 10, and the CAP brought one more down after sunrise. TF 38 had soon penetrated deep into the South China Sea, and Admiral Halsey believed the Japanese had been unable to track the movements of the Fast Carrier Task Force. The fleet continued on a southwest bearing and rendezvoused with Task Unit 30.8.10, a subgroup of TG 30.8 that had also slipped into the South China Sea for a fuel-smeared logistical special op. Captain Acuff served as Officer in Tactical Command (OTC) of TU 30.8.10 and led a flotilla of six fast oilers, two escort carriers, and eight destroyers. On the morning and early afternoon of January 11, the oilers used their refueling gear to transfer 171,000 barrels of Navy Special bunker fuel and 253,000 gallons of aviation gasoline to the ships of TF 38, which then steamed into the setting sun towards Cam Ranh Bay.[1]

Meanwhile, Japanese convoy Hi-87 left Takao at dusk on January 10 and steamed for the port of Mako in the Pescadores, an archipelago to the west of Formosa. Convoy commander Rear Admiral Komazawa Katsumi may have hoped that steaming for Mako would allow the convoy to evade the American carrier planes that had been pounding Takao, and this might have been a viable strategy if TF 38 had stayed out in the open Pacific to the east of Formosa. However, TF 38 had now entered the South China Sea, though the admiral remained unaware of this development, and its air groups could reach Mako just as easily as they could reach Takao. Along with the oiler IJNS *Kamoi*, the convoy retained four of its original seven civilian tankers – *Matsushima Maru*, *Mitsushima Maru*, *Tenei Maru*, and *Sarawak Maru*. In addition, the convoy had gained the tanker *Hashidate Maru*. However, the *Mitsushima Maru* only managed to steam for ninety minutes before dropping out of formation with engine problems and returning to Takao, which reduced Hi-87 to just four merchant tankers and the *Kamoi*.

Suzumoku Goni had already survived one trip to Syonan-to aboard the *Hashidate Maru*, and like every man aboard the 10,000-ton ship, he would have known that they would need more than the usual ration of luck to complete the run a second time. He served with a detachment of military gun crews assigned to the civilian tanker, which had hauled 16,000 tons of oil from Singapore to Takao with convoy Hi-82 before reassignment to Hi-87. For Suzumoku and his fellow antiaircraft gunners, the order to pump tanks at Takao and return to Singapore, as opposed to hauling their load of crude back to the relative safety of Moji, would have been as terrifying as it was demoralizing. The Americans seemed to be everywhere. While in port at Takao, Suzumoku had defended the *Hashidate Maru* against low-flying enemy warplanes, which had strafed the ship and bracketed it with bombs that flayed the decks with shrapnel, killing a member of the crew. Suzumoku and the other sailors aboard the *Hashidate Maru* had also seen firsthand what enemy submarines could do to a fully laden tanker despite the best efforts of the escort vessels. Few things burned as fiercely as a tanker full of crude oil, Suzumoku knew, and when the hull plates ruptured, spilling oil into the sea as the ship finally went under, the fire lived on like a terrible monster of war, burning atop the waves and painting the sky with twisting black smears of smoke.

To prevent this kind of fiery cataclysm, eleven warships had left Takao with the *Hashidate Maru* and the other four tankers of convoy Hi-87. This sizeable force included the destroyer *Shigure* and the smaller *Kanju*, flagship of the 7th Escort Convoy, with Rear Admiral Komazawa aboard. Lt. Cdr. Noriteru Yatsui, one of the officers aboard the *Kanju*, could feel the vibration of the engines beneath his feet as he stood on deck, swaying with the pitch and roll of the blacked-out ship. An Etorofu-class escort vessel, the 255-foot *Kanju* had been launched in 1943 at the Uraga dockyards on Tokyo Bay as part of a larger effort to construct a fleet of escort ships capable of countering the American submarines that had become an existential threat to Japan's wartime economy. The prewar Japanese navy had failed to prepare for this strategic vulnerability and had not possessed a single purpose-built escort vessel capable of operating on the open ocean when it went to war against the United States in late 1941. By 1943, the need for dedicated convoy escort vessels had become clear to the high command, which ramped up construction of ships like the *Kanju*. By 1944, over a hundred oceangoing escorts had entered service. Each *kaibōkan* – literally, "sea defense ship" – carried a large stock of depth charges, and many mounted basic radar systems, but the gun packages varied. The *Kanju* carried a typical mix of three 4.7-inch guns and a battery of 25mm antiaircraft cannons.[2]

An eight-year navy veteran, Yatsui had already acquired a full career's worth of combat experience. He had entered the ranks of the IJN before the attack on Pearl Harbor, and after tours of duty with the Naval Air Corps and Southeast Area Fleet, went to navigation school at Yokosuka. He completed his training in November 1943 and received orders for Southeast Asia, where he joined the crew of the light cruiser *Ōi*. In the months that followed, Yatsui plotted courses that took the *Ōi* on a variety of missions to the Andaman Islands, Borneo, Singapore, Penang, Palau, Java, and Davao.

These forays became increasingly hazardous as the tides of war turned in favor of the Allies, however, and on July 19, 1944, the American submarine *Flasher* harpooned the *Ōi* in rough seas to the west of Manila. A pair of torpedoes slammed into the engine room on the port side of the ship, though apparently only one detonated. Still, the blast flung the mainmast over the side and caused the *Ōi* to list to port and settle by the stern. The tough old cruiser took five hours to founder, but finally slipped stern-first beneath the oil-slicked waves along with a third of the crew. After an unsuccessful depth charging of the *Flasher*, the IJN destroyer accompanying the *Ōi* rescued the ship's captain as well as Yatsui and the other surviving crewmembers.[3]

The navy soon reposted Yatsui to Formosa, where he became a staff officer assigned to the 7th Escort Convoy of the 1st Escort Fleet based in Takao.[4] In turn, the 1st Escort Fleet answered to Grand Escort Command headquarters, which the naval high command had established in November 1943 to bring a measure of coordination and cohesion to the nation's maritime protection efforts.[5] Commanded by Rear Admiral Komazawa, a twenty-five-year naval veteran with extensive experience in submarines, the 7th Escort Convoy was not assigned to patrol a specific zone of ocean; rather, it was assigned to accompany specific convoys, which could be heading to such disparate destinations as Manila, Shanghai, or Balikpapan. Like maritime bodyguards, the 860-ton *Kanju* and the other *kaibōkan* assigned to the 7th Escort Convoy provided antisubmarine and antiaircraft defense for convoys of merchant ships running between various points of the shrinking Japanese Empire. In the case of Hi-87, a particularly important convoy, the *kaibōkan* had been reinforced by larger warships like the *Shigure*, which belonged to the 21st Destroyer Division of the 2nd Destroyer Squadron, 2nd Fleet.[6]

After departing Takao in the early evening of January 10, convoy Hi-87 received new orders to bypass Mako in the Pescadores and proceed directly to Singapore instead. In accordance with this new directive, the *Kanju*, *Shigure*, and other escorts shepherded the tankers across the South China Sea towards Hainan on January 11. However, on January 12 mechanical problems with the *Tenei Maru*'s rudder forced the tanker to drop out of the convoy and divert to Hong Kong for repairs. This development also cost the convoy two of its escorts, since Rear Admiral Komazawa had to detach the *CD-13* and *CD-60* to provide protection for the *Tenei Maru*. The rest of the convoy continued south, but while steaming east of Hainan the headquarters of the 1st Escort Fleet at Takao radioed to warn that American carrier aircraft had attacked convoys near Saigon. Rather than continue south into the path of the enemy fleet, headquarters ordered convoy Hi-87 to alter course and head for Hong Kong instead.[7]

Search planes from the carrier air groups of TF 38, which had been hunting for the *Ise* and *Hyuga* along the coast of French Indochina, would likely have discovered convoy Hi-87 if it had continued on its southbound route to Singapore. Diverting to Hong Kong allowed the convoy to avoid immediate detection. The *Ise* and *Hyuga* also remained elusive, as search aircraft failed to locate the two hybrid battleship-carriers in Cam Ranh Bay where navy intelligence had reported them to be. Since the Lingayen beachhead appeared to be safe from attack by IJN surface ships like the *Ise* and *Hyuga*, which seemed disinclined to sortie for the Philippines, Admiral Nimitz granted Admiral Halsey permission to shift his tactical focus to shipping and other targets in the South China Sea. On the morning of January 12, carrier air groups from TF 38 launched air raids against the port area of Saigon and ambushed three different convoys along the S-shaped curve of the Indochinese seaboard.

At sunup, Task Group 38.2 under the command of Rear Admiral Bogan launched Strike 2A against a ten-ship convoy steaming along the coast between Phan Rang and Cape Padaran. Codenamed SATA-05 by the Japanese, the convoy included several vessels that had once flown the flags of Japan's wartime adversaries. The *Kensei Maru*, originally named the *Hin Sang*, had been scuttled by her British owners in Victoria Harbor in 1941 and later refloated by Japanese salvage teams. The minesweeper *W-101* had started life as the half-built HMS *Taitam*, which had been captured in a Hong Kong dry dock and later launched as a prize of war. Commander Lamade would have known the *PB-103* from his days in the Asiatic Fleet, when the Lapwing-class minesweeper had served alongside the *Houston* in Manila Bay as the USS *Finch*. In 1942, the minesweeper foundered in shallow water off Corregidor after a near miss from a bomb ruptured the hull and forced the crew to go over the side. With pragmatic efficiency, the Japanese refloated the *Finch* after the surrender of American forces in the Philippines and sent it out to fight its former owners as the much-modified *PB-103* in 1943. Including the reincarnated *PB-103*, *W-101*, and *Kensei Maru*, SATA-05 consisted of three tankers, two freighters, and five small warships.*

Each fleet carrier in Rear Admiral Bogan's task group – the *Hancock*, *Hornet*, and *Lexington* – contributed a full deck load of planes for the strike against SATA-05. With twenty-five aircraft, the strike package from the *Hancock* remained representative of the deck loads assembled by the other two flattops, with a mix of twelve Hellcats from VF-7, six Helldivers from VB-7, and seven Avengers from VT-7, including one flown by Lieutenant Hunt, the former high-school

---

*Convoy SATA-05 consisted of escort vessels *CD-35* and *CD-43*; submarine chaser *CH-31*; minesweeper *W-101*; patrol boat *PB-103*; tankers *Ayayuki Maru*, *Eiho Maru*, and *Koshin Maru*; and freighters *Kensei Maru* and *Toyu Maru*.

golf champion from Kansas City. He and his fellow torpedo pilots faced more abysmal flying weather – clouds that hung heavy as a wet towel on a pilot's head, interwoven with curtains of rain – but greatly appreciated the robust headwinds that blew down the flight deck as the *Hancock* turned into the wind in preparation to launch its aircraft. As every carrier pilot knew, an additional 5 or 10 knots (6 or 12mph) of airflow could provide enough extra lift to turn a white-knuckle launch of a heavily laden combat plane into a takeoff with a more comfortable margin for error.[8]

Northbound Japanese convoys on the Saigon-Takao or SATA run typically kept the shoreline close in on the port beam, since steaming in shallow coastal waters reduced the threat from American submarines. In the case of SATA-05, however, tracing the coast meant that the convoy lost the chance to ghost into the gray weather out at sea. Rather than low cloud, mist, and fog so dense it blended into the waves, the convoy pushed north at 10 knots (12mph) beneath blue skies flecked with tattered scraps of high cloud. Squinting into the glare of the morning sun, the gun crews enjoyed visibility out to the eastern horizon. Ten miles to the west, they could see the hazy line of the Indochina coast as the deck rolled gently in the mild morning seas. Crowded into their tubs and turrets, their helmets on and their hands smelling of brass and cordite, they likely would have been watching for land-based B-24 heavy bombers rather than American carrier planes. They spotted the incoming formations of smaller single-engine planes easily enough, however, and opened fire as soon as they came within range.

Locating a ten-ship column in CAVU conditions ("clear and visibility unlimited") proved just as easy for the combined strike group from TG 38.2, which operated under the tactical direction of the *Lexington* air group commander. In his capacity as the target coordinator, he chose to send in his own pilots and the *Hornet* air group as the first wave. Like a clean-up squad, Lieutenant Hunt and the rest of the *Hancock* air group would go in as the second wave. Predicting the optimal choice of ordnance for a mission often amounted to educated guesswork, and the VT-7 pilots had hedged their bets and loaded three of their Avengers with 500-pound bombs and four with Mark 13 torpedoes. Unsurprisingly, given his level of combat experience and proven adeptness with torpedoes, Lieutenant Hunt flew one of the Avengers armed with a Mark 13.

A torpedo-plane pilot lining up to drop his fish presented an easy target, as the U.S. Navy had learned to its sorrow. Entire squadrons of torpedo planes had been splashed by fighters and flak while mounting courageous but entirely unsuccessful attacks against the Japanese carrier fleet at Midway in 1942. A torpedo pilot had to fly at low altitude while holding a consistent bearing, maintaining a relatively slow air speed, and keeping his aircraft level to ensure that his fish ran "hot, straight, and normal" when it hit the water. This meant that torpedo pilots needed to be patient and steady, and that they required an aircraft with the power and stability of an Avenger. Pilots also needed the right blend of practice, skill, guts, and luck because, like a knife thrown at a bullseye, a torpedo had to be launched just right to lance its target. A torpedo would malfunction if dropped from too high an altitude, or if released at too high a speed, or if pickled at too high or too low an angle because the pilot had pitched or yawed due to nerves, inexperience, turbulence, or enemy gunfire. In any of these scenarios, the torpedo might swerve off course, or dive into the seabed, or jump up and down out of the water in a dramatic weapons failure that pilots referred to as "porpoising." Every torpedo pilot could tell stories about torpedoes that had broken apart, or detonated prematurely, or leapt out of the sea like a fish with a hook in its mouth. In one remarkable incident, a Marine pilot had watched as his unarmed training torpedo porpoised *over* the deck of the target ship like a skipped rock.[9]

For the VT-20 pilots from the *Lexington*, the Mark 13 proved as squirrely as ever. A quintet of Avenger pilots focused on the tanker riding closest to the coastline, and all five of their 2,200-pound torpedoes misbehaved. One torpedo refused to drop from the open bomb bay, another detonated when it struck the water, and two more sped in circles like giant wind-up toys. A fifth torpedo struck one of the tankers, but produced a disappointingly small explosion. VT-11 from the *Hornet* fared much better, dropping four torpedoes and scoring three hits on two different tankers. Both vessels began to burn and settle into the waves as seawater poured through their breached hull plates.

Lieutenant Hunt and the three other pilots from VT-7 who had torpedoes shackled in the bomb bays of their Avengers executed the final runs of the strike. By this time, more than seventy aircraft from the *Lexington*, *Hancock*, and *Hornet* had unloaded on the convoy and left a trail of broken, beached, and burning ships. All three tankers – the *Ayayuki Maru*, *Eiho Maru*, and *Koshin Maru* – had been hit multiple times and the escort vessels had been thoroughly worked over. Helldiver pilots repeatedly strafed the *PB-103* with their 20mm cannons, and one pilot with superb ship-recognition skills thought the patrol boat bore a striking resemblance to a ship from the U.S. Navy's Bird class, which was the unofficial name for the Lapwing class that included the USS *Finch*. The gun crews aboard the little warship put a two-foot hole in the wing of a Helldiver from the *Lexington*, and gunners aboard the other ships nailed a Hellcat from the *Lexington*. Possibly the pilot had been hit as well, because he executed a rough water landing that left him floating face down in the waves.

By the time Lieutenant Hunt started his torpedo run, the antiaircraft fire from the convoy had slackened to the point where it no longer represented a serious threat to his aircraft. He bored in on the port side of a tanker with a second Avenger pilot on his wing. In the lingo of torpedo pilots, Hunt kept his plane "straight and level" as he lined up on his prey, almost certainly the 2,855-ton Type 2TM tanker *Koshin Maru*. He kept his airspeed at 275mph and brought his Avenger down to 500 feet as sporadic streaks of antiaircraft fire flashed past. To the right of his aircraft, he could see the mainland, and to the left, a tableau of burning ships. When he had closed to within a half mile, he opened the bomb bay door and released his Mark 18. His torpedo ran true, struck the ship amidships, and raised a towering geyser of seawater as it exploded. Meanwhile, his wingman's torpedo slammed into the bow of the same tanker. With its hull torn open, the ship sank rapidly by the bow. A second two-plane element from VT-7 put a torpedo into one of the tankers originally hit by VT-11 pilots – either the *Ayayuki Maru* or *Eiho Maru* – which broke apart like a piñata hit with a baseball bat.[10]

After three hours in the air, Lieutenant Hunt returned his aircraft to the deck of the *Hancock*, where a midmorning headcount determined that all planes launched from the carrier had returned from the mission. In a testament to the rapid pace of air operations during Operation *Gratitude* as well as his proven competence and aggressive spirit, Hunt spent just enough time aboard the *Hancock* for the refueling crews to fill his tanks and the armorers to hoist another torpedo into the bomb bay. At noon, after a two-hour break, he executed the aviation equivalent of a doubleheader when he launched from the *Hancock* to join Strike

2C, the third deck-load strike launched from the carrier that day. Commander Lamade exercised tactical control as the target coordinator for the strike, which would hit a Japanese convoy steaming along the Indochina coast to the north of Qui Nhon. Codenamed Hi-86, the convoy consisted of ten merchant vessels and five warships of the 101st Escort Flotilla. Neither Lamade nor Hunt knew the codenames for Japanese convoys or the nomenclature of Japanese naval units, of course, but then again such details remained largely irrelevant to the *Hancock* pilots and a passing curiosity at best. Pilots focused instead on the life-and-death details that mattered, like the slant of their fuel-gauge needles or the VHF frequency for the lifeguard submarine.

Once again, VT-7 contributed seven Avengers, and once again, the squadron opted for split loadings, with four of the big Grummans hauling 500-pounders and three carrying torpedoes, including the plane piloted by Lieutenant Hunt. His successful torpedo run during Strike 2A had brought his score while flying with VT-7 to three enemy ships and an unknown, but certainly large, number of enemy sailors. Forty-four men had died aboard the *Koshin Maru* alone. In addition to sinking the 325-foot tanker, Hunt had singlehandedly obliterated the landing ship *T-106* in December 1944. He also shared credit for dispatching the light cruiser *Noshiro* in October 1944. By any measure, the U.S. Navy's investment in Lt. (j.g.) Richard L. Hunt had produced some handsome returns.

The Imperial Japanese Navy's investment in Rear Admiral Shibuya Shiro had generated some valuable dividends as well. After graduating from the naval academy in 1916, Shibuya had served on a wide variety of warships and climbed steadily upwards through the naval hierarchy until his promotion to flag rank in October 1944. A month later, the newly minted rear admiral took command of the nascent 101st Escort Flotilla, a special antisubmarine squadron tasked with protecting the strategically vital convoys shuttling between Singapore and the home islands. Shibuya broke his flag aboard the light cruiser *Kashii*, the heart of the squadron, which also included the escort vessels *Daito* and *Ukuru* as well as three coastal defense vessels with names that mirrored their no-frills functionality: *CD-23*, *CD-27*, and *CD-51*. In the final days of 1944, the fifty-one-year-old Shibuya had stood on the bridge of the *Kashii* as his squadron departed from Singapore with the tankers and bulk carriers of convoy Hi-86, bound initially for Saigon, but ultimately for Moji. On January 4, the sixteen-ship convoy reached Saigon and dropped anchor for a five-day port call. Shibuya and the *Kashii* had led the convoy back out into the South China Sea to resume its northward journey on January 9, the very same day that Admiral Halsey had unleashed Operation *Gratitude*.

All had gone well for Rear Admiral Shibuya and his squadron until the morning of January 12, when air groups from TF 38 began hunting along the coast of French Indochina. Aircraft launched from the flattops of Rear Admiral Sherman's TG 38.3 had swarmed the ships of Hi-86 in numbers sufficient to jeopardize the entire convoy. In a pragmatic response that mitigated the damage inflicted by Sherman's aviators, the helmsmen aboard the merchant vessels in the convoy had purposefully run for the beaches lining the coast near Qui Nhon and plowed their bows into the sand. This tactic, apparently carried out with the acquiescence if not the direct endorsement of Rear Admiral Shibuya, prevented damaged ships from going under in deep water. As a result, many of the badly holed ships settled into the sand with their decks above the breakers, awaiting future salvage and repair, while their crews swam ashore and took cover in the sand dunes. Some of the grounded ships burned with a volcanic fury, however, which reduced their salvage value to scrap metal and emitted pillars of oily black smoke that served as homing beacons for the incoming aircraft of Strike 2C.

Commander Lamade assigned the freighters and tankers that had run themselves aground along the shoreline near Qui Nhon to CVG-20 of the *Lexington*, and the merchant vessels beached further up the coast to CVG-11 of the *Hornet*. Like a school of minnows, the five smaller escort vessels of the 101st Flotilla had darted beneath a low shelf of cloud hanging just offshore, which offered a measure of concealment, but the *Kashii* had been caught out in the open between the cloudbank and the coast. Lamade selected the *Kashii* as the target for his own air group, but the presence of such a large enemy warship generated considerable excitement among the pilots in the other two groups as well, since everyone wanted to be in on bagging an enemy cruiser. Pilots from the *Hornet* and *Lexington* either failed to hear or failed to heed Lamade's targeting instructions and descended upon the *Kashii*, which flashed with the muzzle blasts of its antiaircraft batteries. Flying into this maelstrom of tracer rounds and shrapnel proved costly for the *Lexington* pilots, perhaps because they led the charge and thus faced the opening barrage. One F6F-5 took a fatal hit and plunged straight into the water astern of the *Kashii*, while an Avenger managed to drop its torpedo before executing a sudden wingover into the waves and disintegrating.

The *Hancock* air group went in at more or less the same time as everyone else – for the pilots, the entire engagement remained a confused tangle of swooping aircraft and exploding ordnance, making it impossible to know who had actually hit what. Still, though the *Kashii* took multiple hits, Lamade credited his own VB-7 with dropping the bomb that ultimately sent the cruiser to the bottom. An expertly placed 1,000-pound semi-armor-piercing (SAP) bomb ripped apart the fantail and triggered a secondary explosion in the depth-charge magazine. As camera-equipped aircraft from the *Hancock* wheeled overhead like navy-blue vultures, the ship went down stern first, its bow raised high out of the water in a final salute before sliding beneath the waves. Most of the men aboard perished, including Captain Matsumura Midori, who had commanded the ship since March 1944, and Rear Admiral Shibuya. Lamade knew his pilots had sunk an enemy cruiser, but what he did not know was that they had also gutted the 101st Escort Flotilla and killed a flag-rank enemy officer with thirty years of invaluable naval experience.

Lieutenant Hunt had already claimed one cruiser at Leyte Gulf, and doubtless would have been pleased to bag a second one. However, he and the other two VT-7 pilots with torpedoes in their bomb bays lost sight of each other in the overcast offshore, and they ended up making uncoordinated individual attacks against the merchant vessels instead. Coming out of the east, all three pilots executed successful drops, but none of their torpedoes connected with the target ship.

Bombs and torpedoes expended, Lieutenant Hunt and the *Hancock* pilots chased the escort vessels hiding beneath the cloudbank and strafed the grounded ships scattered along the sandy shoreline. Motionless, often abandoned, and blazing like beachside bonfires, the stranded vessels made for easy targets. VF-7 pilots alone burned through 8,000 heavy machine-gun rounds. Lieutenant Lloyd E. Newcomer and his wingman made five strafing runs, a performance that any fighter pilot would be pleased with, but Lieutenant George E. Kemper outdid them both by making *ten* passes. Ultimately, Kemper concluded that the abundance of targets exceeded the capacity of his ammunition trays.

VB-7 pilots ripped into ships with their 20mm cannons, while the VT-7 pilots turned their multipurpose Avengers into gunships and shot up several of the surviving escort vessels with their .50-caliber wing guns. In the rear of the Helldivers and Avengers, the gunners banged away opportunistically whenever they had a clear shot. Even Commander Lamade got in on the action with his 5-inch rockets.

Despite the fire and smoke engulfing their ruined ship, however, a diehard crew of gunners aboard one of the beached and burning hulks tried their best to keep the fight from devolving into an entirely one-sided affair. They took a bead on a VB-7 Helldiver and nearly sliced off its wing when they sent a slug into its wing root. Fortunately for the pilot, the Beast had a robust airframe worthy of its nickname, and the badly damaged dive-bomber held together for the 120-mile run back to the fleet. Lieutenant Charles E. Golson, the ACI officer for CVG-7 who compiled the aircraft action report filed after the strike, felt the episode drove home a point worthy of capital letters. "The lesson learned," he or his yeoman typed, holding down the caps key: "NEVER UNDERESTIMATE THE ENEMY."[11]

Shootin' Star

On January 12, 1945, Rear Admiral Bogan had ordered the air groups of TG 38.2 to destroy two luckless Japanese convoys midway up the S-shaped coastline of French Indochina. On the same day, Rear Admiral Radford of TG 38.1 dispatched his air groups to the bottom curve of the S. As part of this effort, the *Yorktown* and other carriers from the task group sent Strike 1A to Cap St. Jacques and Strike 1B to Saigon, where the air groups found plentiful targets in the river of the same name, which wound past the city and served as its anchorage. Optimum conditions for dive-bombing allowed VB-3 from the *Yorktown* to fly its most successful mission since the re-formed squadron had left Pearl Harbor in October 1944. All seven VB-3 pilots who flew Strike 1B scored at least one hit on a ship, including the light cruiser *Lamotte-Picquet*. Though the nonoperational Vichy warship still flew the French flag, U.S. Navy intelligence assumed it to be under Japanese control and therefore considered it a legitimate target. VB-3 left the cruiser rolled over on its side in the river mud. Much to the disappointment of Lieutenant Lavender and the five other VB-3 pilots slated to fly Strike 1C, however, the final mission of the day shifted the focus from Saigon to Tourane Bay on the coast of central Indochina.

In preparation for launch, Lieutenant Lavender sat in his cockpit, which smelled of paint, engine exhaust, lubricating oils, sea salt, and his own sweat. With the wings folded down, his Helldiver had a wingspan just shy of fifty feet and a length of nearly thirty-seven feet, including the oversized tail rudder that many pilots joked was big enough to steer a battleship. In the bomb bay, a 1,000-pound bomb hung from the shackles, but a careful triangulation of total aircraft weight, length of takeoff roll, and flight duration allowed Lavender's plane to tote an additional 250-pound bomb as well as 378 gallons of fuel. Once the eleven Hellcat pilots assigned to Strike 1C had launched, Lieutenant Lavender and the other five VB pilots prepared to leave the *Yorktown* as well. When the flight deck officer gave the wind-up signal, the first VB pilot in the launch order spun up his four-bladed propeller to a blur while standing on the hydraulic brakes, listening intently to the hammering of the fourteen cylinders in the twin-row radial engine, eyes sweeping the gauges arrayed before him on the instrument panel. After acknowledging the signal to launch, he commenced his takeoff roll knowing that his heavily loaded Helldiver would need every stallion of its 1,900-horsepower engine to overpower gravity when it hurtled off the heaving bow of the *Yorktown*. As usual, his SB-Deuce sank below the level of the *Yorktown*'s bow when it left the flight deck, but the big warplane soon steadied itself and started powering aloft as the pilot banked away from the carrier. Lieutenant Lavender performed the same maneuver when he launched, and then he and the other five VB pilots formed up with eleven Hellcats and five TBMs and headed for the coast of French Indochina, which lay some 290 miles distant.

Weather conditions soon deteriorated into a solid mass of overcast cut by rain, forcing the *Yorktown* pilots to go in on the deck. Like ghost ships, two Japanese warships materialized out of the haze and put up a barrage of tracer fire, but Lieutenant Lavender and the other aviators assigned to Strike 1C ignored this provocation and continued towards Tourane, as per their mission briefing. However, when the ceiling dropped to 150 feet and threatened to press straight down to the foam-flecked wave tops, the strike leader scrubbed the attack on Tourane. Even if they managed to find the port or the shipping reported to be in the vicinity, the pilots all knew they would not be able to see any targets in zero-zero conditions and, moreover, might shake hands with a mountain or succumb to vertigo and fly straight into the waves. By the time the strike leader gave up on finding Tourane, the *Yorktown* planes had ventured within fifteen miles of landfall and flown out of the soup. With visibility much improved, the pilots began tracing the coast in search of convoy Hi-86, their secondary target. The *Yorktown* contingent soon encountered air groups from TG 38.2, which had sunk the *Kashii* and pounded the merchant vessels strung along the coast near Qui Nhon.

Flying under an overcast sky with a ceiling of 5,000 feet, Lieutenant Lavender and the other VB-3 pilots surveyed a maritime wasteland punctuated by smoke plumes that boiled up like gigantic exclamation marks from the decks of burning ships. Oil slicks undulated on the swells, and foamy breakers slopped against motionless hulks grounded in shallow water. Banking overhead, Lavender observed nine tankers and freighters in their death throes, plus a single surviving escort vessel under way two miles offshore.

For the next forty-five minutes, the *Yorktown* pilots as well as aviators from other air groups circled over the wreckage of convoy Hi-86, periodically peeling off to strafe, rocket, torpedo, and bomb whatever ship still had enough hull above water to make it worth the ordnance. The low ceiling precluded dive-bombing, so Lavender and his fellow VB pilots split into two-plane sections and opted for glide-bombing runs instead, using their Mark 8 illuminated gunsights to try to pitch bombs into ships that had already been hammered multiple times during the strike led by Commander Lamade. Hampered by the low visibility, their inexperience in glide-bombing, and the lack of coordination among the different air groups overhead, the VB-3 pilots scored just one bomb hit even though they had dropped on stationary vessels that had foundered in shallow water with decks awash or been purposefully run into the sand. One 250-pound bomb smacked into a burning freighter grounded 100 yards from shore, which expanded the flames, but previous hits had already damaged the ship so severely that one more bomb strike made little difference.

Once each VB-3 pilot had released his payload, he circled around to strafe with his 20mm wing guns. In the rear seat, the gunners snapped off quick bursts with their twin M1919s, taking care not to riddle their own tail in the process. The .30-caliber machine guns lacked an interrupter mechanism to prevent them from shooting into the vertical stabilizer, so gunners like Jean Balch had been extensively drilled at Naval Air Gunners School to fire at angles that avoided hitting their own aircraft.[1] Lieutenant Lavender and the other pilots proved more adept at strafing than low-level bombing and poured hundreds of 20mm rounds into burning and beached transports as well as the lone escort vessel offshore. After withstanding numerous near misses, a 500-pound bomb strike on the stern courtesy of VF-3, and a vicious strafing from numerous aircraft, the warship finally caught fire and started steaming in circles due to an apparent loss of steering control. As the *Yorktown* pilots withdrew from the battle space, other air groups moved in to finish off the escort vessel and the crippled transports. Of the twenty-five warships and merchant vessels in convoy Hi-86 and SATA-05, just three badly shot-up escort ships remained afloat at the end of the day.

Lieutenant Lavender landed at 6:00 p.m. with a hundred gallons of fuel still in the tanks, an empty bomb bay, cordite streaks on his wings from the muzzle blast of his 20mm wing guns, and not a single hole in his aircraft. In the rear seat, Balch pulled up his goggles and started unfastening himself from his rotating gunner's seat. The two Texans had just survived their seventh bombing mission, and compared with what they had experienced over Manila Bay, enemy fire had not been much of a threat. VB-3 pilots had observed very few muzzle flashes winking from the ruined convoy, and only the occasional pulse of tracer fire. They guessed that the sailors manning the antiaircraft guns had either been killed during earlier airstrikes or been forced to abandon ship. In the crowded airspace over the convoy, collisions with friendly planes, particularly those from other air groups, had presented a greater risk to Lavender and Balch than enemy flak. As events would prove, friendly fire presented yet another hazard for American aviators along the coast of French Indochina.[2]

On the morning of January 12, five B-24 Liberators rumbled aloft from Luliang, an airfield secreted deep in the Chinese hinterland. One of the Liberators aborted the mission shortly after takeoff, but the remaining four ships formed up for a long overland flight to Cam Ranh Bay on the Indochinese coast. The B-24s belonged to the 373rd Bomb Squadron of the 308th Bomb Group (Heavy), which had racked up an impressive number of combat sorties since its deployment to China in the spring of 1943. As the only heavy bomb group assigned to the 14th Air Force, the 308th served as an airborne jack-of-all-trades for General Chennault. The four squadrons of the 308th mounted conventional high-altitude bombing raids, ran reconnaissance flights, made resupply runs over the Himalayas to India, and dropped antiship mines into the Yangtze River and Victoria Harbor. On a few occasions, the pilots of the 308th had even brought their big four-engine bombers down on the deck to strafe enemy infantry. The sea sweep, however, remained one of the group's most common mission types. During these long-range patrols, which could last more than ten hours, the bomber crews hunted for Japanese ships in the South China Sea, often at night with the aid of radar-guided low-altitude bombing (LAB) systems. The mission on the morning of January 12 called for a daylight sea sweep, though, perhaps because the aircraft assigned to the mission lacked the radar equipment that facilitated nocturnal bombing runs. Regardless of whether a sea sweep occurred during daylight or darkness, the mission brief remained the same: sink any and all Japanese ships detected in the South China Sea.

The South China Sea now belonged to the thirteen fast carriers of TF 38, of course, though whether this critical piece of intelligence had been passed along to the 308th Bomb Group remained unclear. Presumably, the U.S. Navy had briefed General Chennault on Operation *Gratitude*, but this briefing would necessarily have been short on tactical details. He might have received a big-picture overview, but the day-to-day maneuvering of the fast carriers would have been unknown to him. Even if the navy had been so inclined, keeping Chennault apprised of the movements of the fleet would have inevitably involved so much lag-time that the reports would have been of little value. For its part, the 14th Air Force had supplied the navy with a steady flow of intelligence on Japanese ship movements, much of it collected during sea sweeps flown by the Liberator crews of the 308th. Ironically, however, the B-24 pilots assigned to fly the mission along the Indochina seaboard on January 12 – a mission that would generate exactly the kind of intelligence that typically got passed along to the navy – had apparently never been informed of the presence of American carrier task groups in the South China Sea.

The 308th Bomb Group had been striking targets in Indochina since mid-1943, so for the forty men aboard the four B-24s a sea sweep along the coast of the Japanese-occupied French colony amounted to business as usual, albeit of a deadly and dangerous kind. The pilots, navigators, and bombardiers had been briefed to start their patrol at Cam Ranh Bay and then work their way northwards up the coast of French Indochina in search of maritime targets of opportunity. When the B-24s reached the vicinity of the bay, however, they encountered a pair of blunt-nosed fighter aircraft, which slashed past in a high-speed gun run. In the distance, the B-24 crews spotted at least two dozen more single-engine aircraft. Acting on the assumption that these aircraft belonged to the JAAF and that the Japanese pilots would soon swarm the outnumbered B-24s, the flight leader ordered his formation to lighten its load and make a run for it. All four bombers jettisoned their 500-pounders over open water and ran for the convenient haven of a nearby cloudbank. Some of the gunners opened up with their .50-calibers, but their fire soon tapered off as they identified the approaching aircraft as a mix of U.S. Navy F6Fs and TBMs.

At 2:54 p.m., the four B-24s had turned up on the radar screens of Rear Admiral Sherman's TG 38.3, which included the *Essex*, *Ticonderoga*, and *Langley*. Fighter director officers (FDOs) aboard the carriers had immediately vectored pilots from the CAP to intercept the presumed Japanese bogeys. Just six minutes after the initial radar contact, two Hellcat pilots from the *Ticonderoga* had tally-hoed the B-24s and identified the bombers as friendly. Aircraft from TG 38.3 made no further attacks on the quartet of Liberators, though a division of Hellcat pilots from either the *Ticonderoga* or the *Essex* shadowed the B-24s in an unsuccessful attempt to discern the tail markings on the mystery aircraft. To their frustration, the Hellcat pilots found that the bombers sported no readable numbers or other insignia that might indicate their unit. Radio contact proved fruitless as well, so the fighter pilots finally broke off and let the B-24s withdraw from the Cam Ranh Bay area. All four Liberators returned safely to Luliang, where the crews reported that the U.S. Navy had trespassed on the traditional hunting grounds of the 14th Air Force.

Three hours after the edgy encounter between the four Liberators from the 373rd and the Hellcats from the *Ticonderoga* and *Essex*, the radar operators aboard the *Langley* and then the *Essex* detected yet another unidentified aircraft in the vicinity of Cam Ranh Bay. Unbeknownst to anyone in the task group, the radar echoes were bouncing off the aluminum airframe of a B-24J from the 374th Bomb Squadron, a sister unit to the 373rd. First Lieutenant Robert E. Churgin served as the aircraft commander of the B-24, which its crew had nicknamed the *Shootin' Star*. Like so many of the B-24 crews flying out of Chinese airfields, they had turned their aircraft into a flying art installation.

In large capital letters, they had painted "Shootin' Star" on the fuselage just below the cockpit windows, along with a pin-up girl perched on a five-pointed star. To complete their masterpiece, they had emblazoned the signature trademark of the 14th Air Force on the nose below the gun turret: an open shark's mouth lined with rows of pointy white teeth. Lieutenant Churgin and his crew had been briefed to fly a long-range reconnaissance mission from Cap St. Jacques to Cam Ranh Bay, and like the crews from the 373rd, the men aboard the *Shootin' Star* apparently had no inkling that the U.S. Navy had roared into the South China Sea with the fury of a hundred-year typhoon.

After a few minutes on the scopes, the radar signature of the unidentified aircraft faded into the greater landmass of the Indochinese coast. As a precaution, the FDO on the *Essex* ordered an understrength division of three Chance Vought F4U-1D Corsairs from the CAP to orbit in the path of the presumed Japanese snooper. Based aboard the *Essex*, the Corsair pilots belonged to VMF-124 and VMF-213, the only U.S. Marine Corps squadrons attached to the fast carriers of TF 38.

Led by Capt. Edmond P. Hartsock, the Corsair pilots soon caught sight of the bogey to the south of Cam Ranh Bay. The three pilots would later report that they had held their fire and flown beside the unknown aircraft out of concern that it might be American. Waggling their wings, the Marine pilots said they had attempted to identify themselves and make contact via radio, but received only tracer fire from the waist gunners in response. They also claimed they had been unable to discern any identifying markings on the four-engine plane. Perhaps events had unfolded as the Marines described, but the plausibility of their story remained open to question, since few aircraft were more ubiquitous on Pacific airfields than the B-24 and its navy doppelganger, the PB4Y-1. Hartsock himself had escorted B-24s while flying in the southwest Pacific, so he would have certainly recognized a Liberator if he had flown alongside one. Moreover, in addition to the shark mouth, pin-up girl, and English-language nickname painted on its nose, the *Shootin' Star* bore the standard stars-and-bars insignia on its fuselage and wings. Since careful inspection would have revealed the *Shootin' Star* to be a friendly aircraft, the tale about diligently trying to establish contact with the mystery plane may have been concocted post-mission to avoid possible disciplinary action. The more likely scenario was that the three Corsair pilots had assumed they had a four-engine Japanese flying boat in their gunsights and then did what they had been trained to do. They closed in for the kill. The fact that the waist gunners aboard the presumed enemy aircraft began firing at the Corsairs would have only confirmed the assumptions of the Marine pilots that the aircraft was hostile.

Given the extensive national media coverage of the famed Black Sheep Squadron, which flew the Corsair, the crew of the *Shootin' Star* would almost certainly have been familiar with the unique profile of the F4U. Still, they would not have been expecting to encounter Corsairs during their mission and would have been anticipating Japanese fighter aircraft instead. Perhaps the gunners thought they faced an exotic new model of Japanese pursuit plane, or perhaps they never even noticed the odd crimp of the wings and simply assumed that any fighter aircraft operating along the Indochina coast would have a Japanese pilot in the cockpit. Either way, they gripped their gun handles and did what *they* had been trained to do. Lieutenant Churgin and his copilot, meanwhile, plunged towards the refuge of the clouds hanging above the ocean surface in an attempt to evade the three fighters. General Chennault would later claim that a member of the crew had radioed, "Being attacked by U.S. Navy planes." If so, at least some of the men aboard the B-24 had managed to recognize the Corsairs as friendlies.

Since the gunners aboard the *Shootin' Star* had opened fire, Captain Hartsock and his wingman had no reason to reconsider whether they faced an enemy aircraft. They executed a high-speed gun run that targeted the right front quarter of the B-24, which began to trail smoke. The third Corsair pilot, coming in from behind the plane, drilled the Liberator with his .50-caliber wing guns, setting the port wing root aflame. Seconds later an explosion aboard the *Shootin' Star* inflicted mortal damage. The nickname for the B-24 proved tragically apt as the burning aircraft continued its diving turn and disappeared into the cloud layer masking the corrugated surface of the South China Sea.

None of the Corsair pilots followed the B-24 down through the undercast, so nobody witnessed the final moments of the *Shootin' Star*. Perhaps the plane simply continued its dive straight into the swells, killing the entire ten-man crew on impact and slicking the waters with aviation fuel. Alternatively, perhaps Lieutenant Churgin and his copilot had enough control of the doomed aircraft to attempt a water landing, though this would have been a truly desperate move because B-24 pilots all knew that, unlike the low-winged B-17, the high-winged Liberator tended to break up when ditched. If any crewmembers had managed to bail out or to swim free from the fuselage before the waves swallowed the shattered Liberator, they soon perished while floating in the open sea.*

Just four minutes had elapsed between the initial tally-ho of the *Shootin' Star* at 6:46 p.m. and the death dive of the stricken bomber. At 6:51, the three Marine pilots radioed that they had splashed an Emily – the Allied codename for the Kawanishi H8K2 – but upon landing back aboard the *Essex*, the worried trio of pilots reported to their ACI officer that they might have downed a B-24.[3] Within twenty-four hours, photo technicians had developed the gun camera footage from the three Corsairs, which depicted the unmistakable silhouette of a twin-tailed, four-engine B-24 Liberator. The final frames showed the aircraft plunging towards the sea at the spear tip of a long javelin of smoke that pointed nearly straight down. Some of the navy pilots aboard the *Essex* opined that their Marine counterparts had been overeager in mistaking a friendly B-24 heavy bomber for an enemy H8K2 flying boat. Both aircraft had four engines and a similar fuselage profile, but the H8K2 had dead-giveaway pontoons hanging from the wings and a traditional tail design with a single vertical stabilizer. No pontoons dangled from the wings of a Liberator, of course, and the aircraft featured a distinctive twin-rudder tail configuration. On the other hand, some navy pilots admitted, the B-24 had picked a fight with the Corsairs, so the Marine pilots could hardly be blamed for reacting like the fighter pilots they were and pressing their gun buttons. In the high-stakes drama of air combat, hesitation could get a pilot killed or provide the opening for a *kamikaze* to immolate sailors by the hundreds. Still, there would have to be an investigation for what had clearly been a friendly fire incident involving USAAF and U.S. Marine Corps aircraft.

In China, meanwhile, the 374th Bomb Squadron filed a missing air crew report (MACR) for the *Shootin' Star*. It remained standard USAAF procedure to file an MACR whenever an aircraft went missing, regardless of the reason, and the template-style form provided blanks

---

*The ten men aboard the *Shootin' Star* were declared dead on January 13, 1946.

for pertinent information, including numerous serial numbers – for the aircraft, for the engines, for the machine guns, and, of course, for the ten crewmembers. The form listed the men aboard the *Shootin' Star* as missing in action and noted that the plane had disappeared without making further contact after setting out from Luliang for the South China Sea. As indicated in the MACR and other documents, the 308th Bomb Group remained unaware of any final radio transmissions from the *Shootin' Star*, and consequently the unit assumed that enemy fire or operational mishap had caused the loss of the aircraft. None of the paperwork ever mentioned the U.S. Navy.[4]

12

The Most Frightening Thing

The army crew of the *Shootin' Star* had stumbled into an all-out assault on the Indochinese coast by the naval air groups of TF 38, which had destroyed more than forty Japanese ships by sundown on January 12, 1945. On January 13, Admiral Nimitz ordered Admiral Halsey to move the fleet to the north end of the South China Sea so that his carriers would be in position to block any attacks on the Lingayen beachhead by the surviving IJN battleships and cruisers. Potentially, IJN warships such as the super-battleship *Yamato* could steam south from the home waters of Japan, while other capital ships could sortie north from Singapore, which intelligence now considered the likely location of the elusive *Ise* and *Hyuga*. In the worst-case scenario, an attack by IJN battleships would come from both directions simultaneously. Should the IJN choose not to move against the Lingayen landings, however, Halsey had permission to unleash his carrier air groups against port facilities, shipping, and airbases along the south China coast as well as on Hainan and Formosa.[1]

In preparation for whatever combat operations lay ahead, the ships of TF 38 once again focused on the carefully choreographed process of taking on fuel from the fast oilers of Captain Acuff's TU 30.8.10. Bludgeoning through heavy seas at 10 knots (12mph), the oilers transferred 198,000 barrels of Navy Special and 796,000 gallons of avgas on January 13 and 14. Admiral Halsey and TF 38 then continued steaming on a northwest bearing up the South China Sea towards Hainan and Hong Kong. Acuff, meanwhile, planned to rendezvous with a relief service group and swap his empty fast oilers for eight fully laden AOs.[2]

Meanwhile, convoy Hi-87 entered Hong Kong waters on the cold, overcast morning of January 13. Officers standing watch and sailors in the gun tubs watched the crenelated profile of Hong Kong Island materialize out of the haze like some kind of hallucinatory dreamscape. Lieutenant Commander Yatsui aboard the *Kanju*, antiaircraft gunner Suzumoku Goni on the *Hashidate Maru*, and everyone else aboard the ships of Hi-87 had defied the odds and escaped detection by the carrier pilots and submariners of the U.S. Navy.

However, other eyes were watching the movements of the Japanese navy and merchant marine. From his prison-yard vantage point on the Stanley Peninsula, Ray Jones focused his binoculars and peered out to sea. To his surprise, he spotted a convoy of Japanese ships. The vessels steamed past Jones's vantage point above Tweed Bay on the east side of the Stanley Peninsula. The convoy caused a stir among his fellow prisoners, because while numerous Japanese ships had called on Hong Kong in the early days of the war, they had become increasingly rare due to the depredations of American submarines, airdropped mines, and radar-guided B-24s. With a pencil, Jones jotted down the details in his journal for January 13, 1945: "Convoy of 4 tankers 9 destrs & 1 cruiser off Tweed Bay."[3]

Jones had no way of knowing he had spotted convoy Hi-87, but he had the naval training to identify enemy warships when he saw them. He also had a keen eye for detail, no shortage of time, and a pair of binoculars that his Japanese captors had never shown any interest in confiscating. As it turned out, his journal entry had been pretty close to the mark. The convoy did, in fact, include four tankers. Jones had misidentified the escort vessels and over-counted them by one, however. Rather than a cruiser and nine destroyers, as he had thought, the convoy escort actually consisted of a destroyer and eight smaller warships.

By noon, the *Kanju* and the rest of the ships in the convoy had entered the haven of Victoria Harbor, where they joined the *CD-13*, *CD-60*, and *Tenei Maru*. The *Sarawak Maru*, the smallest of the tankers, headed for the wharves fringing the western shore of the Kowloon Peninsula and eased alongside Pier 3, which had belonged to the Hong Kong and Kowloon Wharf and Godown Company before the war.[4] The larger 10,000-ton tankers *Hashidate Maru*, *Matsushima*

Maru, and *Tenei Maru* joined the navy oiler *Kamoi* at the mooring buoys off Kennedy Town, a district on the northwest coast of Hong Kong Island.* Aboard the *Hashidate Maru*, Suzumoku Goni sized up Victoria Harbor and concluded it looked like a decidedly more peaceful port than Takao. Lieutenant Commander Yatsui likely had no such illusions, however, since the *Kanju* and the other escort vessels had anchored in a circle around the tankers, the highest value targets for any American air attack. In addition to the *kaibōkan*, other naval vessels in port included the IJNS *Hasu*, an obsolete destroyer dating to World War I, and the landing ship *T-108*. Both vessels would add their guns to the air-defense effort.

A motley assemblage of steel-hulled merchant vessels, some of them ex-Chinese or ex-British, had already sought the protection of Victoria Harbor when convoy Hi-87 arrived. Many of them had been bottled up in port for months by the American antiship mines lurking in the harbor channels, the paucity of coal and bunker fuel, the trepidations of sailors fearful of going to sea, and the general collapse of the Japanese merchant marine. At the mooring buoys off Kennedy Town, the *Hida Maru* and *Okinoyama Maru No. 5* swung with the tide. Other merchant ships in port included the *Anri Go No. 2*, *Choko Maru*, *Dosei Maru*, *Hakushu Maru No. 2*, *Heikai Maru*, *Katsuura Maru*, and *Sekko Maru*. The tanker *Yamasachi Maru* – also known as the *Yamako Maru* or *Sanko Maru* – hugged the quay at the Tai Koo dockyard, where the *Ankai Maru* rested in dry dock like an anesthetized whale, and a small army of welders, riveters, carpenters, and pipefitters – most of them local Cantonese – had nearly completed work on the *Yokai Maru*. In total, nearly forty steel-hulled ships of various types and tonnages had anchored, moored, or docked in Victoria Harbor, which also contained numerous small wooden vessels, including the forty-ton *Nanshu Maru*.[5] A sizeable flotilla of tugs, lighters, launches, and ferries as well as civilian junks and sampans further cluttered the coves, piers, and typhoon shelters of the harbor, which had the feel of a maritime refugee camp.

*Sources are unclear about the position of the *Hashidate Maru* on January 13, 1945, but it seems likely that the tanker moored with the *Matsushima Maru*, *Tenei Maru*, and IJNS *Kamoi* off Kennedy Town.

Lieutenant Commander Yatsui had always believed that maneuverability remained a ship's best defense and had worked to organize convoys accordingly.[6] When in port, however, maneuverability became a moot point, and he knew that antiaircraft defenses mattered the most. In Hong Kong, these defenses remained robust, since shore-based flak batteries on both sides of the harbor and on Stonecutters Island would supplement the convoy's own guns. In addition, Yatsui could see from his vantage point aboard the *Kanju*, which had taken up station 1,000 feet from the nearest tanker, that Hong Kong's topography would benefit the defenders as well. Gunners aboard a ship at sea had to guard against air attack from all directions, but gunners aboard a ship in Victoria Harbor could predict the flight paths of incoming American warplanes. They knew that low-flying aircraft would have to enter the harbor through the narrow straits to the east and west, which could be covered by automatic antiaircraft weapons of the sort crewed by Suzumoku Goni and his comrades. Pilots flying above 3,500 feet – the minimum margin needed to clear Hong Kong's highest peaks – could approach from any direction, of course, though an approach from the sea remained most likely. Regardless of the direction, however, pilots would still have to descend to a lower altitude to execute their attacks, and this maneuver would be hindered by the mountains that ringed the harbor like a natural palisade, particularly during pull-outs at the bottom of a bomb run. Rather than haul back on the stick and try to claw back up and over the mountains, which made them easy targets, the pilots would have to escape on the deck through the flak curtains shielding the eastern and western approaches to the harbor.

Though Suzumoku Goni and all the other antiaircraft gunners aboard the ships of convoy Hi-87 stood ready, no American warplanes appeared over Hong Kong during the afternoon of January 13. Lieutenant Commander Yatsui and just about everyone else aboard the ships of convoy Hi-87 no doubt experienced a considerable degree of relief when the sun finally dipped below the mountainous profile of Lantau Island and nightfall dropped a protective cloak over Victoria Harbor. Moji and the home islands must have seemed very far away, and the hard-drinking sailors aboard the tankers would have long since recovered from their final night of carousing before setting sail for Syonan-to. Against their own grimly calculated odds, Suzumoku and the tanker crews had eluded the enemy submarines and carrier planes and made it as far as Hong Kong. Sailors and officers alike stood watch that evening, but the night passed as uneventfully as a prewar port call. However, the appearance of a four-engine patrol bomber the next morning shattered any hope that the convoy would remain undetected behind the mountains that screened Victoria Harbor.

Lt. Paul F. Stevens and Crew Two had lifted off from Tacloban that morning to execute a standard search mission in their PB4Y-1. They would fly a thousand miles out to the China mainland, went the mission brief, where they would then bank and fly north along the coast for 200 miles before heading back out to sea for the thousand-mile cruise back to Leyte. A pair of auxiliary fuel tanks mounted in the forward bomb bay made such long-range missions possible. Each of these tanks held 390 gallons of aviation fuel, which increased the fuel capacity of the PB4Y-1 to 3,400 gallons and allowed the aircraft to fly fourteen-hour patrols. The tanks would self-seal if punctured by a bullet or shard of shrapnel and could be jettisoned in an emergency, though pilots considered this a dicey move because when the crew removed the release pins the tanks could snag and wind up hanging halfway out of the bomb bay.[7]

The PB4Y-1s flown by Lieutenant Stevens and the other pilots of VPB-104 carried a reduced bombload on extended missions since the extra gas tanks in the forward bomb bay weighed 5,400 pounds when topped up with avgas. Typically, Stevens and the other PPCs flew with 1,000 to 1,500 pounds of ordnance in the two aft bomb bays. Though they carried 100-, 250-, and 500-pound GP bombs in varying mixes, by the start of 1945, large maritime targets had become relatively rare, and PPCs preferred to carry 100-pound bombs because they worked well against the small coastal vessels they typically encountered along the China coast. Sometimes patrol bombers also carried 100-pound AN-M8 incendiary cluster bombs for use against wooden-hulled ships, though this required landing the bomb on the deck or superstructure. A near miss with a general-purpose bomb could damage or even sink a small wooden ship, but a near miss with an incendiary accomplished nothing at all, making them unpopular with some PPCs. Like all the PPCs, Stevens sometimes opted to carry 500-pounders for use against larger steel-hulled ships, but he invariably carried some 100-pounders as well for small game. Exactly what constituted the most suitable bombload remained a point of contention throughout the deployment of VPB-104, but the debate had become irrelevant with the issuing of the order not to carry any bombs while on patrol. When Stevens departed Tacloban that morning, he had two topped-up auxiliary fuel tanks in the forward bomb bay, but nothing at all in the aft bomb bay.[8]

Lieutenant Stevens and the other pilots of VPB-104 tracked ships for a living, so they had quickly discovered that the carrier task groups of TF 38 had sortied into the South China Sea. They picked them up on radar, observed the telltale comb of their wakes, and sometimes approached close enough to identify the different classes of warships arrayed in concentric rings – flattops in the bullseye, a circle of cruisers and battleships, and an outer phalanx of destroyers. Stevens and his fellow PPCs dreaded stumbling upon a carrier task group, but they nonetheless often did because they were not privy to the tactical movements of TF 38. In such encounters, the CAP came gunning for the presumed enemy bogey, hell bent on instigating a friendly fire incident. Stevens knew from experience that he could survive an encounter with Japanese fighters, but he doubted he could survive a tussle with a division of Hellcats. "Make no mistake about this," he would later write. "Coming upon one of our Fast Carrier Task Forces was the most frightening thing a patrol plane could encounter."[9]

When Lieutenant Stevens had crossed the South China Sea and reached the mainland, he executed a fly-by of the neutral Portuguese colony of Macau, which occupied a narrow peninsula some forty miles southwest of Hong Kong at the mouth of the Pearl River delta. On previous missions, Stevens and other PPCs from his squadron had reported the presence of Japanese ships and seaplanes at Macau, which led them to view the city's neutrality as a meaningless legal definition that had no bearing on the facts on the ground. On this day, however, Stevens and his crew failed to spot anything afloat at Macau other than the usual collection of sail-powered civilian junks.

From Macau, Lieutenant Stevens cut across the mouth of the Pearl River estuary towards Hong Kong, where he intended to conduct a ship count in Victoria Harbor. He brought his PB4Y-1 down to the deck and let the jagged profile of Hong Kong Island fill his windshield, then throttled up to full military power and surfed up the side of the mountainous island to maximize surprise and minimize exposure to antiaircraft fire. He popped over the spine of the island and hurtled back down towards the harbor, which offered up a bonanza of Japanese vessels of all sizes. A week after discovering convoy Hi-87 in the South China Sea, Stevens and his crew had located the convoy yet again, this time while in port. They counted a light cruiser, two destroyers, two destroyer escorts, seven freighters, and four tankers. For the second time, they had misidentified the *Shigure* as a light cruiser and promoted escort vessels to destroyers. They had also undercounted the number of warships, but they had accurately tallied the four 10,000-ton tankers, which ranked as the highest priority targets in Victoria Harbor.

Lieutenant Stevens and his crew remained on the alert for enemy fighter aircraft, since they could see the aircraft revetments and runways at Kai Tak airfield. The Japanese had painted the tarmac in camouflage colors, though the bomb craters pocking the field suggested this paint scheme had done little to fool the bombardiers of General Chennault's 14th Air Force. No Japanese aircraft chose to contest Lieutenant Stevens's run over the harbor and the mottled colors of the Kai Tak runway, however, so he continued north along the islands and bays of the China coast before swinging back out to sea for the final leg of his wedge-shaped search pattern.

Much to their alarm, Lieutenant Stevens and his crew soon caught sight of two different carrier task groups prowling offshore. To avoid interception by friendly fighters, Stevens ordered his radioman to broadcast their friendly identity over VHF as they continued across the South China Sea through shifting combinations of mist, cloud, rain, and fog.[10] Every man aboard would have been wondering if a CAP had been vectored out to dispatch the fat blip lighting up the radarscopes in a fleet carrier's Combat Information Center (CIC). Somewhere out there in the grayness lurked the bogeyman, and everybody strapped inside the bucking innards of Lieutenant Stevens's rain-washed patrol bomber knew what kind of aircraft he would be flying. He wouldn't be sitting in the cockpit of a Zero. He would be piloting a made-in-America Grumman F6.

Blanket Missions

Admiral Halsey and his staff envisioned a two-day series of strikes once the fleet had taken up station off Formosa. Starting at dawn on January 15, 1945, Hellcat pilots would fly fighter sweeps over Canton and Hong Kong and along the south China coast up to Amoy and Swatow. However, the bulk of the fighter sweeps and all of the airstrikes by the dive-bomber and torpedo-bomber squadrons would focus on Formosa and the Pescadores. On January 16, the fighters would continue to cover enemy airfields, but the airstrikes would shift to Canton, Hong Kong, and Hainan.[1]

In accordance with Admiral Halsey's plan, Vice Admiral McCain instructed his task-group commanders to ready their VF squadrons for fighter sweeps on the morning of January 15. As the name implied, a fighter sweep was an all-Hellcat operation. However, the purpose of a sweep could vary from hunting for targets of opportunity to hitting preselected targets. In this case, however, the pilots would "blanket" enemy airbases and destroy any aircraft that could threaten TF 38 or interfere with airstrikes by the dive-bomber and torpedo-bomber squadrons. Halsey ordered two of his carrier task groups to focus on the Pearl River delta, a region that encompassed the inland river city of Canton and the coastal ports of Hong Kong and Macau. Rear Admiral Radford, commander of TG 38.1, would cover the airbases at Canton. Rear Admiral Bogan, commander of TG 38.2, received orders to blanket airfields and seaplane bases at the mouth of the Pearl River delta, including Kai Tak at Hong Kong. Halsey ordered Rear Admiral

Sherman, commander of Task Group 38.3, to blanket airfields along the China coast to the north of Hong Kong, particularly at Amoy and Swatow. All three of the task groups would also send Hellcats to Formosa to clear the skies and runways of enemy aircraft. Once the VF pilots had established air superiority over Formosa and Hong Kong, the task groups would send in the dive-bombers and torpedo bombers to smash shipping and port facilities. Additional fighter sweeps would maintain air superiority by continuous blanketing of enemy airfields as well.[2]

As instructed by Vice Admiral McCain, Rear Admiral Bogan assigned targets to the fighter squadrons aboard the carriers of TG 38.2. On the morning of January 15, VF-20 from the *Lexington* would cover Kai Tak airfield at Hong Kong. VF-11 from the *Hornet* would provide additional muscle for the sweep over Kai Tak, but also handle four auxiliary airfields to the north of Hong Kong. The *Hancock* would dispatch Hellcats from VF-7 to bolster the sweep over Kai Tak and to blanket targets to the south of Hong Kong, including the airfield on the island of Sanchau, the airstrip at Chungshan, and the seaplane base at Macau.

The Fast Carrier Task Force operated in a theater where every land mass, from the tiniest atoll to the sprawling vastness of the Chinese mainland, belonged to belligerent powers. Macau remained the one exception, a tiny thread of peacetime neutrality woven into the ragged folds of a conflict that spanned the Pacific Ocean and the Asian continent. Macau remained the one place in all of Asia that the U.S. Navy could not count as ally or enemy, the one place that stood on the sidelines as Asia burned. In the European theater, American fighter pilots and bomber crews fought an air war over a continent divided into a patchwork quilt of belligerent and non-belligerent powers. Large chunks of Europe remained neutral territory – Switzerland, Sweden, Spain, Portugal, Ireland, Turkey. The USAAF briefed its crews accordingly and forbade overflights of neutral territory, but gave a tacit nod to the notion that a B-17 crew over Germany with two engines shot out and no hope of making it back to the field in England might consider diverting to the haven of Switzerland. Internment by the Swiss beat a Nazi POW camp, went the unstated calculus.[3] In the Pacific, such briefings never happened, because in the Pacific no nations had taken a neutral position on the war. Every country and colony had taken sides, with the minor exceptions of the Portuguese territories of Timor and Macau. The Japanese had invaded Timor in 1942, which turned the colony's non-belligerent status into a moot point, but Macau remained neutral and unoccupied.

For Admiral Halsey, Portuguese neutrality remained just one of the many variables to factor into the complexities of Operation *Gratitude*. He had learned to keep his focus on the strategic panorama and on making critical command decisions, however, while leaving the more granular tactical details to his subordinates.[4] The specifics for dealing with Macau's neutrality thus fell to Rear Admiral Bogan, whose task group would establish air superiority over a region of southern China that included the Portuguese colony. On January 13, Bogan sent Halsey and Vice Admiral McCain a communique that explained how he planned to instruct the ACI officers aboard the *Hancock* to brief the VF-7 fighter pilots assigned to blanket missions over the Pearl River delta. Bogan's message read: "Since Macao is owned by neutral Portugal unless otherwise advised plan to brief pilots to inspect peninsular and adjacent waters for aircraft and seaplanes. No attacks to be made unless aircraft are seen and then only on aircraft and air installations."[5]

Both Halsey and McCain concurred with the briefing plan proposed by Bogan, who then sent instructions to Captain Robert F. Hickey, the skipper of the *Hancock*. Communique 130735 established the rules of engagement for any *Hancock* pilots flying missions near Macau: "Since Macao is owned by neutral Portugal brief all pilots that no attacks are to be made on Macao or shipping within two miles thereof unless Japanese aircraft or shipping are on [sic] Macao or in those waters in which case attack will be limited to those aircraft and ships. Pilots will inspect Macao for aircraft but will not fly over it."[6]

On January 14, Admiral Halsey gave Vice Admiral McCain the green light for launching his carrier air groups the next morning. As TF 38 moved towards Formosa in the early morning hours of January 15, however, McCain recommended turning the fleet around and canceling the day's strikes due to the monsoon weather that had reduced visibility and generated heavy seas. After considering this recommendation, Halsey directed that the fleet should continue its run north to Formosa despite the adverse conditions for air operations. TF 38 would be in range of enemy air attack even if it reversed course, Halsey concluded, and destroying Japanese air assets and shipping at Formosa remained of major strategic importance. With characteristic aggressiveness, Halsey ordered his air groups to prepare for airstrikes against Formosan targets and for fighter sweeps along the China coast regardless of the weather.[7]

By the predawn hours of January 15, the flattops of TF 38 had reached a position about 250 miles to the southeast of Hong Kong and just 170 miles from Formosa.[8] Sunrise broke over the gray-hulled warships at 8:03, revealing a turbulent ocean under gunmetal skies. Plane handlers aboard the TG 38.1 carriers *Yorktown* and *Wasp* under Rear Admiral Radford's command prepared twenty-eight Hellcats for a sweep of the Canton airfields. The carriers *Hornet*, *Hancock*, and *Lexington* of Rear Admiral Bogan's TG 38.2, meanwhile, prepared to launch another twenty-eight Hellcats for similar missions against airfields in the Hong Kong area. For both of these blanket missions, the goal would be to gain and maintain local air superiority by proactively eliminating enemy warplanes before they could attack the fleet or interfere with the Helldivers and Avengers that would execute the follow-up strikes. The nature of the mission called for flexible combat loadings that would allow the Hellcat pilots to take on enemy pilots in air-to-air combat or take out enemy aircraft on the ground. Of the fifty-six Hellcats scheduled for the sweeps over Canton and Hong Kong, nine would go in with guns only, twenty-one would tote a 500-pound bomb, and twenty-four would carry rockets. Most of the pilots with rockets under their wings hauled the standard 5-inch high-explosive model, which weighed in at ninety pounds, but a few lucky aviators packed the heavier 5-inch High Velocity Aerial Rocket (HVAR), a weapon so pyrotechnically spectacular that awestruck pilots had nicknamed it the "Holy Moses."[9]

The Hellcats from the *Hancock*, *Hornet*, and *Lexington* began launching for the Hong Kong sweep in the morning twilight, with the last planes leaving the rain-washed flight decks at eight in the morning. Mechanical issues forced two pilots to abort the mission, leaving twenty-six planes for the 250-mile run to Hong Kong, which was a third longer than the hops that would be flown for the strikes against Formosa that morning. VF-11 from the *Hornet* led the sweep as the three squadrons wormed under ceilings as low as fifty feet, and the pilots squinted into visibility that often shrank to less than a mile. The overcast began to lift as the Hellcats approached the China coast, however, which allowed them to climb to a more tactically advantageous 6,000 feet. This decision to ascend to a higher altitude soon paid off when the VF-11 pilots spotted five aircraft flying below them at low altitude, apparently inbound to Hong Kong from Formosa.

Leaving the squadrons from the *Hancock* and *Lexington* to fly top cover, the six VF-11 pilots from the *Hornet* dove on the formation of presumed enemy aircraft. As the pilots closed the distance, they identified a twin-engine L2D transport – the Japanese version of the Douglas DC-3 – with an escort of four A6M navy fighters. When the A6M pilots spotted the incoming F6Fs, they reacted like inexperienced aviators with far too few hours in the cockpit. Rather than take advantage of the A6M's legendary acrobatic performance and attempt to outmaneuver the Hellcats, the rookie pilots simply tried to outrun the far more experienced American aviators on the deck. With ruthless efficiency, the *Hornet* pilots lined up behind each of the fleeing A6Ms and dispatched them with well-aimed bursts from their six .50-caliber wing guns. A pair of F6F pilots then shot out the engines of the transport plane, which lost a wing and cartwheeled into the spume with enough violence to ensure there would be no survivors. Operation *Gratitude* had now claimed a second Japanese officer of flag rank. Rear Admiral Shibuya had gone down with the *Kashii*, and Vice Admiral Hatakeyama Koichiro, a flag officer important enough to rate an A6M fighter escort, numbered among those killed in the crash of the L2D.[10]

The three squadrons continued towards Hong Kong, broke through the edge of the weather front, and emerged into hazy sunlight some five miles from the coast. Fishing junks speckled the rippling surface of the ocean, which outlined the rocky offshore islands with brilliant white necklaces of surf. The Hellcats from the *Hornet* as well as the *Hancock* and *Lexington* began arriving over Hong Kong at 9:30 a.m. No Japanese fighter aircraft contested the airspace over the harbor, but antiaircraft gun crews put up a vigorous barrage, particularly over the concentration of tankers and escort vessels moored at the western end of the anchorage. As per their mission orders, the Hellcat pilots from all three squadrons ignored the plethora of maritime targets and proceeded to bomb, strafe, and rocket the hangars and revetments at Kai Tak for the next thirty minutes. Though some claims doubtless overlapped, the VF pilots believed they had destroyed eight aircraft on the ground, including three planes rocketed in a single large revetment. However, whether the aircraft had been flightworthy or even whether they had been real aircraft as opposed to decoys constructed of rice paper and bamboo remained an open question.

After making their runs on Kai Tak, the VF-11 pilots from the *Hornet* scouted the auxiliary fields to the north of Hong Kong, but only located two of the four airstrips. After determining that both fields appeared to be empty, the *Hornet* pilots headed back to the fleet. The pilots from the *Hancock* and *Lexington* did not execute a similar detour to the south of Hong Kong to check out the fields and seaplane ramps at Chungshan, Sanchau, and Macau. Perhaps out of fuel concerns, they banked out to sea instead. By noon, every pilot assigned to the fighter sweep had returned safely to the flattops of TG 38.2, and only one of them unbuckled from a battle-damaged Hellcat that would need repairs.[11]

The two squadrons assigned to hit the Canton airfields – VF-3 and VF-81 – reached the mainland without encountering any Japanese aircraft, though two pilots aborted the mission for mechanical reasons – a loose hood lock and a faulty artificial horizon – not long after launch from the *Yorktown* and *Wasp*. With twenty-six aircraft, the formation bypassed Hong Kong and flew inland in clear visibility. By 9:40 a.m., the navy pilots could see the sinuous Pearl River and the runways of Tien Ho and White Cloud, the main airbases of the badly depleted JAAF air units in southern China. At this point at least four pilots of the 9th Sentai dove out of the sun from high altitude and bounced the much larger formation of Hellcats. While the American pilots all flew the same make and model of aircraft, the JAAF formation appears to have been a mongrel one equipped with the Ki-43 Hayabusa, the Ki-44 Shōki, and perhaps even the Ki-84 Hayate. In the ensuing dogfight, two pilots from the 9th Sentai bailed out of their mortally wounded aircraft and the unit lost its commanding officer, Capt. Kobayashi Isao, who had just taken the helm three weeks before when the previous commander had been killed in action. Having cleared the skies without taking any losses, the Hellcat pilots made runs on Tien Ho and White Cloud and claimed to destroy six aircraft on the ground. For good measure, some of the pilots then machine-gunned small craft on the Pearl River.[12]

While returning from Canton, all of the *Yorktown* pilots as well as two of the *Wasp* pilots strafed, bombed, and rocketed the ships arrayed down the length of Victoria Harbor. Ensign Joseph G. Scordo – Joe to his squadron mates – and at least one other pilot believed they had scored bomb hits on the tankers, while two more pilots claimed rocket strikes on a tanker and an escort vessel. However, none of these hits could be confirmed because the pilots encountered such an unexpectedly dense curtain of antiaircraft fire that they chose not to make a second run on the harbor. In total, eight Hellcat pilots heard bullets and shrapnel puncture their planes with a sound that they likened to the rattle of rocks hitting the fenders while speeding down a gravel road. For seven of the pilots, the hits inflicted nothing more severe than the aeronautical equivalent of flesh wounds. However, the flak eviscerated the vital organs of the eighth Hellcat piloted by Ensign Scordo. After punching his burning belly tank, Scordo headed back towards the fleet in the hopes he could close the distance before he went down. However, he ended up ditching several hundred yards from a beach somewhere to the southwest of Victoria Harbor as his squadron mates orbited overhead. Some of these pilots reported that Scordo never rolled back his canopy and went down with his plane, while other pilots from the *Wasp* claimed they had observed him in the water, without a raft but within sight of several Chinese fishing junks. All of the other Hellcats from the Canton fighter sweep returned to *Wasp* and *Yorktown*, with the last pilots snagging the wire at 1.20 p.m.[13]

The fighter sweeps flown that morning marked the first time that aircraft from the U.S. Navy had pummeled Hong Kong. However, the wail of the air-raid siren had long been a familiar sound in the occupied colony, which General Chennault's 14th Air Force frequently targeted. In December 1944 and January 1945, the 118th Tactical Reconnaissance Squadron (TRS) under the command of Lt. Col. Edward O. McComas flew more missions to Hong Kong than any other squadron in the 14th Air Force. On the morning of January 15, the squadron sent sixteen P-51 Mustangs into action over the Pearl River delta. Eight pilots strafed the Canton airbases, while another eight Mustangs buzzed into Victoria Harbor on the deck to skip-bomb Japanese shipping just after the last Hellcats had vacated the airspace over Hong Kong. Major David H. Houck, who had just joined the squadron and was scheduled to relieve Lieutenant Colonel McComas as its commander, numbered among the pilots. The army aviators did not coordinate their mission that morning with their navy counterparts, since the navy brass shared the details of fast-carrier operations on a need-to-know basis, and the 118th TRS most definitely did not need to know. As the loss of the *Shootin' Star* had so vividly illustrated, even General Chennault and his staff remained out of the loop when it came to the tactical operations of TF 38.

If the inbound pilots of the 118th TRS remained unaware that navy squadrons had already been in action over Hong Kong that morning, they also had no idea that convoy Hi-87 had taken refuge in the port, and consequently they ran full-throttle into an unexpectedly dense flak barrage courtesy of the Imperial Japanese Navy. The P-51C flown by Major Houck flared like a giant match, ascended to 1,000 feet, and then did an abrupt wingover into the harbor. A second Mustang piloted by 2nd Lt. Galen C. Theobold trailed a line of smoke as it streaked eastwards just a few feet above the harbor and disappeared. Two more P-51s flown by 1st Lt. Frank S. Palmer and 2nd Lt. Daniel Mitchell succumbed to antiaircraft fire during the fighter sweep over the Canton airbases, bringing the day's losses to four aircraft and four pilots missing in action, with Major Houck presumed dead. None of the twelve pilots who returned to Suichuan airfield reported the presence of U.S. Navy aircraft or noticed that the Japanese ships in Victoria Harbor had been damaged by airstrikes earlier that morning. As far as the Mustang pilots of the 118th TRS were concerned, they had been the only squadron to put any planes over the Pearl River delta that day.[14]

A Complete Failure

No warship afloat packed more combat power than the Essex-class fleet carriers of the U.S. Navy. Paradoxically, however, the fleet carriers remained uniquely vulnerable to enemy attack. A warship as large as an American fleet carrier presented a large and distinctive target profile, for one thing. No armor undergirded its wooden flight deck, either. Ranks of highly combustible warplanes often filled its hangar deck, and a warren of magazines and fuel bunkers honeycombed its interior. However, no greater moment of vulnerability occurred for a fleet carrier than the minutes just before the launch of a full deck-load strike, when rows of aircraft packed folded wingtip to folded wingtip jammed the aft end of the rectangular flight deck like a string of giant firecrackers. A single enemy bomb or *kamikaze* aircraft could instantly transform this assemblage of armed and fueled warplanes into an inferno that could consume the entire ship. Such had been the fate of the Japanese flattops during the Battle of Midway. Launching a strike with utmost speed thus became a survival imperative for the captain of a fleet carrier, and his deck crews worked at the pace of an Indy 500 pit crew to ready planes for flight. Assisted by small tractors and specially modified jeeps equipped with tow bars, the plane handlers used the elevators to bring aircraft up from the hangar deck and maneuver them into their position in the launch order. To ensure the longest deck run possible on the forward flight deck, the planes had to be spotted on the aft flight deck in a tightly interlocked grid that used as little space as possible. Every foot of flight deck mattered, and the handlers pushed the rearmost planes so far aft that their tailwheels stopped just short of round down.

Aboard the *Yorktown* on the morning of January 15, 1945, the process of spotting the aircraft for Strike 1B at the aft end of the ship began while the flight deck officer was still launching Hellcats for the Canton and Formosa fighter sweeps from the forward flight deck. Squalls continued to blow across the length of the ship, soaking the flight deck officer, the plane handlers, and the 20mm antiaircraft gunners standing in the balcony-like "galleries" mounted along the edges of the flight deck. Peering out from beneath the brims of their helmets, the gunners could see the other carriers of their task group – Rear Admiral Radford's TG 38.1 – rolling in the heavy seas as navy-blue aircraft lifted off from their decks in rapid succession. In the screen surrounding the carriers, the battleships and cruisers shouldered through the high seas like brawny men pushing their way down a crowded sidewalk, while the smaller tin cans pitched and bobbed in the swells. The vulnerability of the carriers to air and submarine attack necessitated such a muscular escort, though the fact that the fast battleships of the U.S. Navy now served primarily as antiaircraft protection for fleet carriers signaled the primacy of the flattop over the dreadnought.

Unlike the ready rooms in earlier generations of U.S. Navy fleet carriers, those in Essex-class fleet carriers like the *Yorktown* had been specifically designed with pilot comfort in mind. A carrier depended upon its air groups, and the design of the ready rooms reflected the need to provide naval aviators with a combination clubhouse and workspace that would keep them well rested, focused, and ready to fight. Rather than the dim, poorly ventilated compartments of the prewar carriers, the ready rooms aboard the *Yorktown* featured rows of leather recliners arranged auditorium-style to face the briefing area at the front of the room, with its chalkboard, squawk box, and teleprinter synched with the air plot room up on the signal bridge. The brightly lit ready rooms also featured air conditioning, a rare luxury aboard U.S. Navy warships.[1] Lieutenant John Lavender and the other pilots of VB-3 would likely have been sitting in their leather recliners during the run-up for Strike 1B, navigation chart boards and coffee mugs in hand, though they would have felt anything but relaxed as they prepared for another dicey mission over open water and enemy territory. Standing at the front of the room, perhaps with a clipboard or stick of chalk in hand, the squadron ACI officer would have delivered a preflight briefing to his audience of amped-up combat pilots. They were going to visit the port city of Takao this morning, the ACI officer would have explained, and they could expect the usual combination of piss-poor flying weather and hellacious antiaircraft fire. Though equipped with creature comforts, the maritime architects had not neglected practical considerations when designing the pilot ready rooms, as evidenced by the fact that each ready room had been placed in close proximity to where the plane handlers typically spotted the squadron's aircraft on the flight deck. When ordered to man their planes, Lavender and his fellow aviators hustled quickly up through connecting passageways to the deafening noise of the flight deck, where the plane handlers had spotted, fueled, and armed their Helldivers.

At 8:30, less than thirty minutes after the departure of the morning fighter sweeps, a dozen VF-3 pilots assigned to Strike 1B began launching from the *Yorktown* and forming up overhead into divisions of four aircraft. The planes carried a mix of 500-pound bombs and 5-inch rockets, the generic combat loading for Hellcats serving in a fighter-bomber role. A fourth division designated as Photo 1B flew a quartet of camera-equipped F6F-5P photo ships, each lightly loaded with belts of machine-gun ammunition and rolls of unexposed film.

Thirty-six pilots, turret gunners, and radio-gunners left the *Yorktown* at 8:40 in a dozen VT-3 Avengers. None of the planes hauled a torpedo, however. Instead, each carried a mix of 100-pound and 500-pound GPs suitable for a target-saturated environment like Takao, where a pilot needed an all-purpose weapon that would work equally well on a Sugar Charlie, a steam locomotive, or a chemical factory. Despite their ungainly appearance and considerable size, all twelve Avengers cleared the deck in less than five minutes.

VB-3 occupied third place in the launch order, with twelve planes and twenty-four men. Each pilot in the squadron flew with the same gunner on every mission, barring illness or injury, so Jean Balch once again strapped himself into the rear cockpit of Lieutenant Lavender's Helldiver. Aircraft from TF 38 had pounded Takao on multiple occasions, but this would be the first time that the two Texans had flown a strike against the city, which scuttlebutt as well as the prestrike briefing described as ripe with targets, but also well defended with shore-based and ship-mounted antiaircraft guns. To further complicate their eighth bombing mission, Lavender had been warned to watch out for barrage balloons festooned with dangling beards of steel cable that could slice the wings from a plane. Takao would most likely be socked in as well, making the balloons all the more difficult to avoid. By now, Balch had grown used to the atrocious flying weather that had dogged Operation *Gratitude* and missions to Formosa in particular. As the ACI officers had made clear during the prestrike briefing, the aviators of VB-3 could expect business as usual from a meteorological standpoint, which meant broken clouds at 500 feet and solid cloud cover from 800 feet on up. Flying would be challenging, but hardly impossible, so at 8:45 a.m. Lieutenant Lavender and eleven other VB-3 pilots throttled up and careened in quick succession down the rain-slicked flight deck. To the officers and sailors watching from the island – the naval term for the carrier's superstructure with its Tinkertoy collection of ladders, masts, platforms, rigging, searchlights, radar dishes, and radio antennas – each plane seemed to disappear off the bow of the ship like a stone kicked over the edge of a cliff. Moments later, each of the planes reappeared as it gained altitude in a bank away from the ship, revealing the white stars-and-bars on the navy-blue wings.

Led by Commander Lowe, the skipper of CVG-3, the group orbited the *Yorktown* until every plane assigned to the strike had launched and formed up. Lowe then commenced the 120-mile run into the target zone with seventy-five men under his command, a number roughly equivalent in personnel to a pair of reinforced infantry platoons or the crew of a fleet submarine. Like everyone else in VB-3, Lieutenant Lavender flew at 500 feet through intermittent light rain that further reduced his already limited ability to see other aircraft and distinguish up from down. Turbulence smacked the airplane around, and streaks of rain slid along the sides of the cockpit canopy like quicksilver. As the three squadrons approached the coast of Formosa, they climbed through solid overcast until they emerged into clear sky sandwiched between two cloud layers. When pilots dipped a wing to look downwards, they could see the undercast floating at 5,000 feet, and when they glanced up through the cockpit canopy, they could see another layer of clouds hanging at 8,000 feet.

Flying between the stratified layers of cloud, the group circled over Takao in hopes of finding a sufficiently expansive break in the undercast to facilitate a glide- or dive-bombing attack. Pilots caught occasional glimpses of ships through rips in the fabric of the cloud blanket, but the vessels immediately slid back into the mist like tricks of the eye. To dissuade the American pilots from viewing these openings in the clouds as invitations to push forward on the stick and head downstairs, Japanese antiaircraft gunners began blocking the infrequent gaps that opened up in the clouds with flak barrages – a tactic that the pilots of VT-3 in the larger and slower Avengers judged as particularly effective.

The Japanese gun crews, who no doubt found it unnerving to hear the American planes droning unseen in the clouds above, resorted to firing straight up through the overcast. VB-3 pilots could not observe the guns below, but they could see the shells exploding in colored puffs all around them. This suggested the presence of Japanese naval vessels somewhere under the clouds because, as American naval aviators had learned, the IJN used colored smoke as an aiming device. Such a technique only worked when the gunners could actually see the explosions of their shells and adjust their fire accordingly, but they still managed to consistently place flak bursts at the same altitude as the VB-3 planes. This caused Lavender and many of the other dive-bomber pilots to speculate that some of the guns might be radar guided, which caused more than a little concern. They knew that a direct hit from a shell fired by the dual-purpose main gun of an IJN warship would disintegrate a Helldiver and its crew. Near misses packed considerable lethality as well, and could put the fear of God into a pilot and more than a little shrapnel into his airframe. One chunk of metal banged into the cowling of a Helldiver flown by Lt. Fink, a pilot who often flew in the same section as Lavender and Balch, and it seemed only a matter of time before another shell inflicted more severe damage on a Helldiver or simply wiped it out like a chalk eraser swiping a figure on a blackboard, leaving nothing behind but a puff of dust.

After forty-five tense minutes of orbiting with the rest of the air group, Lt. Roger L. Jenkinson – known as "Jenk" to his fellow pilots, who often addressed each other by abbreviated versions of their last names – plunged through a promising hole in the undercast. Lt. (j.g.) Joe Vercelli followed his section leader, while the third pilot in the three-plane section, perhaps understanding the perilous nature of such a headfirst dive into an un-reconnoitered battle space, chose to remain above the clouds. Lt. Vercelli's plane popped out of the clouds over open water some four miles west of Takao's outer harbor. He circled in an attempt to locate Lt. Jenkinson, but neither Vercelli nor his gunner could spot him. Lt. Vercelli did see Takao in the distance, however, and acting on the assumption that Lt. Jenkinson had flown in that direction, Vercelli popped back into the clouds until he estimated he had flown over the harbor. Then he nosed into a forty-five-degree glide, dropped out of the overcast, and lined up on a mid-sized freighter while simultaneously watching for the barrage balloons that floated at 1,500 feet like gigantic jellyfish. Vercelli released all three of his bombs just as it seemed that every automatic cannon in the entire harbor opened up on him. He nearly got his tail shot off when a 25mm shell struck the leading edge of one of his horizontal stabilizers, shredding the tail and fuselage aft of the gunner's position. Vercelli hauled back on the stick as the bomb bay doors vibrated shut, zoomed up into the gauzy embrace of the clouds, and rejoined Lieutenant Lavender, Lieutenant Fink, and the rest of VB-3 at the rendezvous point.

Due to the low ceiling, the copious antiaircraft fire, and the barrage balloons that turned the harbor into an aviation obstacle course, Commander Lowe judged that low-level attacks would lead to aircraft losses that would exceed the value of any damage his air group could inflict on the enemy at Takao, as the experience of Lt. Jenkinson and Lt. Vercelli had certainly proved. Lowe gave the order to execute level bombing runs from above the clouds, a command that included the rocket-armed Hellcats. Flying between 5,000 and 7,000 feet, all three squadrons dropped on what they estimated to be the port's epicenter. The pilots calculated their aiming point based on radarscope images of the coastline, quick glimpses of the harbor whenever the clouds thinned out, and the quadrant of sky most heavily planted with the multicolored blossoms of exploding flak shells. Drop on the antiaircraft guns, the American fliers figured, and the bombs would hit whatever the Japanese had positioned the guns to defend.

By 1:20 p.m., the *Yorktown* had recovered every plane from Strike 1B and Photo 1B with the exception of number 111, the SB2C-4 piloted by Lt. Jenkinson, which had simply disappeared. Lt. Fink made it back despite the oil line hemorrhaging inside his engine cowling like an aneurism, and Lt. Vercelli brought his mangled Helldiver home as well. His SB2C-4 avoided the usual fate of badly damaged aircraft – an unceremonious shove over the side – but had to endure the amputation of its signature oversized tail empennage and replacement with a new tail section.

After a 250-mile roundtrip flight and four and a half hours strapped to an armored seat, dodging shell bursts or flying blind on instruments in zero-zero clouds layered like a triple-decker birthday cake, the aviators of CVG-3 were exhausted. Despite their fatigue, the pilots of VT-3, who flew versatile radar-equipped Avengers as suited to level bombing as to torpedo runs, remained optimistic that the ordnance they had released over the target zone – an impressive 118 bombs in total – had managed to land on something or somebody worth taking out. However, the frustrated tone of the aircraft action report for VB-3 reflected the loss of Lt. Jenkinson and his rearseatman, John P. Scrafford, ARM1c, who had both gone missing after initiating a foolhardy, if unquestionably courageous, attack on Takao. Exasperated by the poor flying weather and having to fire rockets through the cloud cover, an amateur-hour waste of ordnance that amounted to a blindfolded man throwing darts at a dartboard the size of a penny, the ACI officer who debriefed the pilots of VF-3 described Strike 1B as "a complete failure."[2]

Due to worsening weather conditions out at sea as well as over Formosa, Admiral Halsey canceled all follow-up strikes scheduled for the afternoon. The air groups of TF 38 had inflicted significant damage to targets at Formosa and the Pescadores, but the operations that morning had cost the fleet twelve aircraft, including the Helldiver flown by Lt. Jenkinson at Takao and the Hellcat flown by Ensign Scordo at Hong Kong.[3] On Halsey's orders, TF 38 battened down the hatches and steamed away from Formosa towards the south China coast. If the weather cooperated, Halsey intended to launch strikes in the morning against targets at Hong Kong, Canton, and Hainan.

––––––––––––

Aboard the *Kanju*, flagship of the 7th Escort Convoy, Lieutenant Commander Yatsui parsed the casualty reports coming in from the other ships of convoy Hi-87. Several of the *kaibōkan* had been mauled that morning by the enemy fighter aircraft, but the damage appeared to be superficial. More significantly, four of the five tankers had avoided serious damage. If the tankers had been fully loaded, Yatsui knew that they might have been set afire, but all five carried nothing except saltwater ballast. Still, near misses from bombs had damaged the *Hashidate Maru* severely enough that its captain decided to leave the mooring buoys and move to the Hong Kong and Whampoa dockyard for repairs. While no ships had been lost, rocket hits and strafing by heavy machine guns had caused thirty to forty casualties among the IJN sailors and merchant marine crews.[4]

At sunset, Lieutenant Commander Yatsui and the men of convoy Hi-87 breathed a sigh of collective relief. They had been granted a reprieve by the unruly gale offshore, but they knew that the Grummans would reappear in the morning if the seas settled down. The next assault would almost certainly include dive-bombers and torpedo aircraft, too. If by some chance the Americans did not return, convoy Hi-87 would weigh anchor and continue its journey south to Syonan-to. Either way, January 16 would be a dangerous day for the 7th Escort Convoy and the tankers it had been charged with protecting.

Target 8

By early morning on January 16, 1945, the warships of TF 38 had moved to a position southeast of Hong Kong, and weather conditions had improved enough to permit the resumption of carrier operations. Aboard the *Hancock*, one of the four flattops assigned to Rear Admiral Bogan's task group, the fighter pilots of VF-7 assembled in Ready Room 4 at 5:00 a.m. The pilots had been issued charts of the target zones and special survival gear for Operation *Gratitude*, including China-Burma-India theater shoulder patches for their flight suits, packets of Nationalist Chinese currency, and *Pointie Talkie* phrasebooks that made it possible for an English-speaking pilot to communicate with a Chinese-speaking rescuer and vice-versa. Many pilots received small American flags or, perhaps more usefully, small silk Nationalist Chinese flags embroidered with Chinese characters that identified the bearer as an American flier who should be given aid and assistance.[1] American airmen referred to the little flags as "blood chits," and army pilots of the 14th Air Force sewed them to the backs of their leather flight jackets. In addition to this specialized paraphernalia, which remained in such short supply that many aviators never received a blood chit or a *Pointie Talkie*, the pilots also carried their standard survival equipment. This gear varied from one flier to the next, but typically included a .38-caliber revolver with tracer ammunition, a hunting knife, a life jacket, a dye marker pouch, a parachute harness, and a "jungle kit" worn under the backside of the life jacket. Officially known as the M-592 Back Pad Kit, the rectangular pouch contained a rain poncho, a mosquito head net, sewing needles and thread, a first-aid kit, sunburn ointment, fishing hooks and line, a flare gun, waterproof matches, a compass, a machete, a signal mirror, a whistle, pints of canned water, rations, and various other items of use to a downed aviator. Each pilot would fasten his parachute to his harness before takeoff, and once airborne he would sit on the uncomfortable combination of his parachute and uninflated one-man life raft, both of which he hoped he would never have to use.

At 5:30 a.m., Lt. G.B. Gose, the ACI officer for VF-7, briefed the pilots scheduled to fly the first blanket mission of the day. Gose had in turn been briefed by Lieutenant Golson, ACI officer for CVG-7. Standing in front of the pilots as the air grew gauzy with tobacco smoke, Lieutenant Gose reviewed the orders to strike Chungshan airfield (designated as "Target 7"), the seaplane base at Macau (designated as "Target 8"), and the airfield on Sanchau (designated as "Target 9").[2] Gose also informed the pilots that Macau was a neutral possession of Portugal. Lieutenant Golson, who was not present in the ready room, further emphasized the neutrality of the colony when he read the order from Rear Admiral Bogan restricting attacks on Macau to enemy aircraft and ships over the squawk box to the pilots.[3]

Lieutenant Golson and Lieutenant Gose knew very little about Macau and relied on intelligence documents that provided only the most basic of information about the colony's aviation facilities, which were said to consist of an auxiliary seaplane station that had served the prewar flying clipper service of Pan American Airways. One intelligence bulletin stated that the seaplane base was in a Portuguese colony, but reportedly used by Japanese aircraft.[4] Consequently, the briefing officers told the pilots that Macau had been occupied by the Japanese and that its aviation facilities accommodated Japanese military aircraft. Neither statement was true, however. The briefing officers also erroneously believed that Macau had an airfield in addition to the seaplane base, and they shared this information with the pilots as well. Moreover, the briefing officers were not aware that Macau actually had *two* seaplane bases – the Pan American station and the nearby Center for Naval Aviation, which belonged to the Portuguese navy.

Further confusion resulted when the ACI officers aboard the *Hancock* failed to brief the VF-7 pilots according to Rear Admiral Bogan's orders. A blanket mission as understood by Lieutenant Golson and Lieutenant Gose as well as the second ACI officer for VF-7, Lt. (j.g.) Henry

Helmers, was a fighter sweep with a broad mandate to destroy enemy aircraft wherever the Hellcat pilots found them – in the air or on the ground – as well as any installations that might service or conceal these aircraft, such as hangars, runways, and revetments. Captain Hickey of the *Hancock* and his air group commander, Commander Lamade, shared this understanding of blanket missions. Experience during previous combat missions had taught Lamade and the pilots of VF-7 that the Japanese often hid their aircraft around the perimeter of airfields, and that the only way to "dig out" these aircraft was to rocket and strafe all structures in and around an airbase.[5] In other words, Lamade and his aviators considered it standard procedure to attack airfields regardless of whether they observed any enemy aircraft. Presumably, Rear Admiral Bogan knew this, which explained why he had ordered that pilots be briefed that they could only hit Macau if they spotted *visible* aircraft on the ground. This directive from the admiral did not make it into the briefing, however, leading the VF-7 pilots to conclude that they had carte blanche to shoot up the seaplane bases at Macau regardless of whether they observed any floatplanes.

At the conclusion of the briefing in Ready Room 4, the twelve VF-7 pilots assigned to the morning fighter sweep headed topside, stepped out into the blustery ocean drizzle, and clambered into the cramped confines of their cockpits. Engines coughed blue-gray exhaust plumes that streamed away towards the stern, and propellers began to spin until they blurred into transparent discs. The deck crews started pulling chocks at 7:35 a.m. as the *Hancock* steamed into the wind in preparation for launching the blanket mission assigned to VF-7. Engines roaring at full throttle, the first rocket-laden F6F-5s hurtled down the length of the flight deck, wobbled out over open water, and lifted into the overcast sunrise. In the poor visibility, however, the pilots failed to rendezvous as planned, and the twelve Hellcats broke into two separate groups that proceeded separately towards the mainland.

Lt. George E. Kemper led the first group of five aircraft, while Lt. Lloyd E. Newcomer commanded the second group of seven aircraft. Both men had penned numerous combat missions into their logbooks. A former VT-7 pilot, Kemper had undergone fighter training and transferred into VF-7 when the *Hancock* had slimmed down its contingent of torpedo planes in favor of more Hellcats in December 1944.[6] Kemper and Newcomer had both acquired a reputation as aggressive pilots who went right down on the deck to shoot things up. In marathon fashion, Kemper had executed *ten* gun runs in a row against the 101st Flotilla off the coast of Indochina, which demonstrated his fearless persistence in the face of enemy antiaircraft fire as well as his careful fire control.

Meanwhile, another two dozen F6F-5s from the *Lexington* and *Hornet* formed up over TG 38.2, assumed a northwesterly bearing, and commenced the 170-mile run to Hong Kong. As the pilots well knew and very much appreciated, the relatively short hop would reduce the potential for running out of fuel on the return leg. Moreover, any pilot unlucky enough to leave Hong Kong in a gut-shot aircraft would have a fighting chance of making it back to the fleet, or at least making it far enough out to sea to ditch near one of the radar-equipped picket destroyers – referred to as "Tomcats" – positioned along the flight path between the carriers and Hong Kong. In addition to providing early warning of any incoming Japanese "snoopers" and serving as navigational beacons for carrier aircraft, the picket destroyers functioned as search and rescue vessels for downed naval aviators.

A pilot who came down in the water between the target zone and the fleet could also hope for rescue by a trio of lifeguard submarines, the USS *Sea Dog*, USS *Sea Robin*, and USS *Guardfish*. Since mid-1943 every major carrier strike had been supported by at least one rescue submarine, and by 1945 serving as part of the "Lifeguard League" had become a primary duty of the submarine fleet. Submariners had fished hundreds of "zoomies" from the Pacific, often while under fire close to enemy-held islands. When injury or shock left an aviator helpless in the waves, bobbing in a Mae West but unable to swim or grasp a rope, teams formed from a submarine crew's strongest swimmers dove over the side to complete the rescue. The presence of lifeguard submarines did wonders for pilot morale and certainly earned the gratitude of navy aviators. After the lifeguard submarine *Skate* had retrieved pilots from the *Lexington* who had gone into the drink during an airstrike on Wake Island in October 1943, the "Lady Lex" had radioed to the submarine, "Anything on the *Lexington* is yours for the asking. If it's too big to carry away, we will cut it up into small parts!" If a pilot from the *Lexington* or any of the other carriers sending air groups to Hong Kong had to ditch, fellow pilots would use the VHF lifeguard frequency to vector one of the three lifeguard submarines to the downed aviator's location.[7]

Skippered by Commander Douglas T. Hammond, the aptly named USS *Guardfish* had departed Pearl Harbor on its tenth war patrol on November 26, 1944. Known throughout the submarine fleet for its reputation as a ship killer, the *Guardfish* had earned two Presidential Unit Citations for previous war patrols – a distinction claimed by only one other Pacific Fleet submarine. A previous commander of the *Guardfish* had even earned the Navy Cross – the navy's most prestigious decoration for valor in combat – after claiming seven enemy ships during the submarine's eighth war patrol.[8] However, after seven weeks at sea, much of it in enemy waters, the "G-fish" had failed to sink so much as a sampan, and Commander Hammond faced the unhappy possibility of ending his patrol with no enemy vessels to his credit. In accordance with orders from Commander, Submarine Forces, U.S. Pacific Fleet, the *Guardfish* suspended offensive operations and switched over to lifeguard duty off Hong Kong on January 13. Though frustrated by the prospect of what submariners called a "dry run," the crew recognized that they could still score a first for the *Guardfish* by plucking their inaugural downed aviator from the waves, if need be by sending their best swimmers over the side with lines tied around their waists. With a bit of luck Commander Hammond and his crew would soon have their first zoomie ensconced in the officer's wardroom with a smoke in one hand and a mug of strong coffee in the other, perhaps fortified with a tot of medicinal brandy. At sunset on January 16, the *Guardfish* would set course for Guam and the end of its patrol. Any rescued zoomies would enjoy an all-expenses-paid cruise to Apra Harbor, where the navy would have to figure out how to reunite the disembarking pilots with their carriers.[9]

Pushing on through intermittent rainsqualls, the *Lexington* pilots of VF-20 arrived over the Hong Kong area at approximately 8:30 a.m., where they found CAVU conditions. After a fruitless search for airborne targets, they opted to rocket and strafe Kai Tak, where they shredded three aircraft of doubtful operability on the ground. As the squadron left the area, several pilots made gun runs on a radio station on the south side of Hong Kong Island. The VF-11 pilots from the *Hornet* arrived overhead at 9:30 a.m., had no better luck finding any JAAF planes in the air, and subjected Kai Tak to another round of strafing. However, the *Hornet* pilots suspected they might be punching more holes in nonoperational wrecks, including some the *Lexington* pilots had already used for target practice. One pilot took some hits in the engine compartment and belly tank, but his machine remained airworthy enough to make the run back to the fleet.

As the fighter sweeps from the TG 38.2 carriers *Lexington* and *Hornet* hit Kai Tak, a second group of Hellcats from the TG 38.1 flattops *Wasp* and *Yorktown* arrived over Canton at 8:30 a.m. For the next hour, a joint formation of twenty-eight Hellcats from VF-3 and VF-81 orbited the Canton area in the company of two Helldivers from VB-3, Lieutenant Lavender's outfit. Commander Lowe, the former skipper of VB-3 who now commanded all of CVG-3, had become a proponent of using pathfinder aircraft to scout targets in advance. For this reason, he had saddled up in an SB2C-4 and accompanied the fighter sweep over Canton, where he identified and assigned targets for the incoming planes of Strike 2A, scheduled for approximately 9:45 a.m. He and his wingman also used their Helldivers as communications relay aircraft that kept the fighters in touch with the *Lexington* and *Hornet*.[10] Since neither the Hellcat pilots nor Commander Lowe observed any aircraft on the ground at Tien Ho and White Horse, the aviators of VF-3 and VF-81 deposited their 500-pound bombs in an industrial area of the city instead. In the face of moderate but inaccurate flak, they also rocketed and strafed a trio of river gunboats, five tugs, and a slew of barges on the brown waters of the Pearl River.

While Commander Lowe coordinated the fighter sweep over Canton, Lieutenant Newcomer of the *Hancock* arrived over Sanchau airfield at 9:00 a.m. Newcomer and the six Hellcat pilots in his flight did not encounter Japanese aircraft in the air or spot any on the ground, but they followed standard procedure for a blanket mission when they strafed and rocketed hangars that might conceal enemy planes. The seven pilots then proceeded to investigate the auxiliary field at Chungshan, where they found nothing but a dirt airstrip. At this point, Lieutenant Newcomer headed for Target 8 – the seaplane base at Macau.

Portugal's neutrality extended to its colonial possessions throughout the world, including Macau, which by the end of 1941 had been completely surrounded by Japanese-controlled territory. Lisbon's declaration of neutrality had failed to prevent the Japanese from invading Timor, the only other Portuguese colony in the Pacific, in February 1942.

However, tiny Macau remained unoccupied. The United States had honored Lisbon's declaration of neutrality, and for a variety of reasons, the Japanese government had chosen to do so as well.[11] Consequently, the IJA had refrained from an outright occupation, and the Portuguese colonial administration remained in control of the city. To emphasize Macau's neutral status and ensure that the enclave escaped future Japanese occupation, Lisbon reduced its military presence in the colony. With the exception of the tiny 135-ton gunboat *Macau*, all naval vessels had been withdrawn to Portugal by May 1942.[12] During the same year the navy mothballed the only military aircraft in Macau – a squadron of five Hawker Osprey naval seaplanes.[13] The hilltop fortresses that had accreted over centuries of Portuguese rule belied the fact that Macau retained only a modest garrison of 500 men with few heavy weapons.[14] Though sufficient for internal policing and border security, the garrison would never have been able to offer more than token resistance to a Japanese invasion of the colony.

Macau maintained its tenuous neutrality under the administration of Governor Gabriel Maurício Teixeira, a career naval officer. Teixeira's colonial government faced a massive refugee crisis as thousands of civilians fled wartime violence in southern China and tripled Macau's prewar population.[15] Refugees arrived from Hong Kong as well, including a substantial number of British nationals who fell under the care of British Consul John Pownall Reeves, whose consulate Teixeira had allowed to remain open in accordance with Macau's neutral status. Teixeira's administration began selling government-owned equipment and other goods to the Japanese or on the black market to keep the government running and feed the refugees.[16] During an extreme food shortage in 1943, for example, the government sold the gunboat *Macau* to the Japanese for ten tons of rice.[17] Pedro José Lobo played a key role in these dealings in his powerful position as head of the government's Central Bureau for Economic Services.[18] Under Lobo's direction, the bureau stored government property destined for the black market in the navy seaplane hangar on the Macau waterfront.

Completed in March 1941, the Center for Naval Aviation sat on reclaimed land along the coast of the Outer Harbor beneath a ridgeline topped by the iconic Guia Hill lighthouse.[19] The complex included a hangar and a seaplane ramp for trundling aircraft down to the water's edge. The prewar Pan American station – a complex that included a modest one-story building for arriving and departing passengers, a wharf, and a small refueling shed – stood just down the coast to the west of the naval facility.[20] By January 1945, Consul Reeves believed that the Osprey seaplanes had been removed from the naval hangar and sold to the Japanese.[21] However, a collection of historic memorabilia earmarked for a future maritime museum remained in the hangar at this time.[22] Government property cached in the hangar for eventual sale on the black market included steel and iron frames, nails, cables and wire, the occasional church bell, and other scrap metals.[23] A stock of aviation gasoline that had likely been purchased from Pan American remained the most valuable item in the hangar, however. The fuel-starved Japanese military remained the presumed future buyers of the scrap metal and gasoline, which could be bartered for rice or other essential commodities.

Consul Reeves flew the Union Jack proudly at the consulate, though he knew that after the fall of Hong Kong, Malaya, and Singapore at the start of the war his increasingly tattered standard had become the only British flag left in East or Southeast Asia. Reeves spent much of his time looking after the often-destitute British subjects who had fled occupied Hong Kong, though he also attended to British and American property in Macau and negotiated the complicated intersection of intelligence agencies in a city known as the Casablanca of Asia. He maintained links to the British Army Aid Group (BAAG), a special operations unit based in the Pearl River delta region of southern China. The core of the BAAG consisted of British and Chinese members of the HKVDC and other military units in Hong Kong who had fled the colony after its capitulation to the Japanese in December 1941. They possessed the requisite insider knowledge of the local terrain as well as the linguistic skills to run covert missions in Hong Kong, with a particular focus on intelligence gathering, aiding escapees from the colony, and assisting downed U.S. aviators. BAAG agents often entered Macau as well, as did civilian and military operatives who claimed allegiance to the Portuguese, or to the Japanese, or to the Nationalist Chinese, or to the Communist Chinese, or to the Wang Jing Wei puppet government, or to various triad gangs and pirate bands, or to several of these groups at the same time. All this kept Reeves on his toes.

Macau had certainly suffered during the war years, with refugees literally starving to death in the nooks and crannies of its cobblestone alleyways, but due to its neutral status the city had never once been bombed. Perhaps for this reason, Consul Reeves failed to appreciate the imperative to take cover when the five F6F-5s led by Lieutenant Kemper arrived over Macau. The pilots spotted the seaplane hangar as they circled overhead, but did not observe any Portuguese or Japanese aircraft on the ground or in the air. Figuring that enemy planes could be in the hangar, Lieutenant Kemper nosed over into a dive. More excited than afraid, Reeves stood out in the open by the seaplane ramp. Enthralled, he watched the five Hellcats bear down on the seaplane base to commence what more savvy observers immediately recognized as a strafing run. He saw the wings begin to flash and heard a rapid popping sound as a barrage of .50-caliber slugs punched into the Macau Naval Air Service hangar and the Pan American station. Moments later, the American planes pulled out over the water and disappeared in the direction of Sanchau.

At 9:20 a.m., Lieutenant Newcomer reached Macau after he had finished investigating the empty field at Chungshan with the other six pilots in his flight. Newcomer reached the same conclusion as Lieutenant Kemper and assumed the seaplane hangar concealed Japanese aircraft. All seven pilots in his flight strafed the hangar and set it afire with the standard mix of armor-piercing, tracer, and incendiary rounds. Newcomer and the other pilots agreed that the black smoke rippling out from the hangar suggested burning aircraft and aviation gasoline, which validated their assumption that the building had been used to hide Japanese planes.

Consul Reeves, who had imprudently failed to take cover after the first attack, had once again come under fire and narrowly escaped with his life. His more sensible Portuguese friends had chosen to hug the earth, however. As the drone of aircraft engines faded into the distance, they stood up, dusted themselves off, and muttered indignantly about the American violation of Macau's neutrality. They informed Reeves that multiple rounds had pocked into the ground behind him as he stood watching the action, unaware of how close he had come to catching a machine-gun slug powerful enough to tear him in half. A somewhat chastened Reeves walked over to the Pan American station, where he began counting bullet holes. Fire trucks arrived to deal with the burning hangar, and onlookers began collecting the spent shell casings that had been ejected from the wings of the American warplanes.[24]

At 9:30 a.m., Lieutenant Kemper's flight of five F6F-5s returned to Macau after overflying Sanchau. The pilots reconnoitered the burning seaplane hangar and judged that Target 8 had been destroyed. As they observed the hangar, the pilots took some inaccurate antiaircraft fire, though the location of the weapons could not be determined and none of the aircraft sustained any damage. The two groups of Hellcats led by Lieutenant Kemper and Lieutenant Newcomer then headed back out to sea towards the fleet.

By noon the Hellcats from the morning fighter sweeps over Hong Kong, Canton, Sanchau, and Macau had returned to the five carriers that had launched them. As Lieutenant Kemper entered the landing circle for the *Hancock*, he double-checked that he had turned off his gun switch, rolled back his cockpit canopy, and locked it in the open position. Then he dropped his tail hook, extended his landing gear, and lowered his flaps. He reduced his airspeed to less than 100 knots – or 115mph, though naval aviators had no use for miles per hour – as he approached the carrier from astern and overflew the boiling trail of phosphorescent sea foam left in its wake. Kemper kept his eyes locked on the landing signal officer and watched for either a wave-off or a signal to chop the throttle, drop onto the deck, and snag the arresting wire. Touching down on a flattop always risked a crash, but Kemper and the other eleven VF-7 pilots all landed with no more than the usual drama. In total, sixty-seven Hellcats from two task groups – Radford's TG 38.1 and Bogan's TG 38.2 – had executed fighter sweeps over the Pearl River delta that morning, and every last one had returned.[25]

Fifteen to Twenty Seconds of Flotation

Admiral Halsey's incursion into the South China Sea had been codenamed Operation *Gratitude*, but the airstrikes on Hong Kong and Canton on January 16, 1945, would not receive such memorable designations. Operational orders instead followed standard navy practice and referred to the missions as Strike A, Strike B, Strike C, and Strike D. Strike A and Strike B would go in during the morning hours after the Hellcat pilots flying the blanket missions had established air superiority, while Strike C and Strike D would pile on in the afternoon. Night fighters would close out the show with rearguard sweeps designed to catch any Japanese aircraft attempting to hit the fleet at sunset – prime time for *kamikaze* attacks – or after nightfall. The job of pounding Hong Kong fell to the air groups of TG 38.1 and TG 38.2, which would fly separate but coordinated strikes against Hong Kong. TG 38.1 would fly Strike 1A, 1B, 1C, and 1D, while TG 38.2 would fly Strike 2A, 2B, 2C, and 2D.

In a ready room aboard the *Yorktown*, Jean Balch learned that he had drawn Strike 1C, slated for the early afternoon, and that he would be flying with John Lavender once again. In preparation for the mission, Balch slid the modest wad of Nationalist Chinese currency he had been issued into his wallet, where it would be ready to fund his escape and evasion efforts if he had to bail out over Hong Kong. He had qualified on pistols and shotguns in August 1944, so he knew how to handle the .38-caliber Smith and Wesson revolver that he tucked into his shoulder holster. He also knew how to handle the pair of dice that he kept handy for anyone who wanted to throw a game, which was just about everyone in the airmen's ready room. Throwing some craps provided a welcome distraction for the gunners, who relied on nicotine and camaraderie to keep their nerves in check.

At 9:45 that morning, the first planes assigned to Strike 1A entered the airspace over Canton. Orbiting over the city in the pathfinder Helldiver, Commander Lowe assigned targets to the fifty-eight incoming aircraft from three TG 38.1 carriers – the *Wasp*, *Yorktown*, and *Cowpens*. The *Wasp* sent fourteen F6F-5s and the *Yorktown* dispatched another twenty from VF-3, with most of the thirty-four aircraft carrying a mix of 5-inch rockets and 500-pound bombs. In addition to Commander Lowe and his wingman, the *Yorktown* provided seven SB2C-4s from VB-3, each laden with 250- and 500-pound bombs. The *Yorktown* also dispatched eight Avengers from VT-3, and the *Cowpens* contributed another seven. Since they would be targeting airfields, the TBM pilots from the *Cowpens* and *Yorktown* hauled a mix of AN-M30 100-pound and AN-M64 500-pound GP bombs.

The Hellcat pilots dutifully strafed and rocketed the Canton airfields, where they chewed up a dozen derelict and dummy aircraft, and four of the TBM-1C pilots from the *Cowpens* strung their bombs across the revetments. Commander Lowe and the other eight VB-3 pilots put their bombs into the Whampoa dock area, but the crews reported no subsequent fires or secondary explosions. The *Yorktown* TBM-1C pilots struck the same target with similar results. On the return leg from Canton the Hellcat pilots from the *Wasp* who still had ordnance to drop went after the tankers in Victoria Harbor along with three Avenger pilots from the *Cowpens*. Boring in on the big merchant ships proved more difficult than expected, as the pilots found themselves flying into a storm wall of antiaircraft fire that painted the sky in a hallucinatory rainbow of colored tracers and shell bursts. After scoring what they believed to be multiple hits, the Hellcat and Avenger pilots hightailed it out of Victoria Harbor with a newfound appreciation for its antiaircraft defenses.[1]

Aircraft began dropping out of formation as the strike force retired from Hong Kong. Lt. (j.g.) Hugh V. Sherrill from the *Wasp* had been badly shot up during the attack on the tankers, but he managed to fly his stricken Hellcat more than a hundred miles out to sea before going into the drink. He water-landed fifty miles short of the fleet near the picket destroyer USS *Brush*. Sherrill soon found himself enjoying the hospitality of the sailors who had hauled him aboard like a prize fish. They would eventually return him to the *Wasp* in exchange for the standard finder's fee – twenty-five gallons of ice cream.[2]

Ensign George W. Clark and his crew would have been worth seventy-five gallons of "gedunk" – navy slang for ice cream – but they never made it as far as the tin cans. Clark had monitored his redlining engine temperature as he flew his Avenger on a southeasterly course towards Macau, where he could see a smoke plume rising from at least one burning building. His Turkey had been hit over Canton by what he figured had been a 25mm cannon shell, which had struck some vital organs beneath the cowling. Clark concluded that he would never make it back to the fleet with an engine hemorrhaging oil and vibrating so violently that it threatened to tear itself apart. He used the interphone to warn his turret gunner and radio-gunner that he planned to make a water landing while he could still control the airplane. An armored panel separated Clark from the two men in the rear of the plane, so he knew that he would not see them until the spray settled and they scrambled free of their quick-sinking TBM. According to pilot handbook specs, they could hope for fifteen to twenty seconds of flotation before their plane went under.[3] Jettison hatches, Clark ordered, and then rolled back his canopy, yanked his shoulder harness tight, and detached himself from his parachute pack.

In the gun turret, Donald E. Mize, Aviation Machinist's Mate Third Class (AMM3c), would have worked a pair of red handles that released a circular panel on the side of his bulletproof glass turret. Like a giant Plexiglas Frisbee, the panel would have then whirled out into the slipstream. If he had sufficient time, Charles G. Myers, ARM3c, would likely have abandoned his cramped position aft of the bomb bay and climbed up into the middle compartment behind the pilot's armored bulkhead, where he would have been in a more survivable position that offered quicker and easier egress once the plane hit the water. Since crewmen did not normally ride directly behind the pilot, the middle compartment lacked a seat as well as an interphone jack, which meant Myers would no longer have been able to communicate with Clark up in the front office. Hemmed in by the radio gear, autopilot equipment, oxygen cylinder, and other apparatus that filled much of the compartment, he would have been forced to peer out the side of the cockpit and judge for himself when the plane was about to furrow into the waves. Alternatively, if Myers had not received sufficient warning time to move up into the middle compartment, he would have remained in the belly compartment and yanked a single handle that pulled out the hinge pins of the small side door on the fuselage. With a shove, the hatch would have fallen free of the aircraft as a rush of wind filled the compartment, which would flood quickly once the plane splashed down. Regardless of his location in the plane, Myers would have braced himself for a wheels-up crash into corrugated waters that could claw a belly-landing plane to shreds.

Feathering in over the waves, Clark put the flaps up, eased the stick back to get the tail in the water, felt the plane shudder and stall, and bounced his TBM-1C into the swells three miles northeast of Macau. As the pilots of four Hellcats and an Avenger orbited protectively at low altitude, Clark, Mize, and Myers all emerged from their crashed torpedo plane. One of the downed airmen flipped the quick-release latch on a small compartment door forward of the gun turret, pulled out a case holding an uninflated life raft, and triggered the CO_2 containers. Within seconds, the buoyancy chambers had inflated and all three men had scrambled into the three-man raft. Moments later, their aircraft disappeared beneath the surface, its tail upended like the fins of a diving whale. A small junk soon approached the life raft, and the three Americans climbed aboard at the urging of its occupants. After a final exchange of waves with the pilots circling the junk, Ensign Clark slit the sides of the raft with his survival knife and sank it. Then the trio of aviators ducked below deck to get out of sight as the aircraft overhead departed for the fleet.

Clark and his two gunners found themselves aboard a junk captained by a fisherman named Pang Meng.[4] As a way of introduction, Clark presented his silk blood chit, which featured the Nationalist Chinese flag and Chinese characters that identified Clark as an American flier in need of assistance. Pang seemed impressed by this offering of bona fides, as did the other Chinese aboard the little vessel – two Cantonese passengers, plus a woman and young girl whom Clark took to be Pang's wife and daughter. To show his goodwill, Pang offered rice wine, betel nuts, cigarettes, and candy to the American fliers. Clark regretted that his survival gear did not include a *Pointie Talkie* phrasebook, since the three Americans did not speak Chinese and Pang did not speak

English. Despite the lack of a Chinese–English phrasebook to bridge the linguistic barrier, Pang managed to communicate that he would take the Americans to Macau, and that they should hide themselves beneath the bilge boards until he gave them the all clear. Clark assented to this plan, and Pang concealed them in the bowels of the junk. With a creak of rigging, Pang set sail for Macau.[5]

———

At roughly the same time that the air groups from TG 38.1 pummeled Canton during Strike 1A, the air groups from the TG 38.2 carriers *Hancock*, *Hornet*, and *Lexington* arrived over Hong Kong to execute Strike 2A. In military parlance, the occupied colony qualified as a target-rich environment. The bonanza of high-value military assets included the airbase at Kai Tak, multiple oil storage facilities, rows of waterfront warehouses known locally as "godowns," barracks and communications facilities, and a host of small shipyards. However, the enclave's three major dockyards, which could construct and overhaul all but the largest of vessels, ranked at the top of the target priority list along with the tankers of convoy Hi-87.

Located on Hong Kong Island, the Royal Navy dockyard – now repurposed as an IJN repair facility known as the No. 2 Naval Working Department – sat just to the east of Statue Square in Victoria City, the urban center of Hong Kong.[6] Completed in 1903, the walled complex included a nine-acre tidal basin dredged to a low-tide depth of thirty feet. Protected from the harbor chop by a sturdy seawall, ships could ease into the basin and nuzzle up against the quay for repairs, reprovisioning, and recoaling or refueling. An adjacent 550-foot dry dock could handle smaller warships, such as destroyers and submarines. Under IJN management, the dry-dock work gangs patched holes in the hulls of vessels that had been roughly handled by U.S. submarine captains and General Chennault's bomber pilots.[7]

The Tai Koo dockyard, the second of the three major dockyards, occupied a fifty-acre expanse of reclaimed land at Quarry Point on the northeast coast of Hong Kong Island. When it first commenced operations in the opening decade of the twentieth century, nautical experts rated the dockyard as one of the most advanced shipyards in Asia. Equipped with a massive dry dock that could swallow a 685-foot ocean liner, and an array of slipways, machine shops, and mobile cranes that rolled on train rails, the dockyard shared its harbor-front location with a sister enterprise, a sugar plant known before the war as the Tai Koo Sugar Refining Company. Collectively, the refinery and shipyard blended into one large industrial complex, formerly owned and operated by the colonial firm Butterfield and Swire, but now serving the needs of the Japanese Empire.[8]

Across the harbor in Kowloon, the Hong Kong and Whampoa Dock Company took up much of the Hung Hom Peninsula with its sprawling conglomeration of slipways, dry docks, machine sheds, sawmills, paint shops, godowns, and staff housing. Often referred to as the "Kowloon docks," the complex ranked as one of the largest shipyards in East Asia. A giant 100-ton hammerhead crane capable of plucking a steam locomotive from the deck of a cargo freighter towered so prominently over the dockyard that it had become a local landmark. When viewed from the right angle, the angular girders of the hammerhead crane contrasted with one of the harbor's most well-known natural features: the leonine profile of Lion Rock in the Kowloon hills.[9]

By the start of 1945, acute shortages of electricity, aluminum, brass, bronze, copper, cast iron, kerosene, coal, rivets, and just about everything else needed to construct and maintain metal-hulled ships had forced the dockyards to scale back their operations. Production at Tai Koo Sugar had ended as well due to the cessation of raw sugar imports from the Philippines and the Dutch East Indies. Bombing raids by the 14th Air Force had bludgeoned the dockyards in 1944, further reducing their ability to service Japanese warships and freighters. Construction of new ships had largely shifted to building wooden-hulled vessels that could shuttle supplies up and down the China seaboard.[10] Many of these diminutive coastal vessels rolled down the slipways at the smaller shipyards that fringed the coast of Hong Kong Island and Kowloon, including the Cosmopolitan dockyard at Tai Kok Tsui, not far from the rectangular expanse of the Sham Shui Po POW camp. The camp fronted the harbor near the Cosmopolitan dockyard and the Standard Oil storage facilities at Lai Chi Kok. Further to the west, the tanks of the Texaco Oil Works clustered near the shoreline at Tsuen Wan. On Hong Kong Island, the piers of two prewar firms – the Asiatic Petroleum Company and the Standard-Vacuum Oil Company – still stood along the shoreline of Causeway Bay, though their oil tanks had burned when the Japanese stormed Hong Kong Island in 1941.

Twenty-three Hellcats, ten Helldivers, and twelve Avengers from the TG 38.2 carriers *Hornet* and *Lexington* carried ordnance suited to busting their assigned target, the Tai Koo dockyard. When the pilots first caught sight of the installation, which broke up the curving coastline of Hong Kong Island with its distinctive ruler-straight lines and right angles, they observed several ships nestled in the dry dock and slipways, plus a small freighter pressed up against the quayside. At about 9:40 a.m., the forty-five aircraft started their demolition work.

Coming out of the sun, the Helldivers nosed over at 9,500 feet and commenced a seventy-degree dive. In the back seats, the gunners lay on their backs looking up at the heavens, while in the front seats the pilots pressed forward against their shoulder harnesses. At 2,000 feet, the pilots released their bombs and pulled back hard on the stick with both hands as the G-forces mashed them into their seats and blotted out their vision. The Avenger pilots, meanwhile, came in at a shallower angle for glide-bombing runs that added their payloads to the destructive rain. While each of the six Avenger pilots from the *Hornet* carried four 500-pound bombs apiece – a loading that VT-11 pilots referred to as "four five hundreds" – the *Lexington* pilots each toted a single AN-M66 2,000-pound bomb, the heaviest ordnance available. Spewing rockets and tracer fire, four Hellcats followed the Avengers and Helldivers. The entire dockyard vanished beneath a pall of dust and smoke raised by incendiary machine-gun rounds, 5-inch rockets, and dozens of bombs. With so many aircraft over Tai Koo, some of the Hellcat pilots shifted their attention to maritime targets of opportunity that ranged in size from fifty-foot motor launches to 500-foot tankers. They also strafed a junkyard assortment of airplane carcasses at Kai Tak, lobbed a few 500-pounders into the Cosmopolitan dockyard and, as they headed back out to sea, expended their excess ammunition in a gun run on the Waglan lighthouse.[11]

As the *Lexington* and *Hornet* squadrons pounded the Tai Koo dockyard, the air group from the *Hancock* commenced its attack on the triangle of tankers moored off Kennedy Town. In total, the *Hancock* air group included fifteen F6F-5s, four SB2C-3s, and eight TBM-1s and TBM-3s. The four VB-7 Helldivers carried three different configurations of bombs that had been determined based on launch order back on the *Hancock*. Because the first Helldiver pilot had a shorter takeoff run due to the deck space taken up by other aircraft arrayed behind him, he carried a single 1,000-pound bomb to ensure he could reach minimum takeoff speed during his truncated roll down the flight deck. However, the next two pilots had a bit more space for their takeoff run, which meant they could build up more airspeed and enjoy a higher margin for error when they sped off the bow of the carrier, so they toted a 1,000-pounder plus a single 250-pound bomb. The fourth aircraft had an even longer takeoff run and departed with a 1,000-pounder plus *two* 250-pound bombs. Collectively, the Helldiver pilots sent all eight bombs hurtling towards the three tankers anchored between Kowloon and Hong Kong Island and likely scored hits on the *Kamoi* and either the *Matsushima Maru* or *Tenei Maru*.

The four VT-7 pilots from the *Hancock* who carried the only torpedoes allocated to Strike 2A commenced a rather perilous run against the *Kamoi* and one of the other tankers, which required a low-altitude approach through the western mouth of the harbor in the face of voluminous flak. Flying in parallel formation, the Avenger pilots released their Mark 13s on a trajectory designed to guarantee a hit, since if the torpedoes missed the tankers they would simply speed across the harbor and detonate their 600-pound Torpex warheads among the Kowloon wharves. However, the aircrews could not confirm any torpedo explosions and suspected they had dropped four "mudders" that had plunged nose-first into the bed of the relatively shallow harbor, which also happened to be at low tide. Four bomb-laden Avengers, meanwhile, churned up the wreckage of the Tai Koo dockyard with sixteen 500-pounders.

One division of VF-7 Hellcats peeled off to investigate the air facilities to the south of Hong Kong that their squadron mates had blanketed earlier that morning. Between 9:45 and 10:15 a.m., the Hellcat pilots overflew the airfields at Sanchau and Chungshan as well as the seaplane facilities at Macau, where they observed the burning floatplane hangar. However, they saw no enemy aircraft on the ground or in the air, so they stayed upstairs and took a series of reconnaissance photographs before returning to the *Hancock*.

The other eleven VF-7 fighter pilots bombed and rocketed the tankers and escort vessels as well as the Tai Koo dockyard. Four of them also strafed Kai Tak, where they perforated four aircraft – or aircraft wrecks – tucked into revetments. After making their bomb runs on the ships of convoy Hi-87, another four pilots continued on to Sanchau, where they rocketed one of the hangars. As they departed Hong Kong, two pilots could not resist the enticing profile of Waglan lighthouse. Due to its isolated position on a rocky isle to the southeast of Hong Kong Island, Waglan presented pilots with their last chance to use any unexpended ordnance before making the 170-mile run back to the fleet. In this case, the leftovers included a 500-pound bomb and thousands of .50-caliber rounds. Built to absorb the fury of a South China Sea typhoon, however, the fifty-two-foot cast-iron tower absorbed the pyrotechnic storm unleashed by the two VF-7 pilots and remained battered but upright. The Americans had destroyed many things that morning at Hong Kong, but the Waglan lighthouse was not one of them.[12]

Raymond and Marjorie Jones in
Skegness, England, in 1939.
(Rae Shaw)

SOC-3 Seagull pilots Ensign Walter
G. Winslow, Lt. John D. Lamade, and
Lt. Thomas B. Payne aboard the cruiser
USS *Houston* in the Philippines, October
1941. (NHHC)

TF 38 aircraft carriers USS *Wasp*, *Yorktown*, *Hornet*, *Hancock*, and *Ticonderoga* at anchor
at Ulithi Atoll in December 1944, shortly before the start of Operation *Gratitude*.
(Getty Images)

Lt. (j.g.) Richard L. Hunt. (Missouri Valley Special Collections, Kansas City Public Library, Kansas City, Missouri)

TBM-3 Avenger no. 124, the plane flown by Lt. Hunt during his final mission over Hong Kong on January 16, 1945. (US Navy)

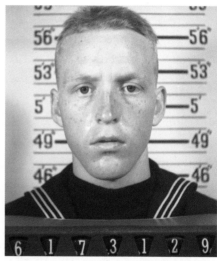

Crewmen beneath the open bomb-bay doors of a TBM Avenger prepare to load a 2,000-pound bomb, the same weapon carried by Lt. Hunt and Lt. Scobell during their ill-fated sorties over Hong Kong. (NHHC)

Jean F. Balch, c. 1942. Balch later flew in an SB2C-3 Helldiver flown by Lt. Ted Lavender and was shot down over Hong Kong. (NPRC)

An SB2C-3 Helldiver of VB-7 of the USS *Hancock* flies over one of the many Japanese ships destroyed along the coast of French Indochina during Operation *Gratitude*. (Getty Images)

TBF Avengers from VT-4 of the USS *Essex* approach the coast of French Indochina on January 12, 1945. (NHHC)

F6F Hellcats prepare to launch from the deck of the USS *Hornet* in 1945. (NHHC)

Above F4U-1D Corsairs and TBM Avengers on the flight deck of the USS *Essex* during Operation *Gratitude*. (NHHC)

Left U.S. Navy PB4Y-1 patrol bomber similar to the aircraft flown by Lt. Paul F. Stevens over Hong Kong and Macau. (NHHC)

Below 1st Lt. John F. Egan (back row, sixth from right) with fellow pilots of the 118th TRS in October 1944, some two months before he was shot down over Hong Kong. (USAAF)

1st Lt. Egan flew a P-51B-7 nicknamed *Lady Jane* on the day he had to bail out over Hong Kong. *Lady Jane* had been transferred to the 118th TRS at the end of 1944, but still wore the markings of the 26th FS when it was shot down.
(Shirley Moyle, courtesy of Chris Davis)

Pilots in their ready room aboard the USS *Hornet* study chalkboard map of targets at Hong Kong in preparation for airstrikes flown on January 16, 1945. (NHHC)

Carrier planes from TF 38 bomb and strafe the Tai Koo dockyards on Hong Kong Island, January 16, 1945. (Getty Images)

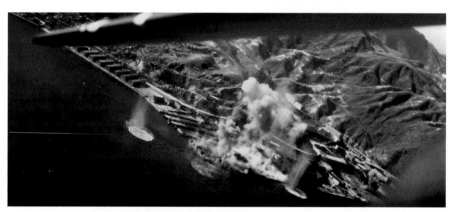

Photo taken by the rear-facing radioman-gunner in a Helldiver shows near misses exploding in the water off the Tai Koo dockyard, with the aircraft's right horizontal stabilizer in the foreground. (Getty Images)

Japanese tankers and escort vessels under attack in Victoria Harbor on January 16, 1945. Kennedy Town on Hong Kong Island can be seen in the background. (Getty Images)

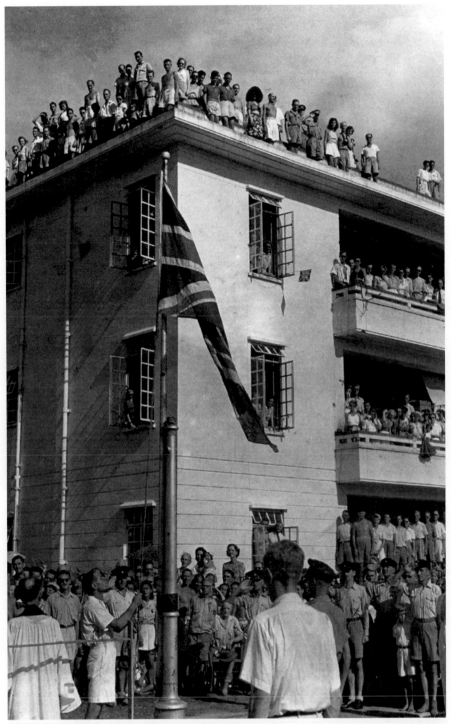

Ray Jones raises the Union Jack during the flag-raising ceremony at the Stanley camp that marked the liberation of Hong Kong in September 1945. (Getty Images)

Above A bomb – likely a 1,000-pounder dropped by a Helldiver – explodes alongside the *Kamoi* in Victoria Harbor. (Getty Images)

Left The Pan American Airways station at Macau, which was strafed by U.S. Navy fighter aircraft on January 16, 1945. (Pan American World Airways Records, Special Collections, University of Miami Libraries)

Below The author at the wreck site of Lt. Hunt's TBM Avenger in 2019, holding a fragment of the aircraft wing or fuselage. (Author)

Intense to Unbelievable

The missions over Hong Kong on January 15, 1945, had cost the 118th Tactical Reconnaissance Squadron two pilots, including Major Houck. Two additional pilots had been shot down over Canton on the same day. These losses left the squadron without its incoming squadron commander, but robust pilot morale and a steady supply of replacement aircraft meant that the unit could still put two dozen P-51s into the air. Disrupting Japanese supply lines remained a primary mission for the squadron, which sought to blunt the momentum of an IJA ground offensive that threatened to overrun its base of operations at Suichuan airfield. On the morning of January 16, four Mustangs targeted bridges just forty-five minutes by air from Suichuan, and later that day four more planes bombed and strafed Japanese-occupied towns in the same area. As these missions unfolded, Lieutenant Colonel McComas, his senior pilots, and his intelligence staff worked on plans for a fighter sweep against JAAF airfields in the Shanghai area, which the squadron expected to attack the next day. McComas had not forgotten about Hong Kong, however, and ordered four pilots to make another run into Victoria Harbor.

By this point, the pilots of the 118th TRS may well have been aware that their navy brethren had roared into the South China Sea like unexpected party guests.* However, if the squadron had in fact received

---

*It remains unclear whether the 118th TRS knew of the presence of U.S. Navy aircraft in the Hong Kong area. There is no mention of the U.S. Navy in the FIRs filed after the 118th TRS flew missions to Hong Kong on January 15–16 and in the squadron history for November 1944 to January 1945. However, in a postwar memoir, 118th TRS pilot Frederick A. Lanphier recollects that the pilots knew that the navy had been flying airstrikes against Hong Kong.

intelligence alerting them to the presence of U.S. Navy carrier planes, this information failed to dissuade Lieutenant Colonel McComas from planning another raid on Hong Kong despite the heightened risk of a friendly fire incident. The 118th also underestimated the scale of the Japanese convoy that had dropped anchor in Hong Kong, as evidenced by the fact the squadron assigned just four planes, albeit heavily armed ones, to take on a dozen warships, five armed tankers, and numerous shore-based antiaircraft guns. The ninety-minute flight from Suichuan would not require drop tanks, which allowed the ground crews to shackle two 500-pound bombs to the wings of each Hong Kong-bound Mustang. Meanwhile, the pilots received their preflight briefing. They could expect CAVU conditions, they were told, and a very hot reception from the Japanese. The game plan called for the pilots to race into the harbor at an altitude of just ten feet to foil shipboard antiaircraft batteries that would not be able to depress their barrels low enough to start registering any hits on the wave-hugging Mustangs. Popping into the harbor like a school of flying fish might reduce the number of gun tubes that could be brought to bear, but both the briefers and the briefed understood that such tactics would reduce rather than eliminate the threat of enemy flak. Consequently, the mission parameters called for the pilots to make a single skip-bombing run and then flee the harbor at full throttle before the enemy gunners could chop them up.

First Lieutenant John F. Egan served as the flight leader for the mission to Hong Kong. An experienced combat pilot, "Jack" Egan had participated in previous airstrikes on the Japanese-occupied city and acquired a working knowledge of its complex topography as well as a wary respect for its defenses. At 9:20 in the morning, he lifted off from the runway in a P-51B nicknamed *Lady Jane*. Second Lieutenant Coleman N. York flew on Egan's wing, and together the two pilots comprised the first subunit of the formation, referred to as an "element." Two additional P-51s piloted by 1st Lt. Robert G. Murray and 2nd Lt. Richard P. Chouinard comprised the second two-plane element.

By coincidence, the four pilots reached Hong Kong during the intermission between Strike A and Strike B, which eliminated the threat of another army-navy friendly fire incident. Though every Japanese gun crew remained on high alert for more carrier aircraft, the arrival of the land-based P-51s seemed to catch them by surprise, perhaps because the Mustangs ripped into the harbor from the north at high speed and an altitude so low that their prop washes generated wakes worthy of a flotilla of PT boats. The Japanese gunners recovered quickly, however, and with unlimited visibility and no U.S. Navy planes to divide their fire, were able to focus their attention on the lone flight of P-51s. Lieutenant Egan and the other three pilots immediately realized that flying on the deck would not protect them from the antiaircraft guns mounted aboard what they would later describe as "flak ships." To suppress the incoming fire, all four pilots started strafing as they lined up on a target, their .50-caliber rounds crisscrossing through the incoming enemy fire to rip into ship and sailor alike.

Lieutenant Chouinard dropped his bombs on or very close to the *Kamoi*, which began to burn as the hull and superstructure flashed with the impact of his tracer rounds. Lieutenant Murray released his 500-pounders next and believed he scored a fatal blow with a pair of waterline hits on an escort vessel, though in fact he had only managed a near miss. The Japanese proved to have better aim and scored multiple hits on Murray's aircraft, but none of them struck the vulnerable liquid coolant system, the Achilles' heel of the inline-engine P-51.

Lieutenant Egan targeted an escort ship south of Stonecutters Island, but his bombs overshot and then he became a target himself as rounds ripped into his P-51B, blasting away half his left aileron and the top of his cockpit canopy. Smoke began streaming out from the root of the right wing, which now sported a sizeable hole. Nobody observed Lieutenant York's bomb run against a freighter, least of all Lieutenant York. He knew better than to climb and bank for a peek at his handiwork, since such a maneuver would have exposed his Mustang's vulnerable underbelly and offered the Japanese the largest possible target profile.

Lieutenants Murray, Chouinard, and York cleared out of Victoria Harbor and assembled at their predetermined rendezvous point, but the three of them lost sight of Lieutenant Egan's aircraft in the process. After some opportunistic strafing of a steam locomotive on the Kowloon–Canton Railway line, which did not enjoy the protection of the flak umbrella over the harbor, the trio of pilots cruised to the north until Suichuan airfield slid into view below. Each pilot would likely have dropped his landing gear and executed a high-speed, two-wheeled touchdown on the long main runway, a maneuver that would have balanced his aircraft between earth and sky, or from a mechanical point of view, between flying and driving. On a runway with sufficient length, and particularly when flying a damaged aircraft that might behave as unpredictably as a maverick stallion, pilots preferred such an approach because it preserved the power and lift necessary to abort if the landing went badly. As the tires of the main gear sped along the lengthy expanse of the gravel runway, the pilot could evaluate whether he liked the feel of the landing and performance of the aircraft. Depending on his instincts, he could either pull back on the stick and go back to flying, or chop the throttle and start driving as the tail dropped and the last of the three wheels kissed the rough surface of the airstrip. Regardless of how they landed, however, Murray, Chouinard, and York all made it back to terra firma. They taxied towards the revetments, shut their planes down, and prepared to report that the squadron had lost yet another comrade – the third in two days – over Hong Kong.

After losing visual contact with his wingman, Lieutenant Egan radioed that he had been hit as he circled around the south side of Hong Kong Island in a counterclockwise direction. He crossed over the straits leading into the eastern mouth of the harbor and barely managed to claw his way over the Kowloon hills before he had to bail out above the rugged rural terrain of the New Territories at just 400 feet. His chute slammed open and he bounced with the snap of a yoyo while his Mustang drifted off into the haze like a child's lost kite. As he twirled beneath the inverted cone of his parachute and watched the ridges, gullies, paddies, inlets, islands, and bays of China rush up to meet him, 1st Lt. John F. Egan prepared to mount a one-man American invasion of Japanese-occupied Hong Kong.[1]

Less than an hour after the departure of Strike 1A and 2A, the carriers of TG 38.1 and TG 38.2 began launching aircraft for Strike 1B and 2B, which would target the Tai Koo dockyard. The TG 38.1 formation consisted of twenty-five Hellcats and fifteen Avengers from the *Yorktown*, *Wasp*, and *Cabot*. A second strike force from the *Hancock*, *Hornet*, and *Lexington* of TG 38.2 added another seventeen

Hellcats, seven Helldivers, and fourteen Avengers. This put a grand total of seventy-eight aircraft over Tai Koo at roughly the same time. To further complicate matters, the seventy-eight pilots came from thirteen individual squadrons spread across six different air groups, which in turn were evenly split between two separate task groups. With no shared strike coordinator to assign targets and sequence attacks, the situation in the congested airspace over the dockyard soon degenerated into a confused free-for-all. Pilots began nosing over into their dives, and as they hurtled earthwards, midair collisions presented nearly as great a risk as the intensifying antiaircraft fire. A rapid series of uncoordinated and overlapping attack runs smothered Tai Koo in a massive display of high-explosive overkill that included AN-M66s carried by four TBMs from the *Hancock*. Three of these Avenger pilots deposited their 2,000-pound blockbusters into the Tai Koo dry dock, where they reported blowing out the massive bulkhead gates. A fourth pilot diverted to the Hong Kong and Whampoa dockyard across the harbor in Kowloon, where he dropped his M66 on a dry-docked ship.

Having reduced the Tai Koo dockyard and the adjacent sugar refinery to a cratered and burning shambles, the two strike forces headed back out to sea to their prearranged rendezvous points. Nobody turned out to be missing as the squadrons regrouped south of Hong Kong, and only one pilot reported flak damage to his aircraft. However, fuel exhaustion forced one TBM pilot from the *Wasp* to ditch within the screen, where the destroyer *Samuel N. Moore* performed an efficient rescue of all three crewmen.[2] During recovery operations, as seventy-seven aircraft touched down on the carrier decks at intervals as short as thirty seconds, an SB2C-3 pilot from the *Hancock* punched his dive-bomber into the crash barrier. Such operational mishaps amounted to the cost of doing business in the carrier aviation trade, and the deck crews went to work on untangling the pranged dive-bomber from the steel cables of the crash barrier with practiced efficiency.[3]

Using a standard five-page form, the ACI officers began filling out aircraft action reports after debriefing the pilots. Each report described a combat mission flown by an individual squadron or, in some cases, an entire air group. Among other things, completing this paperwork required the ACI officers to record the volume of light-, medium-, and heavy-caliber antiaircraft fire over the target by typing an "X" in one of four boxes: none, meager, moderate, or intense. ACI officers talking to jittery pilots found themselves typing "X" in the "intense" box for all three calibers of weaponry. The narrative portion of the aircraft action reports provided the ACI officers with further opportunity to describe the technicolored violence of the antiaircraft fire at Hong Kong. The ACI officer for VT-22 of the *Cowpens* wrote that one Avenger pilot had been so awestruck by the gun show over Victoria Harbor that he felt it exceeded the navy's rating system for measuring enemy antiaircraft defenses. The flak, the pilot said, had not been merely intense; it had, in fact, been "intense to unbelievable."[4]

Three Planes Down

American naval vessels had begun the war with outmoded and ineffective antiaircraft guns and munitions, but the U.S. Navy had perfected the art of shipborne antiaircraft defense by 1945. When Japanese aircraft punched through the CAP of radar-vectored Hellcats, the Fast Carrier Task Force relied upon a battle-tested trio of weapon systems that provided concentric rings of antiaircraft fire at long, medium, and close ranges. An incoming bogey would first have to face long-range fire from the 5-inch dual-purpose guns carried by virtually every ship in the fleet, from destroyers to fleet carriers. These volleys could be lethally accurate because the 5-inch guns fired a mix of Antiaircraft Common (AAC) shells with mechanical-time fuzes set to explode at the same altitude as the targeted warplane and variable-time (VT) shells fitted with radio-proximity fuzes that detonated when they detected the close presence of an aircraft.[1] In essence, the VT-fuzed shells functioned as a simple form of smart munition, and when hundreds of 5-inch guns fired at approaching enemy aircraft, the resulting barrage could knock down planes at a devastating rate.

An incoming aircraft that survived the 5-inchers and came within medium range would then be targeted by hundreds of twin- and quad-mounted Bofors 40mm cannons, which could shield the fleet with an umbrella of automatic shellfire. While VT fuzes small enough to fit inside the two-pound projectiles fired by the Bofors had not yet been developed, this hardly mattered since a quad mount could spit out hundreds of shells per minute.[2] Pedestal-mounted Oerlikon 20mm cannons provided a final layer of close-in defense, bolstered in some cases by smaller numbers of .50-caliber machine guns. Sailors knew that when they heard the chatter of these rapid-firing weapons they had best brace for impact because an enemy pilot had penetrated the flak screen and reached the antiaircraft equivalent of pointblank range.[3] Within seconds something would likely explode – perhaps the aircraft, perhaps a bomb, or in the case of a *kamikaze* attack, perhaps the ship, plane, and bomb would go up together.

A fast-carrier task group could throw out a spectacular volume of antiaircraft fire, much of it from the battleships that functioned as armored antiaircraft platforms armed with, in addition to their main batteries, twenty 5-inch guns and variable combinations of 20mm and 40mm cannons that exceeded well over a hundred gun tubes. Fleet carriers also carried 5-inch guns and numerous 20mm and 40mm cannons. Cruisers and destroyers packed plenty of antiaircraft weaponry as well, and they steamed in formations that allowed for thickly interwoven fields of fire with very few holes. In the eye of this tracer-streaked hurricane of outgoing ordnance cruised the carriers, the bullseye targets for enemy aviators. Aircraft that penetrated the CAP and the flak curtain could cause catastrophic damage to a flattop pregnant with warplanes, munitions, and aviation gasoline, but relatively few enemy pilots had the right combination of luck, skill, and tactical advantage to get through.

While the antiaircraft defenses of the U.S. Navy had evolved since Pearl Harbor, the antiaircraft capabilities of the IJN had remained largely unchanged since the start of the war. The armament of the ships in convoy Hi-87 reflected the inadequacy of IJN air defenses. The 4.7-inch main-battery cannon carried by many of the escort vessels in the convoy remained a capable dual-purpose weapon system, for example, but the IJN had never developed radio-proximity fuzes. Instead, the 4.7-inch guns fired conventional antiaircraft shells with mechanical timing fuzes set to explode at a preset altitude, making them far less effective than the VT shells fired by American warships, which would explode when they detected an aircraft regardless of the altitude. The escorts and tankers also carried the 25mm Type 96 cannon, a ubiquitous automatic weapon mounted aboard virtually every IJN warship and many merchant vessels, often in triple-barrel gun mounts. Based on a prewar French design, the Type 96 suffered from numerous shortcomings, including rates of elevation and traverse that could not keep pace with enemy aircraft, gunsights that performed poorly against speedy single-engine planes, limited capacity magazines that slowed the rate of fire, and severe vibration that skewed the accuracy of the guns.[4] In terms of range, accuracy, and hitting power, the 25mm remained roughly equivalent to the 20mm cannon used by the USN for close-in defense. The ships of convoy Hi-87 had also been equipped with varying numbers of 13.2mm Type 93 heavy machine guns and even some 7.7mm light machine guns, though these weapons packed even less punch than the 25mm cannons. With no radio-proximity fuzed shells for the 4.7-inch guns, inadequate fire-control equipment, and no medium-range automatic antiaircraft cannon like the Bofors 40mm, the IJN simply could not match the layered and highly lethal antiaircraft defenses of the U.S. Navy.

Deficiencies in Japanese air-defense weaponry had undoubtedly saved the lives of American pilots assigned to the strikes on Hong Kong and Canton that morning. Still more aviators had likely been saved by the mediocre performance of the Japanese gun crews, who had failed to maintain the kind of coordinated barrage fire that could chew up incoming aircraft like a gigantic meat grinder. Despite the impressive volume of shells pumped into the air that morning, the flak had been consistently inaccurate and scored very few hits. TF 38 had lost just two planes to antiaircraft fire. An additional five aircraft had returned to the fleet with battle damage, all of it repairable, and one Avenger from the *Wasp* had ditched due to fuel exhaustion. By the grim logic of fast-carrier operations, this represented a sustainable rate of attrition, particularly since destroyers had picked up four of the seven downed airmen. The ACI officers, the air staff, the squadron and group commanders, and especially the pilots hoped they would experience a similarly light loss rate during the strikes on Hong Kong planned for that afternoon.

The Japanese had other ideas, however. Taking advantage of the unexpected midday lull in the action, gun crews aboard the *Shigure*, the *Kanju*, and the other escort vessels hauled shells up from the magazines and carried wounded comrades down to the casualty stations. They helped extinguish fires onboard and grabbed quick meals of rice balls and green tea. Crucially, the gap between American airstrikes provided time for the Japanese to reconfigure their air-defense tactics to compensate for the inadequacies of their antiaircraft weaponry. Rather than fire individual guns at individual aircraft, as had been done that morning with little success, the ships of convoy Hi-87 would instead fire a coordinated box barrage of shells fuzed to explode at predetermined altitudes. When the American squadrons arrived over Victoria Harbor at an altitude sufficient to clear the surrounding ridgelines, which rose sharply from sea level to 1,800 feet on Hong Kong Island and even higher in the New Territories, they would be forced to dive through layers of exploding flak shells. From a cockpit perspective, the descent would be analogous to punching down through a series of cloud layers, except in this case each layer would consist of multicolored flak puffs rather than banks of white water vapor. As the pilots continued to head downstairs they would collide with massed streams of fire from the 25mm cannons, which could be cranked so far back they could shoot virtually straight upwards. By the time the pilots hauled back on the stick at the bottom of their dive, assuming they had survived the maneuver, they would also be under fire from the relatively short-ranged 7.7mm and 13.2mm machine guns manned by shipboard gunners like Suzumoku Goni aboard the *Hashidate Maru*. At this point, the planes would be caught in a murderous crossfire from the escort vessels, the armed merchant ships, and the antiaircraft batteries positioned along the northern coast of Hong Kong Island, the shoreline of Kowloon, and Stonecutters Island. Any American aircraft that came in on the deck would face a similar reception, as had been the case with the Mustangs from the 118th TRS. Like mosquitoes flying into a spider's web, the American carrier planes would buzz straight into a net woven from thick strands of flak fire.

At three in the afternoon, as the warning klaxons wailed aboard the ships of convoy Hi-87, the air groups from Rear Admiral Radford's TG 38.1 and Rear Admiral Bogan's TG 38.2 arrived to execute strikes 1C and 2C. Sixty-one aircraft from the TG 38.1 carriers *Wasp*, *Yorktown*, and *Cowpens* joined eighty-one aircraft from the TG 38.2 carriers *Lexington*, *Hancock*, and *Hornet*. Both task groups supplied their own target coordinators, with Commander Lamade of CVG-7 from the *Hancock* serving as the coordinator for TG 38.2. However, the two coordinators operated independently, which meant the air groups from

TG 38.1 and TG 38.2 had no mechanism for coordinating strikes 1C and 2C. As a result, some 140 warplanes from both air groups executed disjointed attacks from all directions on the same set of targets – the tankers and escort vessels, the Royal Navy dockyard, and various shore installations along the coast of east and west Kowloon. The shift in Japanese air-defense tactics came as a nasty surprise, and the well-coordinated antiaircraft fire knocked down multiple planes from both air groups. Strike 1C losses for Radford's TG 38.1 exhibited an odd symmetry, with each carrier losing one plane. Moreover, these losses included all three aircraft types involved, with one Avenger, one Hellcat, and one Helldiver failing to return to the task group.

The *Cowpens* sustained the first loss when an Avenger piloted by Lt. Billy B. Laughren of VT-22 went into the harbor with all hands. Another TBM from the same squadron got shot to pieces, with a hole a foot in diameter punched through the wing. A machine-gun round whizzed between the radio-gunner's legs, another cracked through the canopy behind the turret-gunner's head, and two more passed through the front of the cockpit. In total, the plane had been Swiss-cheesed with fifty-four hits of various sizes and severity. In what qualified as an aviation miracle, none of the three airmen aboard sustained any wounds, and the pilot managed to keep his mangled Avenger airborne on a bearing back to the *Cowpens*, where he landed the wreck without mishap.[5]

The *Wasp* sustained the second loss when Lt. (j.g.) Albert Basmajian of VF-81 nosed over into a rocket run from 14,000 feet and hurtled into the flak thrown up by the escort vessels ringing the tankers. Shrapnel eviscerated the undersides of his Hellcat and punctured the belly tank as he dropped through the barrage. Basmajian held his dive and released his rockets at 3,000 feet before pulling back on the stick and streaking full-throttle out of the western mouth of the harbor with smoke in the cockpit and his drop tank trailing a snake of burning aviation fuel. His engine quit as he flew south past the dumbbell-shaped island of Cheung Chau, forcing him to execute a dicey dead-stick water landing near Lingting Island.[*] In preparation, he rolled back the cockpit canopy and locked it in place. Presumably, he also unfastened his parachute

---

[*]Lingting Island is known today as Wailingding Island.

from his harness and tightened his shoulder straps and waist belt. The pilots flying on Basmajian's wing advised him to release his burning drop tank, but he was apparently unable to do so – or in the tunnel-vision focus of his imminent crash simply forgot to yank the requisite handle. He kept the landing gear up, but likely lowered the arrestor hook as per standard procedure to help him judge when the plane was just a few feet above the water. When he felt the hook drag through the waves, or simply judged that he had run out of altitude, he stalled the plane and dropped the Grumman into the sea. At this point, the drop tank slung beneath the aircraft apparently caught a wave and ended any hopes of a smooth belly-slide into the sea. The impact of the landing shattered the Hellcat into multiple pieces, though Basmajian sustained no injuries and wasted no time in getting out of his cockpit. In a matter of seconds, he unbuckled, vaulted out onto the wing, reached back into the cockpit to grab his life-raft pack, and then kicked off into the saltwater as the plane began to melt into the sea. Fearful of the suction from the sinking fuselage, Basmajian swam clear before triggering the CO_2 bottle for the raft, which inflated with a snap of unfolding plastic. He pulled himself into the bathtub-sized raft under the watchful eyes of his comrades in VF-81, who orbited overhead while monitoring their fuel gauges.[6]

The *Yorktown* lost the third plane, an SB2C-4 with the number 104 painted on its fuselage and twenty-four-year-old Lt. (j.g.) John H. Lavender in the cockpit. In the rear-facing backseat, twenty-one-year-old Jean F. Balch, ARM3c, had his canopy open and his twin .30-caliber machine guns ready to fire. Eleven other Helldivers from VB-3 bucked in the turbulent air around them, each laden with a bombload of 1,250 pounds. As the shoreline of Kowloon slid past far below and the ship-spangled harbor came into view, Lavender tipped number 104 into a dive from 13,000 feet. Balch plummeted towards the harbor on his back, his guns pointing nearly straight up, as Lavender kept his Mark 8 bombsight aligned on one of the Japanese tankers. He released their payload at the bottom of the dive, a maneuver so aerodynamically violent that the pullout could buckle wing panels, and then they flew into a blizzard of flak. With a flash, the bomb bay caught fire. Milliseconds later the engine quit, oil trailed out from the cowling in a long black ribbon, and the roar of the R-2600 gave way to a terrifying silence and the whistle of the slipstream. Lavender failed to respond over the intercom and Balch assumed he had been killed or incapacitated. When Balch glanced at his altimeter, it read 600 feet, and he had been told to assume that if it read 600, he was actually at 350 feet.

Acting on instinct and adrenaline, Balch pushed himself up and out of the open back cockpit. Moments later number 104 slammed into a mountainside on Hong Kong Island with Lavender still strapped in the cockpit. Whipped about by the snap of the opening chute, Balch saw buildings whirling below him and caught kaleidoscopic views of the harbor sparking with pyrotechnic violence. Rifle bullets started tearing through his parachute canopy as he drifted towards the shoreline of Kennedy Town. He hit the side of a bombed-out building, the air puffed out of his deflating parachute, and he dropped into a pile of coiled-up chicken wire for a relatively soft landing.

After unsnapping his harness, Balch attempted to pull down his parachute, which had snagged on the side of the building like a giant signal flag announcing the arrival of an American airman in Hong Kong. A Chinese civilian soon appeared from a doorway that led into an intact portion of the building, and since the two did not share a common language, Balch showed him his blood chit. The Nationalist flag on the chit clearly pleased the Chinese man, who helped Balch conceal his parachute in a basket attached to a shoulder-pole. As they completed wadding up the parachute canopy, two Sikh men peered into the building through a blown-out window. Balch had no idea what the three men discussed, or even what languages they used, but he could tell that the conversation was not between friends.

Dismissing the Sikhs, the Chinese man guided Balch back through the doorway and into the undamaged wing of the building. Balch found himself in a small room equipped with nothing more than a tiny table and a chair. A fishing pole stood in one corner. An elderly woman and a pregnant young woman with a toddler gave Balch a set of clean but threadbare civilian clothes and a straw hat that failed to hide his blond hair. Balch stripped off his flight suit and empty holster – his .38-caliber revolver had been jerked loose during the bail out and gone spinning into the harbor – and stuffed them into the other basket on the shoulder-pole. Then he put on his ill-fitting disguise over his navy-issue dungarees.

Pushing open a green-painted door, the Chinese man led Balch down a narrow alleyway and into the shell of another wrecked building, where he gestured that Balch should hide behind a sheet of corrugated metal propped up against an inside wall like a lean-to. Balch wanted to get further away from his landing point, but he lacked a *Pointie Talkie* and had no way of communicating this desire to his benefactor. In fact, Balch only knew two words in Chinese – "Chiang Kai-shek" and "Chungking" – but he could not even pronounce these words in a way that his rescuer could understand. Seeing no alternative, Balch settled in behind the lean-to with his feet in the dead ashes of someone's campfire. Not much later he heard a chorus of excited yelling. Through a nail hole in the corrugated metal, Balch saw eight Japanese soldiers with their long Arisaka rifles trained on his hiding spot.[7]

19

Triple X

Strike 1C had cost the *Wasp*, *Yorktown*, and *Cowpens* a trio of aircraft, but Strike 2C exacted an even greater toll from the air groups embarked aboard the *Lexington*, *Hancock*, and *Hornet*. The *Hornet* alone lost two aircraft and four men from its twenty-two plane strike package, which included eleven F6F-5s, a half-dozen SB2C-3s, and five Avengers. In accordance with orders issued by Commander Lamade, the task-group target coordinator, the Helldivers and one bomb-laden Avenger went for the Hong Kong and Whampoa dockyard, where they missed the ships tied to the piers but sent bombs hurtling into the slipways, godowns, and machine shops. As the other four Avengers swept over Stonecutters Island to execute a torpedo run on the tankers, Lt. (j.g.) Edwin W. McGowan's TBM took multiple hits, wobbled out of formation, and went into the water. A thousand yards out from the target ships, the remaining three Avengers launched two fish at one tanker and a third at an escort vessel. One torpedo may have hit the stern of a tanker, though the crew that dropped the weapon could not confirm this, and the other two torpedoes likely drilled into the mud of the harbor floor.

As the Helldiver and Avenger crews made their attack runs, the F6 pilots from the *Hornet* buzzed around the harbor, rocketing and strafing the tankers and escort vessels, the oil tanks at Lai Chi Kok, the Hong Kong and Whampoa dockyard, the Green Island Cement plant, and Kai Tak airfield. Spotting the telltale wake of a vessel to the east of the harbor in Junk Bay, two Hellcat pilots swooped down on the *Nanshu Maru* and splintered its wooden hull with .50-caliber rounds.

Tracers and armor-piercing incendiaries set beam and plank ablaze as they punched holes in the little ship, which soon began to founder.

When the *Hornet* pilots had expended their rockets, bombs, and torpedoes as well as 3,000 rounds of .50-caliber ammunition, they left the target zone and formed back up at the prearranged rendezvous point over open water south of Hong Kong. A headcount determined that the TBM flown by Lieutenant McGowan had failed to make the rendezvous. A second Avenger pilot could barely keep his plane in the air as its engine trailed smoke and the oil pressure dropped, suggesting damage to the cylinder heads. Fellow pilots flying alongside could see that enemy fire had shredded the rudder and port elevator and that oil had whipped back from beneath the engine cowling to smear the fuselage.

Ensign Matthew J. Crehan and Lt. Cdr. Robert E. Clements, the executive officer of VF-11, banked back over Kowloon to search for Lieutenant McGowan's plane. When they failed to find the wayward Avenger in the air over Victoria Harbor or to spot any downed crewmen in the water, the two pilots opted to strafe Kai Tak, where antiaircraft fire raked the belly of Crehan's F6F-5 and ignited the drop tank. Smoke began to fill the cockpit as Crehan cleared the harbor, released his belly tank, and made a beeline for the fleet with Clements on his wing. His plane continued to trail a dirty smear of smoke, which told him the undersides of his aircraft had caught fire. Making it back to the *Hornet* seemed unlikely, but every air mile he could fly towards home plate would close the distance to the nearest lifeguard submarine or picket destroyer. With luck, he would be able to ditch, climb into his life raft, and be recovered by sub or tin can. Crehan had ditched during a failed attempt to land aboard the *Hornet* in November 1944, so he knew what it was like to put a plane in the water. The procedure wasn't all that complicated in an undamaged aircraft with enough gas to keep the propeller spinning. As one of his fellow *Hornet* pilots would later say with a wry chuckle, "ditching was just like landing, except you kept your wheels up."[1] However, as Crehan would have been well aware, water landings required a degree of flight control that would be difficult to muster in a gut-shot and burning Hellcat.

In any case, Crehan only managed to fly ten miles out to sea before the engine roughened up and snakes of fire began to writhe around the cockpit. He was still too high to ditch when the flames killed the engine and forced him to bail out at an altitude of 7,000 feet. Crehan slid back the canopy, yanked out his radio lead, and unfastened himself from his armored seat. Then he rolled the plane over on its back, tumbled out into the open air, and pulled his ripcord. Lieutenant Commander Clements watched as fire engulfed the rear of Crehen's aircraft and the tail section disintegrated. Meanwhile, Crehan's chute snapped open, and seconds later the ensign splashed down safely near Tamkan, a rocky islet in the Lema Archipelago south of Hong Kong.

After shucking his parachute harness and popping the CO_2 cartridges of his Mae West, Crehan waved to Lieutenant Commander Clements as he bobbed in the swells. Circling overhead, Clements could see that Crehan had lost his life raft, so he radioed one of the TBM pilots to drop an extra raft. However, the bundle failed to inflate when it hit the water, most likely because the impact had knocked the CO_2 bottle loose. Clements then tossed out his own raft, which similarly malfunctioned. He continued to orbit his downed pilot, radioing for a rescue submarine and firing warning shots at sampans in the area. When his fuel gauges told him he had thirty gallons left, Clements waggled his wings and headed towards the carriers waiting somewhere over the horizon. Crehan watched the Hellcat melt into the haze. He understood that he had just arrived in that liminal gray zone where no pilot ever wanted to be, an in-between space summed up by a single phrase in U.S. Navy typescript: "Missing in action."[2]

Strike 2C punished the *Lexington* air group as well, which lost two planes and five men over Victoria Harbor. As ordered by Commander Lamade, sixteen Hellcat pilots from VF-20 strafed, bombed, and rocketed the tankers and escort vessels, while five Helldivers from VB-20 targeted a vessel at the Royal Navy dockyard. A canopy of flak bursts hung over the target as the Helldiver pilots commenced their dive from 14,000 feet. On the way down the lead plane piloted by Lt. (j.g.) John E. Tsarnas lost a wing and went straight into the harbor, while shrapnel tore into two more of the dive-bombers. Of the five VT-20 pilots who attempted low-level torpedo runs, two thought they scored hits on a freighter, another thought his torpedo might have struck an escort vessel but failed to detonate, the fourth pilot discovered that his recalcitrant fish had failed to release, and the fifth pilot, Lt. (j.g.) Donald F. Seiz, went down with his TBM-1C, which likely crashed and burned among the godowns of the Kowloon wharves not far from the pier where the still-unscathed *Sarawak Maru* had docked.

During the run back to the fleet, the VF-20 pilots searched unsuccessfully for an American aviator reported to be down in the water south of Hong Kong Island – this would have been either Lieutenant Basmajian or Ensign Crehan – and then landed without incident on the *Lexington*. Though reduced in number by the loss of two aircraft, the Helldivers and Avengers also made it back to home base. However, one of the flak-punctured SB2C-3s had been so badly holed that the plane handlers stripped it of useful parts and equipment, pushed it to the edge of the flight deck, and jettisoned it. Airfields had plenty of space for hangar queens, but flattops most definitely did not, and aircraft damaged beyond repair invariably went over the side.[3]

———

Commander Lamade's air group – CVG-7 of the *Hancock* – fared even worse during Strike 2C than the air groups from the *Hornet* and *Lexington*. Lamade brought twenty-nine aircraft to Hong Kong, including his own two-plane target coordinator flight, eight Hellcats from VF-7, eight Hellcats from VBF-7, four Helldivers from VB-7, and seven Avengers from VT-7. Like a flock of predatory blue birds, they punched out of the storm front and emerged into hazy skies to the southeast of Hong Kong. From an altitude of 13,000 feet, the air group crossed over the eastern coast of Hong Kong Island and started descending towards the smoky bowl of the harbor at about 3:00 p.m.

Lieutenant Hunt and Lieutenant Scobell flew in a four-plane division of VT-7 torpedo planes, with Scobell flying just behind and below Hunt. Hellcat pilots could whip out all kinds of barnstorming acrobatics, and Helldiver pilots routinely tipped over into near-vertical dives. Avenger pilots like Hunt and Scobell flew an aircraft with a much more modest performance envelope, but what the TBM lacked in maneuverability it made up for in stability. Hunt and Scobell could tuck themselves right up against each other if they wanted, cozy as two locomotives running side by side down parallel tracks. Any pair of competent pilots could fly for hours with just a few feet between the wingtips of their TBMs, which had the power and steady aerodynamics needed for precision flying, and Hunt and Scobell had long since exceeded the merely competent. Even in a smooth-riding machine like the TBM, however, flying close formation demanded a pilot's continual attention and reduced his ability to perform other vital functions, like watching for enemy aircraft. For this reason, Hunt and Scobell would likely have widened the distance between their aircraft as they approached Hong Kong, and their four-plane formation would have spread out in preparation for combat.[4]

Two enlisted crewmen rode in the rear of Lieutenant Hunt's plane, which had been loaded with a single 2,000-pound bomb. In the tunnel compartment in the fuselage aft of the bomb bay, Gene Barrow from Harrison, Ohio, played multiple roles that called for him to work the radio, assist with the preparation and release of the payload, and fire the rear-facing .30-caliber machine gun. He would also observe the results of their bomb run, since his gunport window would provide him with an ideal vantage point for watching their blockbuster impact whatever luckless ship Lieutenant Hunt chose to demolish. Hunt's usual gunner and Barrow's good friend Alfred Dejesus had been injured by flak shrapnel during a torpedo run against a Japanese convoy off Takao on January 3, 1945. Louis W. Gahran, AOM2c, had joined the crew as the replacement gunner. He had apparently been living in Watertown, Massachusetts, when he enlisted in Boston in November 1942, though his roots stretched down the East Coast to New Jersey. Just twenty years old, Gahran worked a .50-caliber machine gun in a bulbous turret so cramped he went without his parachute pack, which he stowed down in the tunnel with Barrow.

Lieutenant Scobell also carried two crewmen aboard his Avenger, which hauled the same one-ton bomb as Lieutenant Hunt's aircraft. At age twenty-seven, Scobell would have seemed impressively old to his crew. His gunner, John F. Gelnaw, AOM1c, had just celebrated his twenty-first birthday in December 1944, which made him a year older than the radioman-gunner, William P. Walton, ARM3c. Gelnaw hailed from Cuyahoga County in Ohio, while Walton came from Talco, a Texas town known for its oil boom and subsequent bust. Both men had enlisted in late 1942, when the outcome of the conflict seemed uncertain, and the battle with Japan seemed like an existential one for the United States. Two years later, strapped into a Grumman for yet another mission, they would have viewed an Allied victory as inevitable, though the timing would still have remained unclear – sometime in 1946, perhaps.

Despite their differences in rank and their diverse geographical roots, all six men aboard the two aircraft piloted by Lieutenant Hunt and Lieutenant Scobell had a great deal in common. All six were Americans at war, and like the vast majority of men in Admiral Halsey's fleet, all six were naval reservists. All six were white, and all six came from Christian religious backgrounds. All six were in their twenties, all six were combat veterans despite their young age, and all but one would die at Hong Kong.

In the Stanley Military Internment camp, Ray Jones had been watching aircraft pass overhead since just after sunrise. The air raids had lasted all morning, and after a long midday break, had resumed in the afternoon. The internees noticed that the aircraft had been flying in from the ocean that day and withdrawing to the southeast, a bearing that took them out over the South China Sea. They had never seen American planes do this before, which caused them to wonder if the single-engine aircraft came from the American carrier fleet. Some internees even began talking optimistically about an Allied amphibious landing on Hong Kong Island.[5]

At about 3:00 p.m. Jones heard the drone of aircraft engines and soon caught sight of a formation of planes crossing over the mountainous spine of Hong Kong Island. As he watched with many of the other internees in the camp, the formation began descending towards the harbor hidden on the other side of the ridgeline as splotches of colored smoke dotted the sky, spraying out invisible bee-swarms of shrapnel. Jones saw two of the aircraft fold into each other for a moment over Mount Parker, merge in a blossom of fire, and then break apart in a spray of debris. Flaring like meteors, the aircraft hurtled towards the saw-toothed mountains as the rest of the formation crossed over the island and descended towards the harbor. Perhaps the two aircraft had been tossed into each other by the shell bursts, the internees guessed, or perhaps they had collided while trying to avoid the heavy barrage. Perhaps a one-in-a-million shot had exploded an antiaircraft shell between the two planes and killed two birds with one stone.

Two airmen attempted to bail out, but one got his parachute wrapped around the tail assembly and went down with his plane. Jones caught sight of a second parachute popping open, however. An aviator swung beneath like a pendulum, each swing tracing a final arc of freedom before he faced the bayonets waiting below.

In what must have been an instinctual reflex action, Lieutenant Hunt had hurled himself out of his cockpit through sheets of orange flame. A second later, he pulled his ripcord, which opened his parachute pack. He trailed a ribbon of nylon panels and cord, and then his shroud scooped open like an air brake to arrest his fall. Hunt spiraled down towards a valley fenced by boulder-studded ridgelines, his flesh and clothes smoking. A blurry mix of sluiceways, dams, bridges, reservoirs, and streams whirled beneath his feet. Though he saw no other parachutes, he might perhaps have seen the burning mountainsides that marked the endpoint of number 124 and the TBM flown by his friend Lieutenant Scobell.

Scobell would almost certainly have been the aviator who snagged his parachute on the tail of his aircraft, since as the men assigned to the torpedo squadrons of TF 38 had learned to their sorrow, the pilot was often the only person to survive when circumstances forced a crew to bail out of a stricken TBM. The window of time for escaping from a burning Avenger could be measured in seconds, and while this might be sufficient for the pilot, who could pull the emergency canopy release and toss himself over the side, the design of the aircraft precluded easy exit for the two men stationed in the rear of the plane.

In a TBM, an armored partition behind the pilot's seat separated the pilot from the turret gunner and radio-gunner in the rear of the aircraft. The gunner stowed his parachute pack down in the belly compartment, because the cramped confines of his gun turret precluded wearing a bulky pack during flight. Once a TBM started to go down the gunner had to drop himself into the belly compartment, a maneuver that required he first swing open an armored shield that protected him from enemy gunfire. Once in the belly compartment, the gunner had to retrieve his pack from where it hung above the hatch door and harness up. Meanwhile, the radio-gunner would have to jettison the side hatch before the two men could plunge out into the blue, one man at a time. Such an operation took precious seconds under the best of circumstances, and the four men in the rear of the TBMs flown by Lieutenant Hunt and Lieutenant Scobell faced what certainly amounted to the worst of circumstances – fire and smoke, the centrifugal force and disorientation of a spinning aircraft, and very little time. They might have been injured or burned as well. Gene Barrow and Louis Gahran in Hunt's plane and John Gelnaw and William Walton in Scobell's TBM never made it out the side hatch before their planes slammed into the rocky slopes above the reservoirs of Tai Tam Valley.[6]

General Chennault's 14th Air Force had been bombing Hong Kong for years and had lost numerous aircraft in the process, but the internees in the Stanley camp had never witnessed the destruction of American airplanes before. This made the spectacle of the flaming Avengers all the more shocking.[7] As the internees watched in horror, two black smoke plumes boiled up from the hills while Lieutenant Hunt descended beneath his parachute canopy.[8] Four of the surviving VT-7 Avengers continued over the spine of Hong Kong Island and dropped out of sight, leaving the internees to guess their fate, while a fifth pilot veered out of formation to avoid the collision between the planes flown by Hunt and Scobell. He crossed over Deep Water Bay on the south side of Hong Kong Island, and since he had no hope of rejoining his squadron before its run on the tankers on the opposite side of the island, opted to target the Aberdeen dockyard instead. This one-plane raid involved just a single bomb, but as it happened to be a 2,000-pounder, it produced a cataclysmic eruption of fire, smoke, and debris. A few seconds later, Ray Jones and everyone else in the Stanley camp heard the echoing rumble of the blast.

After crossing over Hong Kong Island, the four remaining Avenger pilots from the original seven-plane formation descended towards the harbor in forty- to fifty-degree dives. Two of them lobbed 2,000-pound bombs at the *Kamoi* and either the *Matsushima Maru* or the *Tenei Maru*, but could claim nothing more than damaging near misses. A third TBM dropped on a freighter tied up to the quay at the Royal Navy dockyard, and a fourth pilot opted to level a sizeable chunk of the Kowloon waterfront with his one-ton bomb. At the same time, the four VB-7 pilots from the *Hancock* nosed their Helldivers over at 10,000 feet and hurtled towards the tankers in the face of heavy antiaircraft fire.

All of the pilots dropped their payloads on either the *Matsushima Maru* or the *Tenei Maru*. At least one bomb struck amidships, the pilots claimed, and rekindled the smoldering fires aboard the already blackened ship. As the Avengers and Helldivers went in, the Hellcat pilots made glide-bombing runs with their 500-pounders and then sledded down to the deck to strafe and rocket the escort vessels. Along the way, two pilots from VBF-7 disappeared – shot down over Tai Tam Valley or the harbor – and three more took multiple flak hits.[9]

Ordnance expended, the CVG-7 pilots cleared out of the harbor and formed up at their predetermined rendezvous point, where Commander Lamade detached a division of four VF-7 Hellcats under the command of Lt. E.W. Niebling to sweep enemy airfields south of Hong Kong. Lamade had originally planned to assign eight Hellcats to this sweep, but he chose to divert four of these fighters to cover a reported ditching. Lamade no doubt hoped the aviator down in the water would prove to be one of his missing Hellcat pilots. In all probability, however, the report referred to Ensign Crehan from the *Hornet* or Lieutenant Basmajian from the *Wasp*, who had both come down in the swells south of Hong Kong.

During the preflight briefing for Strike 2C, Lieutenant Golson, Lieutenant Gose, and Lieutenant Helmers, the ACI officers for VF-7 and CVG-7, had instructed Lieutenant Niebling to continue blanketing air installations at Sanchau, Chungshan, and Macau, which had been covered by the flights led by Lieutenant Kemper and Lieutenant Newcomer earlier that morning. During their debriefing the two lieutenants had reported that they had *not* observed any enemy aircraft at Macau, but that they had attacked the seaplane base as ordered and set it ablaze. The ACI officers had apparently failed to modify their prestrike briefings for Lieutenant Niebling and the other VF-7 pilots flying Strike 2C, even though the actions by Kemper and Newcomer violated the original directive from Rear Admiral Bogan to strike Macau *only* if pilots observed aircraft out in the open. Consequently, the seaplane base in neutral Macau – Target 8 – remained on the roster of air facilities to be blanketed by VF-7 during Strike 2C.

Between 3:00 and 3:30 p.m., the four F6F-5s led by Lieutenant Niebling arrived over Sanchau, where they made one strafing pass on the empty airfield. The hangars had already been mauled during the strikes by VF-7 earlier that day, so the pilots settled for torching two small buildings with .50-caliber incendiary rounds. All four pilots then banked back to the north towards Macau, where they noted the same absence of enemy aircraft. Lieutenant Niebling placed the burnt-out seaplane hangar in his Mark 8 gunsight, pressed his gun button, and felt the jackhammer recoil of his six .50-calibers. Pedro José Lobo and his son Rogerio, who had been surveying the damage to the hangar and its contents, heard the roar of aircraft engines and sprinted for cover as Niebling and his wingman opened fire. Heavy machine-gun rounds perforated the shell of the hangar and thoroughly sieved Lobo's government-owned Dodge sedan, though he and his son survived the raid without injury. Several local police officers drew their pistols and popped off a few shots, which Rogerio thought rather ridiculous.[10]

The other two Hellcat pilots in Lieutenant Niebling's division opted to make a strafing run on the Pan American station and one of its outbuildings, a small wooden shack at the water's edge that the navy pilots believed to be a refueling facility. Slugs ripped pieces out of both structures, and Consul Reeves would later claim that 211 bullets had struck the buildings.[11] The two Hellcat pilots also strafed what they suspected to be aircraft revetments. Though protective structures of this type had never been constructed in Macau, the fortress walls of the Sao Francisco Barracks featured circular bastions, and possibly the pilots mistook these open-topped constructions for aircraft revetments. Alternatively, the pilots may have been shooting at a different target that resembled a revetment and inflicted collateral damage on the barracks in the process. Regardless, streams of .50-caliber machine-gun fire raked the barracks, which housed soldiers from the Portuguese garrison.[12] After making a single strafing run against targets in Macau, Lieutenant Niebling and the other three pilots hit Sanchau one more time before heading back to the fleet.[13]

After touching down on the *Hancock*, Lieutenant Niebling pulled himself out of his cockpit, his hind-end sore from sitting on his life-raft pack with its pokey CO_2 inflator bottle, but otherwise no worse for wear. He soon learned that many members of his air group had not been so fortunate. In addition to the two Avengers that had collided over Hong Kong Island and the two Hellcats that had disappeared over Tai Tam Valley or Victoria Harbor, a third F6 had succumbed to battle damage during the run back to the fleet and ditched seventy miles offshore. All three VBF-7 pilots remained missing in action, as did the six men aboard the crashed VT-7 Avengers. No other air group from TF 38 had sustained such heavy losses over Hong Kong. The midair collision of the Avengers flown by Lieutenant Hunt and Lieutenant Scobell seemed particularly bad luck since VF-7 had lost its commanding officer, Lieutenant Commander Leonard J. Check, in a midair collision with his wingman over Formosa on January 4.[14]

After debriefing the pilots who had flown Strike 2C, Lieutenant Golson and the other ACI officers aboard the *Hancock* compiled the aircraft action report for CVG-7. As Golson or his yeoman typed up the "Enemy Anti-Aircraft Encountered" section of the form, he pounded the "X" key three times in all caps for emphasis – "XXX" – in the boxes that indicated the pilots had encountered "intense" antiaircraft fire of light, medium, and heavy caliber. Flak of triple-X intensity remained an apt description. In just a few minutes of action over Hong Kong the *Hancock* had lost five aircraft and nine airmen, which amounted to a grievous loss rate of one out of every six aircraft launched for Strike 2C.[15]

The Man in the Harris Tweed

At about the same time that Jean Balch realized he had been cornered by what appeared to be an impromptu firing squad, sixty-two pilots from the *Lexington*, *Hancock*, and *Hornet* prepared to execute Strike 2D as the mountainous bulk of Hong Kong Island loomed out of the haze in front of their bulletproof windshields. Strikes A, B, and C had involved air groups from both TG 38.1 and TG 38.2, but Strike 2D would be carried out by the air groups from TG 38.2 alone. All three of the air groups – CVG-7 of the *Hancock*, CVG-11 of the *Hornet*, and CVG-20 of the *Lexington* – had struggled to assemble full deck loads for the final strike of the day. In part, the shortage of available pilots and planes for Strike 2D stemmed from the fact that the aviators assigned to Strike 2C – including Commander Lamade – were still in the air. Other planes had been slated for the CAP or taken down to the hangar deck for repairs. Despite the depleted state of the squadrons, however, the three air groups managed to assemble a fighter-heavy strike package that included nine VF-7 Hellcats from the *Hancock*. In total, the fighters numbered thirty-two F6F-5s, three F6F-5Ps, and two older F6F-3s, which had become rather rare birds in the air groups of TG 38.2. Aside from the trio of photo ships, the Hellcats had been loaded as fighter-bombers with 500-pound bombs and 5-inch rockets. In addition, each F6 carried the standard 2,400-round ammo load for its six .50-caliber wing guns.

The three air groups also pulled together a dozen bomb-laden TBM-1Cs for Strike 2D, though they included just three machines from hard-hit VT-7, the torpedo squadron from the *Hancock* that had lost the Avengers piloted by Lieutenant Hunt and Lieutenant Scobell during Strike 2C. VB-7 had also been drained by the pace of combat operations and like VT-7 could muster only three aircraft for Strike 2D. Collectively, the trio of air groups readied thirteen SB2C-3s, most loaded with typical combinations of 1,000-pound and 250-pound bombs totaling 1,500 to 2,000 pounds. However, two Helldivers from the *Hornet* launched with 2,500 pounds worth of ordnance on board – a pair of 1,000-pounders matched with a pair of 250-pounders. This ambitious loading pushed the envelope for the SB2C-3, a plane that could be challenging to fly under the best of conditions, and ranked as the heaviest bombload hauled to Hong Kong by an aircraft from TF 38.

The strike force approached the target zone from the south and, depending on the squadron, overflew either the northeast or southeast corner of Hong Kong Island before banking for a sequence of east-to-west attack runs down the length of the harbor at 4:45 p.m. Most SB2C and TBM pilots zeroed in on the tankers and escort vessels, but determining who had hit what amounted to guesswork due to the sheer number of detonations – over a hundred bomb explosions and at least as many rocket blasts – as well as the sustained antiaircraft fire, not to mention the fact that immediately after release the Helldiver and Avenger pilots streaked out of the western entrance of the harbor to escape the flak. After strafing and rocketing the Lai Chi Kok oil tanks and Cosmopolitan dockyard without any apparent results, the Hellcat pilots targeted the Texaco oil facility at Tsuen Wan, where they scored a bullseye. Several large oil tanks ignited like giant Sterno cans, and the resultant blaze spawned a roiling black plume that spiraled above the already smoke-choked harbor. Everything seemed to be on fire, and a pall of haze and smoke draped over Hong Kong like a funeral shroud. Visibility deteriorated to the point that pilots from the *Lexington* believed the Japanese had cranked up land-based chemical smoke generators to mask the ships in the harbor.

Throughout the afternoon, the gunners aboard the *Kanju* and the other escort vessels had been repeatedly raked with .50-caliber slugs and blown off their feet by rocket blasts. They had been eviscerated by bomb shrapnel, deafened by explosions, and drenched by near misses that raised towering geysers of seawater. Despite this hammering of ship and sailor, despite the fires rippling out of holes punched through bulkheads and hull plates, despite the blood sloshing across the decks like buckets of spilled paint, despite the sailors moaning their last words in the gun tubs as they lay ragdoll-limp among the spent brass – despite all this the antiaircraft gunners aboard the shot-up *kaibōkan* continued to swat American planes out of the sky. They had no sure way to determine how many enemy aircraft they had hit, but they had witnessed enough planes plunging into the harbor to keep them at their guns.

Strike 2D had, in fact, been costly for the air groups of TG 38.2. At least three aircraft returned to the task group with battle damage, and the plane handlers on the *Hornet* had to shove one hopelessly riddled SB2C-3 over the side. Three more planes failed to return at all, with each carrier in the task group losing one machine. Ensign Richard E. Wilson of the *Hornet* went down with his F6F-5 while in a dive over the target. After shedding a wing, the Avenger piloted by Lt. Marvin L. Leedom of the *Lexington* spun into the water and disintegrated. Leedom had been the cabinmate and close friend of Lieutenant Seiz, who had been lost earlier that afternoon when his Turkey had crashed into the godowns along the Kowloon waterfront during Strike 2C. Lt. (j.g.) Charles S. Snead of the *Hancock* never pulled his burning SB2C-3 out of its dive and plunged into the harbor. Though six men had been aboard the three downed aircraft, fellow pilots observed just a single parachute. Alvin W. Hughes, the nineteen-year-old gunner aboard Lieutenant Snead's Helldiver, had managed to throw himself out of the cockpit just before the dive-bomber drilled into the sea. He hurtled through the flames trailing from the plane, roasting his face and neck in the process, and pulled his ripcord. Hughes had bailed out at very low altitude, and he slapped into the greasy waters of the harbor just seconds after his chute opened.[1]

Despite the effectiveness of the Japanese antiaircraft defenses, however, the tankers of convoy Hi-87 had been bombed, rocketed, and strafed throughout the day. Like the Avenger from the *Cowpens* that had absorbed fifty-four flak hits and kept on flying, however, the tankers obstinately refused to sink. Similarly, just as the pilot from the *Cowpens* had never given up on his riddled Avenger, the crews of the tankers showed a similar resoluteness and remained aboard ship instead of taking to the lifeboats. Still, while the *Kamoi* and *Matsushima Maru* remained afloat, they had both been reduced to a smoking shambles, and the *Tenei Maru* had listed heavily to port with its stern under water. At the Hong Kong and Whampoa dockyard, the *Hashidate Maru* had also suffered considerable damage. Only the *Sarawak Maru* had escaped the deluge of bombs and rockets, perhaps because its smaller size and berth at the Kowloon wharves made it difficult for the American pilots to spot. Casualties among the tanker crews had been substantial, though Suzumoku Goni had managed to stay alive. He and the other gunners aboard the *Hashidate Maru* believed they had downed a trio of Grummans.[2]

Though the American airmen had focused on the tankers and warships of convoy Hi-87, they had attacked other merchant ships and naval vessels in the harbor as well. The little *Nanshu Maru* had been destroyed by strafing, and the landing ship *T-108* had been pounded into scrap metal. Several small freighters had been sunk, including the *Hakushu Maru No. 2* and the *Anri Go No. 2*. The *Sekko Maru* – formerly the *Chekiang* of the prewar China Navigation Company – had also been sent to the bottom. The *Okinoyama Maru No. 5*, the *Hida Maru*, the *Yamasachi Maru*, and the *Dosei Maru* had all taken varying degrees of damage. In addition, the American air attacks likely damaged three merchant ships that had been under construction or repair in the dockyards, including the *Ankai Maru*, *Heikai Maru*, and *Yokai Maru*. Some of these vessels could be salvaged, but not easily or quickly, since the heavily bombed dockyards would have to be returned to service first and ship-building materials remained in short supply.[3]

Luck continued to favor the destroyer *Shigure*, which suffered only superficial damage topside, but the vintage destroyer *Hasu* had taken a beating and would need extensive repairs. The escort vessel *Nomi* had lost seven men when a bomb or rocket slaughtered the crew manning the aft 4.7-inch gun battery, which lacked armored protection for the gunners. Machine-gun fire and shrapnel had flayed the escort vessels *CD-60* and *Shinnan*, killing two crewmen aboard the latter vessel and wounding another eighteen. Casualties among the gun crews and bridge officers of the 7th Escort Convoy had been severe and included Lieutenant Commander Yatsui, who had been seriously wounded at 2:30 p.m. when American planes strafed the *Kanju*. Despite the extended thrashing by the U.S. Navy, however, all of the escort vessels in Victoria Harbor remained afloat with most of their barrels still manned and trained skywards in anticipation of additional raids by American aircraft.[4]

On shore, meanwhile, Japanese patrols fanned out to investigate reports of downed American aviators. In Kennedy Town one squad cornered Jean Balch, who stepped out from behind the sheet of corrugated metal where he had been hiding and raised his hands in surrender. A well-dressed Chinese man in a suit of Harris Tweed appeared to be in command of the soldiers, and he ordered his men to search Balch's pockets. The man examined the contents of Balch's wallet, which contained no identification cards of any sort, but did reveal that the airman had come from the *Yorktown*. Since Balch had neglected to wear his dog tags, he remained an anonymous, if obviously American, prisoner. However, though the man in tweed spoke English, he never bothered to ask for his captive's name. Instead, he ordered that Balch be taken to a waiting car.

Their bayonets leveled like pitchforks, the squad of soldiers marched Balch out of the wrecked building to a Pontiac station wagon. Balch recognized the two Sikhs standing by the car – they were the pair that had argued with the Chinese man who had helped him hide his parachute. Balch figured the Sikhs had turned him in to the man in the tweed suit, who Balch assumed must be in the pay of the Kempeitai, the much-feared Japanese military police.

"Where did you get the clothes?" the man in tweed asked Balch as they all stood by the Pontiac.

"Stole them from a clothesline," Balch told him, and pointed. At the end of the street a coil of barbed wire had been swung aside to allow traffic to pass during the day, and Balch assumed at night it would be stretched back across the street to block access to the waterfront. Fresh laundry had been laid over the wire to dry in the sun.

Without indicating whether he accepted this explanation, the man in tweed asked Balch where he had touched down in his parachute. Balch told him about a hundred yards from where he had been apprehended. The man then had Balch retrace his steps back towards where he had landed, but when he asked the airman for further directions, Balch refused to provide them based on the excuse that he did not know the neighborhood. This reply earned him an expertly applied blow to the side of the head from the man in the tweed suit, who clearly knew where and how to hit prisoners – smacks to the side of the head could be painful and disorienting, but they left few marks and inflicted no lasting injury.

As the two Sikhs and the man in the Harris Tweed searched the surrounding area for anyone who might have helped Balch during his abortive attempt to escape and evade, four soldiers pushed Balch into the station wagon and clambered in beside him, leather belts creaking and rifles clunking against the metal sides of the car. Looking towards the front of the vehicle, Balch saw the words "Hong Kong Hotel, Ltd." emblazoned on the horn button in the center of the steering wheel. He doubted, however, that he would be going to a hotel. Some of his guards knew some English, and as they waited in the back of the Pontiac, they passed the time by subjecting Balch to their own interrogation.

"Do you know Deanna Durbin?" one of them asked.

Balch figured they were asking if he knew *about* the famous Canadian movie star and singer, not whether he knew her personally, but decided to respond literally to the question instead. "No," he said.

"Do you know Joe Louis?"

Though every sailor and aviator in the U.S. Navy had heard of Joe Louis, the world heavyweight-boxing champion, Balch simply said, "No."

While the guards allowed Balch to keep the Chinese currency that he had been issued before leaving the *Yorktown* as well as some stray American coins in his pocket, they confiscated his navy pocketknife and his pair of dice. They asked for a demonstration of how the dice worked, and Balch obliged with a game of craps. If they had been betting for ownership of the Pontiac, Balch reckoned that he would have been the proud owner of a station wagon looted from the Hong Kong Hotel.

To Balch's dismay, the two Sikhs and the man in the tweed suit soon returned with the Chinese man who had given Balch the civilian clothes. They tossed him into the station wagon and the driver started the engine of the Pontiac. As they motored uphill, a wall collapsed into the street ahead, and a microsecond later the roar of a bomb rocked the station wagon on its springs. After a smoothly executed but rapid U-turn, the driver took them back downhill to the harbor and motored along the quay. In the second or two before the guards smacked him in the head and told him not to look, Balch caught a morale-boosting glimpse of multiple ships burning in the harbor.

Balch had no idea where they were going, of course, but most likely the Pontiac carried him to either the Central Police Station compound or the Supreme Court building, which had both been requisitioned by the Kempeitai. As the driver brought the station wagon to a halt at their destination, another bomb fell nearby. The resultant explosion lifted an entire tree and tossed it aside like a piece of straw caught in a gust of wind. Balch saw the root ball whirl through the air in a colossal spray of dirt, dust, splinters, and smoke. Moving quickly, the guards yanked Balch from the Pontiac and hustled him to a tiny cell. After a short interval, they returned with a blindfold and handcuffs. They then hauled Balch up a staircase and pushed him down onto a chair for his first interrogation, which consisted primarily of yet more smacks to the side of his head and a few desultory questions. Men in military boots – the inept blindfolding ensured Balch could see his own feet as well as the footwear of his guards – manhandled him out of the interrogation room and made him kneel. Balch wondered if he was about to receive a bullet in the back of the head.

Instead, the guards put him in a motorcycle sidecar, and after a short journey along streets he could not see due to his blindfold, transferred him to the back of a truck. Balch felt the truck grind up and then back down a steep and winding roadway. After what seemed like a very long journey, he found himself in an interrogation room in Stanley Prison. The guards left him in handcuffs, but they removed his blindfold. A military officer and two enlisted men sat behind a table, and a pregnant young Chinese woman brought them a pot of tea and a package of Pirate-brand cigarettes emblazoned with a picture of a Spanish galleon. A desk stood in one corner, and, rather ominously, a water-filled bucket with a length of wet rope occupied the other corner.

Balch stood before the table for a four-hour interrogation mediated by one of the enlisted men, who served as interpreter. The initial questions focused on when Balch had been born and where he had gone to school. Eventually the questions zeroed in on the USS *Yorktown*. His inquisitors knew he had come from the *Yorktown* because they had examined the contents of his wallet, but they also knew the *Yorktown* had been sunk during the Battle of Midway in 1942 and seemed unaware that a new ship with the same name had been built to replace it. At this point, the interrogation took a turn for the worse. When asked if Balch knew where he was, he made the mistake of saying no, and in response to this uncooperative answer, two guards shoved a pole under one armpit and threaded it behind his back and under the other armpit. With a grunt, the guards lifted the pole and left Balch suspended from the ceiling with his arms still bound behind him. Balch then received a thorough thrashing with the wet rope and a wooden club, all the while feeling like his arms were about to pull from his shoulders. When the Japanese judged he had been sufficiently punished for his unwillingness to be more forthcoming, or perhaps when they simply grew tired and lost interest in the whole affair, a pair of guards dropped Balch to the floor, yanked out the pole, and dragged him back to a cell, where they flung him down onto the concrete floor like a sack of rice in a granary storeroom. Then they slammed the door.[5]

The Bombing of Bungalow C

In the late afternoon, Rear Admiral Sherman's TG 38.3 sent aircraft to Hong Kong for the first time. The strike package consisted of thirty-two Hellcats from the *Essex, Langley,* and *Ticonderoga.* Air groups from all three flattops had mounted CAPs over the fleet and sent missions to Formosa and Hainan on January 15 and 16, 1945, but they had not participated in the strikes against targets in the Pearl River delta. Consequently, the Hellcat pilots from TG 38.3 headed for Hong Kong with a limited understanding of the target zone and its defenses.

A dozen F6F-5 pilots from VF-80 launched from the *Ticonderoga* on a fighter sweep, which meant they could select targets of opportunity for their 500-pound bombs and wing guns once they reached Hong Kong. When the pilots arrived just before 5:00 p.m., they circled Hong Kong Island to assess possible targets. Weather conditions remained ideal, with clear visibility out to fifteen miles. Fires glowed along the shoreline of western Kowloon, where the Texaco oil facility continued to belch rolls of black smoke, and a grayish plume rising thousands of feet into the air likely marked the crash site of the TBM-1C flown by Lieutenant Seiz from the *Lexington.* Still more fires burned on Hong Kong Island, particularly on Ko Shing Street in Sheung Wan, where the wreckage of an American aircraft continued to blaze.[1] Hindered by the pall of smoke obscuring the harbor, the pilots failed to spot the undamaged *Sarawak Maru,* though they did manage to determine that the other four tankers had been hit by earlier raids, leaving them either awash, aflame, or both. In addition, the pilots failed to spot any

Japanese aircraft on the field at Kai Tak, so they ruled out both the tankers and the airbase as viable targets. As they traced the shoreline of Hong Kong Island, the VF-80 pilots spotted a small merchant vessel at Sai Wan and another tucked away in Repulse Bay. Releasing their bombs at 2,000 feet, the *Ticonderoga* pilots only managed to churn up circles of white foam around the two vessels, which remained afloat but badly sieved by 6,200 rounds of .50-caliber ammunition. Perhaps deciding that he wanted to aim at a bigger target, one pilot dropped on the Tai Koo dockyard instead. His 500-pounder would prove to be the last bomb dropped on Tai Koo by the aircraft of TF 38.[2]

At roughly the same time that the fighter sweep had taken off from the *Ticonderoga*, a dozen F6F-5s from VF-4 roared aloft from the *Essex*. Fighting Four had launched on short notice, which precluded a thorough briefing, and the ACI officers had instructed the Hellcat pilots to select their own targets at Hong Kong despite their limited understanding of the tactical terrain. Unlike every other Hellcat squadron sent to Hong Kong that day, the *Essex* pilots had been loaded up with 1,000-pound bombs for a shipping strike. For this reason, they scouted Victoria Harbor and made targeting decisions quite different from those of the *Ticonderoga* pilots. Rather than go for smaller, undamaged ships, the *Essex* pilots opted to target the four badly damaged tankers as well as the Royal Navy dockyard and Cosmopolitan dockyard. Rattled by the unexpectedly heavy antiaircraft fire and hemmed in by the vertical topography of the harbor, the pilots rolled over into sixty-degree dives from 15,000 feet. After punching through three layers of flak, the pilots released at a cautious 5,000 feet and then used both hands to pull back on the stick for a high-G pullout. Helldiver pilots typically released at 2,500 feet and often failed to score, so a mile-high drop by fighter pilots all but guaranteed a miss no matter how big the target, but nobody hung around to confirm this due to the blistering flak. All twelve of the VF-4 Hellcats cleared out of the harbor at high speed and regrouped south of Hong Kong Island, where it turned out that one particularly unflappable lieutenant had chosen to retain his thousand-pounder at the bottom of his dive when he realized that he would almost certainly overshoot his target. As he winged back out to sea with the rest of his squadron, he opted to hurl his M65 against the last available target: the much-abused Waglan lighthouse.[3]

Like the pilots from the *Ticonderoga*, the eight VF-44 pilots launched from the *Langley* had been ordered to fly a fighter sweep and had discretion to choose targets at will. Lt. Carland E. Brunmier led the first division of four Hellcats, while Lt. Alva N. Abernathy commanded the second division. The two lieutenants had acquired considerable combat experience while flying with VF-44, not to mention decorations like the Navy Cross and the Distinguished Flying Cross, though like most carrier pilots they were only in their twenties. The youngest fliers in the squadron, in fact, were just twenty years old. Abernathy and Brunmier knew their business, from the performance envelopes of their Hellcats to the lethality of the various types of weaponry they could carry. For the sweep over Hong Kong, four Hellcats toted a 500-pound bomb, and four hauled six 5-inch rockets, a combat loading that suited the flexible nature of the mission.

When the two lieutenants first arrived over the target zone they led their divisions on a circuit around the mountainous center of Hong Kong Island, which allowed them to observe numerous fires burning along the shoreline of Victoria Harbor and a cauldron of flak boiling below them between 5,000 and 15,000 feet. Though the smoke and haze impeded visibility, the *Langley* pilots made the same damage assessment that the *Ticonderoga* pilots had: the tankers had been bombed out, the dockyards had been pulverized, and the airfield at Kai Tak had been abandoned. Seeing no targets of value on the north side of the island, Brunmier and Abernathy chose to hit targets on the south side, where they identified a complex of Japanese barracks on the Stanley Peninsula. They also observed a Sugar Charlie aground on the western coast of the peninsula with a salvage lighter alongside.

Lieutenant Brunmier attempted to glide-bomb the tanker but missed the target. A second pilot in his division discovered that his 500-pounder would not release, which meant he would have to burn more avgas than expected as he hauled the quarter-ton weapon back to the fleet. He had sufficient fuel reserves to cope with this development, but if the carriers had been further out to sea and he had been at his maximum range, the extra weight might have meant ditching by a lifeguard submarine or picket destroyer. The two pilots in Lieutenant Brunmier's division with rockets under their wings took their shots as well but failed to score any hits. Brunmier and the rest of his division then wheeled around for two more runs, launching still more rockets that went wide of the mark, though incendiary rounds fired from the wing guns set the lighter ablaze.

As Lieutenant Brunmier and his division worked over the vessels in Stanley Bay, Lieutenant Abernathy led his division in an attack on what he assumed to be a Japanese military base but was actually Stanley Prison and the adjacent compound for the Stanley Military Internment Camp, which housed Ray Jones and 2,400 Allied civilians. Lieutenant Abernathy's division made three runs on the prison and the camp, dropping two bombs and firing ten rockets. Abernathy's division then made two strafing runs on the tanker and salvage lighter as soon as Lieutenant Brunmier's division had cleared out of the airspace over Stanley Bay. However, despite the attention of eight Hellcats and the expenditure of one bomb, twelve rockets, and at least 2,000 rounds of 12.7mm machine-gun ammunition, the two vessels showed little sign of damage. Moreover, a disappointed Lieutenant Abernathy noted that the fire aboard the lighter had quickly burned itself out. Meanwhile, Lieutenant Brunmier's division, which had already expended its heavy ordnance in a fruitless attack on the tanker and lighter, made a final gun run against the buildings of the camp and prison.[4]

Most internees had been confined to their quarters by the Japanese, but those who had been caught outdoors at the start of the air raid had scrambled into ditches or ducked behind the nearest stone wall. Despite the risk of angering the camp guards, not to mention the hazards posed by the American warplanes, many internees could not resist watching the kaleidoscopic airshow of whizzing dark-blue aircraft and crisscrossing lines of pink tracer rounds. One of the inmates in Stanley Prison peeked out his cellblock window and witnessed the thorough perforation of freshly washed prison laundry by a strafing Hellcat. Prisoners had spread the laundry out on the ground to dry in the pale winter sun, and the inmate theorized that the prison uniforms resembled prone soldiers when seen from the air. Several rockets detonated against the southeast corner of the prison walls near the camp hospital, where many of the windows shattered as the staff hurled themselves to the floor. Shrapnel or bullet fragments wounded one internee who had been caught outside while grinding rice. Tracer rounds ignited dry grass and underbrush around the camp. Bullets slapped into the walls of buildings, leaving an acne-like spray of gouges, and plaster fell from the ceilings to coat internees in a dust as fine as confectionary sugar. Soon a second internee caught some shrapnel. Then the entire camp reverberated with the concussion of a massive explosion. Internees lying on the floor of Bungalow A felt the blast wave ripple the concrete slab beneath them like a shaken rug. They knew a bomb had landed close by – so close by, in fact, that they counted themselves lucky to be alive. Soon they heard cries of anguish and alarm from the direction of Bungalow C.

Perched on the side of a slope, the front windows of Bungalow C overlooked the cemetery and Stanley Bay, as did the windows on its western side. The eastern flank of the building faced the incline that led up to Bungalow A and the main hall of St. Stephen's, however. In the narrow space between the bungalow and the hillside stood a garage. Bungalow C had been on the front line during the battle for Stanley in 1941 and suffered extensive damage, though the internees assigned to live in the bungalow had done their best to clean and repair the battered residence. When the airstrike began at least eighteen people had taken cover inside the one-story bungalow and its garage, which offered scant protection from machine-gun fire and even less from a quarter-ton bomb or a 5-inch rocket that packed a punch comparable to the high-explosive shell fired by the 5-inch main battery of a destroyer.[5] However, the internees had nowhere else to go, since the camp lacked even the most rudimentary of air-raid shelters.

A bomb likely dropped by Lieutenant Abernathy's division had fallen between the bungalow and the garage. The resultant blast wave ripped through the bungalow and hurled those inside out onto the front lawn. Rescuers found the bodies of their fellow internees sprawled on the ground outside the bungalow, and at first glance, many of the victims appeared to be sleeping. They were, however, quite dead, and it appeared that nearly everyone had died from the concussion of the blast wave. One man, however, had been decapitated. Though damaged, the bungalow remained structurally intact, but the explosion had blown out the brick walls of the garage and brought the concrete roof down on top of the women huddling inside. The rescuers spotted an arm protruding from the rubble and eventually pulled four corpses from beneath the wreckage. Stretcher parties carried five more internees with injuries of varying severity towards the hospital, but one died on the way. In total, the bombing had killed nine men and five women.

Ray Jones had taken cover elsewhere in the camp and did not witness the destruction of Bungalow C firsthand, though he saw the Hellcats from the *Langley* roaring past at low altitude and heard the staccato rattle of machine-gun fire and the deep whump of the detonating 500-pounder. "Local spots machine gunned & bombed," he wrote that evening, and added that both Stanley Prison and St. Stephen's College within the camp boundaries had been targeted. "C Bungalow hit," he continued. "14 killed, 4 injured. All clear 6.30pm." Jones then listed the names and ages of the dead internees. He knew many of them, though none had been as close to him as Gwen Flower or Steve and his wife Mary. For Jones and everyone else in the Stanley camp, the bombing had been a painful reminder of their acute vulnerability and just how little they really mattered.[6]

Jones and the rest of the internees believed with almost complete unanimity that the airstrike on Bungalow C had been an unintentional act. They believed that the American pilots had hit the bungalow accidentally while responding to ground fire, since Japanese soldiers atop Stanley Prison – a facility directly adjacent to the Stanley camp – had fired machine guns at the Hellcats. Other shooting from within the camp boundaries included rifle and pistol fire from the camp guards, who were under orders to shoot their weapons at enemy aircraft and in deference to these orders took potshots at American warplanes regardless of whether they were actually in range. At least one Japanese officer yelled defiantly at the American aircraft while slashing the air with his sword. Internees also reported that machine guns and a larger antiaircraft weapon concealed in Stanley Village fired at the Hellcats, as did a mobile antiaircraft gun positioned on the road to Stanley Fort, which ran below Bungalow C. Other internees believed the bungalow had been hit by ordnance intended for the tanker and salvage lighter in Stanley Bay, given the proximity of the vessels to Bungalow C.[7]

Like everyone else in the Stanley camp, Jones exonerated the American pilots and placed the blame for the bombing of Bungalow C squarely on the Japanese. He reckoned that firing on the American aircraft from positions in or near the camp had been a clear invitation for the strafing, rocketing, and bombing that had followed. Moreover, the Japanese camp administration had consistently refused to grant the internees permission to construct air-raid shelters of any sort, and as a result, the internees had been forced to take refuge in the buildings where they lived, such as Bungalow C. The Japanese had been similarly disinclined to grant internee requests to mark the camp with white crosses that could be seen from the air by American pilots, though the

Hongkong News would later report that the camp had been clearly marked with white crosses. Always quick to spot a propaganda opportunity, the newspaper also inflated the number of casualties. "Jap paper reports 49 killed & injured here in camp & that all buildings have white crosses on them," Jones wrote. "Lying yellow bastards. They do not tell the people why our planes had need to come so close to Camp."[8]

The Allied prisoners at Sham Shui Po had become quite adept at judging the relative weights of American air raids, which like the interminable roll calls had become a regular feature of camp life. Both guards and captors alike had learned that the lone high-flying reconnaissance plane from the 14th Air Force that regularly appeared over the harbor – nicknamed "Albert" by the prisoners – could be safely ignored. Bombing and strafing of Kai Tak or other distant targets by low-flying P-51s presented relatively little risk. High-altitude visits by B-24 heavy bombers proved more nerve-wracking, since the prisoners found it difficult to judge their intended target, and shrapnel from the big 120mm antiaircraft guns ringing the harbor often fell into the camp. All prisoners agreed that the most dangerous attacks focused on the Cosmopolitan dockyard and the Lai Chi Kok oil tanks, which occupied positions along the coast on both sides of the camp. Airstrikes on ships moored near Stonecutters Island also presented a serious hazard to the prisoners.

Like the civilian internees at the Stanley camp, the POWs at Sham Shui Po had been repeatedly denied permission to build air-raid shelters despite the camp's proximity to high-value targets. While some prisoners occupied a pair of four-story barracks known as the Jubilee Buildings, which offered the protection of concrete walls but the disadvantage of a large target profile, most of the men lived in flimsy one-room barracks lined up in rows that just begged for a strafing. When the air-raid siren had gone off and the first U.S. Navy planes appeared overhead just after morning roll call, the guards confined all prisoners to the barracks.

With the guards distracted by the American warplanes and unable to enforce the regulation that forbade prisoners from observing airstrikes, the POWs watched the raids unfold with a violence that left them alternatively jubilant and scared witless. Those men with sea-facing windows enjoyed panoramic views of the harbor and could clearly make out the *Kamoi*, *Matsushima Maru*, and *Tenei Maru* with their cordon of escort vessels off the coast of Kennedy Town. As each wave of American planes arrived, they watched the antiaircraft guns on Stonecutters Island open fire along with the batteries aboard the escort vessels. They witnessed the collision of the two TBMs from the *Hancock* over Hong Kong Island and saw several American planes go into the harbor, including one that plunged into the water not far offshore from the camp. They saw the failed torpedo runs as well as some memorable dive-bombing attacks, and by sundown could count nine different smoke plumes rising from various points along the harbor, with the largest boiling up from the Texaco oil facility at Tsuen Wan.

While the Japanese and Formosan sentries stayed under cover and occasionally sniped at passing American aircraft, Sgt. Maj. Honda – a guard respected by the prisoners for his evenhanded treatment – remained out in the open for much of the day, leaning on the scabbard of his sheathed sword. Unmoved by the low-bursting flak and the rain of shell casings from the Hellcats streaking past, he stoically watched the destruction of convoy Hi-87. After he had stood statue-like through one of the heaviest airstrikes, the prisoners let out a spontaneous cheer in his honor. Honda nodded slightly in response, and continued to lean on his sword as a steady drumbeat of explosions rolled across the harbor.

Shrapnel fell into the camp throughout the day and punctured barracks roofs in a spray of wooden splinters and fractured roof tiles. One prisoner found a brass nosecone on the floor of his barracks, while another got knocked across the room by a piece of shrapnel that lodged harmlessly in the pages of the journal in his breast pocket. Despite the hail of flak splinters and spent antiaircraft rounds, the prisoners suffered only two shrapnel injuries and just one fatality – a sergeant who died of heart failure brought on by a raging case of malaria rather than the cacophonous terror of an all-day air raid.[9]

Though the American aircraft never singled out the camp for attack, the prisoners frequently heard the telltale whoosh of an incoming bomb or rocket meant for the nearby Cosmopolitan dockyard. One errant bomb or rocket struck the seawall of the camp, while another detonated on Castle Peak Road, which the prisoners agreed was just a bit too close for comfort. "The racket was tremendous," one thoroughly frazzled prisoner wrote in his diary that evening, "and it was a very wearing day."[10]

The Results Were Not Commensurate
with the Losses

Task Force 38 withdrew from its position to the south of Hong Kong at 7:00 p.m. on the evening of January 16, 1945. In heavy seas, the fleet began steaming towards Luzon on the opposite side of the South China Sea, though the night-flying squadrons of TG 38.5 remained in operation over the Pearl River delta. The *Enterprise* and *Independence* launched four radar-equipped F6F-5Ns apiece for special patrols known as "zipper" flights. Pilots assigned to these missions extended the blanketing of enemy airfields into the twilight hours, which covered the withdrawal of the squadrons that had flown Strike 2D and the final round of fighter sweeps from the *Essex, Langley*, and *Ticonderoga*. Prowling over the Hong Kong and Canton runways during the hours bracketing sunset, the eight Hellcat pilots engaged one Ki-43 and one Ki-44 over Canton. They also caught a twin-engine transport plane after it landed at Kai Tak. The Hellcat pilots reported all three aircraft as destroyed, bringing the likely total of enemy planes shot down over the Pearl River delta on January 15 and 16 to eleven. Four more F6F-5N pilots launched from the *Enterprise* for a post-sundown "heckler" mission, which called for harassing the JAAF airbases after nightfall. After failing to locate any airborne Japanese aircraft, the quartet of Hellcats strafed and rocketed searchlight positions at Tien Ho and White Cloud airfields.

As if to underscore the hazardous nature of nocturnal carrier operations, the twelve Hellcats sent aloft for the zipper flights and heckler mission lost four aircraft and two pilots. One *Enterprise* pilot from the heckler flight – Lt. (j.g.) Robert F. Wright – simply disappeared, while another pilot from the zipper mission – Ensign Erwin G. Nash – flew into the water aft of the *Enterprise* while landing in the dark at 10:00 p.m., with vertigo the suspected cause. A third *Enterprise* pilot flipped his Hellcat into the crash barrier but emerged from the wrecked plane without injury. Another pilot destroyed his F6F-5N in a similar barrier crash while landing on the heaving deck of the *Independence*, demolishing two forward-spotted aircraft in the process. In total, four mangled aircraft had to be jettisoned from the night carriers. A fifth pilot damaged his engine and propeller in a less dramatic barrier crash, which meant his Hellcat went down to the mechanics on the hangar deck rather than over the side.[1]

The lifeguard submarine USS *Guardfish*, meanwhile, had been battered by the same rough weather that had bedeviled TF 38. The high seas had wrecked the sub's radio antenna and then washed two jury-rigged temporary antennas overboard as well, which had compromised the ability of the ship to send and receive radio transmissions. Commander Hammond and his crew had occasionally heard the garbled voices of American pilots over the radio, but they never spotted any friendly aircraft. At one point, the *Guardfish* cruised through a spill of green dye of the sort a downed aviator might use to mark his position in the waves. Possibly, the dye had been released by Lt. (j.g.) Newell O. Maxwell of VBF-7, who had ditched some seventy-five miles offshore from Hong Kong after his aircraft had been shot up while executing Strike 2C with the *Hancock* air group. An accompanying pilot had observed dye on the water after Maxwell made his wheels-up landing in rough seas but never located anyone in the water. The lookouts aboard the *Guardfish* had never caught sight of a life raft or a pilot in the waves, either, though they did spot plenty of Chinese junks. Closer inspection confirmed the battered wooden vessels carried nothing more dangerous than nets and a haul of fish. With no rescued airmen aboard, the *Guardfish* departed the South China Sea and set course for Guam, where it would end its tenth war patrol.[2]

Over a two-day period, the air groups of TF 38 had struck shipping, warships, port facilities, and airbases at Hainan, Amoy, Swatow, Formosa, the Pescadores, Canton, Macau, and Hong Kong. Naval aviators had flown more than 1,100 sorties against these targets, including nearly 600 sorties against Hong Kong and Canton alone.[3] Pilots had expended more than a thousand bombs, torpedoes, and rockets while attacking targets around Victoria Harbor, including dockyards, fuel depots, tankers, naval escort vessels, and Kai Tak airfield. Despite the high sortie rate and impressive bomb tonnage, however, the Hong Kong strikes had proven to be a disappointment for the exhausted airmen of TF 38. In the opinion of more than a few pilots, too many aircraft had been lost and too little damage had been inflicted. "The plain unvarnished truth is that the results were not commensurate with the losses," stated the commander of VB-7, the Helldiver squadron aboard the *Hancock*. Though he was specifically referring to his own air group's experience during Strike 2C, pilots across the entire fleet echoed his opinion in the aircraft action reports compiled by the ACI officers.[4]

The heavy flak and tight terrain of Victoria Harbor had been a deadly combination, as the commander of VB-7 made clear. "The topography of the Hong Kong area permitted a concentration of fire so intense," he said, "that it is surprising any planes got through."[5] Commander Lamade, who led the *Hancock* air group, echoed his subordinate's assessment. "Thought must be given as to the practicability of sending dive-bombers into heavily defended land-locked harbors, where approaches and retirements are limited," Lamade wrote. "New methods of attack must be planned for carrier based aircraft when hitting such objectives if the personnel losses are to be cut down." Lamade spoke from bitter experience, as his air group had lost twenty-six pilots and aircrew since October 1944, including eleven at Hong Kong.[6]

As noted in numerous action reports, the midday lull between strikes had given the Japanese time to adjust their antiaircraft tactics. As a result, while losses during the morning had been unexpectedly light, with just two aircraft brought down by enemy fire, during the afternoon the casualty rate had been shockingly heavy, with fifteen aircraft lost, including six planes from CVG-7 of the *Hancock* alone. Commander Lamade voiced his frustration with the long intervals between each strike, which he believed had contributed to the high loss rate:

As has been repeated time and time again, too much time prevails between strikes over one objective. The schedules should be so arranged that task groups can dove-tail their schedules so that there is a constant hitting power <u>OVER</u> the target at all times. A maximum of thirty minutes should be set for time between strikes on the target.[7]

As Lamade surely knew, however, the interval between Strike B in the morning and Strike C in the afternoon had lasted for nearly four hours.

What Lamade could not have known was that the gap between Strike B and C had been wide enough for the 14th Air Force to fly four P-51s into Victoria Harbor without the navy even noticing, which suggested that the blanketing of the airspace over Hong Kong had been full of holes. This ragged coverage would not have come as a surprise to Lamade, who felt that blanket missions flown during Operation *Gratitude* often involved too few aircraft covering too many airfields. He wrote, "Territories assigned to an Air Group for 'blanketing' are sometimes ridiculous in extent." As an example, he noted that at one point VF-7 had been tasked with blanketing Luzon airfields spread over 8,400 square miles, at times with just eight Hellcats.[8] This tendency to assign modest numbers of pilots to blanket missions that covered large swathes of airspace had been the rule during the strikes on Hong Kong as well, though the limited enemy air activity had compensated fortuitously for this deficiency.

In post-strike action reports many aviators opined that their loadings had been inadequate for the missions assigned. The Hellcat pilots believed that they had been given the wrong mix for busting ships – too few 500-pound bombs and too many 5-inch rockets, which had proven ineffective against shipping. The Avenger pilots, meanwhile, criticized the decision to send them in with Mark 13s, particularly at low tide in a well-defended harbor too shallow for torpedo runs. "It is considered that a torpedo attack in a place like Hong Kong Bay is suicidal to say the least," asserted the action report for the *Hornet*, which argued that torpedoes should only be used against vessels at sea in coordination with strafing attacks by F6Fs to suppress antiaircraft fire. In the report's view, shore-based gun positions could not be as easily neutralized as ship-based flak guns, which meant that torpedo runs in bays and harbors would likely face devastating crossfires from entrenched antiaircraft weapons.[9]

Based on their experience at Hong Kong as well as over Formosa, Indochina, and the Philippines, Commander Lamade and other air group commanders argued for paring down strike packages from three aircraft types to two – F6F fighters and fighter-bombers plus SB2C dive-bombers *or* TBM torpedo planes, but not both. Going in with fighters, fighter-bombers, dive-bombers, and torpedo planes made for unwieldy formations, due to the varying speeds, ranges, ceilings, and other performance factors of the different aircraft types. Lamade advocated for adding more Hellcats and retiring the bulky TBMs, which required considerable deck space even with their wings folded. Not all air group commanders agreed with this assessment, however. The *Ticonderoga* air group argued against replacing its complement of TBM-3s with additional SB2Cs, for example.[10] Still other commanders continued to view the combined air group – fighter, dive-bomber, torpedo plane – as essential to successful combat operations. Vice Admiral McCain, meanwhile, had long called for replacing the SB2C with more Hellcats and Corsairs, which could serve as fighters or bombers depending upon tactical requirements. Many air group commanders as well as the rear admirals leading the fast-carrier task groups supported the addition of more fighter-bomber squadrons, as did McCain, but they argued that the VBF pilots would need specialized training *before* joining the air groups of TF 38.[11]

Many action reports singled out poor target coordination as a major problem – perhaps *the* problem – that had reduced the effectiveness of the strikes on Hong Kong. The target coordinators for each strike had the difficult job of assessing which squadrons under their control should hit what targets, and then adjusting and reassigning targets as needed in reaction to how things played out. While some action reports questioned the performance of the task-group target coordinators, the key criticism centered on the fact that there had never been a target coordinator for the *entire* task force. As a result, while there had been coordination *within* the strike forces launched by individual task groups, there had been little coordination *between* the strike forces from the different task groups. Chaos over the target zone had been the inevitable result, with multiple squadrons from different air groups diving on the same targets simultaneously. This had increased the risk of midair collisions and forced pilots to pay more attention to dodging friendly aircraft than on keeping targets aligned in their Mark 8 gunsights. Additionally, the lack of task-force level coordination as well as the sometimes-poor coordination within a task group meant that some squadrons had gone in alone with limited numbers of aircraft, which had allowed the Japanese to concentrate their antiaircraft fire. In some cases, the vulnerable low-flying Avengers had made torpedo runs without adequate support from the Hellcats or Helldivers. In addition, the lack of target coordination at the task-force level had inevitably caused air groups to focus on the highest priority targets. As a result, too many aircraft had piled in on the tankers, while too few had lined up on the escort vessels. Moreover, the Tai Koo dockyard had received far too much attention during Strike A and B, leading to target overkill.

"There will always be a poor target selection when two or more task groups hit a small area such as Hong Kong without a target coordinator for the whole task force," stated the commander of the air group aboard the *Hornet*. "It is strongly recommended that a target coordinator be assigned for the whole task force."[12] Commander Lamade echoed this assessment and advocated for a "Flying Field Marshal" who could take on the role of fleet-wide target coordinator and have command authority over all strikes flown by the task force.[13]

The execution of the strikes against Hong Kong had been flawed in their conception, many of the pilots concluded. Lack of coordination aside, hitting Formosa and Hong Kong simultaneously had diluted the power of the air groups, often referred to as the main batteries or "Sunday punch" of the carriers. In addition, too many aircraft had been assigned to search missions and CAPs over the fleet on January 16, leading to a further shortage of aircraft available for strikes against Hong Kong. The commander of the *Hornet* air group, for example, noted that only 55 percent of the group's aircraft had been available for the Hong Kong strikes because so many planes had been slated for CAPs and search flights, some of which duplicated the efforts of B-24 and PB4Y-1 squadrons based in China and the Philippines.[14] Due to the poorly coordinated strikes and low aircraft availability, wave after wave of small to midsized strikes had hit Victoria Harbor. However, Japanese antiaircraft defenses had become increasingly deadly as the day went on, which suggested that sending in a series of less than full-scale strikes throughout the morning and afternoon with breaks in between for the flak gunners had been a costly strategy. "Over well defended targets," an action report for the *Hancock* air group stated, "coming back again and again simply results in pilots being shot down without appreciable increase in damage to targets."[15] Rather than sending in waves of relatively modest strikes preceded by fighter sweeps, the *Hancock* pilots suggested sending in just one or two all-out strikes by several hundred aircraft to maximize force and achieve tactical surprise. Essentially, they were advocating for the same strategy used by the IJN at Pearl Harbor, where six carrier air groups had put eight heavily armored battleships out of commission in a two-wave surprise airstrike. In contrast, TF 38 had employed *thirteen* carrier air groups, but lost the element of tactical surprise on the morning of January 15. The four strikes sent in the next day had only managed to wreck four tankers, plus a handful of small-fry naval and merchant vessels.[16]

Moreover, VF-7 pilots from the *Hancock* had strafed neutral Macau three times, while VF-44 pilots from the *Langley* had killed fourteen Allied internees in Hong Kong and injured at least six more. Things had even gone bad for the lifeguard submarine USS *Guardfish*. As the *Guardfish* approached Guam on January 24 at the end of its tenth war patrol, Commander Hammond and his executive officer mistook the silhouette of the rescue and salvage ship USS *Extractor* for the outline of a surfaced Japanese submarine. Commander Hammond fired four Mark 18 torpedoes in the half-light of dawn and scored two hits. Fatally holed, the wooden-hulled vessel kicked up its stern with its twin screws still turning and then plunged beneath the waves bow first, taking with it six American sailors and the reputation of an accomplished submarine captain. After surfacing, the *Guardfish* rescued the captain of the *Extractor*, Lt. Horace M. Babcock, and seventy-two crewmen.[17] Since both ships belonged to the U.S. Navy, the friendly fire incident – the first of its kind – would remain an in-house problem investigated by the navy and for the navy during a court of inquiry to be held aboard the seaplane tender USS *Curtiss* in Apra Harbor, Guam. In contrast, the strafing runs on neutral Macau had all but guaranteed strong protests from Portugal, which precluded an in-house inquiry. Any investigation would have to involve not just the navy, but also a small army of diplomats and politicians in both Washington and Lisbon.

Nobody in TF 38 thought about what London would say about the bombing of the Stanley internment camp, since nobody in the navy seemed to know that American carrier planes had killed British noncombatants in a small building known as Bungalow C. The eight VF-44 pilots from the *Langley* who had attacked targets in and around the Stanley Peninsula certainly had no idea that they had killed any civilians, much less Allied civilians. The casualty count could easily have been higher, given the amount of ordnance expended. One pilot had been unable to release his bomb due to a technical malfunction, and one of the rocket-armed aircraft had carried four instead of the usual six rockets. Therefore, in total the eight Hellcats had dropped three 500-pound bombs, launched twenty-two 5-inch rockets, and fired approximately 5,500 .50-caliber rounds while attacking targets on the Stanley Peninsula and in Stanley Bay. The bomb-damage assessment in the *Langley* action report stated that a tanker and lighter had been "rocketed and set afire." As for the land targets, the report stated, "On 16 January, barracks at Hong Kong were rocketed and two 500# GP hits made."[*] The report noted that the barracks were "seen to smoke" and concluded that the buildings had been "rendered unserviceable" by the bombing.[18] In all likelihood, Bungalow C had been hit by one of the two 500-pound bombs dropped by the pilots in Lieutenant Abernathy's division of Hellcats, who assumed they were targeting a Japanese barracks.

Rather than an accident, as Ray Jones and the internees believed, the bombing of Bungalow C had been an intentional act by the pilots of VF-44. However, the airstrike had not been a premeditated attack on civilians, as claimed by the stories published in the *Hongkong News*. Rather, the pilots had thought they were attacking legitimate military targets – a small ship with a lighter in attendance and a barracks compound. According to the aircraft action report compiled by the squadron ACI officer, Lt. (j.g.) E.E. Speight, the pilots had never targeted any antiaircraft positions. The pilots stated that they had not encountered medium or heavy flak over the Stanley Peninsula, and while they did notice antiaircraft fire from machine guns and small arms, they judged this ground fire to be single-X "meager." In short, they had never observed any antiaircraft weapons worth attacking, so the bomb that hit Bungalow C had not been meant for a Japanese gun position, as many of the internees assumed. Rather, it had been meant for a building within the camp fence or Stanley Prison.

Possibly the bungalow had been hit by the single bomb dropped by Lieutenant Brunmier on the grounded tanker in Stanley Bay, though this scenario remained less plausible. Had such an errant bomb strike

---

[*]In U.S. Navy action reports, "#" was often used as an abbreviation for "pound."

occurred, it likely would have been observed by Brunmier or the other pilots in his division and been included in the tally of bomb hits on the presumed barracks compound. The aircraft action report, however, recorded Brunmier's bomb as an unambiguous miss that, presumably, detonated in the water. A rocket strike remained another possibility, though eyewitness internee accounts consistently stated the bungalow had been struck by a bomb. Whether the pilots had aimed specifically at Bungalow C or another building within the camp perimeter and whether they had used a bomb or rocket remained open questions, but largely beside the point when considered in the larger context of the airstrike, which had purposefully targeted camp and prison buildings.

As the aircraft action report made clear, the pilots had never been confused about the location of their targets. They had understood that they were attacking targets in Stanley Bay and on the Stanley Peninsula, presumably because Lieutenant Speight aboard the *Langley* had briefed them on the geography of Hong Kong Island. Exactly why the VF-44 pilots had identified the Stanley camp as a military facility therefore remained unclear, particularly since action reports filed by other aircraft carriers after the strike on Hong Kong suggested that intelligence officers knew of the location of prison camps in Hong Kong. Some and perhaps even most of the pilots assigned to fly missions over Hong Kong had been briefed on the location of the Sham Shui Po and Argyle Street POW camps. Chalkboard drawings of Victoria Harbor studied by pilots aboard the *Hornet* before the airstrikes featured prominent white rectangles that marked both camps, for example. As a result of this briefing and similar ones conducted in ready rooms across the fleet, pilots from TF 38 had never once attacked the Sham Shui Po POW camp despite its proximity to significant targets like the Cosmopolitan dockyard and the Lai Chi Kok oil storage facility.[19] Intelligence officers had apparently known the location of the civilian camp at Stanley as well. The action report for the aircraft carrier USS *Cabot* contained, for example, an aerial photograph of the Stanley camp taken by one of its aircraft on January 16. Intelligence staff had unambiguously captioned the photo as "Camp Stanley, Allied POW Camp on Hong Kong."[20]

Despite the ready availability of accurate intelligence information on prison camps in Hong Kong, however, the VF-44 aircraft action report for the airstrike on Stanley Bay and the Stanley Peninsula made no mention of the Stanley camp or prison. Similarly, the action report for the *Langley* that summarized the airstrikes launched by the ship's air group during Operation *Gratitude* never mentioned the camp or prison at Stanley. Possibly Lieutenant Speight and the other ACI officers aboard the *Langley* had known of the Stanley camp but had been unable to adequately brief the pilots due to the rapid pace of combat operations on January 15 and 16. Alternatively, the pilots might have been briefed but misunderstood the location of the camp, or simply failed to recognize the information as important. The fact that many maps of Victoria Harbor – including the chalkboard mockups of the sort used in the *Hornet* ready room – did not include the southern coast of Hong Kong Island and the Stanley Peninsula would not have helped.[21]

Regardless of the reason, however, the Hellcat pilots of VF-44 remained unaware of the presence of Allied civilians on the Stanley Peninsula. Since the pilots had been assigned to fly a fighter sweep during which they could select targets of opportunity, the resultant friendly fire incident was not surprising. The incident and its deadly outcome was not inevitable, however, and likely stemmed from the failure of the ACI officers to adequately brief VF-44 pilots on the location of prison camps in Hong Kong. Such a briefing failure remained plausible, particularly in the context of the briefing errors that had caused so much confusion about Macau's neutral status and led to multiple airstrikes on the Portuguese colony. The Japanese, however, shared in the culpability, since the camp administration had not allowed the internees to construct air-raid shelters or to mark the camp with white crosses, which might have convinced the VF-44 pilots to break off their attack. In the final analysis, the bombing of Bungalow C and the resultant deaths of fourteen Allied civilians had been entirely preventable.

23

The Navy Department Deeply Regrets to Inform You

At the Stanley camp everything remained in short supply – shoes, salt, tea, toothbrushes, and all the other accoutrements of peacetime civilian life. Internees tasked with the burial of the fourteen people killed at Bungalow C sewed the bodies up in rice sacks, since building coffins would have reduced the camp's precious supply of plank wood, much of it stripped from floors and window frames and all of it needed to fuel the cooking fires of the camp kitchen. At 4:00 p.m. on January 17, 1945, just twenty-four hours after the bombing, the burial detail lowered the bodies into a communal grave and covered them with a blanket of rust-orange soil. Only close family and friends attended the burial service along with Catholic and Protestant clergy, but the entire camp planned to attend a Sunday memorial service four days later.

Three hand-carved tombstones marked the location of the graves along the southern edge of the Stanley cemetery. The grave markers listed the names of the dead, who ranged in age from thirty-seven to fifty-seven and represented a broad cross-section of prewar expatriate life as well as the camp community. Some had served in the colonial administration, such as the multilingual Stephen Balfour and building inspector Adam Holland of the Public Works Department. Others had worked for local firms, such as Albert Dennis and Alexander "Alec" Hyde-Lay, both employees of Dodwell and Company. Aileen "Penny" Guerin had worked as a passenger and shipping agent for Butterfield and Swire, while Oscar Eager had served as the Company Secretary of the Hong Kong Land

Investment Company. Sydney Bishop had been employed by the Green Island Cement Company in Hung Hom, Margaret Davies – "Peggy" to family and friends – had been a schoolteacher, George Stopani-Thomson had been in the pay of the Hong Kong Electric Company, and George Willoughby had worked as a pharmacist for Watson's.

Entire families had been shredded and splintered by the bomb blast. Alec Hyde-Lay and his wife Betty had died together, and so had Edward and Mabel Searle. An American citizen, Edward had declined repatriation aboard the *Gripsholm* in 1942 so that he could stay in the camp with his British wife. Stopani-Thomson, Bishop, and Dennis all left widows who had been evacuated to Australia before the start of the war, and two of the men left children behind as well. Holland's death amplified the grief of his three adult children, who had already lost their mother to a Japanese bullet during the invasion of Hong Kong in December 1941. Eager's death compounded the sorrow of his daughter-in-law, a widow who remained in the camp with her four children. Her husband had died defending Hong Kong when his motor torpedo boat went down with all hands in Victoria Harbor on December 19, 1941. Isabella Johnson had already buried her husband, who had died of tuberculosis in October 1944. He had been buried in the Stanley cemetery, and now his wife Bella had also been laid to rest in the same cemetery beneath a granite headstone carved with the words, "Killed during an air raid 16 January 1945."[1]

Convoy Hi-87 had been reduced to a single tanker, the *Sarawak Maru*. The vessel had been berthed at Pier 3 on the Kowloon waterfront, and this had apparently allowed it to escape the attention of U.S. Navy pilots briefed to hit tankers riding at anchor in the harbor. In the company of four escort vessels, the *Sarawak* cast off its lines at 7:30 p.m. on January 17, just a few hours after the burials at the Stanley camp. Under cold and clear weather conditions, the *Sarawak* left Victoria Harbor and set course for Singapore as part of the redesignated convoy Hi-87A. The escorts included the destroyer *Shigure* as well as the smaller escort vessels *CD-13*, *Miyake*, and *Kanju*, though Lieutenant Commander Yatsui had been left behind in Hong Kong with scores of other injured personnel. The dead went to Stonecutters Island, where gravediggers interred the remains of at least 150 Japanese naval and merchant marine personnel killed during the air raids.[2]

Task Force 38 had withdrawn from its position off Hong Kong, which allowed convoy Hi-87A to slip south to Hainan. Two days later the ships reached the port of Yulin on the southern tip of the island, where the *Sarawak Maru* embarked 440 men from the IJA, and the gunners aboard the escort vessels replenished their stock of 25mm antiaircraft shells. After taking on precious bunker fuel and additional provisions, the five-ship convoy resumed course for Singapore at dusk on January 20.

On January 16, meanwhile, TU 30.8.10 under the command of Captain Acuff rendezvoused off Mindoro with a relief service group, codenamed TU 30.8.11, to swap its six empty oilers for eight AOs brimful with bunker fuel and avgas. Acuff remained in the South China Sea with TU 30.8.11, which in addition to the eight oilers included two transport carriers, two escort carriers, nine destroyers, and a single plucky destroyer escort. TU 30.8.10 exited the South China Sea via the Surigao Strait, which bisected the southern Philippine islands and offered the most expedient course back to Ulithi, where the oilers would be reloaded for future at-sea deliveries.[3]

Captain Acuff and TU 30.8.11 linked up with TF 38, which had plowed across the South China Sea towards the Philippines on January 17, but heavy seas and 50mph winds precluded replenishment at sea. Accompanied by the service group, TF 38 carved a zigzagging course in search of calmer weather, which it finally found offshore from Luzon on January 19. All eight oilers commenced refueling operations while the transport carriers deployed new aircraft to the fast carriers. VB-3 pilots from the *Yorktown* retrieved three SB2C-4s from the transport carriers to make up for the losses suffered by the squadron during Operation *Gratitude*. At the same time, replacement personnel came aboard via breeches buoy to fill in for the pilots and gunners who had been shot down in January, including John Lavender and Jean Balch.[4] After transferring the fuel, men, and machines necessary for continuing the grim business of war, TU 30.8.11 disengaged from TF 38 and prepared to exit the South China Sea by threading the Surigao Strait.

The battlewagons and flattops of TF 38 continued on a northern bearing towards the gap between Formosa and Luzon, a wide-open doorway that offered the sea room necessary for a task force consisting of nearly a hundred ships. On the night of January 20–21, the fast carriers exited the South China Sea the same way they had come in, via the Luzon Strait. Every warship that had gone into the South China Sea with TF 38 and the special service groups of TG 30.8 had come out again, a bit battered by the heavy swells in some cases but entirely unscathed by enemy action. No enemy aircraft had ever made it closer than twenty miles from the fleet, in fact. IJN submarine skippers and the wily captains of the *Ise* and *Hyuga* had never even tried to approach TF 38. The two battleship-carriers had remained at anchor near Singapore, their truncated flight decks empty of aircraft. None of the IJN cruisers and destroyers in Singapore had sortied for the Philippines either.

At dawn on January 21, Admiral Halsey ordered another round of strikes against targets on Formosa from a position to the east of the island in the open Pacific. At this point, the good luck of TF 38 finally ran out. A pair of *kamikaze* aircraft plowed into the fleet carrier *Ticonderoga* at noon, killing 143 members of the crew and curtailing further flight operations, while the light carrier *Langley* sustained minor damage from a 100-pound bomb that killed one particularly unlucky sailor. Another *kamikaze* damaged the destroyer *Maddox*, which had to leave the fleet for repairs at Ulithi. Aboard the *Hancock*, a 500-pound bomb carried by one of its own TBM Avengers accidentally detonated on the flight deck, killing more than fifty members of the ship's complement, but efficient damage control allowed the carrier to resume flight operations later that day. On January 22, the fleet raided Okinawa and other islands in the Nansei Shoto chain at the extreme southern end of the Japanese home islands, and then TF 38 retired to Ulithi and Operation *Gratitude* drew to a close. While damage to the warships of TF 38 had been relatively light – one fleet carrier and one destroyer out of action and a second fleet carrier damaged but still operational – casualties among the carrier air groups had been heavy, with ninety-two aircraft shot down and another ninety-eight lost to causes other than enemy action. A total of 161 pilots and airmen had been listed as killed in action or, in the majority of cases, as missing in action.[5]

Twenty-one aircraft had been shot down by antiaircraft fire over Hong Kong and Canton on January 15 and 16. Sixteen of these planes had come from TF 38, with five more from the 118th Tactical Reconnaissance Squadron of the 14th Air Force. In addition, the TBMs piloted by Lieutenant Hunt and Lieutenant Scobell of the *Hancock* had been lost in a midair collision over Hong Kong Island that had likely resulted from antiaircraft fire as well. An F6F-5N had vanished during a nocturnal mission over the Pearl River delta, cause unknown. Six more planes had been wrecked in carrier landing accidents and other operational mishaps. At least one battle-damaged plane had been jettisoned as well, bringing the total bill to thirty-one aircraft. The human cost had been far more grievous, with forty-one American pilots and airmen classified as missing in action – five from the army and thirty-six from the navy – after they failed to return from strikes on Hong Kong and Canton on January 15 and 16.

Across the United States, telegrams addressed to the spouses, parents, and siblings of men lost over Hong Kong arrived from the navy. In all caps, each telegram delivered the same stark message, identical except for the name and rank of the missing aviator. In Abilene, the parents of Jean Balch received an eighty-four-word telegram from Vice Admiral Randall Jacobs, Chief of Naval Personnel, that read as follows:

> The Navy Department deeply regrets to inform you that your son Jean Felton Balch Aviation Radioman Third Class USNR is missing following action while in the service of his country. The Department appreciates your great anxiety but details not now available and delay in receipt thereof must necessarily be expected. To prevent possible aid to our enemies please do not divulge the name of his ship or station.[6]

Commanding officers followed up on the telegrams with their own letters to family members of the men who had disappeared over Hong Kong. Understanding that the designation of missing in action could foster unrealistic hopes, Commander Lowe of VB-3 wrote to the parents of Lieutenant Lavender to offer his condolences and an unvarnished assessment of their son's fate:

> You have by this time doubtless received the telegram from the Secretary of the Navy containing the sad news concerning John, or "Lav" as he was called by most of us. I wish that it were possible for me to offer you more cause for hope than was conveyed in the telegram but regret that nothing has been heard of him since the date he was lost. I am writing this letter to give you, whose loss is greatest, the deep-felt sympathies of his friends in Bombing Squadron Three.

After providing a brief synopsis of Lieutenant Lavender's final mission over Hong Kong and a promise to write again with details about the settlement of their son's National Service Life Insurance and the shipment of his personal belongings back to Texarkana, Lowe wrote: "Your son was a trustworthy, diligent, sensible, and courageous young man and an excellent pilot. He was liked and admired by every member of the squadron. Believe me when I say that he is a real credit to the squadron, to the Naval Service, and to you."[7]

As his letter made clear, experience had taught Commander Lowe that pilots and aircrew rarely survived a shoot-down over an enemy port, and in actuality the majority of the aviators who had gone missing over the Pearl River delta had, in fact, been killed. However, at least four had been captured, including Jean Balch.

Balch had spent his first night in captivity in a cell in Stanley Prison. He sat on the floor for the entire day that followed without any food or water, and then endured another evening question-and-answer session with the Japanese officer who smoked Pirate-brand cigarettes. This experience went no better than the previous interrogation, and Balch returned to his cell so blood-encrusted that his torn-up shirt and dungarees wound up glued to his flesh like a skin graft.

On the morning of January 18, the guards brought Balch out to an open area of the compound that apparently functioned as the prison laundry. They ordered him to strip down and put on a clean white *fundoshi* – the thong-like underwear worn by Japanese men – and a white kimono. The guards then positioned him so that he faced a prison wall in preparation for, he assumed, his execution by firing squad. As he stood in his white kimono, he heard the guards conversing in Japanese behind him, though he had no way of ascertaining the topic of their conversation. They might have been discussing the weather or they might have been debating whether to kill the American with a sword or a rifle. After what seemed like a very long time, the guards stopped talking and shoved Balch back towards his pile of blood-stiffened clothes. They gestured for him to take off the *fundoshi* and kimono and made it clear that he should put his shirt and navy dungarees back on. Mystified by the etiquette of Japanese firing squads, which appeared to require that condemned prisoners be shot in clean underwear, Balch climbed into a truck as ordered. The guards then loaded up two more American prisoners – Richard Hunt of VT-7 and Alvin Hughes of VB-7, both from the *Hancock*.

Lieutenant Hunt had parachuted into the Tai Tam Valley after his TBM had collided with the machine flown by Lieutenant Scobell during Strike 2C. The sole survivor of the six men aboard the two aircraft, Hunt had been captured shortly after he hit the ground. When the Japanese brought him to Stanley Prison, Hunt had a puncture wound in his fractured left arm and severe burns on his right arm as well as his lower legs. Additional burns marred his chest, back, shoulders, and face. Despite his condition, he received no medical treatment.

Alvin Hughes had bailed out about an hour after Balch and Hunt during Strike 2D and been pulled from the harbor by Japanese sailors, his belly full of saltwater and his neck and face blistered with burns. His rescuers had given him a thorough working over before delivering him to Stanley Prison.[8] Like Balch, Hughes had been a gunner in a Helldiver. Though they belonged to different squadrons, the two airmen held the same rating – ARM3c – and had gone through the same radio and radar training in Memphis and gunnery school in Florida. Most significantly, perhaps, both men came from families rooted in Texas – Abilene for Balch, and Houston for Hughes. At nineteen, the blond-haired, blue-eyed Hughes was the youngest of the three men, and Balch could see that he was terrified of his Japanese captors.

With guards in attendance, the three naval aviators rode up and over the mountainous center of Hong Kong Island. Hunt groaned in pain as the truck shuddered over rough patches of roadway and headed downhill to the harbor, where a launch conveyed the prisoners out to a small warship that had likely been a former member of convoy Hi-87. Handcuffed to steam pipes and stanchions in the bowels of the hull, the three men soon felt the vibration of the engines. When the warship began rolling, they knew that they had put to sea on what they presumed to be the first leg of a perilous journey to a POW camp in Japan.[9]

Hunt, Balch, and Hughes had all been forced to bail out over Hong Kong Island or Victoria Harbor. However, a number of pilots had been able to nurse wounded aircraft either inland or out to sea before ditching or pulling the ripcord, including Ensign Crehan of VF-11. He had abandoned his burning Hellcat, parachuted into the water near the Lema Archipelago south of Hong Kong, and then started swimming towards a distant smudge of land that never seemed to get any closer.

After three hours of dogpaddling in his Mae West, strong hands reached down from a fishing junk to haul Crehan from the water like an exotic fish. Forgoing the bounty offered by the Japanese for downed American fliers, the junk crew presented its catch instead to the local communist military outfit, the Hong Kong and Kowloon Independent Brigade (HKKIB). A guerrilla unit consisting of Cantonese irregulars fighting on their home turf, the HKKIB remained well positioned to facilitate the escape and evasion of American aviators. As soon as Crehan stepped foot on dry land, a detachment of guerrillas from the HKKIB shepherded the ensign to the village of Ping Shan in the New Territories. There they introduced him to Merrill Ady, the former missionary who had been interned in the Stanley camp at the start of the war and then repatriated aboard the *Asama Maru* with most of the American civilians in 1942. A fluent Chinese speaker, he had been eager to return to China, and an assignment with the American Office of Strategic Services (OSS) had proven the most expedient way to get there. Along with OSS agent Ady, who had just turned forty-nine, Crehan also met his much younger guest: 1st Lt. John F. Egan, the Mustang pilot from the 118th TRS who had been hit by flak over Hong Kong on January 16 and bailed out over the New Territories. He had landed in some brush pinned to the side of a steep slope, uninjured aside from a bloody but superficial head wound. Like Crehan, Egan had been collected by the communists and brought to Ady, who impressed both pilots with the miracle of his perfect Chinese. Ady also possessed a radio, which allowed him to report that both Egan and Crehan were alive and in friendly hands.

Accompanied by the multilingual OSS agent and a bodyguard of communist soldiers, Crehan and Egan began their "walkout," a term used by 14th Air Force pilots to describe the arduous overland journeys of downed pilots who had trekked through Japanese lines to the safety of free China. On March 11, Ady and the communists handed the two pilots over to a unit of Nationalist guerrillas, who in turn passed the army-navy duo on to agents of the BAAG. On March 13, the BAAG presented Crehan and Egan to Lt. Cdr. Saxe P. Gantz, a U.S. Navy officer attached to yet another special operations unit known as Naval Group China. By March 28, the exhausted pilots had reached Kunming, headquarters of General Chennault's 14th Air Force. Like so many of Chennault's missing-in-action aviators, Ensign Crehan and 1st Lt. Egan had returned from the dead after an epic walkout.[10]

24

Houseguests

Pang Meng worked the ropes and rudder with his callused hands as the ramparts of the Fortaleza da Barra beneath Barra Hill slid past to his starboard. For centuries, the iron cannons of the Portuguese fortress had guarded Barra Point at the mouth of Macau's Inner Harbor against pirates and rival colonial powers, though by 1945 the waterfront battlements had become a military anachronism. Portuguese neutrality rather than force of arms had protected Macau from invasion by the Japanese military, though plenty of Japanese agents operated in Macau – Kempeitai, military intelligence, and diplomats, plus the local triad gangs, pirates, and informants in their pay. Pang knew he would have to be vigilant. His junk ghosted silently past the sleepy Portuguese navy yard next, and soon the red walls of the A-Ma Temple hove into view as his vessel, which served as his livelihood as well as his home, slipped into the Inner Harbor on the morning of January 17. Cocooned beneath the bilge boards, Ensign Clark and his two crewmen could hear the water gurgling against the wooden planks of the hull. Pang breathed easier now that he had reached the relative safety of Macau. He had wagered his life that he could get the Americans to the Portuguese colony without interception by the Japanese and without his Cantonese passengers betraying the presence of the human contraband stowed away below deck. His passengers wanted to turn the Americans over to the Japanese for the bounty – rumored to be the equivalent of 20,000 U.S. dollars – but Pang had refused to consider any deal with the "turnip heads." He convinced the two passengers to remain silent by reminding them that the blood chit carried by the Americans promised a handsome reward for anyone who helped them escape from the Japanese and their puppets.[1]

Pang secured the junk to a pier, and an elderly Chinese man who claimed to own the vessel came aboard. He examined the blood chit provided by Ensign Clark and agreed to forward a message penned by the American to Consul Reeves, who received the note with considerable skepticism. In a city where wartime intrigue swirled thicker than the joss smoke at the A-Ma Temple, Reeves knew he could not accept the missive at face value. He subjected the note-bearer to an extended interrogation before accepting Clark's message as genuine. Reeves sent instructions that the American airmen should consign their flight suits to the deep and change into the local garb that the British consul would arrange to have sent to them. Once they had donned their disguises, Reeves would have his driver bring them to the British consulate in his car that evening. In gratitude for their assistance, Clark gave Pang and the other two men on the junk a .38-caliber revolver, two knives, and some of the escape-and-evasion cash that Clark had been issued before leaving the *Cowpens*.[2]

In the early evening, Pang landed the three aviators on a wharf, where two men – one Chinese and one Portuguese – waited in the British consul's sedan. After a short drive through the narrow, labyrinthine streets of Macau, Ensign Clark and his two crewmen arrived at the consulate on a steeply pitched backstreet known as Calçada do Gaio.[3] They wore ill-fitting Chinese clothes, and one of the men walked in barefoot. Though hungry, unkempt, and smelling of bilge water, the Americans were uninjured and in good spirits. Reeves rewarded Pang with 1,000 Macanese patacas and bought the silence of his two passengers by dolling out similar cash payments to each of them.[4]

A party ensued behind the shuttered windows of the British consulate, which enjoyed the protection of Nationalist Chinese bodyguards detailed to protect Reeves from an assassin's bullet. He had already dodged one attempted hit by an unidentified sniper, either Japanese or someone in their pay. The gunman had aimed at the study window of the consulate and fired two rounds, which had missed Reeves but punched two neat holes through the door of a carved blackwood cabinet.[5] The shell holes that had been drilled into the Avenger flown by Ensign Clark had been far less tidy, but he and his two crewmen nonetheless had much to celebrate. They had survived a flak-induced water landing, and they had avoided apprehension by an enemy who routinely tortured and executed captured American fliers. Moreover, they had enjoyed their first shower and proper meal since their launch from the *Cowpens*. For his part, Reeves appreciated having new conversational partners, since he had not talked to anyone from "outside" in three years. He certainly had a great deal to catch up on, from the latest war news to the current hit songs.[6]

The next day Reeves arranged a surreptitious tour of Macau for his American guests, the itinerary of which included the burnt-out hangar at the Macau Naval Aviation Center. He also moved the three aviators from the consulate to *Skyline*, the house on Penha Hill that served as the residence for Reeves, his wife Rhoda, and their eight-year-old daughter Letitia. A house that functioned as the headquarters of Japanese military intelligence in Macau sat just a few hundred feet away, though this proximity hardly mattered since the Japanese could have been anywhere in the diminutive colony and still have been counted as neighbors.[7]

Later that evening a bedraggled Lt. (j.g.) Albert Basmajian joined Reeves and his three fellow aviators at *Skyline*, where he recounted an escape-and-evasion story quite similar to the one told by Clark and his two crewmen. He had drifted in his life raft after ditching his F6, unsure of his next move, while a division of Hellcats from VF-81 buzzed overhead. Though he did not know how long he could remain undetected, the Japanese had apparently failed to notice that he was down in the water. Other more observant eyes had spotted the lone figure in the raft, however, and two hours after Basmajian had scrambled free of his sinking Grumman a young Chinese boy in a hat and blue denim approached in a sampan not much larger than the aviator's one-man raft. Basmajian and the boy shared no common language, but the lieutenant judged that he could trust the youth and accepted the invitation to climb into the sampan.[8]

With the ease of someone who had grown up on the water, the boy sculled the sampan with life raft in tow to a nearby island – probably Lingting, but perhaps one of the islets to its south – where his family's junk swung at anchor with the tide. The boy's parents ushered Basmajian below deck and hid him beneath the bilge boards between the ribs of the hull. He spent the night on the junk, which set sail at dawn and headed west as the rays of the morning sun painted its raised stern with light.

At noon, the junk anchored near another island, and a guerrilla leader from the HKKIB or its parent unit, the East River Column, came aboard, apparently to confirm that the boy and his family had, in fact, hauled an American pilot from the sea. Satisfied with Basmajian's bona fides, the leader soon departed, but another guerrilla fighter boarded the ship at dusk and communicated to Basmajian that he would be taken to Macau. The junk raised sail after nightfall and arrived at the Portuguese colony just after midnight on January 18. An elderly man that Basmajian understood to be the owner of the fishing junk came aboard, and the lieutenant explained that he wanted to make contact with Nationalist troops or agents of the British or Americans.[9]

Though Basmajian would not have known this at the time, the old man had already helped deliver Clark, Mize, and Myers to Consul Reeves and was likely an agent of the BAAG, or the Nationalists, or the Portuguese.[*] The man arranged for a note from Basmajian to be delivered to Reeves, who sent his own note back to the lieutenant on the letterhead of the British consul. The note asked Basmajian several questions about navy terminology to test his authenticity. Basmajian answered the questions and returned the note to Reeves, who found the answers convincing. The consul penned a reply to the American that instructed him to change into whatever Chinese clothes he could find in preparation for an evening pick up. As instructed, Basmajian smeared his face with soot and changed into the rough-spun clothing worn by the junk crews. After nightfall, two boys led him through a series of narrow alleys to a parked car, which belonged to the consul. A pair of armed Chinese agents drove Basmajian to the front door of the British consulate. There he met Reeves, who offered him food and drink as well as a shower and clean civilian clothes. They then drove up to Skyline, where Basmajian met Ensign Clark and his crew.[10]

As the party continued at Skyline, Reeves conducted a postmortem on the destruction of the seaplane hangar and cache of aviation fuel. Rumors of uncertain origin now claimed that Consul Reeves had conspired with the U.S. Navy to destroy the fuel supply in the naval hangar and prevent its purchase by the Japanese. He found this notion ridiculous, since he would not have needed to requisition the services of

---

[*]The age and identity of the elderly man remains unknown.

a carrier air group to destroy the aviation fuel when the flare of a single well-placed match would have done the job. However, he did wonder why Macau had been subjected to three airstrikes in a single day. Clark and Basmajian explained that their air groups had not been assigned missions involving Macau, and that this likely explained why the ACI officers back on the *Cowpens* and the *Wasp* had never briefed them on Macau's neutral status or familiarized them with the Portuguese flag. Reeves concluded that the American pilots who had inflicted so much violence on the seaplane facility had never been briefed on Macau's neutrality either. He figured they had assumed the entire Pearl River delta belonged to the Japanese, and that any airfield or seaplane base in the region was fair game.[11]

As British consul, Reeves devoted a great deal of his time, energy, and financial resources to the welfare of the 10,000 British subjects who had fled Hong Kong and taken refuge in Macau. At the request of the U.S. State Department, he also rendered aid to American civilians who had taken haven in the colony and represented American business interests.[12] However, he dabbled in BAAG-related intrigues as well, so he knew whom to contact for help with spiriting his visitors out of Macau. He also maintained a close relationship with Governor Teixeira, who telephoned Reeves on January 19 to inquire about the rumors that several American aviators had arrived in Macau. Reeves knew that the governor could be trusted, so he readily admitted that he had four U.S. Navy aviators under his care, adding that he had concocted a rather implausible cover story that they were American civilian road engineers trapped in Macau by Japanese advances in Kwangtung Province. The rules of neutrality required that Teixeira intern American pilots who entered Macau, since releasing them would be seen as aiding the Allies, but he agreed to overlook the presence of the American airmen if Reeves could promise to quickly and discreetly smuggle them out to free China.[13]

Shortly thereafter, Colonel Sawa Eisaku pressed Governor Teixeira about the stories he had heard about American aviators hiding in Macau. Sawa commanded the Kempeitai detachment in Macau, which made him one of the most dangerous men in the colony. Understanding the stakes, the governor replied that any tales about American fliers amounted to just another idle rumor, and that he remained, of course, entirely unaware of any Allied pilots in Macau.

Despite this stonewalling by Teixeira, Reeves understood that his four aviators needed to vacate Macau as soon as possible, and that they would have to travel by sea because the Japanese kept careful watch on the colony's only border gate.[14]

Liang Yun-chang, the senior BAAG operative in Macau, prepared an escape plan with a rogue's gallery of accomplices that included José Maria "Jack" Braga, a covert agent and general manager of the Macau Water Company; a Nationalist guerrilla leader named Wong Kau; and Captain Alberto Carlos Rodrigues Ribeiro da Cunha, the chief of police in Macau. The ad-hoc team also included Pedro José Lobo, who had apparently chosen to forgive the U.S. Navy for machine-gunning his Dodge. For his part, Reeves pilfered the wardrobe of a businessman who had left Macau before the war and collected a mix of tweed suits and Palm Beach suits for the American airmen complemented by green porkpie hats.[*][15] Two sedans picked up the well-dressed aviators in the early morning hours of January 21, and Reeves and his wife had to say goodbye to the four young Americans, whom they had come to know on a first-name basis as Al, George, Don, and Chuck. A police officer drove one of the getaway cars, which facilitated the short drive down to the waterfront during the nightly curfew enforced by his comrades. As an unobtrusive cordon of trusted police kept watch, the four naval aviators boarded a Chinese junk, which soon ghosted out of Macau's Outer Harbor with a creak of rigging and the snap of a much-patched sail. Like Ensign Crehan and 1st Lt. Egan, the four houseguests of the British consul followed a well-established escape route and eventually made their way to free China.[16]

Consul Reeves received much of the credit for the operation. One BAAG officer summarized the escape-and-evasion story of the four American aviators in a top-secret report that ended with considerable praise for the British consul. "As far as can be seen from here," the officer stated, "the main credit goes to Reeves who diplomatically stuck his neck out to help the men in question and to whom I would take my hat, if I still had one, off for a very fine job of work."[17] Whether the

---

*One source suggests that the suits and porkpie hats came from the wardrobe of Frederick J. Gellion, the managing director of the Macau Electric Company who spent the war years in San Francisco. Gellion allowed Reeves to move into his home, Skyline, during the war.

BAAG officer had loaned out his hat or simply lost it to a stiff Chinese breeze remained unclear. However, BAAG officers did find themselves continually loaning out precious British uniforms to downed American pilots who arrived at BAAG offices clad in Chinese peasant motley or flight suits so ripped and filthy they could never be sufficiently patched or laundered. One message sent to Kunming from the advance headquarters of the BAAG requested the return of clothing provided to Ensign Crehan and 1st Lt. Egan, who had walked out with Merrill Ady, the OSS agent. Unlike Reeves, the OSS operative could not draw upon a wardrobe of spare suits and in fact possessed only the clothes on his back, so it fell to the BAAG to scrounge up uniforms befitting a navy ensign and an army first lieutenant. "Please recover our clothes loaned to them whilst theirs [are] being cleaned," said the rather plaintive note from BAAG advance headquarters.[18] The Palm Beach suits and porkpie hats sported by Basmajian, Clark, Mize, and Myers provoked considerable sartorial envy from the underdressed special operators of the BAAG, who lamented their own threadbare Chinese-cut suits. Service with the BAAG certainly had its rewards, but stylish attire did not number among them.

Eager Beavers

The hours just before dawn on January 24, 1945, found the submarine USS *Blackfin* cruising on the glassy surface of the Gulf of Siam under the command of Lt. Cdr. William L. Kitch, who stood on the open bridge atop the conning tower with the officer of the deck. Several lookouts were perched higher up in the periscope shears, alert for any sign of enemy ships or aircraft. At 5:02 a.m., the sailors operating the SJ surface-search radar reported two pips at a range of eleven miles. Lieutenant Commander Kitch immediately alerted the two other American submarines in his patrol area, the USS *Besugo* and the USS *Hardhead*. He then went to battle stations and increased speed to 17 knots (20mph) so that he could maneuver into attack position before sunrise caught his submarine on the surface. Kitch and the *Blackfin* had left Freemantle on January 2 for the ship's second war patrol with two dozen Mark 18 torpedoes and a complement of seventy-five men, all of them eager to savage Japanese ships. After three weeks at sea, they knew that their chance had finally come when they had closed to eight miles, and the mystery pips on the radarscope differentiated into one large and four small enemy vessels.

Lieutenant Commander Kitch and the crew of the *Blackfin* had found convoy Hi-87A, which had continued south from Hainan, traced the shoreline of Indochina, and pushed on across the Gulf of Siam. The early morning hours of January 24 found the blacked-out convoy moving down the coast of the Malay Peninsula at a speed of 14 knots (16mph). Like bodyguards huddling around a man marked for assassination, the destroyer *Shigure* and the escorts *Kanju, Miyake,* and *CD-13* ringed the tanker *Sarawak Maru*. Every measure had been taken to detect the presence of American submarines. Radar operators monitored mast-mounted Type 22 radar, soundmen pinged with active sonar, and lookouts with binoculars swept the horizon, which glowed with a luminous predawn indigo to the east.

"We are attacking on the surface," Lieutenant Commander Kitch radioed the *Besugo* and *Hardhead* at 5:50 a.m. Twenty minutes later, with the *Sarawak Maru* dead ahead and just a mile away, Lieutenant Commander Kitch ordered his fire-control team to launch three torpedoes. As soon as this first spread of fish had cleared the bow tubes Kitch shifted his attention to the *Shigure*, which had been steaming on the port quarter of the tanker while pinging with its active sonar. The destroyer had now closed to within a half mile of the *Blackfin*, which meant Kitch could not swing around to use his stern tubes on the *Sarawak* without first taking out the *Shigure*.

By this point Lieutenant Commander Hagiwara and the crew of the *Shigure* had detected the presence of an American submarine that may have been the *Besugo* commanded by Cdr. Thomas L. Wogan, who had started tracking the convoy after receiving the initial contact report from the *Blackfin*. However, the lookouts and radar operators aboard the destroyer never spotted the low, predatory profile of the *Blackfin*, or at least failed to spot the submarine until it was too late. This allowed Lieutenant Commander Kitch to find a favorable firing solution and launch two torpedoes less than a minute after firing the initial spread at the *Sarawak Maru*. Less than thirty seconds elapsed before one of the Mark 18s struck the destroyer amidships and detonated between the bridge and forward stack. Moments later one of the torpedoes speeding towards the *Sarawak* reached its more distant target and exploded against the number one hold near the bow, though from his position Lieutenant Commander Kitch could not see the hit because the thick scarf of gray smoke wrapping around the *Shigure* blocked his line of sight.

Lieutenant Commander Manubu must have known that the *Shigure* was doomed as the slate-colored smoke cocooning his ship darkened to an angry black. After weathering air attacks at Rabaul, running the gauntlet escorting merchant ships to Truk, and emerging as the sole survivor of the southern column at Leyte Gulf, the warship's long career closed with the most prosaic and ignominious of ends for a destroyer: to be sunk by a submarine, which was a bit like the snake killing the mongoose. In just ten minutes the *Shigure* slipped beneath the lazily viscous swells of the Gulf of Siam, leaving a greasy sheen of wreckage dotted with the heads of men floating in their lifebelts.

As the eastern horizon continued to brighten, the radar operator aboard the *Blackfin* confirmed that one target had vanished from the scope, but that the largest of the enemy ships remained afloat. Determined to sink the *Sarawak Maru*, Lieutenant Commander Kitch fired a third spread of three torpedoes from stern tube number seven, number eight, and, after number nine malfunctioned, number ten at the relatively close range of one and a half miles. Three minutes later he heard and saw a second hit on the stern of the tanker. Kitch then observed a brilliant flash on the deck of one of the Japanese escort ships as its gunners opened fire with a 4.7-inch deck gun. Almost instantaneously, a shell exploded near the *Blackfin* with a substantial boom. Two more followed in quick succession. Though none of the shells had landed close enough to the *Blackfin* to cause any harm, Kitch knew more volleys would soon be on the way. He gave the order to clear the bridge and submerge before the Japanese gunners found the range and put a shell through the pressure hull.

Commander Wogan of the *Besugo* had also been forced to submerge to periscope depth when one of the escorts – most likely the *CD-13* – altered course in his direction with obvious hostile intent. Determined to continue stalking the *Sarawak Maru*, Wogan gave the order to rig for silent running. Instantly the crew shut down fans, pumps, and other machinery that could be picked up on Japanese sound-detection gear. Conversation dropped to a whisper as the stealthy electric motors propelled the submarine towards the enemy tanker. Ten minutes after submerging, Wogan and his crew heard five depth charges rumbling nearby, though not in close enough proximity to harm their submarine. Wogan continued to approach the *Sarawak* at dead slow, but before he could get within two miles of the tanker he heard the blast of two more depth charges, which his crew referred to as "ash cans" on account of their barrel-like shape. When Wogan had closed to just over a mile, four more depth charges literally rocked the submarine on its keel as the fire-control party rapidly calculated a firing solution on the torpedo data computer. At 7:16 a.m., six Mark 18s raced from the bow tubes as Wogan monitored the target through the periscope. A minute later he observed a geyser of smoke and saltwater as the *Sarawak* absorbed a torpedo just forward of the stack.

The crew of the *CD-13* retaliated with five more depth charges. Knowing more ash cans would surely be coming, Wogan dove the *Besugo* to 140 feet. Ten more depth charges followed him down, including some that may have come from the *Kanju* and *Miyake*. When the *Besugo* hovered just above the seafloor at 180 feet, the *CD-13* pinpointed the location of the submarine and dropped four depth charges that detonated close enough to cause minor damage and jolt Wogan and his crew with an adrenaline-fueled, tunnel-vision scare of the sort that only imminent death in combat can produce. Just when it seemed that *CD-13* would score a direct hit, however, the *Besugo* crept away like an undersea phantom, and the sonar operators aboard the escort vessels lost the scent.

Aboard the *Blackfin*, meanwhile, the crew reloaded the torpedo tubes, brought the malfunctioning number nine tube back on line, and celebrated their victory even as they heard the distant rumble of depth charges. Lieutenant Commander Kitch took the submarine back up to the surface at 8:37 a.m. to finish off the *Sarawak Maru*. However, while he spotted a tanker and an escort zigzagging in the approximate location where he had torpedoed the *Sarawak*, the two vessels were making 16 knots (18mph). Kitch concluded that he had sighted a second tanker, since he doubted the *Sarawak* could absorb multiple Torpex warheads and still maintain such a speed. Before he could close to firing range, however, the SD air-search radar detected an unidentified aircraft approaching, which forced Kitch to sound the dive klaxon and take the *Blackfin* back under the waves. He knew he had likely lost his chance to attack the tanker, since his submarine could not make anything close to 16 knots when submerged. Kitch brought the *Blackfin* back up to the surface ninety minutes later and immediately saw that he would never catch up with the tanker before it reached the safety of Singapore, where the shallow waters and harbor defenses precluded submarine attacks.

Lieutenant Commander Kitch had in fact spotted the *Sarawak Maru*, which had continued south under its own power in the company of the *CD-13*. By this point, convoy Hi-87A had divided itself in two, with the *Kanju* and *Miyake* doubling back in search of the missing *Shigure*. The two *kaibōkan* soon discovered survivors from the sunken destroyer drifting in an oily debris field and took some 270 men aboard, including Lieutenant Commander Manubu, who had apparently concluded that going down with his ship would not help the Japanese war effort. However, his headcount determined that thirty-seven members of his crew had been lost with the *Shigure*.

At dusk, the *Blackfin* observed two escort vessels of a size and profile that matched the *Kanju* and the *Miyake*. In turn, the lookouts and radar operators aboard the two warships spotted the surfaced American submarine and sounded the alert. Gun crews manning the forward batteries opened fire with their 4.7-inch deck guns, which packed sufficient destructive power to disable or even sink a submarine with a direct hit. All five salvoes fell short of the *Blackfin*, however, though the enthusiastic shellfire nonetheless prompted the officer who would compile the submarine's war patrol report to opine, "These people are certainly eager beavers with their deck guns." Since Kitch thought it imprudent to close on the surface while under fire, and in any case had orders to take up a lifeguard station for downed pilots off Saigon, he broke off the engagement and watched the two warships melt into the gathering darkness.

The *Kanju* and *Miyake* rejoined the *CD-13* and the *Sarawak Maru* after the skirmish with the *Blackfin*. Though Lieutenant Commander Kitch and Commander Wogan believed they had torpedoed the *Sarawak* three times, the tanker could still steam under its own power at a brisk pace, which suggested the vessel had actually absorbed fewer hits. Ringed by a diminished phalanx of escorts, the *Sarawak* proceeded south down the Malayan coast without further incident. On January 26, ten days after leaving Hong Kong, the *Sarawak* and three escort vessels – all that remained of convoy Hi-87 – straggled into port at Singapore. The *Sarawak* put in for repairs at the Seletar Naval Base and the survivors of the *Shigure* came ashore, including Lieutenant Commander Hagiwara, who would later assume command of the destroyer *Kashi*.[1]

The saga of the *Sarawak Maru* and the fast tanker convoys had not yet ended, however. At the Seletar Naval Base the 101st Repair Unit, which had put the *Sarawak* back together the last time it had rendezvoused with an American torpedo, worked to patch the holes punched in the vessel's hull.[2] By mid-March the *Sarawak* had been repaired and assigned to northbound convoy Hi-88J, the last of the fast tanker convoys to attempt to run the blockade back to Japan. Laden with 4,400 tons of crude, 690 tons of rubber, and 116 tons of tin, the *Sarawak* departed Singapore on March 19 and promptly triggered a magnetic mine that ripped open the hull like a gigantic can opener. Seeing no other alternative, the captain beached the ship. With a creak of buckling hull plates, the tanker settled in shallow water, the decks dry and crew safe, but keel affixed to the muddy glue of the seafloor. Convoy Hi-88J, consisting of six merchant vessels and six naval escorts led by Commander Yasuhiro Hirano, steamed northwards without the *Sarawak*. Three days later the abandoned hulk rolled over to port and slid beneath the waves.[3]

26

Courts of Inquiry

Word of the casualties at the Stanley camp soon reached London via the BAAG and other intelligence channels, though his majesty's government had no desire to point accusatory fingers at the U.S. Navy. The British mourned the fourteen deaths at Stanley but did not lodge any protests with Washington, just as they had not protested at the sinking of the *Lisbon Maru* by a U.S. submarine and the resultant deaths of more than 800 British soldiers who had been taken captive at Hong Kong. The British were realists who understood that total war with the Japanese Empire would inevitably have its share of bloody friendly fire incidents. Moreover, they knew that winning the war would require an unshakeable alliance with the United States. In any case, the British held Tokyo to account for the *Lisbon Maru* and Bungalow C, since the Japanese had failed to mark the ship and camp with the white crosses that would have signaled the presence of Allied POWs and civilian internees.

In contrast to the muted British reaction to the carnage at Bungalow C, the Portuguese government had immediately lodged a protest in response to the American strafing of Macau on January 16, 1945. News of the incident had spread quickly across the globe, and Tokyo radio as well as newspapers in Hong Kong, Portugal, and the United States ran stories on the Macau air raids within twenty-four hours. In front-page articles on January 18 and 19, the *Hongkong News* reported that "Grummans" launched from American aircraft carriers had bombed and strafed Macau three times in one day. According to these news stories, the American "air gangsters" had attacked shipping in the harbor, motor vehicles, a radio station, the seaplane hangar, fortresses, and residential buildings. The stories reported 200 casualties from the raids, including unidentified foreign nationals and ten Portuguese soldiers.[1] In Lisbon, meanwhile, *Diário de Lisboa* and other local media outlets vigorously denounced the bombing of the colony and the resultant violation of Portugal's wartime neutrality.[2] In North America, initial articles from the Associated Press (AP) and the United Press (UP) reported that "unidentified" aircraft had carried out the raids and provoked considerable consternation in Lisbon. In a typical example, the *Miami Daily News* ran an eighty-two-word wire story titled "Raid on Macao Annoys Lisbon." The editors tucked the article away on page 4-A alongside miscellaneous minor news items like "Fuel Shutdown Ends Gay Night Life in Paris" and "Slash in Pork Cost Due Soon."[3] The Portuguese government viewed the incident as far more than a mere annoyance, however, and the U.S. State Department began working to contain the damage to relations between the two countries. By January 21, AP and UP wire stories reported that American aircraft had carried out the airstrikes against Macau and that Washington had officially apologized for the incident. These same stories reported that the raids had killed two civilians and wounded two soldiers, a police officer, and several more civilians.[4] Meanwhile, Admiral Nimitz sent a message to Admiral Halsey on January 23 requesting clarification of what exactly had transpired at Macau.[5]

On January 26 – just ten days after the raids on Macau and the same day that the *Sarawak Maru* reached Singapore – Admiral Halsey appointed a closed-door court of inquiry at the behest of Admiral Nimitz. Halsey ordered the inquiry to focus on the reported violation of Portuguese neutrality by naval aircraft at Macau on January 16. He tasked the court with establishing the facts of the incident, determining culpability, and recommending appropriate disciplinary actions. As fleet commander, Halsey eschewed micromanaging and preferred to delegate tasks when he had officers capable of carrying them out.[6] Unsurprisingly, he did not plan to attend the court of inquiry and assigned Vice Admiral Willis A. "Ching" Lee to lead the inquiry, which also included Rear Admiral James C. Jones, Rear Admiral Thomas R. Cooley, and Judge Advocate Capt. Ira H. Nunn. Lee commanded Battleship Squadron 2 and ranked as one of the navy's most capable battleship commanders. Cooley led Battleship Division 6, and Jones served as the commanding officer of Cruiser Division 17, which meant the court consisted of "blackshoe" navy flag officers who specialized in surface warfare even though the men who would be questioned by the court were aviators or "brownshoe" navy. The blackshoe-brownshoe distinction stemmed from a minor difference in uniforms, but symbolized a long-running and divisive schism in the navy between the more traditionally minded officers who commanded battleships and cruisers and the officers specializing in aerial warfare who commanded carriers, planned and coordinated air operations, and led air groups.[7] Whether the blackshoe composition of the court would influence its findings remained to be seen, but the fact remained that none of the judges was an aviator. In accordance with Halsey's orders, Vice Admiral Lee convened the court's initial meeting aboard his flagship, the battleship USS *South Dakota*, which had anchored at Ulithi with the rest of TF 38 at the conclusion of Operation *Gratitude*.[8] However, since some members of the court had not yet arrived at Ulithi, Lee postponed further proceedings to the following day and adjourned the court.

On the morning of January 27, the court reconvened aboard the *South Dakota* with all members in attendance. By coincidence, an entirely separate court of inquiry convened at Guam on the same day and with a similar mandate, though in this case the friendly fire incident in question involved the torpedoing of the rescue and salvage ship *Extractor* by the submarine *Guardfish* on January 24. Unlike the proceedings at Ulithi, however, the investigation into the loss of the *Extractor*, which at the time of its sinking had been steaming to assist the *kamikaze*-ravaged fleet carrier *Ticonderoga*, remained an internal affair of interest primarily to the navy. In contrast, the bombing of neutral Macau had geopolitical implications, making the court of inquiry aboard the *South Dakota* a high-profile affair with stakeholders outside the navy. Washington was watching, albeit from afar, and so too was Portugal.

The court began with witnesses from the highest levels of command and interrogated eight naval officers, including Captain Hickey of the *Hancock* and his immediate superior, Rear Admiral Bogan, the commander of TG 38.2. On January 28, the court recalled Bogan and Hickey for additional testimony. The court also interviewed Commander

Lamade, and many of its questions focused on communique 130735, which Rear Admiral Bogan had sent to the *Hancock* on January 13. Since this dispatch had instructed pilots to strike Macau *only* if they observed enemy ships or aircraft, the court asked Lamade whether he believed his pilots had been justified in strafing the seaplane installations at Macau even though they had never spotted any Japanese planes. Lamade backed up his men without hesitation or qualification:

> My interpretation of this dispatch, in view of the fact that I have made many attacks on enemy installations and have had numerous indications, that would point out to me that the hangar on which the attack was made would be a likely place for hiding out aircraft. This would seem to be enough authority considering the possibility of concealed aircraft. It is obviously impossible for the pilots to investigate closely prior to striking. In view of the above, I consider the hangar as a legal target.[9]

The court then asked about the briefing procedures for VF-7 pilots aboard the *Hancock* before returning to Commander Lamade's assertion that the seaplane hangar qualified as a legitimate target. The court pressed him on this point and followed up by asking, "Do you still consider you were justified in striking the sea plane base at Macao?"[10]

"Our instructions were to destroy aircraft whenever seen," Lamade replied. "I consider we were justified in striking the hangars found on Macao."[11]

In addition to Commander Lamade, the court also took testimony from the ACI officers – Lieutenants Golson, Gose, and Helmers – who had conducted the prestrike briefings aboard the *Hancock* and the three VF-7 pilots who had led the raids on Macau: Lieutenant Kemper, Lieutenant Newcomer, and Lieutenant Niebling. Captain Hickey made his third appearance before the court as the final witness on January 28. In total, the court asked Hickey some fifty questions, far more than it had asked of any other witness.

The court of inquiry examined a variety of documents during witness testimony and entered them into the record as exhibits 1 through 10. Communiques from Admiral Halsey, Vice Admiral McCain, and Rear Admiral Bogan comprised exhibits 2–7. Exhibit 8 consisted of documents from the *Hancock* that summarized the missions flown over Sanchau, Chungshan, and Macau. Exhibits 1, 9, and 10 included intelligence documents with information pertinent to Macau that the ACI officers had consulted when briefing VF-7 pilots.

The exhibits did not include any photographs, though the court asked witnesses whether photographs had been taken of Macau, and several witnesses believed that they had been. Though no witness volunteered this information, the action report for the *Hancock* indicated that CVG-7 aircraft had taken reconnaissance photos of Macau and other airfields on three separate occasions. In total, the K-17 and K-18 recon cameras carried by CVG-7 aircraft took ninety-one photos of these locales, though the action report did not quantify the number that pictured Macau specifically.[12] In addition, there may have been gun-camera footage of the strikes on Macau. However, the *Hancock* had suffered substantial damage during the accidental bomb detonation on January 21, which had killed more than fifty members of the crew. The blast and fire wrecked the Air Office as well as the Air Intelligence Office and incinerated CVG-7 documents and gun-camera footage, though the record of the court of inquiry did not address this point. The negatives for the ninety-one reconnaissance photographs may have been destroyed as well, though at least one print of a recon photo taken by a VF-7 Hellcat on January 16 survived the destruction of the Air Office and was forwarded on to the Guam-based Photographic Interpretation Squadron 2. However, this photo did not depict the seaplane hangars, and the court might not have been aware of its existence. Regardless of the reasons, the court did not enter any photographs into the record as exhibits.[13]

The court of inquiry adjourned at the end of the day on January 28. Two days later, the court of inquiry for the sinking of the *Extractor* concluded in the wardroom of the seaplane tender *Curtiss* in Apra Harbor. While the court ruled that no criminal offenses had occurred, it also assigned "serious blame" to Commander Hammond, the skipper of the *Guardfish*, and Lieutenant Babcock, the captain of the *Extractor*. However, the court included several fellow submarine officers, and this sympathetic panel of judges may explain why Hammond retained command of the *Guardfish*. Though the court identified a string of errors by Hammond, Babcock, and several other officers that led to the sinking of the *Extractor* and the deaths of six American sailors, the court seemed to view the incident as an unavoidable cost of doing business.

In short, the court saw no reason to cashier a respected submarine skipper like Commander Hammond. There seemed little appetite for punishing Lieutenant Babcock, the skipper of the *Extractor*, either. The navy offered him several different ships, and he chose to take command of a training vessel based on the Hudson River.[14]

The court of inquiry convened to investigate the torpedoing of the *Extractor* had taken four days from start to finish. However, six weeks passed before the court of inquiry for the air attacks on Macau reconvened aboard the *South Dakota* on the morning of March 13, 1945. The delay could be attributed in part to the delicate nature of the inquiry, which required more time to adjudicate, but it also stemmed from the invasion of Iwo Jima on February 19, since the operation involved Vice Admiral Lee as well as his flagship, the *South Dakota*. In a four-page ruling, the court summarized its understanding of what had occurred at Macau on January 16, 1945. The court also offered its opinion on who was culpable for the airstrikes on Macau and recommended appropriate disciplinary action.[15]

The court determined that there had been three separate airstrikes on the seaplane installations at Macau on January 16. All three had been flown by VF-7 from the *Hancock* during blanket missions to the south of Hong Kong, and there had been no additional strikes on Macau by other air groups attached to TF 38. The objective of the fighter sweeps flown by the VF-7 pilots had been to achieve air superiority by destroying enemy aircraft on the ground or in the air. However, the court never addressed the issue of whether the pilots had been ordered to destroy aviation gasoline stores at Macau. The court's silence on this matter suggested that the members of the court as well as the witnesses they examined did not possess specific knowledge about aviation fuel stocks in the Portuguese colony.

Consul Reeves later claimed that the aviation fuel stored in the seaplane hangar amounted to 1,500 gallons. If an accurate figure, the fuel cache would have equaled about thirty 55-gallon drums or just under the amount needed to fill the internal tanks of four F6F-5 Hellcats.[16] Such a modest fuel dump hardly ranked as a target of major significance, though the word on the street in Macau was that the U.S. Navy had specifically attacked the seaplane hangar to deny the fuel to the Japanese. According to this scenario, China-based intelligence operatives had informed the U.S. Navy that the Japanese were storing fuel and other supplies in the hangar, or alternatively, that the Japanese planned to purchase these goods from the Macau government.[17]

However, Vice Admiral Lee and the other members of the court of inquiry never asked about fuel supplies at Macau. In turn, no witness mentioned fuel supplies at Macau during his testimony, though the VF-7 pilots did note that when the seaplane hangar ignited, the resultant smoke plume had been consistent with burning aviation gasoline. None of the documents entered into the record as exhibits discussed aviation fuel supplies at Macau, either. Moreover, the aircraft action reports filed by ACI officers Gose and Golson on January 16, the *Hancock* action report filed on January 25, and the VF-7 war history filed on February 15 made no reference to fuel supplies at Macau. The court also determined that there was no evidence of "unneutral service" by Portugal at Macau, which meant, presumably, that there was no evidence that Macau had been used by the Japanese as a seaplane base and there was no evidence that the Portuguese garrison had fired upon American aircraft. This exoneration of the Portuguese further suggests that the participants in the court of inquiry remained unaware that the colonial administration in Macau had possessed aviation fuel stocks that it intended to sell to the Japanese military. Such a transaction would have been under duress and perhaps forgivable, particularly since Pedro José Lobo likely planned to trade the fuel for rice or other desperately needed commodities. Still, selling military supplies to a belligerent would have broken the rules of neutrality, as the court would certainly have noted.

While Allied intelligence may well have been aware of the contents of the seaplane hangar, it appeared that this information never found its way to the command and intelligence staff of TF 38. Consul Reeves claimed that pro-Axis factions in Macau had attempted to discredit him by spreading the rumor that he had coordinated the attack on the seaplane hangar with the Americans.[18] Many in Macau consequently believed that the U.S. Navy had deliberately targeted the fuel supply, when in fact the pilots of VF-7 had no idea what the seaplane hangar contained. They had destroyed the building on the presumption that it could conceal Japanese warplanes, not because it contained fuel stocks belonging to the colonial administration of Macau.

The court also failed to address the question of casualties on the ground at Macau, though this omission may have reflected a tacit assumption by court members and witnesses that casualties remained a given. Initial media accounts in Portuguese and American newspapers had reported two people killed and at least five wounded during the raids. If members of the court had seen these news reports or heard more exaggerated accounts from radio Tokyo, they failed to mention them during the trial or in court documents. Though the true number of dead and wounded remained unknown to the court, Vice Admiral Lee and the other members likely understood that casualties had in fact occurred.

When it came to the question of assigning blame, the court found that Captain Hickey bore primary responsibility for the failure to brief VF-7 pilots as ordered by Rear Admiral Bogan, and that this failure to brief was the "proximate cause" of all three airstrikes on Macau. The court therefore ruled that Hickey be reprimanded for negligence in obeying orders. In addition, the court recommended that three other officers aboard the *Hancock* be "admonished for their negligence in obeying orders." These officers included Cdr. Whitmore S. Butts, who served as the air officer aboard the *Hancock*, and Commander Lamade, the skipper of CVG-7. Lieutenant Golson, the ACI officer for CVG-7, rounded out the trio of officers singled out for admonishments but spared a more damaging reprimand. By the time of the court's ruling, however, CVG-7 had rotated off the *Hancock* and been replaced by CVG-80, the air group from the badly damaged *Ticonderoga*. By mid-February, CVG-7 had returned to the West Coast with the *Ticonderoga*.[19]

The court did not recommend disciplinary action against Lieutenant Gose and Lieutenant Helmers, the junior ACI officers who had delivered the mission briefings for VF-7. Lieutenant Kemper, Lieutenant Newcomer, Lieutenant Niebling, and the thirteen other VF-7 pilots who had flown the strikes were also found blameless. Possibly, these exonerations represented a tacit admission by the court that pilot fatigue and exhaustion among the ACI officers had played a role in the foul-ups that had led to multiple attacks on Macau. Regardless, the VF-7 pilots did not hold themselves accountable for any wrongdoing. As the war history for the squadron made clear, the pilots believed they had been ordered to hunt Japanese aircraft south of Hong Kong and that their mauling of the seaplane base at Macau had been entirely in line with the mission parameters. The VF-7 war history – a document authored by the squadron's own officers and endorsed by Commander Lamade – recounted the blanket mission flown on the morning of January 16 with jocular glee and made no attempt whatsoever to justify the squadron's actions. After lamenting the dearth of destroyable enemy aircraft at Sanchau, Chungshan, and Macau, the war history described how the Hellcat pilots had "worked over" all three air facilities. Though the war history had been compiled just a few weeks *after* the court of inquiry had taken witness testimony, the pilots of VF-7 clearly remained unrepentant for the airstrikes on Macau.[20]

Admiral Nimitz only partially accepted the recommendations of the court of inquiry. He addressed letters of reprimand to Commander Lamade and Lieutenant Golson for their "negligence and inefficiency in performance of duty" in late March 1945.[21] However, Captain Hickey and Commander Butts were exonerated with Nimitz's approval on the grounds that the failure to brief the VF-7 pilots as ordered remained the fault of their subordinates, specifically Commander Lamade and Lieutenant Golson. The blame would go no higher than the commander of CVG-7, and no lower than the ACI officer for the air group, when it came to the question of culpability for the briefing failure in Ready Room 4.

Killed on a Sunday

In Hong Kong, an entirely different kind of court determined the fate of Major David H. Houck of the 118th Tactical Reconnaissance Squadron. Including Houck, five pilots from the squadron had been shot down over Hong Kong and Canton on January 15 and 16, 1945. Four had taken to their parachutes and eventually walked out, including 1st Lt. Palmer, 2nd Lt. Mitchell, 2nd Lt. Theobold, and, with the help of agent Ady of the OSS, 1st Lt. Egan. Major Houck remained missing in action, however. Fellow pilots had witnessed the plunge of his burning P-51 into Victoria Harbor on January 15, and the sudden, uncontrolled nature of the dive as well as the fact that nobody had observed a parachute led them to believe that Houck had died in the crash. However, the major had actually managed to survive a rather miraculous low-altitude bail out. He had been hauled out of the harbor, sodden but uninjured, and held initially by the Kempeitai, presumably at their headquarters in the Court of Final Appeal building in Victoria City. However, the Kempeitai soon transported the major to Stanley Prison, the usual destination for captured American aviators. Locked in solitary confinement, Houck never saw the three other American aviators – Jean Balch, Alvin Hughes, and Richard Hunt – who had been shot down on January 16 and held at the prison before transport to Japan.

Born in Baltimore in 1914, Major Houck had earned an undergraduate engineering degree from John Hopkins University in 1935 and joined the U.S. Army Corps of Engineers in 1941. However, he had wanted to take the fight to the enemy after Pearl Harbor, so he transferred to the U.S. Army Air Forces. He went through preflight at Maxwell Field and then trained as a fighter pilot at Craig Army Air Field, both in Alabama. He logged hundreds of hours in the cockpit of the PT-23 primary trainer, the AT-6 advanced trainer, the obsolescent P-36 interceptor, and various models of the P-40 fighter. Granted his wings in September 1942, he then served as a flight instructor and rose to the rank of captain before his transfer to the CBI in April 1944, where he served as an operations officer in the CBI Air Forces Training Unit at Karachi and attained the rank of major. In December 1944, he had been transferred to China to take over command of the 118th from Lieutenant Colonel McComas.[1]

Guards periodically hauled Major Houck out of his cell for interrogation sessions led by Major Shii Saburo of the IJA. Shii questioned Houck with the goal of charging him with attacking non-military targets, such as civilian vessels in Victoria Harbor. Houck, however, maintained that he had been attempting to sink a destroyer when his plane went down. Major Shii's interest in charging Houck no doubt stemmed from the fact that he was the highest-ranking American aviator ever captured at Hong Kong. Moreover, Houck was the incoming squadron commander of the 118th TRS, and Shii may have calculated that putting him on trial, with its presumed guilty verdict and death penalty, would have an adverse impact on the morale of a squadron that had inflicted a great deal of pain on the Japanese military.

In addition, Shii may have believed that putting Houck on trial would avenge the recent sinking of the passenger-cargo steamer *Reinan Maru* by American fighter aircraft.* Two Mustangs had pounced on the *Reinan Maru* as it steamed from Hong Kong to Macau on December 24, 1944. Slammed by a pair of 500-pound bombs, the ship had quickly foundered off Lantau Island with heavy loss of life. Some accounts claimed that American pilots had strafed passengers as they clung to floating scraps of wreckage and machine-gunned the vessels that tried to recover survivors. Both the 118th TRS and the 74th Fighter Squadron had been active over Hong Kong that day, and most likely the 118th

---

*The *Reinan Maru* (嶺南丸) was also known as the *Ling Nam Maru*.

had sunk the *Reinan Maru* and the 74th had worked over the ships that tried to rescue passengers in the water.[2]

Hundreds of civilian passengers had been lost with the *Reinan Maru*, including Chan Lim-pak, a wealthy war profiteer and pro-Japanese politician. Chan had been a prominent figure in Hong Kong, where he had served on the Chinese Representative Council, which oversaw the local Chinese population on behalf of the Japanese military administration. A memorial service for Chan had been held in the council chambers on January 11, just four days before the capture of Major Houck, so the *Reinan Maru* incident remained in the forefront of public memory.[3] Major Shii may have figured that by charging Houck the Japanese occupation authorities in Hong Kong could demonstrate to the populace that American pilots would be held accountable for sinking civilian vessels and killing noncombatants.

Major General Fukuchi Haruo fully supported Major Shii's attempt to try Major Houck for war crimes. At the request of Major Shii, the general contacted the legal bureau of the War Ministry in Tokyo to request permission to prosecute Major Houck. The legal bureau granted its consent if the prosecution could provide evidence that American pilots had targeted a civilian ferry. In addition, the trial required the assent of Lt. Gen. Tanaka Hisakasu, the absentee governor general of Hong Kong and commander of the 23rd Army who maintained his headquarters in Canton. Tanaka apparently granted this approval indirectly through Major General Fukuchi, who served as his chief of staff in Hong Kong. Tanaka had granted Fukuchi full authority to act on his behalf in all military matters pertaining to Hong Kong, and had even provided Fukuchi with blank sheets of paper with his signature for this purpose.[4]

On April 5, 1945, nearly three months after hurling himself out of his burning P-51, Major Houck faced a military tribunal convened on the authority of Lt. Gen. Tanaka, though the governor general was not present in the courtroom. Lt. Col. Kubo Nishigai, Major Watanabe Masamori, and Capt. Yamaguchi Koichi served as the judges. However, only Yamaguchi, a member of the Judicial Affairs Section attached to the 23rd Army, had had any legal training. Captain Asakawa Hiroshi served as the prosecutor during the trial, though Major Shii directed his actions. The court provided a civilian interpreter named Nakazawa

Asao, but Major Houck had no defense counsel and could neither call witnesses nor produce evidence. As the judges explained through the translations of Mr. Nakazawa, Houck faced the charge of sinking a thirty-ton Chinese civilian vessel and killing eight noncombatants in violation of the Enemy Airman Act enacted in 1942 by the first governor general of occupied Hong Kong, Isogai Rensuke. Article 2 proved to be the most pertinent: "Those having committed the following acts will be subjected to military punishment: (b) bombing, strafing or attacking in any manner, with intention of destroying, damaging or burning private property of non-military nature."[5]

No witnesses testified during the trial other than Major Houck, who stated he had never intentionally bombed a civilian ship on January 15. Moreover, he stated that he had not observed any other pilot attack a civilian vessel on that date. However, the question of intentionality did not interest either the judges or the prosecutor despite the centrality of intent when it came to establishing guilt under Article 2. In his role as the prosecutor, Captain Asakawa recommended a guilty verdict and the death penalty for Major Houck, who had been following the court proceedings as best he could through the translation efforts of Mr. Nakazawa. At the conclusion of the two-hour court session the guards returned Houck to his cell, and the judges then heard two more unrelated cases before adjourning for lunch.

In their closed-door deliberations, all three judges found Houck guilty of violating Article 2 of the Enemy Airman Act and voted unanimously for the death penalty. However, they noted that Lt. General Tanaka in Canton had the authority to approve the death sentence or, alternatively, commute the sentence to a prison term of ten years to life. Major General Fukuchi made no attempt to bring Tanaka into the conversation, however, and after Major Shii assured him that the American pilot had admitted to sinking a civilian ship, he approved the guilty verdict and death penalty on Tanaka's behalf.[6]

The day after the trial a detail of Indian wardens from Stanley Prison drove Major Houck to the beach at Big Wave Bay, a favorite execution ground on an isolated finger of land that jutted from the southeast coast of Hong Kong Island.[7] Major Shii supervised the execution detail, which also included Capt. Saito Shunkichi, the chief medical officer for POW camps in Hong Kong. Mr. Nakazawa and at least two sergeants and two corporals rounded out the detail.* Major Shii read the charges against Major Houck and announced the guilty verdict and death sentence, which Mr. Nakazawa duly translated for the American officer. The soldiers then blindfolded Houck and covered his head with a white sack, pushed him to his knees, and tied him to a wooden cross on the beach. Major Houck apparently remained silent and offered no resistance as the sergeant delegated one of the corporals to shoot the condemned man with his rifle. Prone on the cold sand with his Arisaka steadied on a sandbag, the soldier took careful aim at the target circle that had been painted on the sack covering Major Houck's head. However, he could not bring himself to pull the trigger and kill a helpless man just thirty feet away. The sergeant then took his place, tucked the rifle against his shoulder, and promptly shot Houck in the forehead. Major Houck hung motionless from the cross as Captain Saito took his wrist to check for a pulse. He then called for another shot. The sergeant chambered another round and fired again, and this bullet proved fatal. Mr. Nakazawa, who had turned away during the execution to face the sea, now pivoted back around and saw that blood had soaked through the white sack over Houck's head. The Indian wardens then untied Houck's body and rolled it into a hole that had been dug in the sand, kicked the cross in as well, and buried them both in short order. Despite the secluded nature of the execution site, which lent itself to unmarked graves, the Japanese made no attempt to hide the location of Houck's body. Instead, they marked Houck's grave with a wooden pillar etched with his name in Japanese, a few hundred feet from the high-tide line.[8]

Rather than execution on a crescent of beach in Hong Kong, Jean Balch of the *Yorktown* along with Richard Hunt and Alvin Hughes of the

---

*Due to illegible documents and contradictory accounts in U.S. military records, the members of the execution party could not be definitively established. As best as can be determined, the party included Major Shii Saburo; Sergeant Imai Morinojo; Sergeant Ono Teruo; Corporal Hirano; Corporal Yamasaki; medical officer Captain Saito Shunkichi; civilian interpreter Nakazawa Asao; and up to six Indian wardens from Stanley Prison, possibly including one named Lal Khan.

Hancock had been shipped like low-priority freight from Hong Kong to Japan via Amoy, Formosa, and Okinawa. Eleven days after they had bailed out over Hong Kong, they reached Ōfuna prison camp outside Yokohama. The secret IJN-run compound held American and British prisoners that naval intelligence classified as high value, including submarine sailors and officers, fighter and bomber pilots, and airmen trained to operate radar and communications equipment. Though the prisoners possessed extensive technical knowledge about everything from sonar to solenoids, the camp itself remained a ramshackle, low-tech affair tucked away on a dirt backroad. Balch and Hughes had to carry the badly injured Hunt in a wheelbarrow from the train station. Upon his arrival at Ōfuna, Balch immediately went into solitary confinement in a wooden cell, where he received a bowl of rice – his first meal since leaving the *Yorktown*.[9]

William Leibold, chief boatswain's mate from the submarine USS *Tang*, which had been lost off Formosa in October 1944, occupied a cell next to the one holding Lieutenant Hunt. Leibold served as an assistant to the man responsible for medical care at Ōfuna, Kitamura Sueharu, who had been nicknamed "the quack" by the prisoners due to his lack of medical training and his sadist tendencies. Prisoners who were pilots aggravated these tendencies in Kitamura, and he consistently tortured Hunt through medical neglect punctuated with beatings meted out in the camp dispensary. Most prisoners figured this thrashing stemmed from Kitamura's rage at the incineration of Japanese cities by American B-29s. Deprived of clean dressings and other basic medical necessities, not to mention badly beaten and terrified, Lieutenant Hunt's condition rapidly deteriorated. Leibold knew that Hunt would not survive without help, since his injured arms meant he could barely feed himself and he had grown so weak that he could no longer stand up to walk to the toilet. His cell stank of infected burns, dirty bandages, and human waste. Since the guards had ordered them not to assist Lieutenant Hunt, Leibold and several other prisoners had to ghost into Hunt's cell whenever the guards weren't in sight and provide a few seconds of comfort – a blanket pulled up to the chin against the winter cold, a murmured word of encouragement, a quick sip of rice gruel. Leibold and his fellow conspirators escaped detection while administering these acts of mercy, but Hunt failed to improve. In late February, he stopped eating and slipped into delirium, terrified by a man he thought was hiding behind his cell door and by memories of his fiery bail out over Tai Tam Valley. Starved, frozen, and suffering from severe burns and broken bones, Lieutenant Hunt died alone in his cell on the evening of February 25. A work detail that presumably consisted of Hunt's fellow prisoners placed his body in a wooden casket and buried it behind the Ryuho-ji Temple opposite the prison compound.[10]

Meanwhile, Balch remained in solitary confinement broken only by interrogation sessions run by IJN intelligence officers. He endured beatings, starvation, disease, filth, isolation, and extreme cold. Psychological torture accompanied the physical mistreatment. Japanese officers and guards routinely told Balch that he would be executed on an upcoming Sunday, for example, apparently because they thought being killed on the Sabbath was a particularly unhappy fate for Christians. However, Sunday after Sunday crawled past, and Balch managed to stay alive. His captors released him from solitary confinement after six months, having apparently concluded that while they could beat useless tidbits of military trivia out of Balch, they could never pound loose top-secret information from a humble air-gunner whose need to know had never extended much further beyond the barrels of his twin .30-caliber machine guns. Balch now had the comradeship of the other Americans in the prison barracks, and he knew from the increasing tempo of "the music" – a term Ōfuna inmates used to refer to American air raids – that the war would soon be over. He just had to survive the remaining Sundays.[11]

28

Ten Centuries

In the predawn darkness of February 25, 1945, Lt. Paul F. Stevens and the other ten men of Crew Two climbed into their PB4Y-1, which stood on the hardstand like a testament to inter-service cooperation. Part army and part navy, his navy-blue patrol bomber now sported a silver tail with the black stripes of a squadron assigned to the 13th Air Force. This aviation Frankenstein had resulted from a midair collision with an Aichi D3A, which had destroyed the Japanese dive-bomber and chewed off an impressive chunk of Lieutenant Stevens's tail assembly. His mangled patrol bomber had held together for the flight back to the Philippines, where the mechanics of Combat Aircraft Service Unit (F) 9 shook their heads in wonder as they inspected the damage. With no PB4Y-1 available to cannibalize, the repair crew salvaged the hind end of a wrecked army B-24.* They bolted the bare aluminum tail assembly to the fuselage of Stevens's aircraft, which wound up sporting a hybrid silver-blue paint scheme because the sunburned mechanics had neither the time nor the paint to address such cosmetic trivialities.[1]

In the Wing Operations Quonset hut that morning, the ACI officer and his team had issued codebooks, assigned search sectors to the crews scheduled to fly that day – during normal operations, a crew flew a mission once every three days – and provided a weather report. Lt. Stevens had

---

*A CASU was a Carrier Aircraft Service Unit, while a CASU (F) was a Combat Aircraft Service Unit.

been briefed to fly a fourteen-hour maritime reconnaissance run along the China coast. On February 1, the brass had rescinded the order forbidding VPB pilots from conducting offensive operations, so Stevens had discretion to attack targets of opportunity during his patrol. In the aft bomb bay, he carried a load of ten AN-M30 100-pound bombs, which VPB pilots referred to as "centuries." As usual, the forward bomb bay held the two auxiliary fuel tanks that made marathon recon missions possible, bringing the weight of the plane to thirty tons.[2]

When Lieutenant Stevens taxied out for takeoff, he could see kerosene pots burning in two parallel rows along the edges of the runway. In the absence of runway lights, the fires guided pilots making early morning takeoffs. From a cockpit vantage point, the pots eventually converged into a single dot of smudgy flame far in the distance, which marked the endpoint of the runway.[3] Stevens noted the time – 0410 hours – and commenced his takeoff roll, the kerosene fires blurring into streaks as the plane accelerated and then falling away out of sight as the wheels lifted from the runway. Once airborne, Lieutenant Stevens banked out over the oily darkness of open water and headed west as Leyte receded like a dream into the inky night sky.

Lieutenant Stevens and Crew Two crossed the South China Sea to the mainland, chased by the sunrise and buffeted by the surly weather. As they approached Hong Kong at 500 feet, they spotted an Aichi E13A floatplane circling over a large transport ship with a single stack amidships. Since any chance for a surprise attack had been lost, Stevens feinted by flying over the horizon and then doubling back on the deck for a skip-bombing run. However, as the distance closed he saw large white crosses painted on the ship's green hull. Unsure what these prominently displayed crosses signified, he aborted the bomb run and decided to go after the floatplane instead. Stevens would later discover that he had made the right call. He and his crew had found the *Awa Maru*, which the U.S. Navy had granted noncombatant status so it could deliver Red Cross supplies to Allied POWs held in Singapore and Java. Whether by design or snafu, VPB-104 had never been notified of the arrangement, and Stevens had come within seconds of violating the safe-passage agreement negotiated between the governments of Japan and the United States.

Lieutenant Stevens settled for chasing after the E13 – a Jake, in the parlance of Allied codenames – but the floatplane pilot banked around Hong Kong Island at low altitude and slipped into the eastern mouth of Victoria Harbor like a wasp into a hive. Though they had lost the floatplane, Stevens and his crew soon spotted a flight of Mitsubishi G4Ms flying several thousand feet overhead. He began climbing towards the twin-engine bombers with the goal of picking off the tail-end Charlie, but then his crew saw the three enemy fighters escorting the bombers. Stevens had acquired a reputation in his squadron as a top gun, but he did not like the odds of a three-on-one dogfight and broke off the pursuit.

Since the northbound Japanese aviators had apparently failed to detect his aircraft, Lieutenant Stevens judged that he could safely approach Victoria Harbor for a ship count. He crossed over the Stanley Peninsula, where he could see one of the 9.2-inch coastal defense guns that the Japanese had captured intact in 1941 and pressed back into service to defend Hong Kong against Allied warships.[4] Then he executed a terrain-hugging flight up the steep southern flank of Hong Kong Island and over the ridges that split the middle of the island like scales on the back of a dinosaur. Low-hanging clouds melted into the ridges and pinnacles, but Stevens had just enough visibility to clear the peaks and make his descent over the northern side of the island. Banking to the east without drawing any fire, he sped down the length of Victoria Harbor as his crew tallied up the vessels in port. Once clear of the anchorage, Stevens circled around to the southeast coast of Hong Kong Island.

As Lieutenant Stevens approached Repulse Bay, a beach-lined crescent of sand that had been popular with the prewar colonial elite, his tail gunner reported over the interphone that a fighter had dropped into their six o'clock like a tail on a kite. Stevens immediately reversed course and identified the bandit as a dark-brown Ki-43-II Hayabusa. Assuming he had correctly identified the aircraft type, the nimble radial-engine fighter may have belonged to the 24th Sentai of the JAAF, which had deployed from Formosa to Hong Kong and Swatow under the command of Captain Koichi Shoji to protect Japanese shipping as it moved along the China coast. Shooting down the troublesome American patrol bombers, in fact, had been part of the unit's mission brief. However, the 1st Escort Fleet had based a handful of A6M fighters at Kai Tak as well, and since the navy A6M – the famed Zero – bore more than a passing resemblance to the army Ki-43, possibly Lieutenant Stevens and his crew had misidentified the enemy aircraft type.[5]

Lieutenant Stevens knew better than to try to outpace a much speedier Japanese fighter plane, since running for it would simply give the enemy pilot the opportunity to position himself for his optimal angle of attack. Instead, Stevens preferred maneuvering to deny his adversary a viable gun run while simultaneously lining his gunners up for the best shots possible, an aerial dance that he referred to as going "round-de-round." Stevens pulled up the nose of his PB4Y-1 to meet the oncoming Hayabusa, which enjoyed a slight advantage in altitude, so that his forward gunners could open fire. Stevens and his copilot ducked reflexively when the top-turret gunner triggered his twin .50-calibers, an action every patrol bomber pilot had learned to dread. While the thin aluminum carapace of the cockpit roof shielded them from the superheated muzzle flashes just above their heads, it offered scant protection from the noise and concussion, which pummeled the entire flight deck. Crouched down in his armored seat, Stevens felt like his head had been split open, though he managed to keep the nose pointed at the incoming enemy bandit so that the gunners could keep hammering away. However, the Hayabusa pilot refused to break off his attack and flashed past at a high rate of speed, albeit without scoring a single hit. Stevens admired the courage and skill of the nameless enemy aviator but appreciated the poor quality of his gunnery even more.[6]

As the Hayabusa pilot banked around the far side of Middle Island in Repulse Bay, Lieutenant Stevens tried to cut him off by flying straight across the rocky islet. However, the Japanese pilot apparently had the same plan for an ambush, and Stevens found himself hurtling straight towards the Ki-43 in what amounted to an airborne game of chicken. He felt the airframe shake with the recoil of the bow guns and the twin fifties positioned just above his head. A fusillade of defensive fire streaked out towards the oncoming enemy fighter, which trailed smoke from its wings. For a happy second, Stevens thought his gunners had hit the bullseye, but then he realized that the smoke came from the muzzle blasts of the enemy pilot's wing guns. Tracer fire crisscrossed between the two aircraft as the Ki-43 bored on in until Stevens thought he was in for another midair collision. At the last moment, however, the enemy pilot jinked to avoid the patrol bomber. Ensconced in his armored gun turret, the bow gunner thought he had put a few rounds into the fuselage of the Hayabusa but knew he had failed to inflict significant damage. Stevens continued maneuvering in the hopes of giving his gunners another shot, but the enemy pilot knew his business and easily shook off the patrol bomber. He disappeared on a heading that would take him in for a landing at Kai Tak, where Stevens wondered what story he would tell the other members of his squadron as they poured each other cups of hot sake that evening.

Though his gunners had burned through their share of machine-gun ammunition, Lieutenant Stevens still had ten 100-pounders in the bomb bay. He had no desire to haul a bellyful of ordnance all the way back to Tacloban, and even less desire to jettison his bombload into the sea. An attack on a ship huddled beneath the flak umbrella covering Victoria Harbor struck him as far too risky, so he settled on a softer target and told his crew they would head for Macau instead. He wanted to see if they could surprise the Japanese vessel that another VPB-104 pilot had observed in the Portuguese colony's Inner Harbor. As Stevens understood it, the neutral territory of Macau consisted of several islands offshore from the city, but not the city itself or its harbor. He therefore assumed that any ships in port amounted to fair game.[7]

Flying on the deck to avoid detection by Japanese radar, Lieutenant Stevens traced the veins of the Pearl River, then doubled back to speed overland towards Macau. Rain, fog, and mist severely restricted visibility, but as he overflew Macau's Inner Harbor at about eleven in the morning the haze parted like a curtain to reveal a pair of presumed Japanese ships. With just a few seconds to set up his attack, he made a tight turn and lined up on what he believed to be a Fox Tare Charlie, the ONI codename for a 300-foot freighter with the superstructure slightly aft of amidships.

PB4Y-1 crews rarely bombed from higher altitudes with their Norden bombsights and usually chose to attack at masthead height instead. Such attacks required skilled coordination between the PPC – who set up the speed, angle, and altitude of the attack – and the bombardier, who chose the optimal moment of bomb release. The bombardier occupied a compartment behind and below the bow turret and when flying just above the breakers used an aiming technique the crews referred to as the "seaman's eye," which relied on visual judgement honed by practice and experience. On most missions, patrol bombers carried bombs fuzed for a four- to five-second delay so that the bombs would not explode instantaneously or on contact. This ensured the plane would not be caught in its own bomb blast, and often maximized damage to the target because the bomb banged into the hull, sank, and detonated below the waterline. Alternatively, the bomb might punch through the hull and explode below deck deep in the guts of the ship. Either scenario could crack a vessel open like an egg rapped against the edge of a frying pan.[8]

To increase the chances of scoring lethal hits, the VPB crews stowed extra 100-pounders on the bomb-bay catwalk or alongside the nose-wheel crawl space. Reloading the bomb shackles during flight required some real muscle work, but it also gave a PPC more high explosives to lob at the Japanese. While stowing loose centuries on the bomb-bay catwalk wasn't exactly regulation, it nonetheless enjoyed the approval of Lt. Cdr. Wright, the commanding officer of VPB-104. On one patrol, Wright took off with ten 100-pound bombs shackled up in the bomb bay and another ten stashed inside the aircraft for in-flight reloads. Like most PPCs, Wright and Stevens tended to be parsimonious with their ordnance and were reluctant to drop a string of two or more bombs against a small vessel when one well-placed century would do the job. Moreover, PPCs were eternal optimists who always figured a bigger ship would come along later in the patrol. In the case of the Fox Tare Charlie at Macau, however, Stevens doubted he would get a second shot because they might not find the ship again in the fog, so he ordered his bombardier to salvo their entire payload.[9]

Though Lieutenant Stevens assumed he had pounced on a Japanese vessel berthed outside Macau's territorial boundaries, he had actually spotted the SS *Masbate* at its berth in Macau's Inner Harbor, which fell within the neutral zone. The complex ownership and operation of the little 790-ton tramp steamer involved multiple stakeholders spread over three continents. In Panama, Wallem and Company had arranged Panamanian registry for the vessel. Wallem, however, functioned as a front company, and the ship actually belonged to the Chinese-owned South China Steamship Company in Hong Kong. In maritime terms, South China Steamship was the "beneficial owner," meaning the firm pocketed the profits for the operation of the *Masbate* less management fees due to Wallem in Panama. To further accentuate the multinational character of the vessel, which had been named after a Philippine island, the ship's master, Trygve "Trigger" Jorgensen, hailed from Norway. Moreover, he captained a Chinese crew and had taken refuge in Portuguese Macau.[10]

Consul Reeves, who retained his sense of humor despite living such a tenuous existence that he had to wear a revolver under his coat, referred to Captain Jorgensen as the "Commodore of the Allied Fleet" in Macau – a flotilla that by 1945 consisted of only the *Masbate*, since the Japanese had purchased or purloined every other vessel in Macau except for the immobile river steamer *Tung Hui.** An influx of refugees had tripled Macau's wartime population, leading to a severe housing shortage, and the *Tung Hui* had been pressed into service as emergency accommodation for Macanese refugees from Hong Kong. They nicknamed their new home "the hulk," which occupied a berth near the *Masbate.*[11]

Lieutenant Stevens had a skilled and experienced bombardier in his crew, but even for a seasoned deadeye the sudden appearance of the ship, the tight turn, and the unexpected order to drop on the *Masbate* amounted to a Hail Mary, the equivalent of a quick-draw pistol shot from a galloping horse. To Stevens's disappointment but not his surprise, most of the stick went long over the target and exploded on land. None of the bombs hit the *Tung Hui*, and some of the centuries detonated harmlessly in the low-tide muck of the Inner Harbor. However, several 100-pounders whistled into the Tamagnini Barbosa neighborhood, a crowded residential quarter ripe for collateral damage. Explosions damaged a Catholic school for the poor. At least one bomb and hundreds of machine-gun rounds slammed into the *Masbate*, killing the ship's cook and wounding several crewmembers. Captain Jorgensen suffered a bloody head wound and nearly lost a leg. His dog perished and his beloved ship was, as his friend Reeves later said with understated humor, "badly dented."[12]

As the commanding officer of VPB-104, Lt. Cdr. Wright felt obliged to add his own assessment of Lieutenant Stevens's mission on the final page of the aircraft action report filed after Stevens and his crew had returned to Tacloban. While squadron commanders signed off on aircraft action reports, the compilation of this routine paperwork normally fell to the ACI officers. The fact that Lt. Cdr. Wright inserted his own comments suggested that he understood the need to justify the actions of his executive officer. Wright stated: "Pilot properly briefed and understood Macao was neutral territory. Maze of islands and sudden appearance of ship resulted in attack. After realizing it was at Macao, pilot properly reported attack upon return to base."[13]

Lieutenant Commander Wright and the squadron's ACI officer both signed the aircraft action report, which made no mention of the

*Also spelled as *Tungwei.*

narrowly averted attack on the *Awa Maru* and chalked up the bombing of the *Masbate* to poor visibility and complex coastal geography. The squadron's war diary compiled four days later echoed this initial assessment: "The weather was very bad with limited visibility and rain showers. With such weather and with the maze of islands along the coast, the position of the attack was very doubtful."[14]

Despite these carefully worded justifications, however, the fact remained that the attack had occurred just five weeks after the strafing of Macau by the Hellcat pilots of VF-7. News of the attack on the *Masbate* reached Portugal within a matter of hours. Just a day after the airstrike, AP stories in American newspapers reported that unidentified planes had hit Macau and reminded readers rather pointedly that the colony had been "bombed in error" by American planes the previous month. As reports claiming nineteen civilians had died during the incident reached Lisbon, the Portuguese government once again protested at the violation of Macau's neutral status by American pilots.[15]

Consequently, Lieutenant Stevens found himself facing a court martial for bombing a ship in neutral Macau. An army colonel arrived to question Stevens and his crew, who had no interest in spending time in the brig. They rehearsed their story about the blinding fog, the navigational disorientation, and the sudden appearance of what they all presumed to be a Japanese ship. Then they stuck to their story. No sir, they all said, they had no idea they were over neutral Macau when the Nipponese ship had popped out of the mist like the Flying Dutchman. After some preliminary questioning of Stevens and his crew that corroborated events as described in the aircraft action report, the colonel concluded he did not have a case. A career officer, Lieutenant Stevens had been flying combat missions since the start of the war, and by the time the court martial investigation began, he had engaged in a dogfight with an H8K2-L flying boat carrying a Japanese admiral. The flying boat escaped from this rare form of air combat between four-engine aircraft but sustained so much damage it had to make an emergency landing on a hostile stretch of the China coast. With Chinese guerrillas closing in, the admiral killed himself to avoid the ignominy of capture.[16] The fact Stevens had been partially responsible for the death of a flag-rank enemy officer appears to have given him a degree of legal immunity for his indiscretion at Macau. The navy dropped the court martial investigation, perhaps because it could not stomach punishing an experienced and aggressive patrol plane commander for an error that could quite literally be blamed on the fog of war.[17]

Six weeks after Lieutenant Stevens had strewn a stick of bombs across Macau's Inner Harbor, a twin-engine PV-1 Ventura from VPB-137 sank a tugboat towing a barge just offshore from Macau on April 7. Since the PPC had just reached his patrol area, he wanted to conserve his load of three 100-pound bombs and six 5-inch rockets. Flying at mast height, he opted to glide-bomb the sixty-five-foot tug with a single century and scored a direct hit amidships. Smoke and debris spurted skywards, and the tugboat foundered so quickly that it slipped beneath the waves before the Ventura could circle around for another run. When they returned to base at Clark Field, which had been recaptured during the American invasion of Luzon, the PV-1 pilots claimed they had sunk a tugboat without any visible Portuguese flag or other symbol of its nationality that had been steaming three miles beyond the boundaries of Macau's Outer Harbor. Both aviators had been briefed on Macau's neutral status, and the squadron commander passed this information up the chain of command until it eventually reached the headquarters of General MacArthur, commander of army and navy air units based in the Philippines. In response to a communication from the Adjutant General at the War Department, MacArthur stressed that the tugboat had been sunk outside Macau's territorial waters and that the PV-1 pilots had been briefed beforehand on the neutral nature of Macau and its harbor. Moreover, it remained unclear if the tug had in fact come from Macau. The explanation apparently satisfied the Adjutant General, as it appears that the flight crew of the PV-1 never faced any form of military discipline. Meanwhile, on June 11 an unidentified but presumably naval aircraft had made yet another unsuccessful bomb run on the SS *Masbate*.[*][18] While it could have been argued that the PV-1 pilots had been at fault for bombing the nameless tugboat and Lieutenant Stevens had been negligent for taking a crack at the *Masbate*, nobody in the upper echelons of the American military establishment showed much interest in making the case. Admiral Nimitz, it seemed, would not be calling for another court of inquiry.[19]

---

[*]Additional airstrikes on Macau may have occurred on April 12 and July 5, 1945. However, to date no scholar has found corroborating U.S. Navy or USAAF documents for these two airstrikes or the June 11 attack on the *Masbate*.

The Bombing of Bungalow A

By the spring of 1945, the war's center of gravity had begun to shift from the Philippines to the volcanic islands that comprised the southernmost extremity of the Japanese home islands. The Fast Carrier Task Force – now designated Task Force 58 under the command of Admiral Raymond A. Spruance – had deployed northwards to support the invasion of Okinawa and would never return to the South China Sea, which had become a strategic backwater. Despite the increasing irrelevance of Hong Kong, however, naval patrol planes from Fleet Air Wing 10 and 17 (FAW 10 and FAW 17) continued to fly daylight missions over the Pearl River delta along with aircraft from the Philippines-based 5th Air Force and the China-based 14th Air Force, leading to frequent air-raid alerts at the Stanley camp in Hong Kong. Like a brawl between tenants in an adjacent apartment, however, much of the action occurred in Victoria Harbor and thus could be heard by the internees, but never seen. However, on occasion the action spilled out into open view. In the early afternoon of March 11, Ray Jones watched a lone American aircraft – one of the new B-29s, in his estimation – harass a tugboat offshore. However, while Jones possessed the ship-identification skills of a former navy man, his expertise did not extend to aircraft recognition. Rather than a B-29, as he thought, the four-engine bomber was a PB4Y-1. Lieutenant (j.g.) Edward M. Hagen, a VPB-104 pilot and squadron mate of Lieutenant Stevens, made three separate runs on the forty-foot minnow of a tug and failed to score a single bullseye, though the tug still took a severe beating after his gunners poured a thousand rounds into its hull.[1]

The continual threat of air attack wore on the nerves of the internees, who remembered the bombing of Bungalow C all too well. Whenever the alarm sounded, Ray Jones could see his own anxiety mirrored in the gaunt faces of Steve, his wife Mary, Gwen Flower, and indeed almost everyone in the camp.[2] Jones now referred to Flower often in his journal, using the initial "G," which meant that some fifteen months after the *first* G had been repatriated to Canada, Jones was again filling his journal pages with frequent references to an entirely different G.

In addition to writing about G and the depleted state of the camp food supply, Jones continued to record ship traffic and air activity in his journal. He made no mention of the *Ise* and *Hyuga*, which many internees had observed on February 14 as they passed offshore with a light cruiser and trio of destroyers.[3] After waiting out Operation *Gratitude* in Singapore, the hybrid battleship-carriers had weighed anchor for Tokyo Bay, their truncated flight decks laden with a cargo of aviation gasoline, rubber, tin, tungsten, and mercury. The internees noted the northbound bearing of the dreadnoughts and correctly surmised they were falling back to the home islands.[*]

"Planes around & bombs dropped early am despite low clouds," Jones penciled the next day. A week later he lamented the pervasive overcast and added, "Plenty plane activity all day despite the clouds."[4] The American air raids had once been cause for jubilation, but this excitement had been tempered by a wary sense of dread after the bombing of Bungalow C. Rather than watch the fireworks and wave at the pilots, as they had done previously whenever the Yanks had showed up in the earlier days of the occupation, everyone now scrambled for whatever protective cover they could find and cursed the Japanese for refusing them permission to build proper air-raid shelters.

To lend some credibility to the bogus claim that the camp had been marked with white crosses before the bombing of Bungalow C, the camp administration ordered the internees to dig cross-shaped ditches and backfill them with light-colored stones or white kaolin collected from a clay seam near Bungalow D. The Japanese military also removed

---

[*]In one of the most remarkable naval escapes of the war, the *Ise* and *Hyuga* successfully ran the gauntlet from Singapore to Japan. American carrier aircraft sank both ships at Kure in July 1945.

the machine-gun positions from Stanley Prison and promised that the camp guards would refrain from sniping at American aircraft with their rifles. In theory, the lack of antiaircraft fire from the camp and the large white crosses inset into the turf would dissuade American pilots from demolishing any more bungalows.[5]

On the second, third, and fourth days of April, Jones heard the drone of high-flying heavy bombers and the distant rumble of bombs falling on Victoria Harbor. He could tell that all three raids had been big ones, but he could only guess as to the targets. Curious for news, he watched as a truck arrived on the evening of April 4 with a load of vegetables for the camp kitchen. Deliveries of the *Hongkong News* had become increasingly sporadic, but that warm April evening the truck brought three copies that had rolled off the printing press earlier that day. As Jones scanned the front page, he noted a brief article on the raid that had occurred the day before. The article reported that antiaircraft fire had downed or damaged three B-24s and that "some damage was caused to vessels on the Japanese side." Jones doubted the claims about the downed B-24s, but since shipping losses nearly always went unreported in the *Hongkong News*, he shrewdly concluded that the raid must have caused significant harm to merchant vessels in Victoria Harbor.[6]

President Roosevelt died on April 12 and word reached the Stanley camp just one day later via rumor and the *Hongkong News*. "Roosevelt dead," Jones wrote tersely. "Truman takes over."[7] For Jones, however, the events of April – the bombing of Victoria Harbor, the change of leadership in Washington – might as well have been taking place on another planet, and his immediate concern centered, as always, on food.

The heavy bomb groups from the 5th Air Force that had carpeted Hong Kong with high explosives at the start of April flew two additional follow-up raids at the end of the month. As Jones had suspected, the April bombings had damaged or destroyed a number of ships in Victoria Harbor, including the escort vessel IJNS *Manju*. With spectacularly poor timing, the *Manju* had arrived at Hong Kong on April 2 with the remnants of convoy Hi-88J, which had lost the tanker *Sarawak Maru* as it departed from Singapore. On April 3, a rain of 1,000-pound bombs dropped by high-flying B-24s had killed more than fifty sailors and officers aboard the *Manju*, which caught fire and sank bow-first near Stonecutters Island. With the foundering of the *Manju*, only four escort ships remained from Hi-88J. All of the convoy's merchant ships had been lost during the run from Singapore to Hong Kong, and none of the escort vessels would ultimately survive the journey home to Moji.[8]

The April bombings had hammered the Cosmopolitan dockyard and Stonecutters Island while also inflicting substantial collateral damage on the tenement housing in Wan Chai and Sham Shui Po, where the Allied POWs could peer through the camp fence and see rescue teams untangling bodies from a smoking jumble of brick, timber, and roof tile.[9] In Happy Valley, errant bombs leveled the Gap Road primary school and the Sikh Temple, killing a leading member of the local Sikh community.* In Causeway Bay, the bombs struck the compound that housed St. Paul's church and a convent for the Order of St. Paul de Chartres, which lost nine sisters to the American bombs. Still more civilians died in the convent's orphanage, homeless shelter, and medical facility known locally as the "French hospital" in honor of the Francophone nuns who ran it.[10]

Despite the malaise caused by continual hunger, Jones and the other internees kept busy with the many chores necessary to fend off starvation, ensure basic health and sanitation, and maintain the camp buildings. In addition, Jones learned in May that the Japanese had finally reversed their long-standing objection to bomb shelters and would allow internee work gangs to dig air-raid tunnels, though the malnourished men assigned to this task made fitful progress with picks and spades. This proved to be risky work, and a collapsing tunnel roof injured at least one internee.[11] Throughout the camp the internees organized themselves into air-raid precaution (ARP) groups and planned for sandbagging designated rooms as bomb shelters.[12] Word reached the camp that the war in Europe had ended with Germany's unconditional surrender on May 7, but the need for ARP groups and blast-proof shelters remained urgent, since the war in Asia was clearly not over. Everyone expected more American airstrikes and, perhaps, an Allied invasion of Hong Kong. The latter expectation was not necessarily a welcome one, since camp rumors whispered that the Japanese would slaughter the internees if an American landing appeared to be imminent.

On June 12, as Jones worked on constructing a frame for suspending a cooking pot in the kitchen of the camp hospital, he watched formations

---

*Gap Road no longer exists and was replaced postwar by the easternmost extension of Queen's Road East.

of four-engine bombers passing by overhead. They looked to be hitting targets around Victoria Harbor again, so Jones and the other internees wondered why they did not hear the crump of exploding bombs.[13] In the days that followed, Jones continued to work in the camp hospital, where he and the rest of his work detail patched up the roof with lumber salvaged from the wreckage of Bungalow C. Rumor soon reported that Causeway Bay had been set ablaze with a new kind of incendiary weapon that burned everything it touched, including seawater. That explained why he had not heard the usual detonations of bombs packed with high explosives, Jones figured, though he had no way of knowing that the 5th Air Force had dropped a new and particularly horrific new weapon known as napalm on Hong Kong for the first and only time.[14] Jones had always been a connoisseur of the war rumors that coursed through the camp, though they had little direct bearing on his own daily existence, which focused on the inadequacies of his caloric intake and the laborious tasks of camp life – mending broken wheelbarrows, digging potato patches, chopping firewood. Jones and the other members of his work detail had the roofing job just about finished by the end of June, but some of the hospital water taps still needed work.[15]

With the exception of the younger children who were growing up in the camp and knew no other reality, most of the internees at Stanley yearned for their comfortable lives before the war while simultaneously feeling increasingly disconnected from them. As the years had crawled past, Jones had certainly found it harder and harder to recall his prewar existence, which had ended when Marj left Hong Kong in 1941 and he had shouldered a Lee Enfield. Despite the passage of time, however, he had not forgotten about his wife and child. Moreover, they had not forgotten about him either, as he continued to receive mail from Marj in Australia. Her postcards, letters, and photographs arrived sporadically and out of sequence, like rare and beautiful birds. Letters could take eighteen months to make the circuitous postal migration from Allied Australia to Axis Hong Kong, where delivery hinged on the caprices of the Japanese occupation authorities. In July 1945, Jones received a letter from Marj dated December 1943. She had included a photograph of Rae, now old enough to attend kindergarten. Jones had been separated from his wife for a half decade of war and incarceration, and he had never even met his daughter. He looked forward to their eventual reunification, writing in his journal, "Soon be with you now Marj darling." However, the immediate problem of survival in the camp made this postwar reassembly of his family seem abstract, a much-desired but hypothetical event so far in the future that it had no more substance to it than the smoke from the camp kitchen fires.[16]

"5 yrs. since Marj went away," Jones wrote on July 5. "I've forgotten what married life was like now." By this time, Jones had fallen deeply in love with Gwen Flower, who appeared to be equally smitten. The affair seemed to lack the emotional seesawing of Jones's first tryst with the Canadian G, which had involved its share of bickering and jealousy. He simply called Flower "sweet," and she apparently reciprocated his affections, perhaps because she shared Jones's intense and immediate need for companionship and normalcy after three years of living in a giant wire cage, herded by men with bayonets and suffering from famishment so acute that eating a banana peel found in the garbage qualified as an unexpected treat. The pairing up of men and women whose spouses remained outside the camp had been cause for gossip in the earliest days of internment, but by 1945 such partnering had largely become accepted and not particularly rare. In the camp, survival remained the end goal, and pooling one's resources – emotional, financial, intellectual, nutritional, and physical – with a new companion helped ensure that survival. Moreover, because such temporary alliances increased the odds of survival, they would also help to ensure the eventual return of each member of the partnership to their legal spouses after the war.[17]

Perhaps because he could not take care of his own family, Jones took care of Flower instead. Like many internees, he had become adept at repairing, repurposing, and making do with the odd bits and assorted scraps that could be scrounged up in the camp. Many of these projects would have absorbed time like a sponge soaked up water, but Jones may well have seen that as a blessing in a camp where boredom frequently pressed down on the spirit like a smothering bank of low-hanging overcast. He made Flower a milk mixer, a garden trowel, and a dustpan. He repaired her sunblind and her mirror. He dug her a potato patch, built her a cucumber frame, ground her rations of rice, chopped her wood, and even "de-bugged" her chair, which surely amounted to a labor of love. He also gave her gifts, some practical, such as homemade shoes or a spoon, and others designed to show his affection, such as a small handmade boat and a flower vase he had fashioned from a .50-caliber shell casing ejected by one of the Hellcats that had strafed the camp in January.[18]

Jones and Flower sometimes met on the flat roofs of the three-story camp buildings, which offered a breath of air and a view of the island-speckled sea. As the summer heat intensified, many of the internees spent their nights on the roofs, where the caress of the sea breeze made sleep come more readily. Undisturbed slumber remained a rarity, however, and not just because the surface of the roof made for an unyieldingly hard bed. Sometimes nocturnal thunderstorms growled out of the blackness to drench the rooftops in a pulsing whirlwind of lighting and rain. On other evenings, the internees would startle awake in the darkness to the drone of an aircraft passing unseen overhead and the rhythmic thump of machine-gun fire in the distance.

American air activity continued during the daylight hours as well, albeit on a much-reduced scale that reflected the shifting of the front lines to the coast of Japan. In July 1945, the 5th Air Force began deploying its fighter and bomber groups from the Philippines to Okinawa and the neighboring island of Ie Shima, where they could be used to bomb Japan in preparation for the endgame invasion of the home islands.[19] Heavy bomb groups still based in the Philippines kept Formosa and the China coast under constant surveillance, as did the navy patrol bomber squadrons. Due to the paucity of significant military targets in the Pearl River delta, major bombing raids ended after a final series of B-24 strikes against Canton in mid-July. From a military point of view, Canton no longer mattered, and neither did Hong Kong. Victoria Harbor had always been the glittering jewel of Hong Kong, but this once-precious asset had lost its value when American submarines and aircraft severed Japan's maritime supply lines. Preoccupied with military operations inside China, the 14th Air Force had scaled back the missions it flew over Hong Kong to reconnaissance flights and intermittent fighter sweeps of modest size. However, the 5th Air Force and FAW 17 continued to fly sorties over Hong Kong on a daily basis despite the colony's irrelevancy to the outcome of the war. Most missions to Hong Kong in summer 1945 consisted of a single high-endurance aircraft, with radar-equipped B-24s flying night intruder sorties and the navy patrol bombers conducting offensive patrols during daylight. Flight crews interdicted the few Japanese vessels still operating in the colony's coastal waters and harassed the garrison, but such missions amounted to a minor sideshow in a bloody carnival culminating far to the north on the home islands.

Given the cessation of major airstrikes against Hong Kong, Ray Jones had reason to hope that there would be no more incidents like the bombing of Bungalow C. On July 25, however, a twin-engine seaplane droned over the camp, dropped a stick of bombs on the compound without attracting any ground fire, and puttered serenely out to sea. Belatedly, the air-raid alarm went off. One bomb smashed through the roof of the main hall of St. Stephen's College and came to rest on the cot of an internee who, quite fortuitously, was not lying down at the time. Even more fortuitously, the bomb failed to explode. Additional dud bombs smacked into the dirt around the college, with at least one nosing into the earth near the makeshift white crosses that the internees had carved into the soil after the demolition of Bungalow C by the U.S. Navy. Two more bombs hurtled towards Bungalow A, which sat just to the south of St. Stephen's, and punched through the roof in a spray of splintered lumber and fractured roof tiles. One bomb landed in the living room without detonating, though it possessed sufficient weight and velocity to do significant damage. The other bomb exploded in the lavatory, where it shattered the plumbing and porcelain, blew out a wall, and injured the occupants of the next room. The wounded collectively represented the epitome of noncombatants: a reverend, a teenage girl, two young children, and their grandmother. By day's end the camp commander, assorted military officers, and representatives from the military governor's office had visited the injured in the camp hospital and expressed uncharacteristic concern for their welfare.

Curiously, only the bomb that struck the lavatory had exploded. Moreover, the internees discovered that the dud bombs – eleven in total – appeared to be of either American or British origin and that some had "100 lbs. 1943" stenciled on the casing. In addition, some of the internees identified the offending seaplane as an American model, though others felt sure they had seen a plane of Japanese design. Few internees knew much about military aircraft in any case, and none of them could claim to be familiar with warplane designs that had come into production after they had been marched through the gates of the Stanley camp in early 1942. Still, the internees recognized the large, slow-flying aircraft as one they had frequently seen flying overhead in the past. Regardless of the aircraft type, many of the internees agreed that a Japanese pilot had been in the cockpit. Jones wrote in his journal later that day: "Jap flying boat dropped practice bombs on St. Stephens & A. Bungalow area. 4 persons injured 12.15pm. The effort would appear to be deliberate, flying & bombing weather being perfect & the plane flew slowly & low."

In blaming the Japanese for the bombing, Jones mirrored popular opinion among the internees, who believed that the attack had been staged as a half-baked propaganda stunt designed to sully the reputation of the United States and drive a wedge between the Americans and the British. However, as Jones noted, the unidentified aircraft, the 92-percent failure rate of the ordnance it had dropped, and the nature of the civilian casualties invited diverse interpretations of what had actually happened. In the last line of his entry for July 25, he wrote, "Many theories by Camp 'experts' re type of bomb, depth charge, identity & type of plane & reasons for the event."[20]

The Japanese certainly had their own opinion about who should be held accountable for dropping bombs on the camp. A series of stories in the *Hongkong News* asserted that the Americans had carried out the attack, and the internees took these stories as further proof that the raid had been staged for propaganda purposes. In an amalgamation of the objective reporting and energetic editorializing that characterized the journalistic style of the paper, the July 26 edition reminded its readers of the perfidy of American airmen: "It will be recalled that the enemy, in his frantic attempts to frighten the civilian populations, made indiscriminate raids on the same camp on January 16 this year, as well as on Macau, while practically the whole French Convent was demolished last April." For all its rhetoric, the *Hongkong News* had a point: American pilots had caused civilian casualties in Hong Kong on numerous occasions.[21]

The internees, however, dismissed the Japanese assertion that the Americans had bombed Bungalow A as an outrageous claim. In doing so, they discounted the argument that if the Japanese had staged a phony raid, they had shown an improbable amount of mercy by using bombs that failed to explode eleven times out of twelve. More live ordnance would certainly have produced a more potent propaganda coup. Moreover, the Japanese had never staged a phony bombing raid before on any of the civilian or military prison camps in Hong Kong, but U.S. Navy aircraft had bombed, rocketed, and strafed the Stanley camp on January 16 and killed fourteen Allied civilians. That the Americans might hit the camp again seemed entirely plausible from the Japanese perspective.

To deepen the mystery, the unmarked seaplane reappeared over the Stanley camp three days after the bombing of Bungalow A, and while the machine still failed to provoke any ground fire, the Japanese did opt to sound the air-raid alarm as it approached. The riddle of the aircraft's identity remained unsolved, however, which made it difficult to assign culpability for the incident. The Japanese regime in Hong Kong had the capability to mount a propaganda operation of the sort theorized by the internees, though whether it had the motivation to do so in the end stages of a lost war remained open to question. No unit assigned to the 14th Air Force on the Chinese mainland flew seaplanes, so General Chennault's command likely remained blameless as well. A detachment of PBY Catalina flying boats from the Royal Australian Air Force had deployed to the Philippines to fly minelaying missions over harbors along the China coast in the spring of 1945. However, these missions had ended on June 1, so the Aussies could be dropped from the lineup of potential suspects.[22] In the Philippines, the 3rd Emergency Rescue Squadron of the 5th Air Force operated a small number of OA-10s, the army version of the navy PBY-5 Catalina, but the unit flew air-sea rescue missions rather than bombing sorties.[23] In addition, the Catalina was a prewar aircraft design, so if the guilty seaplane had been a PBY, some of the internees likely would have recognized it as such. In all probability, the 5th Air Force was off the hook, too. The same could certainly *not* be said of the 7th Fleet, which had squadrons in the Philippines equipped with PBM-3D and PBM-5 Mariner seaplanes, a newer aircraft design that would have been unknown to the internees.[24] FAW 10 and FAW 17 had been dispatching twin-engine Mariners on solo missions to the Hong Kong area for months. Moreover, navy patrol aircraft often carried a bellyful of 100-pound bombs of the sort dropped through the tile roofs of Bungalow A and St. Stephen's. If the offending seaplane belonged to a fleet air wing squadron based in the Philippines, however, the fog of war had intervened to shield that squadron's identity as thoroughly as the mists that often erased the islands of Hong Kong.

On the Beach

Ray Jones spent the first week of August 1945 repairing the roof of Bungalow A. With so much air activity over the camp, he had grown accustomed to monitoring the skies. However, as a former Royal Navy sailor he had maintained a keen interest in the waters offshore as well. Like reading the *Hongkong News*, watching the ship traffic allowed him to glean information about the progress of the war. His binoculars, which he had been trying to sell to raise cash for food, had proven invaluable in this endeavor. During the long years of his incarceration he had observed just about every possible kind of Japanese vessel steam past in the East Lamma Channel, and once he had even seen a four-engine flying boat touch down in Tai Tam Bay. However, the dearth of Japanese ships in the summer of 1945 suggested that things had gone very badly for the Japanese navy and merchant marine.[1]

During the first weeks of August, rumors had been circulating about the end of the war, and some of the more optimistic internees had even begun preparations for packing up and leaving the camp. Jones himself felt increasingly certain that the Allies would soon triumph over Japan just as they had over Germany. There had been plenty of omens pointing to an Allied victory. Deliveries of the *Hongkong News* had ended, for one thing, and Jones interpreted this to mean that the situation had grown so dire for Japan that the editors could no longer spin the news to say otherwise. He figured the Japanese had shut off the newspaper supply to conceal from the internees how badly the war was going for Japan. However, Jones could see that the Japanese garrison intended to continue defending Hong Kong. He could hear work crews blasting tunnels and other defensive positions into the hills. With long bayonets affixed to their rifles, the camp guards drilled for hand-to-hand combat. Small military speedboats trailed wakes near Lamma Island, and the boom tenders continued to maintain the antisubmarine net strung across the East Lamma Channel.

Oceangoing vessels heading for port in Victoria Harbor typically followed the East Lamma Channel that cut between Lamma and the south shore of Hong Kong Island. This meant that vessels transiting the channel passed close by the Stanley Peninsula, allowing ship watchers like Ray Jones to keep track of arrivals and departures. He also monitored the antisubmarine boom, which the Japanese had installed in the channel to foil American submarines. As a form of maritime defense, the submarine boom had the virtue of simplicity, since it consisted of little more than a giant net of steel cable suspended from a series of buoys moored in a line across the channel. The submarine boom presented an effective barrier to submerged submarines, but since the net also blocked the channel to shipping, it had been equipped with a gate in the netting that could be pulled open whenever a friendly ship needed to pass through the channel. Auxiliary naval craft known as boom tenders performed the vital but not particularly glamorous job of operating and maintaining the boom gate in the East Lamma Channel as well as the boom gate in the net the British had originally strung across Lei Yue Mun, the harbor channel on the northeast side of Hong Kong Island.[2]

In August 1945 few military duties in Hong Kong could have been more hazardous than serving on one of the garrison's boom tenders, which remained easy prey for the American patrol bombers that overflew Hong Kong on a daily basis. Flight crews from VPB-104 continued to execute many of these missions, though the squadron had been in theater for so long that the original crews had completed their tours and returned to the United States. In May 1945, Lt. Stevens had rotated home after flying fifty combat missions with VPB-104, bringing his wartime total to an odds-defying 114 missions. With the help of his crew, he had achieved ace status by downing six Japanese aircraft – five by gunfire and one by the blunt-force trauma of a midair collision. Lieutenant Stevens thus joined the rare fraternity of multiengine bomber pilots who could claim the accolades of acedom.[3]

In March 1945, VPB-104 had moved from Tacloban airfield on Leyte to Clark Field, which had become a hub of American air activity since its recapture. As part of this redeployment to the hot and dusty plains of Luzon, the 7th Fleet reassigned VPB-104 from FAW 10 to FAW 17. While the mission brief under this new command remained largely the same, the squadron's flight line underwent a significant change in July when the unit began transitioning from the PB4Y-1 Liberator to the next generation of naval patrol bomber, the PB4Y-2 Privateer. A variant of the B-24 designed specifically for the navy, the PB4Y-2 had been custom-designed for low-altitude maritime patrol work. To improve stability and handling when flying at masthead height, for example, the Privateer featured a single vertical stabilizer rather than the distinctive twin-rudder configuration of the army Liberator. Because fighter attack from below remained unlikely when hugging the waves, the Privateer lacked the belly turret that remained standard equipment on the B-24. All four of the engines had been optimized for low-altitude performance, which meant that the Pratt and Whitney R-1830s lacked the turbochargers necessary for missions flown at high altitudes. As a result, a Privateer could wave hop at a top speed of 300mph, but only operate up to the relatively low ceiling of 21,000 feet. Fully equipped with the latest technological gadgetry, the PB4Y-2 carried a cutting-edge collection of radar, electronic countermeasures, and communications gear. Despite the deletion of the belly turret, the Privateer bristled with twelve .50-caliber guns in four turrets and two waist blisters – a weapons package that outgunned the PB4Y-1 Liberator that Lieutenant Stevens had flown by a substantial margin.

At dawn on the morning of August 14, 1945, a PB4Y-2 taxied out to the end of the runway at Clark Field with Lt. Keith A. Burton in the cockpit as the PPC. Working in well-practiced unison with his copilot, Burton throttled up the four radial engines, released the brakes, and began his takeoff roll. That morning the mission called for a standard 1,100-mile patrol, so his aircraft carried its maximum fuel load and ten 100-pound bombs. Once airborne, Burton flew northwest over the jungles of Luzon, continued out over the South China Sea until the mainland came into sight, and then began his combat patrol along the south China coast. By ten in the morning Burton and his crew had reached Hong Kong, where they found clear conditions ideal for target spotting. They soon noticed a wake in Tai Tam Bay, and upon closer investigation, discovered what they assumed to be a small cargo launch. In fact, they had caught one of the boom tenders, which began running for Tweed Bay, perhaps in an attempt to avoid detection or perhaps out of simple fatalism. Since their vessel was doomed, the sailors aboard may have calculated, self-preservation dictated that they run the ship into the sand and scramble clear before the shooting began.

No air-raid alarm sounded in the Stanley camp, and the low-altitude approach of the patrol bomber caught everyone by surprise. As the internees scrambled for shelter, the guards started banging away at the PB4Y-2 with their Arisaka rifles despite earlier pledges not to fire at American aircraft from within the camp boundaries. Moreover, some of the riflemen stood beside the white crosses that the internees had installed to signal to Allied warplanes that the camp housed noncombatants. A number of internees had been down on the beach that fronted Tweed Bay below the walls of Stanley Prison, and as the PB4Y-2 flashed past with its guns rattling they splashed out of the water, scooped up the children among them, and dropped to the sand or behind the rocks. Reaching the protective shelter of the camp's sturdier buildings would have required a long run up an extended series of concrete steps, and even in top physical shape such a dash would have been an imprudent move during an air raid. In any case, the poorly nourished internees could barely get up the stairs at all, much less get up them at a run. They had no choice but to stay on the terrifyingly exposed beach and hope for the best.

Ray Jones apparently numbered among the many internees who witnessed the entire attack, as later that day he described the air raid by what he presumed to be a B-29 in his journal. Most likely Jones would have been watching from the camp hospital when the patrol bomber caught the boom tender as it motored past Lo Chau To, an islet just offshore from the hospital, beach, and prison.* Some internees believed they saw the tender's crew firing a machine gun at the incoming American plane, which straddled the little ship with four bombs that plunged into the sea like hundred-pound rocks. Fuzed for the usual four-to-five-second delay, the bombs sank and then exploded underwater with enough violence to punch the hull of the boom tender right out of the water. As the shattered tender splashed back down into

---

*Lo Chau To is also known as Tweed Island.

the waves, the warplane circled away to the southeast and disappeared from view. A few minutes later some of the internees caught sight of the bomber as it crossed over the D'Aguilar Peninsula at Windy Gap and sped low across Tai Tam Bay. The forward turrets opened fire, and tracer rounds chewed into the boom tender, which drifted dead in the water. Any machine guns aboard had been silenced, and internees could see the crew jumping overboard.

Lieutenant Burton buzzed the foundering boom tender two more times so that his gunners could get in a few more bursts. Rather than circle around for a fifth strafing run against the tender, which had been so thoroughly sieved that only the natural buoyancy of its wooden-timbered hull kept it afloat, he chose to be parsimonious with his ordnance and banked back out to sea with six centuries still shackled in the bomb bay. Showing similar fire control, the gunners aboard the PB4Y-2 had hammered the hapless ship with 500 well-placed rounds of .50-caliber ammunition. They reported over the interphone that their aircraft had not taken any hits during the attack and that, moreover, they had never spotted any incoming enemy fire.

As the drone of American engines faded into the haze, the boom tender settled into the shallow water off Lo Chau To, leaving an oily circle of floating debris and a dozen crewmen who had leapt into the sea to avoid the merciless strafing attacks. Some of these survivors likely washed up on Lo Chau To, eyes glassy with shock as they crabbed their way over the barnacle-studded rocks, vomiting and dripping blood.[4]

Given the demise of the little boom tender during a one-sided battle with an impressively large and well-armed American bomber, the internees may well have thought it fitting that Japan declared its unconditional surrender the next day. Though they had not been intentionally seeking such an accolade, Lieutenant Burton and his crew – and by extension, Lieutenant Stevens and all the other pilots and airmen who had flown with VPB-104 – could claim the honor of executing the last American airstrike of the war against Hong Kong. The air campaign against Hong Kong had largely been waged by the army pilots of the 14th Air Force, though the 5th Air Force had provided some muscular last-minute backup. Despite the dominant role of the USAAF in the air war above Hong Kong, however, the final offensive sortie against the Japanese-occupied colony had been flown by a patrol bomber of the U.S. Navy.

Forever and A Day

On the afternoon of September 10, 1945, Ray Jones boarded the escort vessel HMAS *Geraldton*, which shuttled him out to where the *Empress of Australia* rode at anchor in Junk Bay. The big troopship had disembarked 2,600 men from the 5358 Airfield Construction Wing of the RAF, who would reconstruct Kai Tak airfield and contribute to the postwar rebuilding of Hong Kong. Jones boarded the *Empress of Australia* along with a thousand other Stanley internees and 900 former prisoners of war from Sham Shui Po. He enjoyed a late dinner onboard, found an empty space to sleep outside on the boat deck, and penned his daily journal entry before turning in for the night. "Goodbye Gwen dearest," he wrote, "for a little while only I hope."[1]

Jones had been able to see the warships from the British Pacific Fleet (BPF) when they anchored offshore south of Stanley on August 29, 1945, two weeks after the capitulation of Japan. Commanded by Rear Admiral Cecil Halliday Jepson Harcourt, Task Group 111.2 included the fleet carrier HMS *Indomitable*, the light carrier HMS *Venerable*, the battleship HMS *Anson*, several cruisers, a half-dozen destroyers, the submarine tender HMS *Maidstone*, eight submarines, and six Australian minesweepers.[2] After refueling in the Philippines and loading up with victuals, medicines, and other relief supplies from American depots overflowing with material originally stockpiled for the invasion of

Japan, the fleet had left Subic Bay and set course for Hong Kong, where Harcourt planned to facilitate the surrender of the Japanese garrison and liberate Allied POWs and interned civilians. As Jones watched in elation, Royal Navy pilots flying Hellcats and Corsairs performed victory rolls over the Stanley camp and an American transport aircraft parachuted medical supplies, cigarettes, chocolate, and a variety of other items into the camp – much to the terror of the children, who expected to be bombed rather than showered with treats.[3]

On the morning of August 30, pilots from the *Indomitable* and *Venerable* executed the first and only Royal Navy airstrike of the war against Hong Kong when they bombed and strafed a flotilla of Japanese *shin'yō* suicide speedboats based on Lamma Island.[4] Meanwhile, the lead elements of Harcourt's fleet threaded the narrow passage at Lei Yue Mun, which at its narrowest point placed the ships within range of Japanese small-arms fire, but all remained quiet as the ships passed through the open antisubmarine boom and entered Victoria Harbor. Armed landing parties soon headed for Hong Kong Island and Kowloon, where astonished Royal Navy sailors stepped ashore to find their own arrival reported in a joint special edition of *The South China Morning Post* and *The Hongkong Telegraph*. A cadre of journalists and editors had resurrected these prewar newspapers, which had been moribund since December 1941. The Japanese-owned *Hongkong News*, meanwhile, had printed its last edition on August 17.

At the Stanley camp, Jones prepared for the flag-raising ceremony that would mark the liberation of Hong Kong. A large group of prisoners from Sham Shui Po arrived at the camp that morning, and at five in the afternoon, Admiral Harcourt and assorted other Royal Navy and Royal Marine personnel drove into the camp in jeeps and DUKW amphibious trucks offloaded from the fleet. The jeeps and amphibians provoked a great deal of interest from the internees, who had never seen these types of vehicles before, as did the astonishing health and vitality of the sailors and marines.

A crowd of internees gathered by the flagpole with the former POWs from Sham Shui Po. Still more internees watched from the balconies and roofs of the three-story camp buildings that had been their homes since January 1942. Rear Admiral Harcourt offered a few remarks, the captain of the *Maidstone* gave a longer speech, and Jones provided the Union Jack, which he had pulled at long last from the innards of his mattress where he had hidden it after surrendering to the Japanese in December 1941. A military bugler sounded attention. Clad in his best shirt and shorts, Jones proudly hoisted the Union Jack that might have cost him his life had it been discovered by his captors. As the bugle notes faded, an east wind gently fanned the flag as the crowd sang "God Save the King," then gave three cheers for the monarch. A representative from each of the other nationalities in the camp then raised their flags – American, Belgian, Nationalist Chinese, Danish, French, Greek, Dutch, Norwegian, Polish, and Russian. The bugler sounded "Last Post" as all flags descended to half-mast in honor of those who had perished during the war years.[5]

Two days later Rear Admiral Harcourt established the British Military Administration (BMA). In an action with obvious parallels to the Japanese roundup of Allied nationals after the fall of Hong Kong in 1941, the BMA placed all Japanese civilians in the Stanley camp, which the Allied internees had quite happily vacated. With the much-needed help of the newly arrived 3rd Commando Brigade, Royal Navy sailors and Royal Marines marched more than 10,000 Japanese POWs into Whitfield Barracks and the Sham Shui Po camp in Kowloon, though the head of the Kempeitai and other suspected war criminals went to Stanley Prison instead.[6]

All Japanese forces in mainland China formally capitulated to the Nationalist Chinese on September 16, 1945. That same day the Japanese garrison in Hong Kong surrendered to the British during a no-nonsense fifteen-minute ceremony at Government House, the residence of the colonial governor that had been modified to suit Japanese architectural tastes during the occupation. Major General Okada Umekichi and Vice Admiral Fujita Ruitaro, the ranking Japanese officers in Hong Kong, handed over their swords and signed the surrender documents in elegant, vertical columns of Japanese calligraphy. In the presence of a Canadian captain, an American colonel, and a Nationalist Chinese general, Rear Admiral Harcourt then signed the surrender documents on behalf of both Great Britain and China in a room dominated by the flags of the United Kingdom and Nationalist China. After three years and eight months of Japanese occupation and American airstrikes, the war had finally ended in Hong Kong.[7]

With the surrender proclamation signed and the former occupiers under lock and key, Rear Admiral Harcourt and the BMA took stock of the colony and its populace. Approximately 1.6 million people had lived in Hong Kong before the Japanese invasion in December 1941, but by August 1945 that number had declined to fewer than 600,000 inhabitants and perhaps as few as 400,000. The Japanese policy of deporting as much of the Chinese population as possible accounted for most of this dramatic population loss. No definitive figures for wartime civilian fatalities existed, but estimates put the death toll from American air raids alone at 10,000 men, women, and children. Other estimates suggested that the Japanese regime had executed over 10,000 residents of Hong Kong as well. While violence had taken many lives, far more civilians had succumbed to disease, malnutrition, and outright starvation. In total, as many as 360,000 residents of Hong Kong may have perished during the war years, though many died outside the colony after expulsion by the Japanese regime. These deaths included civilians of many nationalities, but the vast majority were Chinese.[8]

Bombed, looted, and depopulated, Hong Kong teetered on the edge of famine and epidemic. Given these conditions, evacuating the thousands of newly liberated internees and POWs remained an urgent priority for Rear Admiral Harcourt. Accordingly, the hospital ship *Oxfordshire* docked at the Kowloon wharves and embarked former internees and POWs with tuberculosis, malaria, and other serious maladies, injuries, and conditions. On September 3, just five days after the arrival of Harcourt's task group, the hospital ship left port for Manila with the first batch of repatriates – the term used for Allied soldiers and civilians returning home from Asia for rest and recuperation.[9] Years of captivity under adverse conditions had left the Stanley internees mentally and physically exhausted. Moreover, many of them emerged from the camp unemployed, homeless, widowed, and destitute. For all of these reasons, most of the Stanley internees accepted the offer of repatriation back to their home country, including Ray Jones.

At 7:30 in the morning on September 11, the *Empress of Australia* weighed anchor and departed Victoria Harbor. Ray Jones caught a final glimpse of Hong Kong as the troopship left the protected waters of the colony and ventured out into the rollers of the South China Sea.

Rather than reflect on his experiences in the Stanley camp, he wrote instead about shipboard conditions: "Good food issued, 20 cigs, choc. & soap issued. Hot & sticky on our deck."[10]

From Hong Kong, the *Empress of Australia* steamed to the Philippines. On the morning of September 13, Jones watched the shell-flayed island fortress of Corregidor pass by as the liner entered Manila Bay. He counted more than 150 ships in the bay and watched as landing craft shuttled between them, their wakes breaking against the hulks of half-sunken Japanese vessels. Once the *Empress* had docked, Jones received a Red Cross message from Marj that confirmed she had already returned to England from Australia and would be waiting when he arrived at Liverpool.[11]

Much to Jones's frustration, the *Empress of Australia* remained at anchor in Manila harbor for a week. Though the U.S. military brought the Hong Kong POWs ashore for rest and recuperation, the American authorities prevented the civilian internees from disembarking. Rain periodically washed over the liner, bringing little respite from the tropical temperatures, and Jones soon developed an uncomfortable rash from the heat and humidity. A thousand former POWs newly released from camps in Formosa boarded on September 18, and then two days later the *Empress* left port in the wake of a U.S. Navy minesweeper.[12]

Despite the impressive size of the *Empress of Australia*, Jones found the ship to be almost unbearably crowded during the journey south to Singapore. "It's impossible to be alone anywhere," he wrote in his diary, which he continued to update on a daily basis. He seemed unable to reconcile his desire to reunite with Gwen Flower, whom he dreamed of while sleeping on deck at night, and his duty to return to the wife and daughter he knew only through the outdated snapshots that Marj had enclosed in her letters. He wrote to both his wife and his lover while the *Empress* steamed for Singapore through light seas and patches of drizzle, though he confessed in his journal, "I do almost nothing but think of G."[13]

At Singapore, many of the civilian repatriates disembarked from the *Empress of Australia* so they could switch to other vessels bound for Australia. However, 400 demobilizing naval personnel boarded in their place, and the liner departed Singapore on September 27. After another port call at Colombo, the troopship continued across the Indian Ocean on October 4. Along the way Jones enjoyed the sunsets and porpoises, watched movies – *Forever and a Day* – and lined up to be measured for clothing that would be provided when they reached Port Suez.[14]

The *Empress of Australia* made a brief port call at Aden on October 10 and then continued onwards to Port Suez, where Jones sent a telegram to Marj with an update on his progress. As promised, the supply depot at the Ataka docks issued much-needed new clothes to Jones and his fellow repatriates. After transiting the Suez Canal on October 16, the *Empress of Australia* crossed the Mediterranean, threaded the Strait of Gibraltar, and headed north towards the British Isles. Jones had never lost his sea legs after his fourteen years in the Royal Navy, but many passengers suffered from seasickness in the heavy Atlantic weather.

On the afternoon of October 27, after a forty-eight-day journey, Jones stood on deck as the *Empress of Australia* docked at Liverpool. In the final entry of his wartime diary, Jones wrote, "Am ready to go now." Then he walked down the gangplank to meet his wife, the five-year-old daughter he had never met, and his mother, who would welcome home her only surviving son. Jones and his older brother Alfred had both joined the Royal Navy, but while Jones had left the service prewar, his brother had stayed in and been lost with his ship.[15]

The years of deprivation in the Stanley camp had left every prisoner with psychological scars, though some men and women emerged from the experience with a clear-eyed sense of where they belonged and what they wanted. For Ray Jones, the postwar transition proved far more difficult, and the news of his brother's death would have only compounded the emotional challenges of this wrenching shift from life as a prisoner to whatever came after. His experiences in the camp had unmoored him from his prewar life even while other prisoners had remained firmly anchored to it. Jones seemed intent on continuing his relationship with Gwen Flower and had written her postwar address on a scrap of paper folded away into a secret recess of his diary, but she had understood that he would have to go home to Marj and Rae. Flower sent Jones an atlas as a parting gift and a note telling him that he belonged with his wife and daughter. Marj, however, found the letter, and the devastation that Jones felt at losing Gwen was matched by the sense of betrayal that Marj experienced when she learned of her husband's wartime infidelities. In a fury, she tore up the letter from Flower, not to mention their wedding photos and all of their wartime correspondence. Jones managed to slip his wartime journal to a friend, however, so it survived the combustion that nearly consumed his marriage. In the end, Jones reconciled with Marj, and the hurt and loss that they had both experienced – and that Gwen Flower had no doubt felt keenly as well – became part of the greater mass of grief and anguish inflicted by a global conflict that had stretched from the corpse-filled courtyards of Nanking to the radioactive rubble of Nagasaki. In 1947, Ray and Marj returned to Hong Kong with their young daughter Rae, now seven years old. Like so many repatriates and evacuees who had found their way back to the colony, they hoped to clear away the wreckage of the war, rebuild their lives, and claim their place in Hong Kong's postwar story. The future of the city remained unknown to Ray and Marj, but they wagered with characteristic Hong Kong optimism that it would be a highly prosperous one.*

*In 1952, Raymond and Marjorie Jones had a second daughter, Diana. Jones died of cancer in 1957. He was fifty-one.

Reparations, Reassignments, and Record Jackets

Consul John Pownall Reeves learned of the Japanese surrender while listening to the BBC and immediately rushed outside to swap the faded British flag that flew over the consulate for a newer and much larger Union Jack. In 1943, BAAG agents had smuggled the flag into Macau and delivered it to Reeves, who had resolved that he would only run it up the masthead when the Allies had won the war. The moment of triumph had come at last, and Reeves jubilantly pulled the brightly colored Union Jack to the top of the flagpole, where it unfurled in the sea breeze. Tangible proof of the Allied victory appeared on September 2, 1945, when the frigate HMS *Plym* from Admiral Harcourt's fleet arrived at Macau along with the SS *Fat Shan*. Reeves boarded the *Plym* with Governor Teixeira, indulged in some celebratory gin and whiskey with the ship's officers, and marveled at the diversity of British accents echoing off the gray steel bulkheads.

A Hong Kong–Canton river ferry that had rather miraculously survived the war, the *Fat Shan* had arrived with a delegation of Chinese civilians. Acting on the assumption that neutral Macau must have fared better than occupied Hong Kong during the war years, the delegation hoped to procure a shipment of rice for the city's starving populace. Governor Teixeira approved the release of government-owned foodstuffs from the godowns, and the *Plym* and *Fat Shan* departed for Hong Kong with a shipment of desperately needed rice on September 3.

In the weeks that followed, Reeves began the process of winding down the consulate's wartime operations and making the transition to peacetime. He helped expedite the transfer of medicines and additional rice stocks from the relatively well-off Macau to the gutted shell of Hong Kong, and he facilitated the repatriation of British civilians who had fled to the Portuguese colony during the war years. Most of the British refugees under his care returned to Hong Kong, where many joined the ranks of the repatriates bound for England and Australia. At the end of September, Reeves's wife Rhoda and daughter Letitia boarded the Australian minesweeper HMAS *Fremantle* and departed for Manila on the first leg of their long journey back to England. Reeves and his wife had become strangers to each other, and while the widening of the distance between them might have been inevitable, the stresses of life in wartime Macau had surely accelerated the fissure. Their parting would prove to be permanent.

If Reeves's marriage had reached its endpoint, so too had his time in Macau. In the summer of 1946, a new consul arrived to relieve him of his duties so that he could travel to his next posting in Rome. Reeves packed up his possessions, including the bullet-holed Blackwood cabinet that an unknown assassin had perforated during an attempt on the consul's life. Reeves no longer faced such threats, and he stopped packing the revolver that he had worn continuously during the war years except when bathing or out on the turf playing field hockey.

A summer typhoon howled up the Pearl River delta on the day before Reeves's departure from Macau in August 1946. The flag that Reeves had raised over the consulate to mark the Japanese surrender flapped madly in the rising winds, started to fray, and finally tore loose from the masthead altogether. Reeves found this incident with the flag and the tempest to be richly symbolic of the British Empire, which he knew had been torn to shreds by the winds of war. When Reeves left Macau the next day aboard the HMS *Ranee*, he took the badly shredded flag with him.[1] On the long sea journey to Europe he began work on his memoir, which he titled with understated eloquence as *The Lone Flag*.*

---

*Reeves died in 1978 in South Africa, his home after leaving the Foreign Office.

Meanwhile, the question of who should bear the blame for the airstrikes on Macau in January 1945 had not yet been settled. Admiral Nimitz had addressed letters of reprimand to Commander Lamade and Lieutenant Golson, the commander and senior ACI officer, respectively, of the *Hancock* air group, in late March 1945.[2] However, Captain Hickey of the *Hancock* and Commander Butts, the ship's air officer, had been exonerated with Nimitz's approval on the grounds that the failure to brief the VF-7 pilots as ordered was the fault of their subordinates, specifically Commander Lamade and Lieutenant Golson. Fleet Admiral King, the Commander in Chief of the U.S. Fleet, had never been known for showing much patience when it came to the mistakes and miscalculations of the officers under his command.[3] He concurred with the disciplining of Lamade and Golson, but disagreed about the exoneration of Captain Hickey and Commander Butts. King recommended that letters of admonition be placed in their service records, and this was done on November 14, 1945.[4]

Both Captain Hickey and Commander Butts, who were career naval officers, later petitioned for the removal of the letters of admonition from their personnel file, often referred to as a "record jacket." The Secretary of the Navy approved the removal of the letter of admonition from the file of Captain Hickey – soon to become a rear admiral after more than twenty-five years in the navy – on October 23, 1947.[5] The letter of admonition addressed to Commander Butts – now promoted to the rank of captain – was removed from his service record in April 1949 after a hearing conducted by the Board for Correction of Naval Records on April 13, 1949.[6]

Commander Lamade, a career officer, and Lieutenant Golson, a reservist who had been awarded a Bronze Star for his exemplary service as an ACI officer aboard the *Hancock*, also challenged their letters of reprimand, arguing that the court proceedings contravened existing provisions of the Naval Courts and Boards because only Captain Hickey had been afforded the rights of an "interested party," even though three additional officers received reprimands and therefore also qualified as interested parties. Moreover, both officers argued that the contradictory and confusing orders on January 16, 1945, had all but assured that VF-7 would strike Macau regardless of whether the pilots observed enemy aircraft on the ground. Commander Lamade requested that if the letters of reprimand were to stand, then all blame for the airstrikes on Macau be assigned to him, since he was the commanding officer of the pilots involved. Lieutenant Golson claimed in a lucid three-page letter that while he had misinterpreted unclear orders, and thus failed to properly brief the pilots of VF-7, his actions had not stemmed from any negligence on his part. He fully accepted responsibility, however, and requested that all blame for the incident be attributed to his own failure to correctly interpret and evaluate orders.[7] The court of inquiry documents did not include a reply to the appeals of Lamade and Golson, but documents from the appeal hearing for Commander Butts suggested that the letters of reprimand remained in the service files of both officers. Ultimately, the letter of admonition appears to have done little harm to the career of Commander Lamade, a decorated combat commander who had been awarded the Navy Cross and the Distinguished Flying Cross. In 1951, the navy promoted him to the rank of captain, and he held this rank until his retirement in 1961 after twenty-nine years of service.[8]

As the records from the court of inquiry made clear, the repeated strafing of Macau by VF-7 Hellcat pilots had resulted in part from incomplete and inaccurate intelligence information about the Portuguese colony. While the ACI officers briefing the pilots had understood that Macau constituted neutral Portuguese territory, they had also believed that Macau was under Japanese control and thus a legitimate target. In addition, the airstrikes stemmed from the failure of the ACI officers to address the contradiction between Admiral Bogan's orders and standard doctrine for blanket missions. In other words, if the ACI officers had told the VF-7 pilots assigned to cover Macau that they did *not* have the usual free reign to shoot up enemy air installations regardless of whether they observed enemy aircraft on the ground, the pilots would have known to leave Macau alone when they failed to spot any planes at the colony's two seaplane facilities. Reliable intelligence and more nuanced briefings might well have prevented the airstrikes against the neutral Portuguese enclave. Improvements in the intelligence and briefing procedures for the patrol bomber squadrons based in the Philippines might have also prevented the additional airstrikes on Macau that occurred later in 1945, including the February bombing of the SS *Masbate* by Lieutenant Stevens of VPB-104. Though Stevens had been at fault, his error in judgement had stemmed from inadequate information about Macau's geography and neutrality. In all likelihood, every PPC in the squadron would have dropped on the *Masbate* if given the opportunity, since they all assumed Macau remained under Japanese occupation.

Though both the Norwegian and Portuguese governments would insist that Washington pay up for abusing the *Masbate* and its Scandinavian captain, nobody seemed too interested in determining exactly who had toggled the bombs. His record jacket unblemished by letters of reprimand or other disciplinary actions connected to Macau, Lieutenant Stevens continued his postwar career in the U.S. Navy. Like Commander Lamade, Stevens received the Navy Cross for wartime valor. His career as a naval aviator paralleled Lamade's in other ways as well. He went on to qualify as a carrier pilot, serve as a squadron commander, and like Lamade, assume command of a carrier air group. He and Lamade both rose to the rank of captain as well. When Stevens retired from the navy in 1965, he could look back on a flying career that had started with the bumblebee buzz of a prewar biplane trainer and ended with the sonic boom of a McDonnell Douglas F-4 Phantom.

On August 6, 1945, the Portuguese Foreign Office submitted to the American Embassy in Lisbon a claim for losses suffered during American airstrikes on Macau on January 16, February 25, April 7, and June 11, 1945. Washington did not dispute that American airstrikes on the Portuguese colony had caused a number of casualties, as reported in media accounts appearing in both Portuguese and American newspapers. Moreover, intelligence reports generated *after* the court of inquiry had confirmed that injuries and fatalities had in fact occurred. In May 1945, for example, U.S. intelligence reported that two people had been killed and five injured during the strafing of Macau on January 16, 1945.[9] The U.S. government also accepted that American warplanes had damaged government assets and private property in Macau during the airstrikes. Washington therefore agreed to provide appropriate compensation for all four incidents.

The Portuguese government calculated the cost of damaged and destroyed property in the local colonial currency, the Macanese pataca, and initially claimed losses amounting to three million patacas as a result of the three airstrikes by VF-7 Hellcats from the *Hancock* on

January 16, 1945. These losses included the gasoline and lubricating oil stored in the naval seaplane hangar as well as the hangar itself. The Portuguese also claimed damage to the Dona Maria Fort and "engines" contained inside, though no documents from the court of inquiry or action reports from VF-7, CVG-7, or the *Hancock* substantiated an attack on this fortification, which occupied a ridgetop position not far from the naval hangar and Pan American station. Additional lost property included a government-owned 1937 Dodge Sedan used by Pedro José Lobo. Other damages included unspecified Harbor Office property that likely included the historic maritime artifacts stored in the hangar and property belonging to a pair of corporals, though claimed by the Post Office Department.

The Portuguese government claimed just under 200,000 patacas for the bombing of the Inner Harbor by Lieutenant Stevens and the crew of his PB4Y-1 on February 25, 1945. The claims for compensation included damage to the Fatima Mission, the House of Mercy, and the streets of the Tamagnini Barbosa neighborhood. Private claimants included the owners of the SS *Masbate*, which had been the primary target of the attack, and Trygve Jorgenson, the Norwegian captain of the little steamer, who lodged a greenback-denominated claim of $25,000 for his injuries.*

The Portuguese government did not make any claim for the tugboat that had been sunk on April 7, 1945, by a PV-1 Ventura from VPB-137. No private claimant lodged a request for compensation, either. This suggested that the tugboat had never been homeported in Macau and that the crew had not been Portuguese colonial subjects. In hindsight, it appeared that the decision by the Ventura pilots to sink the tugboat had been justified, since the U.S. Navy's rules of engagement had allowed its pilots to attack all motorized vessels along the coast of southern China, with the exception of clearly marked neutral vessels and hospital ships.

The Portuguese government also claimed 88,000 patacas for a bombing incident on June 11, 1945, by an unknown aircraft that had

---

*In 1948, Wah Shan Shipping Company of Macau purchased the SS *Masbate* from the South China Steamship Company and became its new beneficiary owner. However, the Panama-based Wallem and Company continued as the front-company owner that managed the vessel. The two firms lodged a joint claim for compensation.

targeted the badly battered *Masbate*. On June 15 the *Hongkong News* had published a story titled "Macao Neutrality Again Violated" that reported a lone B-29 had dropped 50kg bombs on the *Masbate* but failed to score any hits, and then strafed local farmers. However, only the USAAF flew the B-29, which served as a high-altitude strategic bomber rather than a patrol bomber designed to attack ships on the deck. In any case, B-29 squadrons had rarely operated over southern China during the war, so the aircraft in question had almost certainly not been a Superfortress. Most likely, the aircraft had been a navy PB4Y-2, which typically carried AN-M30 general-purpose bombs that weighed approximately fifty kilograms. An untrained observer could confuse the PB4Y-2 with the B-29, as both featured four engines, long and slender wings, and a single vertical stabilizer. The mystery aircraft would likely have been based in the Philippines, but the pilots involved remained unknown, their identities and squadron affiliation lost in the reams of wartime paperwork that documented U.S. Navy flight operations. Once again, the colonial authorities lodged a claim for property belonging to the Fatima Mission, which had been damaged by bombs that had overshot the *Masbate*.[10]

In total, the claims by the colonial administration in Macau amounted to 3.3 million patacas. However, War Department investigators dismissed the Portuguese claim as highly inflated and whittled this sum down considerably. The investigators concluded, for example, that the naval hangar had only been 50 percent destroyed by American aircraft. They also found that the Portuguese had based their claim for the fuel and oil stocks on the inflated wartime price they would have demanded when selling these stocks to the Japanese, which the Portuguese government readily admitted the administration in Macau had planned to do. The War Department bean counters based the value of the fuel and oil on its postwar replacement cost instead. They also concluded that the Fatima Mission and House of Mercy had only suffered superficial damage on February 25 and June 11.

Based on the final recommendations of the War Department investigators, the State Department advised Lisbon on October 3, 1947, that just under a million patacas would be paid in compensation to the Portuguese government and 68,000 patacas would be paid to twelve private claimants for a total of 1,063,364 patacas. However, on February 21, 1949, the State Department announced a reduction in the figure for private claimants because Captain Jorgenson had received $5,000 in a separate settlement negotiated between the American and Norwegian governments. At the agreed upon exchange rate of 3.93 patacas to the U.S. dollar, the modified final payment of 1,043,714 patacas totaled approximately $266,000, which would be paid directly to the Portuguese government in Lisbon to disburse as it deemed appropriate to the colonial administration in Macau and private claimants. On May 3, 1949, the Portuguese government accepted this figure but claimed its right to accrued interest. The Portuguese Foreign Office and the State Department eventually settled on 2.5 percent rate of interest, and the State Department formally requested that Congress earmark the requisite funds to pay Lisbon.

In 1950, Congress authorized the Secretary of the Treasury to pay for losses and damages resulting from U.S. air attacks on Macau. In what amounted to a tacit national apology, the U.S. government paid 1,172,762 patacas to settle all claims resulting from American airstrikes on Macau. A fluctuating exchange rate that favored a strong dollar reduced the payment to $202,000, plus additional accrued interest between the point of Congressional authorization and actual payment to the Portuguese government.[11]

Though the War Department had carefully audited the Portuguese claims for compensation for losses suffered at Macau, Washington had never questioned the basic premise that such compensation should be paid.[12] Shortcomings in naval intelligence and pilot briefings had both contributed to the air attacks on targets at Macau. In short, the U.S. Navy had clearly been at fault. The wartime record of the USAAF provided firm support for this conclusion, since the pilots of the 14th Air Force had never once attacked Macau despite flying thousands of sorties over the Pearl River delta from 1942 to 1945.

Ninety-four Pounds

Jean Balch had added about 135 pounds of bodyweight to the load carried by Lieutenant Lavender's Helldiver during its final mission over Hong Kong on January 16, 1945. By summer 1945, his weight had dwindled to less than 100 pounds and his captors were still threatening to kill him on the Sabbath. In the end, however, they decided to transfer him to the prison island of Ōmori instead. They also transferred Alvin Hughes, who had been captured at Hong Kong along with Balch, and Chief Boatswain's Mate Leibold from the submarine *Tang*, who had risked everything in a futile effort to save Lieutenant Hunt. Though the deprivations of Ōmori rivaled those of Ōfuna, the camp offered a morale-boosting front-row seat for watching the fiery drama of Tokyo's destruction by waves of Boeing B-29s. Less than three weeks after arriving at Ōmori, Balch learned that the emperor had surrendered the country unconditionally to the Allied forces. As the camp guards melted away, he knew he would no longer have to fear a Sunday morning firing squad. Hughes and Leibold had made it to the end of the war as well.

Silver-colored B-29s soon began parachuting a bonanza of American plenty into the camp that ranged from clothing to chewing gum. One prisoner nearly died when an airdropped bundle of supplies unraveled in midair and sent a wooden crate of Cashmere Bouquet soap crashing through the flimsy roof of his barracks.[1] Navy landing teams liberated the ecstatic inmates of the Ōmori camp and ferried Balch out to the hospital ship USS *Benevolence*, which took hundreds of Allied POWs aboard for medical treatment. Shipboard doctors diagnosed Balch's ailments, which included pneumonia, pellagra, beriberi, hepatitis, amoebic dysentery, and severe malnourishment. At ninety-four pounds, he had survived his captivity, albeit just barely.

On September 2, 1945, the *Benevolence* dropped anchor alongside the USS *Missouri* in Tokyo Bay, which allowed Balch to witness the surrender ceremony that took place on the deck of the battleship. Six days later, he boarded the USS *Ozark*, a landing ship laden with 950 men collectively referred to as RAMPs, or Recovered Allied Military Personnel. On September 8, the *Ozark* set course for Guam, where Balch and the other RAMPs could receive further medical care, and the army and navy could systematically identify their liberated servicemen and start notifying their families.

Like many of the former POWs, Balch had been declared missing in action. Beyond the basic details of his final mission, his family back in Texas knew nothing of his fate. They shared this agonizing limbo with many other families in the Abilene area. In 1942, the 2nd Battalion of the 131st Field Artillery Regiment, Texas National Guard, had been deployed to Java to help defend the island from the rapidly advancing Japanese military. Different cities in Texas had provided the men for each battery of the battalion, and E Battery consisted largely of men from the Abilene area.[2] Forced to surrender when Java fell to the Japanese, the men of the battalion had vanished into the vast network of prison camps spread across the Japanese Empire. The citizens of Abilene had been waiting for word of their missing sons for more than three years. The army had been waiting as well and had little news to share about the unit, which became known as the "Lost Battalion." Balch, who had gone missing late in the game in 1945, had been just one more local boy swallowed up by the glutton of war. Nobody in Abilene knew that Balch had survived his shoot-down until a telegram reached his parents on September 14. The telegram bore the signature of Vice Admiral Jacobs, the same officer who had originally notified Balch's family that the navy had declared their son missing in action. This time, however, Jacobs had good news to share:

I am pleased to inform you of the liberation from Japanese custody of your son Jean Fenton Balch Aviation Radioman Third Class USNR. You are invited to send him free via this bureau a twenty-five word message. Every effort to effect delivery [of] this message before his return to United States will be made. Further details will be furnished you promptly when received. I rejoice with you in this good news and hope that he will communicate with you at an early date.

Balch's overjoyed parents and sisters replied the same day in a telegram transmitted from Texas to Tokyo via Washington. Somewhere along the way, the original telegram had been shaved down to the permitted maximum of twenty-five words, which required Balch to insert missing words and punctuation when he read the telegram from his hospital bed in U.S. Naval Fleet Hospital 103 on the island of Guam: "Dear son [received] your cable today family together well and extremely happy about your [liberation] call first chance much love from the four of us your family [.]"

On September 16, Balch and his fellow RAMPs reboarded the *Ozark* and settled in for the long trans-Pacific journey home. Seventeen days later, after making just a single port call at Pearl Harbor, the *Ozark* reached the West Coast. Balch received orders transferring him to a naval hospital in Oakland, California, followed by further orders assigning him to another naval hospital in landlocked Norman, Oklahoma. In total, eight months elapsed before the doctors judged that he had recovered sufficiently from his ordeal at Ōfuna and Ōmori. In early 1946, with an honorable discharge, an Air Medal, and back pay from the U.S. Navy, Jean Balch returned to his hometown of Abilene, Texas, and the start of his postwar life.[3]

34

Hungjao Road

Once the surviving prisoners of war had been accounted for, American investigative teams fanned out across the Pacific theater to recover the remains of the many Allied airmen who were still missing. On November 1, 1945, a recovery team led by Staff Sgt. Julian E. Waters of the 4th Platoon, 3045th Graves Registration Company, disinterred Lieutenant Hunt's body from the burial plot behind the Ryuho-ji Temple. The grave proved easy to locate, as it had been marked with a wooden cross bearing Hunt's name and rank in Japanese. Additional information inscribed on the cross indicated that Hunt had died on August 15, 1945, and that his body had been buried by the Japanese navy. Since Hunt had actually died in late February, the August 15 date suggested, perhaps, that the Japanese had erected the cross at the end of the war in a belated attempt to show that they had treated their prisoners of war correctly. Staff Sgt. Waters and the 4th Platoon transported Lieutenant Hunt's remains to the USAAF Cemetery in Yokohama. On the morning of November 2, two chaplains conducted nondenominational burial rites over Hunt's casket before its reburial in grave number 113. In February 1948, the American Graves Registration Service (AGRS) disinterred the casket and placed Hunt's remains in a mausoleum, and in December 1948, as part of the Return of the World War Two Dead Program, the military returned Hunt's stainless-steel casket to the United States at the request of his parents. On a winter's day, Lieutenant (j.g.) Richard L. Hunt Jr. reached his final resting place in Memorial Park Cemetery in his hometown of Kansas City, Missouri.[1]

The Shanghai-based China Theater Search Detachment (CTSD) coordinated efforts to recover the remains of American military personnel on the Chinese mainland. In December 1945, the Canton Sub-Detachment of the CTSD sent recovery teams to Hong Kong to investigate wartime graves and aircraft crash sites. These teams worked closely with the British military in Hong Kong, particularly Graves Registration and Enquiries (GR&E), which had responsibility for recovering Allied war dead in Hong Kong. A substantial number of British, Canadian, Indian, and Chinese soldiers from the prewar garrison had gone missing during the battle for Hong Kong in 1941 and the years of captivity that had followed. Determining the fate of these men fell to the GR&E, which had been combing the colony for both marked and unmarked graves as well as the scattered bones of servicemen who had been left where they had fallen during the confused close-quarters combat that had raged across the ridges and ravines of Hong Kong Island.

In the process of its own investigations, the GR&E had identified a number of locations that might be of interest to the Canton Sub-Detachment, including the grave of an American pilot and the wreck sites for three American aircraft. On January 25, 1946, a search and recovery team led by Tech. Sgt. Richard M.S. Wong and Staff Sgt. Edwin F. Vandenberg drove to Big Wave Bay on the southeast corner of Hong Kong Island to investigate the grave that reportedly held the remains of an American aviator. When the team reached Big Wave Bay, two Cantonese fishermen from the coastal village of Shek O led the two sergeants to a wooden stake that had been engraved with "Major David Henry Houck" in Japanese. A work party supervised by the sergeants started removing the rectangular mound of sand in front of the stake. Soon the workers had unearthed a wooden cross and a body clad in an American military uniform and shoes. Both sergeants concluded that they had recovered the corpse of Major Houck and the cross that he had been tied to during his execution. Sergeant Wong and Sergeant Vandenberg brought Major Houck's body, the execution cross, and the grave marker back to Canton for onward air transport to the American Graves Registration Service-China Zone (AGRS-CZ) at Shanghai. After making a positive identification using dental records, the AGRS-CZ reburied Major Houck's body in grave number 482 in the American military section of the Hungjao Road Cemetery in March 1946.[2]

The Nationalist Chinese had arrested Lt. Gen. Tanaka Hisakasu when he had surrendered at the end of the war in Canton. Before the Chinese could try Tanaka for war crimes, however, the U.S. military commission in Shanghai requested permission to try him first for the execution of Major Houck. With Chinese assent, the Americans took custody of Tanaka and brought him to Shanghai. In August 1946, a military tribunal charged Tanaka and five other Japanese officers with the unlawful trial and execution of Major Houck. In answer to this charge, and presumably as advised by their defense counsel team of American legal officers and Japanese lawyers, all six officers pleaded not guilty. The trial unfolded over a three-week period and included testimony from Mr. Nakazawa, the civilian interpreter who had been present at Major Houck's trial and execution. The tribunal ultimately handed down one not guilty and five guilty verdicts with sentences that ranged from death by hanging to imprisonment for fifty years. Everyone in the courtroom would likely have expected the guilty verdicts, though the one exoneration would perhaps have come as a surprise.

The tribunal initially sentenced Lt. Gen. Tanaka to death by hanging. However, the confirming authority for the commission later disapproved the sentence on the grounds that Tanaka had not been in Hong Kong during Major Houck's trial, had not played a role in the court proceedings, had not been informed of the guilty verdict and death sentence, and had not been told of Major Houck's execution until after it had been carried out. Tanaka still bore indirect responsibility insofar as he had granted his chief of staff, Major General Fukuchi Haruo, unfettered authority to act on his behalf in Hong Kong. However, this was not deemed sufficient for a guilty conviction, much less a death sentence. All this legal wrangling ultimately made no difference, since the Americans returned Tanaka to the custody of the Nationalist Chinese so that he could face a military tribunal in Canton. The tribunal charged Tanaka with a litany of war crimes against the Chinese people that had been perpetrated by the 23rd Army, which he had commanded. The tribunal sentenced Tanaka to death, and with the final approval of Chiang Kai-shek, his execution was carried out on March 27, 1947.

However, the other four officers who had been found guilty by the U.S. military tribunal ultimately escaped the gallows. Major General Fukuchi initially faced the death penalty, but a later reduction of his sentence left him facing life imprisonment instead. The three officers who had served as judges during Major Houck's trial – Lt. Col. Kubo, Major Watanabe, and Captain Yamaguchi – received sentences of life, ten years, and ten years, respectively. Major Shii Saburo, the architect of the indictment against Major Houck, would likely have been found guilty as well, but he had committed suicide while awaiting his day in court. Captain Asakawa Hiroshi, who had served as prosecutor during Major Houck's trial, was found not guilty of any charges because the commission believed he had acted under the orders of Major Shii.[3]

In Baltimore, local men who had gone to war received their discharge papers and came home to a hero's welcome. Nellie White Houck, meanwhile, waited for the military to contact her about the return of her son's remains for final burial in the United States. She had already received several wartime letters from Capt. Oran S. Watts, who had taken over command of the 118th Tactical Reconnaissance Squadron in February 1945, and Major General Edward F. Witsell, the U.S. Army's Adjutant General in Washington. Both men had offered their condolences, testified to the courage and character of Nellie Houck's son, and provided pertinent details of his final mission over Hong Kong and execution by the Japanese.

Based on these personal letters, Nellie Houck knew when, where, and how her son had died. However, she did not know when she would be able to give him a proper burial, so in late 1945 she wrote to the U.S. Army to request information on the whereabouts of her son's remains and whether they would be returned to the United States. The Memorial Division of the Office of the Quartermaster General (OQMG) responded promptly in a letter dated December 21, 1945, but reported that it had not yet received any information about the burial of Major David H. Houck. The Memorial Division promised to contact Nellie Houck when such information became available and added that the War Department would soon receive Congressional authorization for the Return of the World War Two Dead Program.

Implementing the Return of the Dead Program fell to the Army's OQMG, which would coordinate the effort to recover the remains of all American military personnel lost overseas, regardless of their branch of service. When investigative teams recovered and identified a set of remains, the OQMG would contact the next of kin and ask them to choose a final resting place for their son or husband. The OQMG would then ship the remains to the specified burial ground at government expense, in a casket provided by the Return of the Dead Program, and with an appropriate military escort. Tradition and protocol called for an escort from the same service branch and of equal or higher rank to travel with the casket of the deceased soldier, sailor, airman, or marine.[4]

"Your letter states that information pertaining to the burial of the remains of Major David H. Houck had not been received in your office," Nellie Houck wrote in a longhand response to the letter from the Memorial Division. "Perhaps I can help." She then explained that she had received letters from Captain Watts and Major General Witsell, who had described the execution and burial of her son at Big Way Bay, Hong Kong, on April 6, 1945. With matter-of-fact detail that belied what must have been an oceanic expanse of grief, she wrote, "For identification (if beheaded by shooting in the neck) Maj. Houck had a large circular scar under his hair just above his forehead – the size of a silver dollar – also his left hand had [an] inch long scar between forefinger and thumb."

After receiving Nellie Houck's letter, the Memorial Division wrote to the AGRS-CZ in Shanghai and requested a form 1042 Report of Interment or other pertinent documents regarding the remains of Major Houck. In the hopes of facilitating the recovery and identification of the major's body, the Memorial Division explained in its letter that "this office has been advised by Mrs. Nellie W. Houck, mother of Major David H. Houck, that the remains of her son were buried at Big Way Bay, Hong Kong, China on 6 April 1945."

By the time the letter from the Memorial Division reached Shanghai in the winter of 1946, the CTSD had already recovered Major Houck's body and the AGRS-CZ had reburied his remains in the Hungjao Road Cemetery. Several months later, the Memorial Division notified Nellie Houck of this development in a brief letter that stated, "This office promised that upon receipt of burial information concerning your son, you would be advised."

In October of the same year, Nellie Houck responded to the Memorial Division's letter:

Dear Sir:

In accordance with the promise of our Government to return to this country for interment the remains of servicemen who died overseas, if requested to do so, I ask that the remains of my son, Major David Henry Houck, who was imprisoned and later executed by the Japanese, be returned to me as soon as possible. The turbulent conditions in China make this an urgent appeal. I feel that my son has suffered too tragically at the hands of Oriental fanatics to be subject to further indignities in case of civil war in China.

Your letter of July 17 last states that Major Houck is buried in Row A, Grave 482, in the American Military Section, Hungjao Road Cemetery, located on Hungjao Road in Shanghai, China.

Yours very truly,
(Mrs.) Nellie White Houck

In 1947, AGRS-CZ disinterred Major Houck's remains and shipped them from Shanghai to the Territory of Hawaii for temporary interment in U.S. Army Mausoleum No. 2 at Schofield Barracks. In late September of the same year, the U.S. Army Transport *Honda Knot* departed Hawaii with a cargo of specially designed stainless-steel caskets holding the remains of 3,102 American service members killed in the Pacific theater, including Major Houck. Memorial ceremonies in San Francisco marked the arrival of the *Honda Knot*, the first ship to return with American war dead from the Pacific.[5] From the West Coast, a special mortuary train carried the casket containing Major Houck's remains to the Philadelphia Quartermaster Depot. Nellie Houck's son had never married and her husband had died before the war, so the decision about the burial location had fallen to her, though she had no doubt consulted her daughter Elizabeth when choosing one of the three options for a final resting place: an American military cemetery located overseas, Arlington National Cemetery or a similar military graveyard in the Continental United States, or a private cemetery in the Baltimore area. Like the majority of mothers who had lost a son in the fighting overseas, Nellie Houck had chosen to bring her boy home.

On October 27, 1947, Major Houck's casket arrived in Baltimore aboard train number 45 of the Baltimore and Ohio Railroad. On the morning of October 29, after a funeral service in the University Baptist Church opposite from the apartment she shared with her daughter, Nellie Houck buried her son in the Druid Ridge Cemetery on the outskirts of the city. Several years later she commissioned a renowned Baltimore sculptor to commemorate her son with a headstone, which recreated in bas relief the insignias of the uniform he had worn – the oak leaves of a U.S. Army major, a CBI shoulder patch, and, of course, the wings of an American fighter pilot.[6]

Unknowns

In February 1946, a search and recovery team from the Canton Sub-Detachment of the CTSD arrived in Hong Kong to investigate three crash sites that might hold the remains of missing American airmen. In March 1945, Agent Ady of the OSS had reported the location of the first downed aircraft, which had struck a ridge and exploded near the village of Nam Long in an isolated corner of the New Territories. Assisted by the men of Nam Long, the team recovered the remains of five aviators, which forensic analysis later identified as the crew of a B-25J from the 5th Air Force nicknamed *Bold Venture*. All five sets of remains were returned to the United States under the auspices of the Return of the Dead Program for burial in military cemeteries.[1]

Members of a search and recovery team also investigated two wreck sites on Hong Kong Island that they believed marked the crash points for the Avengers flown by Lieutenant Hunt and Lieutenant Scobell, which had collided on January 16, 1945. Hunt had bailed out and been taken prisoner, but the other five men aboard the two aircraft had died when their TBMs slammed into the ridgelines lining the western rim of the Tai Tam Valley. Team members sifted through the two separate debris fields located high above the reservoir on steep ridges that precluded easy access. A gouge in a rocky slope marked the impact point for Hunt's TBM-3, which had been incinerated in a fireball of aviation gasoline. The bent barrel of a .50-caliber machine gun torn free from one of the wings attested to the violence of the crash, as did the fact that the Wright-Cyclone engine had completely disintegrated.

Cylinder heads and other unidentifiable mechanical components lay scattered on the hillside along with the landing-gear assemblies, scraps of rubber, Hunt's armored headrest, Gene Barrow's .30-caliber tunnel gun, the curved armor plating from Louis Gahran's ball turret, rounds of machine-gun ammunition, gauges from the cockpit, and the still-gleaming arrestor hook.[2]

At both wreck sites, the search team collected charred and shattered skeletal remains, which they transported by air to the AGRS-CZ in Shanghai. However, forensic examiners at the AGRS-CZ could not determine the identity of the remains or even say with any assurance how many sets of remains had been recovered, though they presumed the remains belonged to the crew of the Avengers flown by Lieutenant Hunt and Lieutenant Scobell. In the absence of a positive identification, the AGRS-CZ designated what it assumed to be *six* sets of remains as X-73, X-74, X-75, X-76, X-77, and X-78. After a brief ceremony officiated by military chaplains, the AGRS-CZ interred these unknowns in common grave 466 in the Hungjao Road Cemetery on February 28, 1946.

In April 1946, the Office of the Quartermaster General requested that the AGRS-CZ in Shanghai delete X-73 from the group, since Lieutenant Hunt's body had been recovered in Japan. By late 1947, the five unknowns in the group had been officially identified as the crew of the Avengers flown by Lieutenant Hunt and Lieutenant Scobell, and the AGRS-CZ had shipped the remains to the Territory of Hawaii for interment in U.S. Army Mausoleum No. 2 at Schofield Barracks. A review board recommended individual identification of three of the five sets of remains based on dental records, but this recommendation was subsequently overruled on the grounds that the fragmentary remains and limited number of teeth made identification tentative at best. Logic dictated that remains recovered from two separate crash sites should be placed in two separate caskets, and this may well have occurred. However, the military classified the remains from both crash sites as a single group. After considerable delay, these remains arrived in the United States for group burial in Keokuk National Cemetery in Keokuk, Iowa. Lt. (j.g.) Richard C. Scobell; Eugene W. Barrow, ARM3c; Louis W. Gahran, AOM2c; John F. Gelnaw, AOM1c; and William P. Walton, ARM3c, had flown to war together with VT-7, and now they would rest together in peace as well.

Information from the Hong Kong Death and Birth Registration Bureau assisted the investigators from the Canton Sub-Detachment, who learned that the bodies of four American airmen had been buried in a local cemetery in the wake of the airstrikes on Hong Kong by the carriers of TF 38. Two of these bodies had been recovered from Victoria Harbor by the Japanese military on January 16, 1945. According to testimony from witnesses interviewed by the investigators, the Japanese had taken the corpses to the Victoria Public Mortuary after first stripping them of equipment and personal effects that might have revealed their identity. Examiners determined drowning to be the cause of death. The Japanese recovered two more bodies from a wreck site on January 20. One corpse had no head, and both were mangled and burned, which suggested a crash on land rather than in the water, and that the impact and resultant explosion had been the cause of death. Dog tags and anything else that might have identified the bodies had been lost in the crash or confiscated by the Japanese, and witnesses had no knowledge of the wreck site's location. On February 1, 1945, a burial party had removed the bodies from the mortuary and interred all four nameless airmen in a common grave in Kai Lung Wan Cemetery on the southwest coast of Hong Kong Island.*

Investigators from the Canton Sub-Detachment supervised the exhumation of the four unknowns more than a year later on April 4, 1946. The bodies had not yet fully decomposed, which precluded immediate shipment to the AGRS-CZ in Shanghai. The investigative team made the pragmatic decision to let the bodies decompose and dry in the open air, protected by a fence and roof. When this natural process had run its course, a transport plane carried the four sets of desiccated remains to the AGRS-CZ, which designated them as X-337, X-338, X-339, and X-340. On August 1, 1946, the AGRS-CZ buried the four unknowns in a common grave in the Hungjao Road Cemetery. Before reinterring these remains, however, the AGRS-CZ prepared identification dental charts from two intact upper jawbones and sent these forms to the United States for examination by the Dental Professional Division of the Bureau of Medicine and Surgery.

---

*Spelled in CTSD and AGRS-CZ documents as "Kialung Wan Cemetery." The cemetery was replaced postwar by the Wah Fu Public Housing Estate.

The Canton Sub-Detachment of the CTSD ended its work in Hong Kong in the spring of 1946, having recovered the remains of nine of the twenty-eight missing naval aviators lost over Hong Kong during Operation *Gratitude*. Five of these nine sets of remains had been identified, albeit as a group, and four had been designated as unknowns. The CTSD and AGRS-CZ were subordinate units of different commands, and while the two units had coordinated their actions, they had inevitably duplicated their efforts. To avoid this inefficiency, the CTSD was deactivated and its personnel absorbed into the AGRS-CZ in April 1946. The bulked-up AGRS-CZ continued to investigate all unresolved Hong Kong MIA cases, which included at least nineteen naval aviators. The Canton-based Search and Recovery Team Seven of the AGRS-CZ operated in Hong Kong from July to October 1946 and worked in close cooperation with the British GR&E. During this time, however, the two units failed to recover any remains of American airmen, and by the end of 1946 the AGRS-CZ had reached the final stage of its search and recovery efforts.

On New Year's Day 1947, Search and Recovery Team Seven dispatched a two-man investigative team to Hong Kong that consisted of 1st Lt. John J. Sen, an infantry officer on special duty, and civilian interpreter Ignatius J. Law, who could speak Cantonese. Lieutenant Sen had been ordered to make one final investigation of the remaining MIA cases in Hong Kong, which included pilots and aircrew from the USAAF as well as the U.S. Navy. At the Garden Road headquarters of British Land Forces in Hong Kong, Lieutenant Sen and Mr. Law met with Major K. Hussain of the War Crimes Investigation Unit. They hoped Major Hussain would be able to provide possible leads in the remaining MIA cases, and he proved to be more than willing to share pertinent documents. Sen and Law found records confiscated from the Kempeitai at the end of the war to be of particular interest, since the translated "All Prisoners Alphabetical Roll Book" listed the names of inmates incarcerated in Stanley Prison and other facilities in Hong Kong. The accuracy and thoroughness of the roll book remained unknown, however, and none of the names of the missing aviators appeared in the Kempeitai records or any of the other documents provided by Major Hussain.

The major explained that when a plane had come down in Hong Kong during the war the local Chinese rarely had the chance to learn any information about it other than what the Japanese reported to the public through official announcements or local pro-Japanese media outlets like the *Hongkong News*, *Hong Kong Nippo*, and *Hong Kong Yat Po*, published in English, Japanese, and Cantonese, respectively.[3] On at least three occasions, the Japanese had placed wrecked American aircraft on display – a dismembered B-24, the tail assembly of a B-25, and a badly mangled P-40 – in Victoria City, but even then specific details about the pilots and squadrons associated with these war trophies had not been provided to the local population.[4] The Japanese were secretive and not very talkative when it came to downed airmen, explained Major Hussain. Even the Chinese and Indian collaborators who turned in American pilots did not know the names of the men they had handed over to the Japanese. As a result, said the major, the names of captured American aviators were "pretty vague and unknown."

The next morning Lieutenant Sen and Mr. Law went to the office of Major Douglas C. Lightbody, who served as the deputy assistant director of Graves Registration and Enquiries in Hong Kong. As the British equivalent of the American Graves Registration Service, the GR&E had been in operation in Hong Kong since October 1945 and had worked closely with investigative teams from the CTSD and AGRS-CZ. Major Lightbody explained that his unit had systematically searched Hong Kong Island, Kowloon, and the New Territories. Consequently, he felt sure that all Allied war dead had been recovered, including any American war dead. A recent advertising campaign in local newspapers and on local radio stations had asked the public for information about the location of the remains of Allied war dead in Hong Kong, but this bilingual effort had failed to produce any useful leads. "It is almost conclusive proof that this area is cleared," the major said. GR&E had begun shifting its focus from recovery to the permanent reburial of Allied war dead, and construction of a new military cemetery on Hong Kong Island had begun that month for this very purpose. In accordance with British military custom as well as government policy, the remains of British, Canadian, and Indian soldiers who had died defending Hong Kong would be buried locally rather than returned to their home countries.[5] Major Lightbody permitted Lieutenant Sen and Mr. Law to examine GR&E records pertaining to the recovery effort, including a translated Kempeitai document titled "List of Graves of Prisoners of War in Hongkong." None of the names on the MIA case list turned up in this document, however, which suggested that the Japanese had never buried any of the missing aviators. If the Japanese had dug graves for any of the missing men, they had not known their identities and/or had done so outside Hong Kong. Alternatively, the Kempeitai might simply have failed to record the deed.

Lieutenant Sen and Mr. Law submitted their final case reports to AGRS-CZ headquarters in Shanghai on January 17. They closed out seventeen different cases of missing American airmen and recommended the suspension of all search and recovery efforts related to these cases. In the months that followed, AGRS-CZ finalized the case files for the still-missing aviators, convened a Board of Officers to rule on the final casualty status of each missing man, and forwarded the board's recommendations in Casualty Clearance and Case Review letters sent to the Office of the Quartermaster General in Washington D.C. In every case, the board concluded that the locations of the remains of the missing naval aviators were "unknown and untraceable" because they were likely on the bottom of Victoria Harbor or the South China Sea.

Ensign Joseph G. Scordo of the *Yorktown* remained the one possible exception to the lost-at-sea verdict, however, as explained in the pertinent Casualty Clearance and Case Review letter. Two pilots from Scordo's division had flown overhead as he ditched his F6F-3 on the morning of January 15, 1945, and they reported he had never rolled back his cockpit canopy and had gone down with the plane. On the other hand, pilots from the *Wasp* believed he had emerged from the plane, but without a life raft.[6] None of the pilots had a clear sense of where Scordo had ditched, but the letter noted that Scordo had last been seen floating several hundred yards from a beach southwest of Victoria Harbor near some fishing boats. The AGRS-CZ speculated that Scordo had either drowned or been captured by the Japanese. If he had indeed been captured, the AGRS-CZ presumed that he had then been executed and his body disposed of in an unknown location. The Japanese treatment of captured pilots had always seemed capricious. Jean Balch, Alvin Hughes, and Richard Hunt had been shipped to Ōfuna, for example, but Major Houck had been executed in Hong Kong. Quite possibly, Scordo had met a similar fate. Eyewitnesses in Victoria had described how the Japanese had paraded captured American airmen through the streets before their executions, and the Stanley internees had heard similar stories.[7] One of these men may have been Major Houck. Another could well have been Ensign Scordo, though just as plausibly he might have been killed at the moment of his capture. Alternatively, he might have been entombed in his sinking Hellcat. The truth would never be known, and the Board of Officers ruled that despite the ambiguity of how he had perished, his casualty status should be amended to read "killed in action – body unrecoverable."

Meanwhile, the attempt to identify the four unknowns exhumed from the Kai Lung Wan Cemetery in Hong Kong continued. The Dental Professional Division in Washington D.C. had compared dental records for all naval aviators declared missing in action over Hong Kong with the identification dental charts prepared by the AGRS-CZ in Shanghai. This led to the tentative identification of X-337 and X-338 as Lt. (j.g.) Edwin W. McGowan and ARM2c Lawrence C. Schiller from the *Hornet*, who had been shot down while flying a TBM-1C during Strike 2C. To confirm this finding, the AGRS-CZ in Shanghai exhumed the common grave holding X-337, X-338, X-339, and X-340. On January 4, 1947, an examination by Captain Eugene L. Harrison confirmed the identities of X-337 and X-338 as McGowan and Schiller. However, with the exception of the two jawbones used to determine this positive identification, Harrison could not segregate the remains. As a result, the group burial status of X-337, X-338, X-339, and X-340 did not change.

Captain Harrison also concluded that X-339 and X-340 could not be the remains of the third crewman aboard Lieutenant McGowan's TBM, Charles H. Cunningham, AOM1c. Harrison based his ruling in part on the fact that Cunningham had perfect teeth, as proven by his navy dental records, while the skeletal remains associated with X-339 and X-340 included teeth in various states of dental distress. Harrison also determined that the condition of X-339 and X-340 did not match with the condition of the remains for McGowan and Schiller, who had apparently drowned after their TBM spun into the harbor. In contrast, the reports submitted by the search team as well as the condition of X-339 and X-340 suggested that both men had died during a crash and explosion on land. Given the evidence, the AGRS-CZ concluded that Cunningham had died when his TBM plowed into the harbor and that his body had sunk with the plane.

AGRS-CZ officers assumed that X-339 or X-340 were two of the missing American naval aviators from TF 38, but they could not determine which ones. The fact the two unknowns had been extricated from an aircraft that had crashed on land ruled out quite a few of the missing men, however, since witnesses confirmed that many of the aircraft lost during the carrier strikes on Hong Kong had gone into the water. In fact, investigators only had conclusive evidence that the Avengers flown by Lieutenant Hunt and Lieutenant Scobell had come down on land, but CTSD teams had already recovered the remains of the crewmen from these planes. Several additional aircraft may have crashed on land, however. Jean Balch believed his Helldiver had nosedived into a mountainous portion of Hong Kong Island, for example, though just one man – Lieutenant Lavender – would have been in the cockpit. In any case, CTSD never located the wreck site. Since the Avenger piloted by Lieutenant Seiz of the *Lexington* had been reported by some pilots to have crashed into the Kowloon wharves, it remained plausible that X-339 and X-340 could be the remains of two of the three men from his plane. Alternatively, the two unknowns could have been the remains of the men aboard the TBM-1C piloted by Lieutenant Laughren, which may have crashed on Ko Shing Street on Hong Kong Island, or even the missing VBF-7 pilots whose Hellcats were reported to go into the harbor but may, in fact, have been brought down over Tai Tam Valley. Given the range of possible candidates, AGRS-CZ investigators ultimately declined to speculate on the identity of X-339 and X-340.

The AGRS-CZ disinterred the unknowns X-337, X-338, X-339, and X-340 and shipped them as a group to Hawaii, where they were reinterred in U.S. Army Mausoleum No. 2 in April 1947. A skeletal anthropologist at the Central Identification Laboratory determined that the remains included scraps of American military uniforms and bones for four male adults, plus a few additional bones from a fifth male adult, a child of unknown gender, and the toe joints of an animal. The laboratory verified the identification of McGowan's and Schiller's remains and separated them for individual burial. However, even the Central Identification Laboratory, one of the most advanced facilities of its kind in the world, could not determine the identification of X-339 and X-340, which had been badly burned and crushed. To further complicate matters, dental records could not be used to identify the two unknowns, since the incomplete skeletal remains apparently included very few teeth. However, the laboratory did confirm the conclusions reached by the AGRS-CZ that the remains did not include the third man from Lieutenant McGowan's crew, Charles Cunningham. With no possibility of a positive identification, X-339 and X-340 had to be buried as a group along with the orphan bones from the fifth male and the one child.

In 1949, some four years after Admiral Halsey's carrier air groups had darkened the skies over Hong Kong, a flag-draped casket holding the remains of Lt. (j.g.) Edwin W. McGowan arrived at Arlington National Cemetery for an honor-guard burial. Meanwhile, ARM2c Lawrence C. Schiller had been buried in Oak Hill Cemetery in Cameron, Texas, at the request of his family. However, the paperwork for the Hong Kong MIA cases moved at differential speeds through the typewriters, mailbags, and file folders of the military bureaucracy. Final administrative approval from the Quartermaster General to change the ambiguous casualty status for Ensign Richard Wilson and Lieutenant Laughren, who had both disappeared over Victoria Harbor, took nearly six years. In the autumn of 1951, the Quartermaster General and the Navy Department approved a review board's recommendation to amend the casualty status for Wilson and Laughren to "killed in action – remains nonrecoverable." Shortly thereafter, the Return of the Dead Program ended on the last day of 1951. In an effort that had spanned the globe, the 160 million dollar program had recovered the remains of 280,994 Americans from all branches of service.[8] By this time, one war had blurred into another, and as review boards adjudicated the last MIA cases from the conflict with Japan, a new kind of air combat in the skies over Korea had begun generating fresh cases. Many naval aviators had already gone missing, swatted from the sky by MiG fighter jets and Chinese-made antiaircraft guns. More pilots would disappear in the months and years of hard fighting that lay ahead, but when the jet-propelled dogfights finally ended, the search and recovery teams would be back in action once again.[9]

Epilogue

The tempest of war had stripped the peaks of Hong Kong Island to the bone. Desperate for wood to fuel their cookfires, the civilian population of Hong Kong had hacked down the trees that the prewar colonial administration had so painstakingly planted, leaving stumps and scabrous slopes of ochre dirt. The Japanese occupiers had felled trees for fuel and timber as well. Where there had once been slopes of pine forest and stands of bamboo, little remained but boulder and bracken by 1945.[1] With the rocky contours of the island nakedly exposed, prisoners released from the Stanley camp could peer upwards and see the scorched patches of ridgeline above Tai Tam Valley that marked the crash points for the Avengers flown by Lieutenant Hunt and Lieutenant Scobell.[2] Over time, however, the prewar greenery reappeared, lush and verdant. Like a natural balm, the undergrowth soon concealed the wreckage of the two naval aircraft, just as it hid the bunkers, shell craters, and other reminders of a war that the forward-leaning *heung gong yan* – Hong Kong people – had already put far behind them. By 1986, when I first came to Hong Kong in the final years of British colonial rule, the shoreline and lower slopes of Hong Kong Island had been planted with a neon forest of skyscrapers dominated by the futuristic HSBC bank building, but dense subtropical vegetation cloaked the higher elevations of Hong Kong Island.

In the years that followed, I visited Hong Kong frequently in a variety of capacities – as an academic researcher, as a travel writer, as a university instructor, as a transit passenger on layover, and sometimes just as a simple tourist. I often roamed the vibrant backstreets of Hong Kong Island, with their joss-scented temples and raucous wet markets, but

I also explored the island's unparalleled greenspaces, which invariably offered near-vertical climbs and jaw-dropping views that blended city, mountain, sky, and water in a stunning tableau. Hiking map in hand, I spent a lot of time rambling about in the hills, where I kept stumbling upon abandoned military bunkers. Some stood alongside the trails like mute sentinels, their doors bricked up and their back walls notched into the slope of the hillside. Other bunkers equipped with firing slits lurked back in the undergrowth among the creepers and bamboo, their menacing concrete visages blackened with age. I could still see the scars of battle on these mystery fortifications, which had been pockmarked by machine-gun fire and gouged by punishing hits from heavy weapons. These discoveries piqued my curiosity about Hong Kong's wartime history, so I embarked on a more intentional quest to find the many pillboxes, gun emplacements, and other military relics scattered across Hong Kong Island. I also sought to read everything I could about the war years in Hong Kong, and often came across scattered references to American bombing raids on the city. This too piqued my curiosity. I soon discovered that while the battle for Hong Kong in December 1941 and the fate of the colonial garrison had been well documented in memoirs as well as scholarly works penned by historians, nobody had ever written a book on the American air campaign against Japanese-held Hong Kong. I decided to write this book myself, which led to the eventual publication of *Bold Venture: The American Bombing of Japanese-Occupied Hong Kong, 1942–1945*.

In the process of writing *Bold Venture*, which focused on the China-based army pilots of the USAAF, I crossed paths with Craig Mitchell, who had also been researching the American aerial bombardment of Hong Kong, particularly the U.S. Navy airstrikes in January 1945. Born and raised in Hong Kong, Craig was affable, outgoing, and athletically fit. He appreciated a cold beer as well, so we had a lot in common. His research had led him to conclude that the wrecks of as many as five American warplanes were waiting to be discovered up in the hills of Hong Kong Island, possibly with the unrecovered remains of the pilots. By carefully reviewing U.S. Navy documents and making some shrewd educated guesses, Craig pinpointed where he thought the TBM Avengers piloted by Lieutenant Hunt and Lieutenant Scobell might be. After considerable *Indiana Jones*-style bushwhacking through the thick subtropical forest that now cloaked the hillsides rimming Tai Tam

Country Park, he found both aircraft at two separate locations in 2011. He also found the casing for a 2,000-pound bomb at a third location, where it had apparently tumbled from one of the burning Avengers. The police hauled away the bomb casing with a helicopter, but the government showed little interest in the wreck sites. Craig became their unofficial guardian, and he kept their locations secret so that they would remain undisturbed.

At the end of 2019, I traveled to Hong Kong to research my latest book project, which focused on Lieutenant Hunt, Lieutenant Scobell, and the other U.S. Navy pilots who had taken part in the ambitious but flawed carrier raids against Hong Kong in January 1945. As things turned out, I had timed my visit perfectly. The political protests that had been rocking the city had just petered out, so I didn't have to wade through clouds of teargas. The Covid-19 pandemic hadn't kicked in yet, either. Most fortuitously of all, many of my fellow researchers were still in town and had not yet departed for their holiday vacations. With the help of Geoff Emerson, who had written the definitive account of the Stanley camp, I finagled an invite to see Bungalow C, where fourteen Allied civilians had died during the war in an accidental bombing by Hellcats from the USS *Langley*. When I walked out onto the front lawn of the bungalow, which had been repaired postwar as a private residence, I knew that I was standing on the exact place where the dead had been found after the bomb dropped by a Hellcat had exploded in a bouquet of red-hot shrapnel. I could almost see the ghosts standing around me. I wasn't seeing ghosts in the spooky or spectral sense, of course; rather, I was sensing the traces, the fingerprints, and the sometimes not-so-distant echoes that the dead and departed leave behind. I knew that I was standing on the same ground where people whose stories I knew so well had died and died violently, and I felt their presence so powerfully that I could only describe it as if they were, in fact, standing before me as ghosts.

I experienced this uncanny feeling of connection on the cropped front lawn of Bungalow C, and I experienced it again when Craig and I hiked up to the crash site of Lieutenant Hunt's Avenger on a dry December morning. We were accompanied by his dogs, Molly and Ellie, who reminded me of muscular dingoes and served as canine bodyguards against snakes and wild boars. Our uphill trek culminated in a wooded thicket on a steep slope. Rusted .50-caliber machine guns with bent barrels poked from the dirt, as did twisted landing-gear struts, pieces of ammunition feed chutes, engine parts of different shapes and sizes, and other unidentifiable wreckage. We sifted carefully through the debris, much of it half-buried and flaking with rust. A few pieces still wore a coat of navy-blue paint or glinted with chrome. I picked up an intact panel that had likely been part of the fuselage. All the while we could hear the low growl of the urban districts of the island just a few miles away and the rumble-whine of airliners overhead, but there in the undergrowth, dry leaves crackling beneath my feet, I might as well have been deep in an isolated forest. Hong Kong is a place of endless contradiction, as evidenced by the fact that I could be on a jam-packed city sidewalk one minute, but then head up into the hills and within a half hour have a hiking trail entirely to myself. This explained why the debris field from a crashed American warplane with a fifty-four-foot wingspan could remain undisturbed and undetected for more than half a century until Craig and his dogs came along.

Craig had been researching the story of Lieutenant Hunt's Avenger for years, so like me, he felt deeply connected to the wreck site. We both knew the details of the plane that had crashed there: it was a Grumman TBM-3 Avenger, bureau number 73334, assigned to VT-7 of the USS *Hancock*, and identified by the number 124 on its fuselage. We also knew the names of the airmen who had crewed the plane. We knew their stories, and we knew their faces, if only from aged black-and-white photos. We knew where they had been positioned inside the Avenger when it hit the mountainside, so we could connect specific pieces of wreckage to each of the three men in the crew. Unsurprisingly, the plane's armor had survived the crash intact, and we found the triangular steel plate that had served as the armored headrest for Lieutenant Hunt, who had bailed out of the Avenger with his flesh on fire. We identified the gun shield for Gene Barrow's .30-caliber machine gun, knowing he may well have peered over the shield and out the rear window in his final seconds of life. I imagined his last thoughts and how he would have seen the sky and ground pinwheeling crazily as the burning aircraft spun to earth. Likewise, when I examined the curved armor plate from the .50-caliber gun turret, I knew that my hands were touching the same metal that twenty-year-old Louis Gahran had crouched behind in the last moments before he died. Craig pulled a flask of whisky from his backpack, and he poured a few drops onto the ground as an offering to the dead. We toasted Hunt, Barrow, and Gahran as the bamboo stirred in a faint breeze and the mechanized snarl of the city carried over the surrounding hills. Leaving the wreckage as we had found it, we headed downslope, then threaded a ridgeline still pockmarked with the foxholes dug by Japanese infantry during the battle for Hong Kong. As we continued downhill with the dogs crashing ahead in the vanguard, we could see the reservoir and the ridges hemming the Tai Tam Valley like a palisade. Craig thought there might be the wrecks of at least two more aircraft up there, and he aimed to find them. We popped out of the underbrush and stepped onto a side path, which connected to a paved main trail busy with picnickers, joggers, and retirees strolling with transistor radios, all of them entirely unaware of how close they were to a wrecked American warplane.

I left Craig to his search for the other missing planes, flew to Taiwan to conduct additional field research in the port city of Kaohsiung, which had been extensively bombed by the air groups of TF 38 during the war, and then returned home to Michigan, at which point the Covid pandemic swept across the globe. During the lockdowns that followed, I wrote the final draft of *Target Hong Kong* with the ghosts of its characters – Lieutenant Hunt and Lieutenant Scobell, but also Marj and Ray Jones, and Jean Balch and John Lavender – looking over my shoulder. I sought to recount their experiences with the verisimilitude and vibrant prose that they deserved. The pandemic ended before the writing did, but *Target Hong Kong*, at long last, has now been published. I dedicate the book to Lieutenant Hunt, Lieutenant Scobell, and all the other aviators who fought, flew, and sometimes died in the skies over Hong Kong. I can't bring brave men back from the dead, but with the greatest of respect, I have tried to tell their stories in the pages of this book.

Acknowledgments

I always take great pleasure in writing the acknowledgments section, in part because this means I am close to the publication date for a book that has been years in the making. However, what I really like is that I get to gather so many friends, family, and colleagues onto the same pages for a celebration where I can salute the end of a project and thank everyone for helping to make it happen. I have worked with a remarkably generous bunch of people while writing *Target Hong Kong*.

I'll start by thanking Craig Mitchell, a key research collaborator who shared numerous primary source documents and expanded my understanding of how the American airstrikes against Hong Kong unfolded by taking me to the crash site of Lieutenant Hunt's TBM Avenger. Two years after I visited the wreck site, Craig and the Project Avenger team recovered and preserved the wreckage of Lieutenant Hunt's aircraft for future display in a Hong Kong museum. The full story can be found at www.project-avenger.com.

My friend Geoff Emerson arranged for me to visit the campus of St. Stephen's College Preparatory School, site of the wartime Stanley civilian internment camp on Hong Kong Island, and then accompanied me on a tour of the campus. Geoff shared his encyclopedic knowledge of the Stanley camp as we visited the locations that are described in this book, including Bungalow A, Bungalow C, and the Stanley Military Cemetery. Reverend Will Newman graciously allowed me to tour the grounds of Bungalow C, his private residence. I also thank St. Stephen's College for granting me permission to visit its lovely campus.

Stephen Davies and Colin Day, editors of the *Journal of the Royal Asiatic Society Hong Kong*, encouraged me to publish a pair of articles about the U.S. Navy airstrikes on Hong Kong and Macau during Operation *Gratitude*. These pieces appeared in the journal in 2017 and 2018 and are listed in the bibliography. The experience of researching and writing these two articles convinced me to embark on a book project that eventually developed into *Target Hong Kong*. I therefore must gratefully acknowledge that *JRASHK* served as the launch point for this book.

I am indebted to Rae Shaw, the daughter of Raymond and Marjorie Jones, who shared memories of her parents and patiently answered my many questions. I thank David Bellis, the indefatigable and ever-gracious founder of the Hong Kong history website *Gwulo* (www.gwulo .com), for introducing me to Rae and for all the other ways he has assisted my research over the years.

Marlene and Joe McCain shared information and documents pertaining to Commander John D. Lamade's service as a floatplane pilot aboard the USS *Houston*. Bill Beigel helped procure the personnel files for many of the naval aviators whose stories are described in this book. Peter Rose provided invaluable primary documents, including photos of the Pan Am station in Macau.

Speaking with the late Jack diPretoro shaped my understanding of what it was like to pilot a TBM Avenger during Operation *Gratitude*. Jack served with VT-11 aboard the USS *Hornet* and flew seven strikes during the operation, including Strike 2D against Hong Kong. He served twenty-one years in the navy and was still cross-country skiing at age ninety-five. Jack died in 2021 and is buried in Arlington National Cemetery alongside so many of his fellow naval aviators.

I enlisted a cohort of readers to vet my manuscript, point out gaps in the narrative, correct inaccuracies, provide feedback pertinent to their expertise, and generally save me from making embarrassing mistakes. Marty Irons, who is perhaps more familiar with the tactical details of Operation *Gratitude* than any other researcher in the business, served as an invaluable research collaborator, fact checker, sounding board, and morale booster. Colin Day shared his expertise on British Consul John Pownall Reeves and wartime Macau, while Philip Cracknell helped me get my facts straight when it came to the invasion of Hong Kong in 1941. Mark Herber filled me in on the USS *Essex* and its air group. I owe a particular debt to maritime historian Peter Cundall, who helped me to assemble the story of the ill-fated convoy Hi-87 and assisted with translating Japanese ship names. Chris Davis, webmaster of www.118trs .com, once again proved to be an invaluable source of information about the 118th Tactical Reconnaissance Squadron and its pilots.

I am grateful to Central Michigan University for providing the Faculty Research and Creative Endeavors grant that funded the research for this project, including the procurement of archival documents and travel to Hong Kong and Taiwan. My ground crew at CMU provided steady and much-needed support throughout this project as well. Micki Christensen kept efficient track of my research budget. Roy Rowan and Ted Troxell covered my final exam periods when I had to catch a plane to Hong Kong. Aparna Zambare and her fellow research librarians at the CMU Library tracked down dozens of books and other sources, no matter how rare or obscure.

My agent, Anne Devlin at Max Gartenberg Literary Agency, found the right publisher for *Target Hong Kong* with her usual tact and efficiency. I am fortunate to be represented by such a true pro.

My family provided the bedrock support for this project, which they have watched unfold over a span of many years. Much of the writing took place at the kitchen table, and thus *Target Hong Kong* was as integral to our everyday family life as feeding the cats and washing the dishes. My wife Jill gave me space to work while simultaneously providing a nourishing mix of smart advice, good humor, and venison from the deer she hunted on our back forty. My son Kip made sure I came up for air and reminded me that sometimes there are more important things to do than trying to wordsmith a paragraph about the crew compartment of a TBM Avenger. As I worked on this book project, I enjoyed many wide-ranging conversations with my mother, Ellie Bailey, about the complexities of writing and the nuances of history. Her wisdom has shaped this book.

Endnotes

ABBREVIATIONS

AAR – aircraft action report

AFHRA – Archives of the Air Force Historical Research Agency, Maxwell Air Force Base, Montgomery, Alabama

AR – action report

ERC HKHP – Elizabeth Ride Collection, Hong Kong Heritage Project Archives, Hong Kong

FIR – flight intelligence report

IDPF – individual deceased personnel file

JACAR – Japan Center for Asian Historical Records

MACR – missing air crew report

NARA – National Archives and Records Administration

NHHC – Naval History and Heritage Command

NPRC – National Personnel Records Center, St. Louis, MO

OMPF – official military personnel file

SC HKUL – Special Collections, Hong Kong University Library, Hong Kong

TAR – torpedo attack report

UNT OHC – Admiral Nimitz Museum and University of North Texas Oral History Collection

USSBS – United States Strategic Bombing Survey

WD – war diary

WH – war history

Unless otherwise noted, all U.S. Navy documents and MACRs are from the National Archives and Records Administration, but sourced from the online archive www.fold3.com.

CHAPTER 1

1 OMPF for Capt. John D. Lamade, October 31, 1961, NPRC; Joseph L. McCain and Marlene McCain, emails to author, February 21 and 22, 2020.
2 "Navy Hero Related to Altoonans," *Altoona Tribune*, March 14, 1945, 3.
3 AR, *Hancock* (CV-19), December 30, 1944, to January 25, 1945, enclosure A, 17.
4 AAR 61, CVG-7, *Hancock* (CV-19), January 16, 1945.
5 AAR 41, CVG-7, *Hancock* (CV-19), January 3, 1945; AR, *Hancock* (CV-19), December 30, 1944, to January 25, 1945, enclosure A, 7–8.
6 AAR 36, CVG-7, *Hancock* (CV-19), December 15, 1945; AAR 61, CVG-7, *Hancock* (CV-19), January 16, 1945; "Chronology and Narrative," 9, in "History of Torpedo Squadron Seven from 30 August 1944 to 15 February 1945," VT-7, CVG-7, *Hancock* (CV-19), February 16, 1945.
7 Author's interview with Jack diPretoro (ensign, VT-11, CVG-11, *Hornet*), January 19, 2021; Hynes, *Flights of Passage*, 139.
8 AR, *Yorktown* (CV-10), December 30, 1944, to January 23, 1945, enclosure A, 44; WD, *Yorktown* (CV-10), January 1945, 23.
9 Interview with Jean F. Balch, October 12, 1996, UNT OHC, number 1353.
10 "Bombing Squadron Three History through December 1944," VB-3, CVG-3, *Yorktown* (CV-10), part 2, 21; interview with Jean F. Balch, October 12, 1996, UNT OHC, number 1353.
11 "Bombing Squadron Three History through December 1944," VB-3, CVG-3, *Yorktown* (CV-10), part 2, 26–34.
12 AAR 22, VB-3, CVG-3, *Yorktown* (CV-10), January 16, 1945.

CHAPTER 2

1 Emerson, *Hong Kong Internment*, 59.
2 Cameron, *Illustrated History*, 28.
3 Cameron, *Illustrated History*, 192.
4 Mitter, *Forgotten Ally*, 63–66.
5 Mitter, *Forgotten Ally*, 157–64; Tobe, "Japanese Eleventh Army," 208–10.
6 Kwong and Tsoi, *Eastern Fortress*, 151; Macri, *Clash of Empires*, 110, 261; Snow, *Fall of Hong Kong*, 27.
7 Macri, *Clash of Empires*, 90–95.
8 Kwong and Tsoi, *Eastern Fortress*, 74–75, 99–101, 124–25.
9 Alderson, *History of Royal Air Force*, 22, 30.

10   Smith, *Singapore Burning*, 76.

11   Advertisement for C.E. Warren & Company, http://gwulo.com/atom /23852; Endacott and Birch, *Hong Kong Eclipse*, 49; Wong, "Disused Air Raid Precaution Tunnels."

12   Archer, *Internment of Western Civilians*, 38–41; Archer and Fedorowich, "Women of Stanley," 376; Banham, *Reduced to a Symbolic Scale*, 25–40.

13   Rae Shaw, email message to author, February 7, 2021.

14   Raymond Eric Jones, wartime diary, March 15, 1942, transcript in author's collection.

15   Rae Shaw, emails to author, January 17 and February 7, 2021.

16   Rae Shaw, email to author, February 7, 2021.

17   Rae Shaw, emails to author, January 17 and February 7, 2021.

18   Jones, wartime diary, August 2, 1941.

19   All entries from Jones's diary are presented in their original form without alteration or correction. Jones, wartime diary, August 20–21, September 6–7, 1941.

20   Banham, *Not the Slightest Chance*, 6.

21   Gordon, *Fighting for MacArthur*, 26–27.

22   Banham, *Not the Slightest Chance*, 13–17; Kwong and Tsoi, *Eastern Fortress*, 141, 171; Macri, *Clash of Empires*, 303–05.

CHAPTER 3

1   Jones, wartime diary, December 12, 1941.

2   Cracknell, *Battle for Hong Kong*, 72–73.

3   Jones, wartime diary, December 17, 1941.

4   "Warships at Singapore: Coming Visits of Cruisers and Submarines," *Straits Times*, May 24, 1930, 12.

5   "Ashore and Afloat. *Standard* Popular Everywhere!" *Skegness Standard*, date and page unknown; Rae Shaw, email to author, January 17, 2021.

6   Jones, wartime diary, December 24, 1941.

7   Cracknell, *Battle for Hong Kong*, 282.

8   Jones, wartime diary, December 24, 1941.

CHAPTER 4

1   Banham, *Not the Slightest Chance*, 244, 266; Bruce, *Second to None*, 207, 219, 265–70; Endacott and Birch, *Hong Kong Eclipse*, 99–100; Jones, wartime diary, December 24–28, 1941.

2   Jones, wartime diary, December 26, 1941.

3   Banham, *Not the Slightest Chance*, 317–19; Kwong and Tsoi, *Eastern Fortress*, 222; Macri, *Clash of Empires*, 317; Snow, *Fall of Hong Kong*, 81–82.

4   Banham, "Hong Kong's Civilian Fatalities," 33–34; Macri, *Clash of Empires*, 317.

5 Roland, "Massacre and Rape," 57; Snow, *Fall of Hong Kong*, 81–82.

6 Banham, "A Short History," 89, 92; Stericker, *Tear for the Dragon*, 150, 197.

7 Archer, *Internment of Western Civilians*, 32; Archer and Fedorowich, "Women of Stanley," 379, 391; Emerson, *Hong Kong Internment*, 59; Stericker, *Tear for the Dragon*, 158–59.

8 Jones, wartime diary, January 25, 1942.

9 Jones, wartime diary, January 22, 1942.

10 Jones, wartime diary, March 15, April 9, May 4, June 7, and June 24, 1942.

11 Emerson, *Hong Kong Internment*, 65–67.

12 Banham, *We Shall Suffer There*, 55, 60.

13 Banham, *Sinking of the* Lisbon Maru, 253.

14 Anslow, *Tin Hats and Rice*, 129; Jones, wartime diary, October 12, 1942.

15 Jones, wartime diary, November 30, 1942.

16 Jones, wartime diary, December 8, 1942.

17 Jones, wartime diary, December 26, 1942, and January 4 and 6, 1943.

18 Jones, wartime diary, September 12, 1943.

19 Assistant Chief of Air Staff, *Fourteenth Air Force*, 124; Jones, wartime diary, September 12, 1943; squadron history for 449th FS, July 1943 to May 1944, AFHRA, Iris no. 60556.

20 Emerson, *Hong Kong Internment*, 64–71; Hahn, *Hong Kong Holiday*, 275–79; Jones, wartime diary, September 23, 1943.

21 Jones, wartime diary, December 3, 8, and 25, 1943.

22 Jones, wartime diary, December 31, 1943.

23 Jones, wartime diary, January 9, 1944.

24 Jones, wartime diary, September 13, 1943, and February 27, 1944.

25 Emerson, *Hong Kong Internment*, 86; Jones, wartime diary, March 9, April 2, and August 21–26, 1944.

26 Jones, wartime diary, September 20 and October 3, 1944.

27 Emerson, *Hong Kong Internment*, 151–54; Jones, wartime diary, November 25 and 29, 1944; Stericker, *Tear for the Dragon*, 168–69.

28 Little is known about Gwendoline Frances Flower. Basic biographical details are taken from Leck, *Captives of Empire*, 626.

29 Jones, wartime diary, August 27 and December 8, 1944.

30 Charter, *First Shall Be Last*, 474; John Stericker, *Captive Colony: The Story of Stanley Camp, Hong Kong*, chapter 12, pg. 19, unpublished manuscript, September 1945, HKUL SC; Stericker, *Tear for the Dragon*, map inner front cover.

31 Jones, wartime diary, December 25, 1944.

CHAPTER 5

1 Toll, *Conquering Tide*, 328; "Yorktown Historical Report," *Yorktown* (CV-10), April 15, 1943, to September 2, 1945, part 1, 1.

2 Blewett, "History of the Newport News," 283.

3 "Yorktown Historical Report," *Yorktown* (CV-10), April 15, 1943, to September 2, 1945, part 1, 1–2, part 5, 17–18.

4 Hornfischer, *Fleet at Flood Tide*, 321–32; Reynolds, *Fast Carriers*, 204–10; Toll, *Conquering Tide*, 513; Trimble, *Admiral John S. McCain*, 153.

5 "Yorktown Historical Report," *Yorktown* (CV-10), April 15, 1943, to September 2, 1945, part 5, 18–19.

6 IDPF for Lt. (j.g.) John H. Lavender, NPRC.

7 IDPF for Lt. (j.g.) John H. Lavender, NPRC.

8 IDPF for Lt. (j.g.) John H. Lavender, NPRC; Somers, *Lake Michigan's Aircraft Carriers*.

9 OMPF for ARM2c Jean F. Balch, NPRC.

10 OMPF for ARM2c Jean F. Balch, NPRC.

11 "Bombing Squadron Three History through December 1944," VB-3, CVG-3, *Yorktown* (CV-10), part 2, 25; IDPF for Lt. (j.g.) John H. Lavender, NPRC; OMPF for ARM2c Jean F. Balch, NPRC; WD, *Yorktown* (CV-10), September 1944, 1–2, and October 1944, 5–6.

CHAPTER 6

1 Leutze, *Different Kind of Victory*, 231.

2 Leutze, *Different Kind of Victory*, 262.

3 Kehn, *In the Highest Degree*, 111–13, 264; Leutze, *Different Kind of Victory*; Hornfischer, *Ship of Ghosts*, 43.

4 Hornfischer, *Ship of Ghosts*, 463; John D. Lamade, "USS *Houston*: From December 8, 1941 until She Was Reported Missing February 28, 1942"; Joseph L. McCain and Marlene McCain, emails to author, February 21 and 22, 2020, and "Story of the Broome Seagull," 8–10; "Navy Hero Related to Altoonians," *Altoona Tribune*, March 14, 1945, 3; OMPF for Capt. John D. Lamade, October 31, 1961, NPRC; Schultz, *Last Battle Station*, 38–43, 123–24, 127, 129; Winslow, *Ghost that Died*, 18, 86, 102–05.

5 WD, *Hancock* (CV-19), August 1944 and September 1944; "Chronology and Narrative" in "History of Torpedo Squadron Seven from 30 August 1944 to 15 February 1945," VT-7, CVG-7, *Hancock* (CV-19), February 16, 1945.

6 WD, *Hancock* (CV-19), September 1944 and October 1944; WD, *West Virginia* (BB48), September 1944 and October 1944.

7 Hughes, *Admiral Bill Halsey*, 334–35, 338–39; Reynolds, *Fast Carriers*, 243–46; Toll, *Twilight of the Gods*, 50–58, 71–77, 87, 94; Trimble, *Admiral John S. McCain*, 155; Yenne, *MacArthur's Air Force*, 157–59.

8 Toll, *Twilight of the Gods*, 292–93.

9 IDPF for Lt. (j.g.) Richard C. Scobell, NPRC.

10 IDPF for Lt. (j.g.) Richard C. Scobell, NPRC; WD, VT-305, May, June, and July 1944.

11 WD, *Nassau* (CVE-16), October 1944, 5–6.

12 Y'Blood, *Little Giants*, 110–12.

13 AAR 19, CVG-7, *Hancock* (CV-19), October 25, 1944; "Chronology and
Narrative," 5, in "History of Torpedo Squadron Seven from 30 August 1944
to 15 February 1945," VT-7, CVG-7, *Hancock* (CV-19), February 16, 1945;
Mike Crandall, "Forced Landing and Raft Survival Report of Pilot Lieutenant
Scobell," *Remembering Wally*, February 2014, http://rememberingwally
.blogspot.com; WD, *Preston* (DD-795), October 1944, 6–7.

CHAPTER 7

1   Trimble, *Admiral John S. McCain*, 185–86, 195; Reynolds, *Fast Carriers*, 287,
WD, *Yorktown* (CV-10), November 1944, 1–2.
2   "Bombing Squadron Three History through December 1944," VB-3, CVG-3,
Yorktown (CV-10), part 3, 26–28; "Operations against Enemy Shipping in the
Philippines Islands Area, from 11 November to 15 November 1944," *Yorktown*
(CV-10), November 20, 1944; Reynolds, *Fast Carriers*, 287–88; Trimble,
Admiral John S. McCain, 190–91.
3   "Bombing Squadron Three History through December 1944," VB-3, CVG-
3, *Yorktown* (CV-10), part 3, 29–30; WD, *Yorktown* (CV-10), November
1944, 8.
4   Dorr, "Bombing in the Beast," 46–47, 51; Hynes, *Flights of Passage*, 142–43;
Looney and Busha, "Mission into Darkness," 35–36; Reynolds, *Fast Carriers*,
57–58, 131, 226.
5   Dorr, "Bombing in the Beast," 46; Hynes, *Flights of Passage*, 94–95.
6   AAR 4, VB-3, CVG-3, *Yorktown* (CV-10), November 13, 1944; "Bombing
Squadron Three History through December 1944," VB-3, CVG-3, *Yorktown*
(CV-10), part 3, 29–30; "Operations against Enemy Shipping in the
Philippines Islands Area, from 11 November to 15 November 1944," *Yorktown*
(CV-10), November 20, 1944, enclosure A, 2–3, and enclosure D, 2; WD,
Yorktown (CV-10), November 1944, 7–8.
7   AAR 5, VB-3, CVG-3, *Yorktown* (CV-10), November 14, 1944; "Bombing
Squadron Three History through December 1944," VB-3, CVG-3, *Yorktown*
(CV-10), part 3, 30–31; "Operations against Enemy Shipping in the
Philippines Islands Area, from 11 November to 15 November 1944," *Yorktown*
(CV-10), November 20, 1944, enclosure A, 4–5 and enclosure C, 1; WD,
Yorktown (CV-10), November 1944, 9–11; WH, CVG-3, *Yorktown* (CV-10),
January 1945, 1.
8   "Bombing Squadron Three History through December 1944," VB-3, CVG-3,
Yorktown (CV-10), part 3, 31–32; WD, *Yorktown* (CV-10), November 1944,
15–16.
9   "Bombing Squadron Three History through December 1944," VB-3, CVG-3,
Yorktown (CV-10), part 3, 33–34; WD, *Yorktown* (CV-10), November 1944, 21.
10 "Bombing Squadron Three History through December 1944," VB-3,
CVG-3, *Yorktown* (CV-10), part 3, 33–34; Trimble, *Admiral John S. McCain*,
208; WD, *Yorktown* (CV-10), December 1944, 10–20.

11 "Bombing Squadron Three History through December 1944," VB-3, CVG-3,
Yorktown (CV-10), part 3, 34; Trimble, *Admiral John S. McCain*, 216; WD,
Yorktown (CV-10), December 1944, 14; WH, CVG-3, Yorktown (CV-10),
January 1945, 3–4, 28–29.

CHAPTER 8

1 The account of convoy Hi-87 and the story of Suzumoku Goni is based in part
upon maritime historian Peter Cundall's translation of pertinent pages in *Senji
Yuso-sendan-shi* (*History of Wartime Transport*) by Shinshichiro Komamiya. William
G. Somerville prepared the original translation, later modified and annotated in
2020 by Cundall. Translation in author's collection.

2 Parillo, *Japanese Merchant Marine*, 127.

3 Parillo, *Japanese Merchant Marine*, 204.

4 Parillo, *Japanese Merchant Marine*, 113.

5 In addition to sources already noted, details about Japanese ships and convoys
are sourced from the tabular records of movement for individual warships and
merchant vessels found at www.combinedfleet.com.

6 Hara, Saito, and Pineau, *Japanese Destroyer Captain*; USSBS, *Interrogations of
Japanese Officials*, vol. II, 341–51.

7 Toll, *Conquering Tide*, 285.

8 Parillo, *Japanese Merchant Marine*, 120.

9 AAR 9, VB-3, CVG-3, Yorktown (CV-10), January 3, 1945; "Narrative
History of Bombing Squadron Three, 1 January to 31 March 1945," 1–2, and
"Tactical Organization of Strikes 1 January 1945 to 31 March 1945," appendix
A, A-1 to 2, in WH, VB-3, CVG-3, Yorktown (CV-10); WD, Commander 3rd
Fleet, January 1945, 3–5; WD, Yorktown (CV-10), January 1945, 3–5.

10 Paseo High School yearbook, Kansas City, MO, 1938, Kansas City Public
Library, Missouri Valley Special Collections; Scott, *War Below*, 286.

11 "Location of U.S. Naval Aircraft," November 30, 1943 (OP 31 C2 KB, SC
A4-3 VZ), NHHC.

12 Noles, *Twenty-Three Minutes to Eternity*; "War Damage Report No. 45: USS
Liscome Bay (CVE-56)," Preliminary Design Branch, Bureau of Ships, Navy
Department, U.S. Hydrographic Office, March 10, 1944.

13 Hynes, *Flights of Passage*, 113.

14 AAR 36, CVG-7, Hancock (CV-19), December 15, 1945; "Chronology and
Narrative," 9, in "History of Torpedo Squadron Seven from 30 August 1944
to 15 February 1945," VT-7, CVG-7, Hancock (CV-19), February 16, 1945;
Cressman, *Official Chronology*, 593; Joint Army-Navy Assessment Committee,
Japanese Naval and Merchant Shipping, 20; Military History Section, *Imperial
Japanese Navy*, part 8, 217.

15 AAR 21, CVG-7, Hancock (CV-19), October 26, 1944; "Chronology and
Narrative," 5, 9, in "History of Torpedo Squadron Seven from 30 August 1944 to
15 February 1945," VT-7, CVG-7, Hancock (CV-19), February 16, 1945.

16 AR, *Ticonderoga* (CV-14), January 1945, part 6, 7; Thomas, *Torpedo Squadron Four*, 131.

17 AAR 41, CVG-7, *Hancock* (CV-19), January 3, 1945; AR, *Hancock* (CV-19), January 1945, enclosure A, 7.

18 AAR 10, VB-3, CVG-3, *Yorktown* (CV-10), January 4, 1945; "Narrative History of Bombing Squadron Three, 1 January to 31 March 1945," 1–2, and "Tactical Organization of Strikes 1 January 1945 to 31 March 1945," appendix A, A-1 to 2 in WH, VB-3, CVG-3, *Yorktown* (CV-10); WD, Commander 3rd Fleet, January 1945, 3–5; WD, *Yorktown* (CV-10), January 1945, 3–5.

19 IDPF for Lt. (j.g.) John H. Lavender and OMPF for ARM2c Jean F. Balch, NPRC.

20 Hornfischer, *Last Stand*, 88.

21 AAR 13 and 14, VB-3, and AAR 48, VF-3, CVG-3, *Yorktown* (CV-10), January 7, 1945; "Narrative History of Bombing Squadron Three, 1 January to 31 March 1945," 4–5 and "Tactical Organization of Strikes 1 January 1945 to 31 March 1945," appendix A, A-2 in WH, VB-3, CVG-3, *Yorktown* (CV-10); WD, Commander 3rd Fleet, January 1945, 6–8; WD, *Yorktown* (CV-10), January 1945, 9–10.

CHAPTER 9

1 Stevens, *Low Level Liberators*, 70.

2 Paul F. Stevens, oral history interview, National Museum of the Pacific War, October 1, 2000, 4, 25.

3 Stevens, *Low Level Liberators*, 111, 134–35; WD, VPB-104, FAW 10, January 1945.

4 Stevens, *Low Level Liberators*, 11–12, 28, 129.

5 Stevens, *Low Level Liberators*, 42, 65, 103, 129.

6 Stevens, *Low Level Liberators*, 26; Stevens, oral history, 21, 28.

7 Stevens, *Low Level Liberators*, 143.

8 Military History Section, *Imperial Japanese Navy*, part 8, 221; report of war patrol number five, January 5 to 31, 1945, *Picuda* (SS-382), 3–4, 17–18; report of war patrol number eleven, December 19, 1944, to February 15, 1945, *Barb* (SS-220), 4–6.

9 Map of Takao, Formosa, U.S. Army Map Service, 1945, PCL Map Collection, University of Texas Libraries.

10 "Narrative History of Bombing Squadron Three, 1 January to 31 March 1945," 5, in WH, VB-3, CVG-3, *Yorktown* (CV-10).

11 Military History Section, *Imperial Japanese Navy*, appendix B, 263–65.

12 AAR 16, VB-3, and AAR 16, VT-3, CVG-3, *Yorktown* (CV-10), January 9, 1945; "Narrative History of Bombing Squadron Three, 1 January to 31 March 1945," 5–6, in WH, VB-3, CVG-3, *Yorktown* (CV-10); WD, *Yorktown* (CV-10), January 1945, 12–13.

13 Morison, *History of United States*, 159.

14 Reynolds, *Fast Carriers*, 296–97.

15 Thomas, *Sea of Thunder*, 108; Toll, *Twilight of the Gods*, 113.

16 Naval historians have debated whether Halsey assumed tactical command of TF 38, a role that properly fell to McCain. See Reynolds, *Fast Carriers*, and Trimble, *Admiral John S. McCain*.

17 Hughes, *Admiral Bill Halsey*, 338.

18 WD, Commander 3rd Fleet, January 1945, 6.

19 WH, *Hancock* (CV-19), "Engineering Data," appendix A.

20 "Location of U.S. Naval Aircraft," January 16, 1945 (OP 31R, no. 3 45, SC A4 3 0Z), NHHC.

CHAPTER 10

1   WD, Commander TG 30.8, January 1945, 6.

2   Jentschura, Jung, and Mickel, *Warships of the Imperial*, 187; Parillo, *Japanese Merchant Marine*, 95, 98; Stille, *Imperial Japanese Navy*, 24–26; Sturma and Shindo, "Convoy Hi-72," 278, 280–81.

3   Lockwood, *Sink 'Em All*, 200; Military History Section, *Imperial Japanese Navy*, appendix A, 252; report of war patrol number three, June 19 to August 7, 1944, *Flasher* (SS-249), 13–15, 35–36.

4   USSBS, *Interrogations of Japanese Officials*, vol. I, 161–64, and II, 576.

5   Parillo, *Japanese Merchant Marine*, 69; Sturma and Shindo, "Convoy Hi-72," 282.

6   Military History Section, *Imperial Japanese Navy*, part 1, 4.

7   Sources provide incomplete and contradictory information on the movements of convoy Hi-87 on January 10–12, 1945. However, it appears that an initial order to steam from Takao to Mako was countermanded in favor of proceeding directly to Singapore. Lt. Cdr. Yatsui stated that the convoy had reached the vicinity of Hainan when the order came to take refuge in Hong Kong. In contrast, Komamiya omits any mention of Singapore and indicates the convoy was ordered to bypass Mako and proceed to Hong Kong. Komamiya, *Senji Yuso-sendan-shi* (History of Wartime Transport Convoys); USSBS, *Interrogations of Japanese Officials*, vol. I, 162.

8   Thomas, *Torpedo Squadron Four*, 118.

9   Hynes, *Flights of Passage*, 146.

10 AAR 46, VB-11, AAR 52, VT-11, and AAR 108, VF-11, CVG-11, *Hornet* (CV-12), January 12, 1945; AAR 52 and TAR 4, CVG-7, *Hancock* (CV-19), January 12, 1945; AAR 173, CVG-20, *Lexington* (CV-16), January 12, 1945; "Chronology and Narrative," 11, in "History of Torpedo Squadron Seven from 30 August 1944 to 15 February 1945," VT-7, CVG-7, *Hancock* (CV-19), February 16, 1945; Cressman, *Official Chronology*, 608–09; Joint Army-Navy Assessment Committee, *Japanese Naval and Merchant Shipping*, 79–80; Military History Section, *Imperial Japanese Navy*, part 8, 219–21.

11 AAR 47, VB-11, AAR 54, VT-11, and AAR 110, VF-11, CVG-11, *Hornet* (CV-12), January 12, 1945; AAR 54 and TAR 5, CVG-7, *Hancock* (CV-19),

January 12, 1945; AAR 174, CVG-20, *Lexington* (CV-16), January 12, 1945; "Chronology and Narrative," 11, in "History of Torpedo Squadron Seven from 30 August 1944 to 15 February 1945," VT-7, CVG-7, *Hancock* (CV-19), February 16, 1945; Cressman, *Official Chronology*, 608–09; Joint Army-Navy Assessment Committee, *Japanese Naval and Merchant Shipping*, 79–81; Military History Section, *Imperial Japanese Navy*, part 8, 219–21; Parillo, *Japanese Merchant Marine*, 71.

CHAPTER 11

1   Dorr, "Bombing in the Beast," 48.

2   AAR 19, VB-3, AAR 19, VT-3, and AAR 59, VF-3, CVG-3, *Yorktown* (CV-10), January 12, 1945; AR, TG 38.1, TF 38, December 30, 1944 to January 26, 1945; "Narrative History of Bombing Squadron Three, 1 January to 31 March 1945," 7–9, in WH, VB-3, CVG-3, *Yorktown* (CV-10).

3   The designation Air Combat *Information* Officer replaced the earlier designation of Air Combat *Intelligence* Officer. See Trimble, *Admiral John S. McCain*, 121–22. However, the original designation remained in common usage, as evidenced by U.S. Navy documents from 1945 that refer interchangeably to Air Combat Intelligence Officers and Air Combat Information Officers. *Glossary of U.S. Naval Abbreviations* identifies the acronym "ACI" and "ACIO" as "Air Combat Intelligence" and "Air Combat Intelligence Officer," respectively.

4   AR, *Essex* (CV-9), January 3–22, 1945, part 3, 5–6 and part 6, 20; Chennault, *Way of a Fighter*, 333; MACR 11163 for crew of B-24J (aircraft serial no. 42–73249), 374th Bomb Squadron, 308th Bomb Group (Heavy), January 15, 1945; "Organizational History of 308th Bombardment Group (H) AAF," January 1945, "Casualties," 5 and "Missions," 16, AFHRA, Iris no. 81952; Sherrod, *History of Marine Corps Aviation*, 339–40; Thomas, *Torpedo Squadron Four*, 123–25; WD, forward echelons of VMF-124 and VMF-213, Marine Air Wing 44, *Essex* (CV-9), January 1945.

CHAPTER 12

1   Morison, *History of United States*, 169–70; WD, Commander 3rd Fleet, January 1945, 13–15.

2   WD, Commander TG 30.8, January 1945, 7.

3   Anslow, *Tin Hats and Rice*, 199; Jones, wartime diary, January 13, 1945.

4   Detailed engagement reports from September 1944 to July 1945 for armed merchant vessels with initials from "A" to "So" (Japanese syllabary), JACAR, C08030692400, 21–24.

5   AR, *Lexington* (CV-16), December 30, 1944 to January 22, 1945, enclosure A.

6   USSBS, *Interrogations of Japanese Officials*, vol. I, 161.

7   Stevens, *Low Level Liberators*, 41, 117, 154.

8   Stevens, *Low Level Liberators*, 41, 59–60, 154.

9   Stevens, *Low Level Liberators*, 130, 142, 257.
10 Stevens, *Low Level Liberators*, 148.

CHAPTER 13

1   Exhibit 6: Communication 140349 from commander 3rd Fleet to commander TF 38, January 14, 1945, "Record of Proceedings of a Court of Inquiry Convened on Board the USS *South Dakota*," NARA, record group 125: Records of the Office of the Judge Advocate General (Navy), 1799–1953, Records of Select Courts of Inquiry, May 18, 1932–June 1953, case 198-24: "Alleged violation of Portuguese neutrality at Macao by U.S. naval aircraft, January 16, 1945" (NARA identifier 783034).
2   Exhibit 7: Communication 120315 from commander TF 38 to commander 3rd Fleet and commander TG 38.1, 38.2, 38.3, and 38.5, January 12, 1945, "Record of Proceedings of a Court of Inquiry Convened on Board the USS *South Dakota*."
3   McManus, *Deadly Sky*, 244–47.
4   Toll, *Conquering Tide*, 197–98.
5   Exhibit 2: Communication 130225 from Rear Admiral Bogan to Vice Admiral McCain and Admiral Halsey, January 13, 1945, "Record of Proceedings of a Court of Inquiry Convened on Board the USS *South Dakota*."
6   Exhibit 3: Communication 130622 from commander 3rd Fleet to commander TF 38, January 13, 1945; Exhibit 4: Communication 130645 from commander TF 38 to commander TG 38.2, January 13, 1945; Exhibit 5: Communication 130735 from commander TG 38.2 to USS *Hancock*, January 13, 1945, "Record of Proceedings of a Court of Inquiry Convened on Board the USS *South Dakota*."
7   Exhibit 6: Communication 140349 from commander 3rd Fleet to commander TF 38, January 14, 1945, "Record of Proceedings of a Court of Inquiry Convened on Board the USS *South Dakota*"; WD, Commander 3rd Fleet, January 1945, 15.
8   Enclosure H: Track chart of TG 38.2, January 10–20, 1945, AR for commander TG 38.2, December 30, 1944, to January 26, 1945.
9   Campbell, *Naval Weapons*, 169; Reynolds, *Fast Carriers*, 225.
10 Tillman and van der Lugt, *VF-11/111*, 49.
11 AAR 54, VF-7, CVG-7, *Hancock* (CV-19); AAR 115, VF-11, CVG-11, *Hornet* (CV-12); AAR 179, VF-20, CVG-20, *Lexington* (CV-16); all documents January 15, 1945.
12 Hata, Izawa, and Shores, *Japanese Army Fighter Aces*, 71, 313; Millman, *Ki-44 Tojo Aces*, 47.
13 AAR 1-A-1-51, VF-81, CVG-81, *Wasp* (CV-18); AAR 61, VF-3, CVG-3, *Yorktown* (CV-10); both documents January 15, 1945.
14 Bailey, *Bold Venture*, 196–201; FIR 14, January 15, 1945, 118th TRS, 23rd FG; squadron history for 118th TRS, 23rd FG, November 12, 1944, to January 22,

1945; MACR 11636 for 1st Lt. Frank S. Palmer (aircraft serial no. 44–11120) and MACR 11637 for 2nd Lt. Daniel J. Mitchell (aircraft serial no. 43–6751), 118th TRS, 23rd FG, January 17, 1945; MACR 11633 for 2nd Lt. Galen C. Theobold (aircraft serial no. 43–24972) and MACR 11635 for Maj. David L. Houck (aircraft serial no. 44–11103), 118th TRS, 23rd FG, January 18, 1945.

CHAPTER 14

1 Toll, *Conquering Tide*, 302.
2 AAR 20, VB-3, AAR 20, VT-3, and AAR 63, VF-3, CVG-3, *Yorktown* (CV-10), January 15, 1945; AR, TG 38.2, TF 38, December 30, 1944, to January 26, 1945, 21–22; AR, *Yorktown* (CV-10), December 30, 1944, to January 23, 1945, enclosure A, 8, 44; "Narrative History of Bombing Squadron Three, 1 January to 31 March 1945," 9–10, in WH, VB-3, CVG-3, *Yorktown* (CV-10); WD, Commander 3rd Fleet, January 1945, 15–16; WD, *Yorktown* (CV-10), January 1945, 20–21; WH, CVG-3, *Yorktown* (CV-10), April 1945, enclosure B, 6–7.
3 WD, Commander 3rd Fleet, January 1945, 16.
4 USSBS, *Interrogations of Japanese Officials*, vol. I, 162.

CHAPTER 15

1 Exhibit 9: USS *Hancock* Air Intelligence Memorandum 4–45, January 12, 1945, "Record of Proceedings of a Court of Inquiry Convened on Board the USS *South Dakota*"; Stark, *A WWII F6F Navy Fighter*, 34.
2 Exhibit 8: Target Assignments, Annex ABLE Part III, Addendum 1, "Record of Proceedings of a Court of Inquiry Convened on Board the USS *South Dakota*."
3 Testimony of Lt. Charles E. Golson and Lt. G.B. Gose, "Record of Proceedings of a Court of Inquiry Convened on Board the USS *South Dakota*."
4 Exhibit 1: Excerpt from page 21 of CINCPAC-CINCPOA Bulletin 165–44, November 25, 1944; Exhibit 9: USS *Hancock* Air Intelligence Memorandum 4–45, January 12, 1945, "Record of Proceedings of a Court of Inquiry Convened on Board the USS *South Dakota*."
5 Testimony of Captain Robert P. Hickey and Commander John D. Lamade, "Record of Proceedings of a Court of Inquiry Convened on Board the USS *South Dakota*."
6 "History of Torpedo Squadron Seven from 30 August 1944 to 15 February 1945," WH, VT-7, CVG-7, *Hancock* (CV-19), 8.
7 Lockwood, *Sink 'Em All*, 121.
8 Conner, *Nothing Friendly*, 84.
9 Conner, *Nothing Friendly*, 118–19; report of war patrol number ten, *Guardfish* (SS-217), January 26, 1945.
10 "History of Air Group Three (CVG-3) January 1945," enclosure B, 10, in WH, CVG-3, *Yorktown* (CV-10), April 1945.

11 For a discussion of why Japan chose not to occupy Macau, see Gunn, *Wartime Macau*, 25–54.

12 Garrett, *Defences of Macau*, 134.

13 A sixth Osprey crashed on June 26, 1942, killing the two-man crew. Garrett, *Defences of Macau*, 138.

14 Reeves, *Lone Flag*, xxi.

15 Gunn, *Wartime Macau*, 55.

16 Gunn, *Wartime Macau*, 55.

17 Garrett, *Defences of Macau*, 132.

18 Gunn, *Wartime Macau*, 13, 22, 55.

19 Garrett, *Defences of Macau*, 138.

20 Reeves, *Lone Flag*, 186 n23.

21 Reeves, *Lone Flag*, 48.

22 Lopes, "They 'Built' Macau"; Reeves, *Lone Flag*, xxiv; "Sailing in the Waves of History," *Macau News*, May 26, 2016.

23 McGivering, *Macao Remembers*, 77.

24 Armando da Silva, "Hong Kong 16 January 1945: A Rendezvous with History," *UMA News Bulletin*, Fall 2013; Reeves, *Lone Flag*, 99–101.

25 AAR 2-AS-56, VF-81, CVG-81, *Wasp* (CV-18); AAR 55, VF-7, CVG-7, *Hancock* (CV-19); AAR 65, VF-3, CVG-3, *Yorktown* (CV-10); AAR 119, VF-11, CVG-11, *Hornet* (CV-12); AAR 183, CVG-20, *Lexington* (CV-16); all documents January 16, 1945; testimony of Lt. George E. Kemper and Lt. Lloyd E. Newcomer, "Record of Proceedings of a Court of Inquiry Convened on Board the USS *South Dakota.*"

CHAPTER 16

1 AAR 2-A-55, VF-81, CVG-81, *Wasp* (CV-18); AAR 21, VB-3, AAR 21, VT-3, and AAR 66, VF-3, CVG-3, *Yorktown* (CV-10); AAR 32, VT-22, CVLG-22, *Cowpens* (CVL-25); all documents January 16, 1945.

2 WD, *Brush* (DD-745), January 1945, 5.

3 Commanding General, *Pilot's Handbook*, 44.

4 Braga, "Rescued from Certain Death," 1–4.

5 AAR 32, VT-22, CVLG-22, *Cowpens* (CVL-25), January 16, 1945; Braga, "Rescued from Certain Death," 1–4; Commanding General, *Pilot's Handbook*, 43–46; communique from Officer Commanding, BAAG, Yanping, to Commandant, BAAG, re. arrival in Yanping of Lt. (j.g.) A. Basmajian, Ensign G.W. Clark, AMM3c D.E. Mize, and ARM3c C.G. Myers, January 30, 1945; walkout narrative for Lt. (j.g.) A. Basmajian, Ensign G.W. Clark, AMM3c D.E. Mize, and ARM3c C.G. Myers, Headquarters AGAS-China, March 30, 1945.

6 Alternative translations for the No. 2 Naval Working Department include No. 2 Department of the IJN, IJN No. 2 Repair Facility, 2nd Construction Department, and 2nd Naval Construction and Repair Department.

7 Bob Hackett, "History of the IJN's No. 2 Naval Working Department at Britain's Crown Colony of Hong Kong," 2016, http://www.combinedfleet.com/IJN%20No.%202%20Naval%20Working%20Department%20at%20Hong%20Kong.htm; Kwong and Tsoi, *Eastern Fortress*, 34; Melson, *White Ensign*, 45.

8 Cameron, *Illustrated History*, 208; Chiu, *Port of Hong Kong*, 42; Courtald and Holdsworth, *Hong Kong Story*, 40–41; Kwong and Tsoi, *Eastern Fortress*, 34.

9 "1945 HK and Whampoa Docks," https://gwulo.com/atom/20497; Coates, *Whampoa*, 222, 226–27.

10 Hackett, "History of the IJN's No. 2 Naval Working Department"; Ward, *Hong Kong Under Japanese Occupation*, 79–80.

11 AAR 51, VB-11, AAR 58, VT-11, AAR 120, VF-11, CVG-11, *Hornet* (CV-12); AAR 182, CVG-20, *Lexington* (CV-16); all documents January 16, 1945.

12 AAR 59, CVG-7, *Hancock* (CV-19), January 16, 1945; Ha and Waters, "Hong Kong's Lighthouses," 289–90.

CHAPTER 17

1 Bailey, *Bold Venture*, 201–03; FIR 15, 16, and 17, 118th TRS, 23rd FG, January 16, 1945; Lanphier, *WWII Army Air Corps*, 57–60; "Lieut. John Egan of Tiger Fame, Under Chennault, Makes Fighting Seem Fun," *Fort Lauderdale Daily News*, July 19, 1945, 10; MACR 11634, January 18, 1945, and supplemental MACR 11634, January 29, 1945, for 1st Lt. John F. Egan (aircraft serial no. 43–7055), 118th TRS, 23rd FG; squadron history for 118th TRS, 23rd FG, November 12, 1944, to January 22, 1945.

2 WD, *Samuel N. Moore* (DD–747), January 1945, 8.

3 AAR 2-B-57, VF-81 and AAR 1B-16, VT-81, CVG-81, *Wasp* (CV-18); AAR 22, VT-3 and AAR 67, VF-3, CVG-3, *Yorktown* (CV-10); AAR 59, VT-11 and AAR 121, VF-11, CVG-11, *Hornet* (CV-12); AAR 60, CVG-7, *Hancock* (CV-19); AAR 184, CVG-20, *Lexington* (CV-16); AAR VT-24, VT-29, CVLG-29, *Cabot* (CVL-28); all documents January 16, 1945.

4 AAR 32, VT-22, CVLG-22, *Cowpens* (CVL-25), January 16, 1945.

CHAPTER 18

1 Campbell, *Naval Weapons*, 105.

2 Campbell, *Naval Weapons*, 149.

3 Campbell, *Naval Weapons*, 106, 152.

4 Campbell, *Naval Weapons*, 200.

5 AAR 33, VT-22, CVLG-22, *Cowpens* (CVL-25), January 16, 1945.

6 AAR 2-C-58, VF-81, CVG-81, *Wasp* (CV-18), January 16, 1945; communique from Officer Commanding, BAAG, Yanping, to Commandant, BAAG, re. arrival in Yanping of Lt. (j.g.) A. Basmajian, Ensign G.W. Clark, AMM3c D.E. Mize, and ARM3c C.G. Myers, January

30, 1945; evasion and walkout narrative for Lt. (j.g.) A. Basmajian, Ensign G.W. Clark, AMM3c D.E. Mize, and ARM3c C.G. Myers, Headquarters AGAS-China, March 30, 1945.

7 AAR 22, VB-3, AAR 23, VT-3, and AAR 68, VF-3, CVG-3, *Yorktown* (CV-10), January 16, 1945; "Chronology of Bombing Squadron Three, 1 January 1945 to 31 March 1945," 10–11, in WH, VB-3, CVG-3, *Yorktown* (CV-10); interview with Jean F. Balch, October 12, 1996, UNT OHC, number 1353.

CHAPTER 19

1 Author's phone interview with Jack diPretoro, January 19, 2021.

2 AAR 52, VB-11, AAR 60, VT-11, and AAR 122, VF-11, CVG-11, *Hornet* (CV-12), January 16, 1945; Tillman and van der Lugt, *VF-11/111*, 49; walkout narrative for Ensign M.J. Crehan, Headquarters AGAS-China, March 30, 1945.

3 AAR 185, CVG-20, *Lexington* (CV-16), January 16, 1945.

4 Hynes, *Flights of Passage*, 139; Lanphier, *WWII Army Air Corps*, 7.

5 Charter, *First Shall Be Last*, 469; Stericker, *Tear for the Dragon*, 199.

6 Commanding General, *Pilot's Handbook*, 45–46; Ray Panko, "The Mystery of the Middle Seat: The Curious Case of Seating in the Grumman TBF/TBM Avenger," December 20, 2017, https://www.pearlharboraviationmuseum.org/pearl-harbor-blog/mystery-middle-seat/.

7 Charter, *First Shall Be Last*, 468.

8 Anslow, *Tin Hats and Rice*, 201; Banham, *We Shall Suffer There*, 189; Corbin, *Prisoners of the East*, 251–52; George Gerrard, wartime diary, quoted in Stuart Heaver, "Remains of U.S. Airmen Killed in 1945 Crash"; Jones, wartime diary, January 16, 1945; Redwood, *It Was Like This*, 215; Stericker, *Tear for the Dragon*, 200; Wright-Nooth and Adkin, *Prisoner of the Turnip Heads*, 237–38.

9 AAR 61, CVG-7, *Hancock* (CV-19), January 16, 1945.

10 Gunn, *Wartime Macau*, 109; McGivering, *Macao Remembers*, 77; Reeves, *Lone Flag*, 100.

11 Reeves, *Lone Flag*, 100.

12 Lopes, "They 'Built' Macau."

13 AAR 61, CVG-7, *Hancock* (CV-19), January 16, 1945; testimony of Lt. E.W. Niebling, "Record of Proceedings of a Court of Inquiry Convened on Board the USS *South Dakota*."

14 AAR 39, VF-7, CVG-7, *Hancock* (CV-19), January 4, 1945.

15 AR, *Hancock* (CV-19), December 30, 1944, to January 25, 1945, enclosure A, 8.

CHAPTER 20

1 AAR 53, VB-11, AAR 61, VT-11, and AAR 123, VF-11, CVG-11, *Hornet* (CV-12); AAR 62, CVG-7, *Hancock* (CV-19); AAR 186, CVG-20, *Lexington* (CV-16); all documents January 16, 1945; "Lubbock Man, Beaten in Japanese Prison,

Maintains Sense of Humor," *Fort Worth Star-Telegram*, September 3, 1945, 2; Turner and Turner, *Red Wing to Hong Kong*, 210.

2   Cressman, *Official Chronology*, 611; Joint Army-Navy Assessment Committee, *Japanese Naval and Merchant Shipping*, 81; Military History Section, *Imperial Japanese Navy*, part 8, 221; USSBS, *Interrogations of Japanese Officials*, vol. I, 161–64, and II, 576.

3   *China Navigation Company*, 140; Cressman, *Official Chronology*, 611; Joint Army-Navy Assessment Committee, *Japanese Naval and Merchant Shipping*, 81; Military History Section, *Imperial Japanese Navy*, appendix B, 257, 262; Peter Cundall, email to author, November 28, 2019.

4   Cressman, *Official Chronology*, 611; Military History Section, *Imperial Japanese Navy*, part 8, 219; Stille, *Imperial Japanese Navy*, 28; USSBS, *Interrogations of Japanese Officials*, vol. I, 162.

5   Interview with Jean F. Balch, October 12, 1996, UNT OHC, number 1353.

CHAPTER 21

1   Kweilin Intelligence Summary 87, section 2, February 28, 1945, BAAG, ERC HKHP.

2   AAR 68, CVG-80, *Ticonderoga* (CV-14), January 16, 1945.

3   AAR 67, VF-4, CVG-4, *Essex* (CV-9), January 16, 1945; Thomas, *Torpedo Squadron Four*, 171–72.

4   AAR 62, VF-44, CVLG-44, *Langley*, January 16, 1945.

5   Reynolds, *Fast Carriers*, 225.

6   Jones, wartime diary, January 16, 1945.

7   In addition to sources already noted, the account of the bombing of Bungalow C is based on Anslow, *Tin Hats and Rice*, 200–03; Banham, *We Shall Suffer There*, 189–90, 316; Briggs, *From Peking to Perth*, 126–27; Charter, *First Shall Be Last*, 471–77; Corbin, *Prisoners of the East*, 252–56; Emerson, *Hong Kong Internment*, 118–19; Endacott and Birch, *Hong Kong Eclipse*, 215; Gittins, *Stanley*, 138–39; Jones, wartime diary, January 16–18, 1945; Leiper, *Yen for My Thoughts*, 214; Philip G. Cracknell, "Stanley Military Cemetery: A Guide to the Graves of Civilian Internees Who Died at Stanley Internment Camp (1942–1945)," December 2015; Redwood, *It Was Like This*, 214–16; Sewell, *Strange Harmony*, 131–33; Stericker, *Tear for the Dragon*, 199–204; William J. Carrie, wartime diary, January 16, 1945, https://gwulo.com/node/45875; Wright-Nooth and Adkin, *Prisoner of the Turnip Heads*, 87–88, 236–41.

8   Jones, wartime diary, January 18, 1945; "U.S. Airmen Kill & Wound 49 British in Stanley," *Hongkong News*, January 18, 1945, HKUL SC, MF 2521520, reel 6.

9   Banham, *We Shall Suffer There*, 189–90, 316.

10 Banham, *We Shall Suffer There*, 189–90; Corrigan and Corrigan, *Hong Kong Diary Revisited*, 301–05; Ebbage, *Hard Way*, 235–38; Fisher, *I Will Remember*, 171–73; Heywood, *It Won't Be Long Now*, 143; Roland, *Long Night's Journey*, 50.

CHAPTER 22

1 AAR 10 and 11, VFN-90, CVGN-90, *Enterprise* (CV-6), January 16, 1945; AAR II-41, VFN-41, CVLGN-41, *Independence* (CVL-22), January 16, 1945; AR, TG 38.5, January 5–22, 1945.

2 Conner, *Nothing Friendly*; report of war patrol number ten, *Guardfish* (SS-217), January 26, 1945, 20–22; IDPF for Ens. Newell Oneal Maxwell, NPRC.

3 AR, Commander TF 38, October 30, 1944, to January 26, 1945, enclosure B, 25.

4 AAR 61, CVG-7, *Hancock* (CV-19), January 16, 1945.

5 AAR 61, CVG-7, *Hancock* (CV-19), January 16, 1945.

6 Cdr. John D. Lamade, "Comments by Commander Carrier Air Group Seven," CVG-7, *Hancock* (CV-19), January 31, 1945.

7 Cdr. John D. Lamade, "Comments by Commander Carrier Air Group Seven," CVG-7, *Hancock* (CV-19), January 31, 1945.

8 Cdr. John D. Lamade, "Comments by Commander Carrier Air Group Seven," CVG-7, *Hancock* (CV-19), January 31, 1945.

9 AR, *Hornet* (CV-12), January 1–23, 1945.

10 AR, *Ticonderoga* (CV-14), January 3–21, 1945, part 6, 5–6.

11 AR, Commander TG 38.2, December 30, 1944, to January 26, 1945, part 6, 43; Trimble, *Admiral John S. McCain*, 162, 173, 198, 280.

12 Cdr. Robert Emmett Riera, comments re. AARs for January 3–22, 1945, CVG-11, *Hornet* (CV-12), January 25, 1945, 3.

13 Cdr. John D. Lamade, "Comments by Commander Carrier Air Group Seven," CVG-7, *Hancock* (CV-19), January 31, 1945.

14 Cdr. Robert Emmett Riera, comments re. AARs for January 3–22, 1945, CVG-11, *Hornet* (CV-12), January 25, 1945, 2–3.

15 AAR 61, CVG-7, *Hancock* (CV-19), January 16, 1945.

16 AR, *Hancock* (CV-19), December 30, 1944, to January 25, 1945; AR, *Hornet* (CV-12), January 1–23, 1945; AR, *Wasp* (CV-18), December 30, 1944, to January 26, 1945.

17 Conner, *Nothing Friendly*; Lockwood, *Sink 'Em All*, 275–76; report of war patrol number ten, *Guardfish* (SS-217), January 26, 1945, 25–26.

18 AR, *Langley* (CVL-27), December 30, 1944, to January 25, 1945, 38–39.

19 Photo by Lt. Cdr. Charles Kerlee captioned "USS *Hornet* (CV-12)," January 16, 1945, NHHC, catalogue no. 80-G-469297, NH Series 80-G-469000.

20 AR, *Cabot* (CVL-28), December 30, 1944, to January 23, 1945.

21 AAR 62, VF-44, CVLG-44, *Langley* (CVL-27), January 16, 1945; AR, *Langley* (CVL-27), December 30, 1944, to January 25, 1945; Lt. Cdr. R.P. Bond, "History of Fighting Squadron Forty-Four," September 15, 1945.

CHAPTER 23

1 Anslow, *Tin Hats and Rice*, 201–02; Banham, *Reduced to a Symbolic Scale*, 92, 139; Corbin, *Prisoners of the East*, 255–56; Cracknell, *Occupation of Hong Kong*, 143; Emerson, *Hong Kong Internment*, 119; Endacott, *Hong Kong Eclipse*, 215;

Gittins, *Stanley*, 139; Jones, wartime diary, January 17, 1945; Leck, *Captives of Empire*, 615–55; Philip G. Cracknell, "Stanley Military Cemetery: A Guide to the Graves of Civilian Internees Who Died at Stanley Internment Camp (1942–1945)," December 2015; Stericker, *A Tear for the Dragon*, 201–02; William J. Carrie, wartime diary, January 16, 1945, https://gwulo.com/node /45875; Wright-Nooth and Adkin, *Prisoner of the Turnip Heads*, 241.

2 The remains of an estimated 150 Japanese sailors killed during the air raids of January 15 and 16, 1945, were exhumed on Stonecutters Island and returned to Japan in 1966. "Remains of Sailors Exhumed," *South China Morning Post*, May 13, 1966, 1.

3 WD, Commander TG 30.8, January 1945, 8–11.

4 "Chronology of Bombing Squadron Three, 1 January 1945 to 31 March 1945," 2, in WH, VB-3, CVG-3, *Yorktown* (CV-10).

5 AR, commander TF 38, October 30, 1944, to January 26, 1945, "TF 38 Aircraft Losses" and "TF 38 Aviation Personnel Losses," enclosure B, 23–24.

6 OMPF for ARM2c Jean F. Balch, NPRC.

7 IDPF for Lt. (j.g.) John H. Lavender, NPRC.

8 "Lubbock Man, Beaten in Japanese Prison, Maintains Sense of Humor," *Fort Worth Star-Telegram*, September 3, 1945, 2.

9 Scott, *War Below*, 287; interview with Jean F. Balch, October 12, 1996, UNT OHC, number 1353.

10 Chan, *East River Column*, 79–80; Lai, *Hong Kong 1941–45*, 83; Tillman and van der Lugt, *VF-11/111*, 49; walkout narrative for Ensign M.J. Crehan and walkout narrative for 1st Lt. J.F. Egan, Headquarters AGAS-China, March 30, 1945.

CHAPTER 24

1 Braga, "Rescued from Certain Death," 1–4.

2 Braga, "Rescued from Certain Death," 1–4; communique from Officer Commanding, BAAG, Yanping, to Commandant, BAAG, re. arrival in Yanping of Lt. (j.g.) A. Basmajian, Ensign G.W. Clark, AMM3c D.E. Mize, and ARM3c C.G. Myers, January 30, 1945; Gunn, *Wartime Macau*, 153; Reeves, *Lone Flag*, 101; walkout narrative for Lt. (j.g.) A. Basmajian, Ensign G.W. Clark, AMM3c D.E. Mize, and ARM3c C.G. Myers, Headquarters AGAS-China, March 30, 1945.

3 Reeves states in his memoir that Clark and his crew were brought directly to his home; however, BAAG and AGAS-China documents state that they were delivered to the consulate. Also see Braga, "Rescued from Certain Death," 1–4; Gunn, *Wartime Macau*, 153.

4 Sources disagree about the size of the rewards paid to the three men. Braga, "Rescued from Certain Death," 1–4; communique from Officer Commanding, BAAG, Yanping, to Commandant, BAAG, re. arrival in Yanping of Basmajian, Clark, Mize, and Myers, January 30, 1945; Gunn, *Wartime Macau*, 153; Reeves,

Lone Flag, 102; walkout narrative for Basmajian, Clark, Mize, and Myers, Headquarters AGAS-China, March 30, 1945.

5   Reeves, *Lone Flag*, 172–73.
6   Reeves, *Lone Flag*, 101.
7   Walkout narrative for Basmajian, Clark, Mize, and Myers, Headquarters AGAS-China, March 30, 1945.
8   AAR 2-C-58, VF-81, CVG-81, *Wasp* (CV-18), January 16, 1945; communique from Officer Commanding, BAAG, Yanping, to Commandant, BAAG, re. arrival in Yanping of Basmajian, Clark, Mize, and Myers, January 30, 1945; walkout narrative for Basmajian, Clark, Mize, and Myers, Headquarters AGAS-China, March 30, 1945.
9   Communique from Officer Commanding, BAAG, Yanping, to Commandant, BAAG, re. arrival in Yanping of Basmajian, Clark, Mize, and Myers, January 30, 1945; walkout narrative for Basmajian, Clark, Mize, and Myers, Headquarters AGAS-China, March 30, 1945.
10 Walkout narrative for Basmajian, Clark, Mize, and Myers, Headquarters AGAS-China, March 30, 1945.
11 Reeves, *Lone Flag*, 99–100.
12 Day, "Not Just Refugee Relief," 117, 127.
13 Communique from Officer Commanding, BAAG, Yanping, to Commandant, BAAG, re. arrival in Yanping of Basmajian, Clark, Mize, and Myers, January 30, 1945; Gunn, *Wartime Macau*, 153; Reeves, *Lone Flag*, 101; walkout narrative for Basmajian, Clark, Mize, and Myers, Headquarters AGAS-China, March 30, 1945.
14 Communique from Officer Commanding, BAAG, Yanping, to Commandant, BAAG, re. arrival in Yanping of Basmajian, Clark, Mize, and Myers, January 30, 1945; Gunn, *Wartime Macau*, 153; walkout narrative for Basmajian, Clark, Mize, and Myers, Headquarters AGAS-China, March 30, 1945.
15 Colin M. McEwan, "Four U.S. Evaders," 1977, copy in author's collection.
16 Colin M. McEwan, "Four U.S. Evaders," 1977; communique from Officer Commanding, BAAG, Yanping, to Commandant, BAAG, re. arrival in Yanping of Basmajian, Clark, Mize, and Myers, January 30, 1945; Gunn, *Wartime Macau*, 153; walkout narrative for Basmajian, Clark, Mize, and Myers, Headquarters AGAS-China, March 30, 1945.
17 Communique from Officer Commanding, BAAG, Yanping, to Commandant, BAAG, re. arrival in Yanping of Basmajian, Clark, Mize, and Myers, January 30, 1945.
18 Communique (orig. no. R.174) from BAAG Advance Headquarters to BAAG Kunming, March 15, 1945.

CHAPTER 25

1   Military History Section, *Imperial Japanese Navy*, part 8, 219, 221; report of war patrol number three, *Besugo* (SS-321), February 15, 1945, 11–15, 30–31,

46–47; report of war patrol number two, *Blackfin* (SS-322), February 15, 1945, 6–10, 20–25; report of war patrol number three, *Hardhead* (SS-365), February 1945, 14–17; USSBS, *War against Japanese Transportation*, 105.

2 Alternative translations include No. 101 Repair Facility or No. 101 Repair Unit.

3 Military History Section, *Imperial Japanese Navy*, part 8, 226; USSBS, *War against Japanese Transportation*, 105; Williams, "*Amatsukaze,*" 181–89.

CHAPTER 26

1 "Neutral Macao Relentlessly Bombed by U.S. Air Force," *Hongkong News*, January 18, 1945; "Portuguese Soldiers, Third Nationals among Casualties in American Raid on City Quarters of Neutral Macao" and "Air Gangsters," *Hongkong News*, January 19, 1945; all HKUL SC, MF 2521520, reel 6.

2 Gunn, *Wartime Macau*, 166–68.

3 "Raid on Macao Annoys Lisbon," *Miami Daily News*, January 17, 1945, 4-A.

4 "U.S. Offers Apology for Raid on Macao," *Richmond Times Dispatch*, January 21, 1945, 1.

5 WD, Commander 3rd Fleet, January 1945, 25.

6 Hughes, *Admiral Bill Halsey*, 122, 124, 132.

7 Toll, *Conquering Tide*, 323.

8 AR, *South Dakota* (BB-57), December 30, 1944, to January 26, 1945.

9 Testimony of Commander John D. Lamade, "Record of Proceedings of a Court of Inquiry Convened on Board the USS *South Dakota,*" 38.

10 Testimony of Commander John D. Lamade, "Record of Proceedings of a Court of Inquiry Convened on Board the USS *South Dakota,*" 39.

11 Testimony of Commander John D. Lamade, "Record of Proceedings of a Court of Inquiry Convened on Board the USS *South Dakota,*" 39.

12 AR, *Hancock* (CV-19), December 30, 1944, to January 25, 1945, "Photographic Operations," enclosure A, 52–53.

13 Communication 09 0824 from Commander in Chief U.S. Pacific Fleet Advance Headquarters to Commander in Chief U.S. Fleet and Chief of Naval Operations, February 9, 1945; "History of Fighting Squadron Seven," CVG-7, *Hancock* (CV-19), February 15, 1945, 69; photograph captioned "Ao-Men (Macao) Landing Ground, Kwang-Tung Province, China, Sortie *Hancock* 70 of 16 January 1945," Photographic Interpretation Squadron 2, report 368, enclosure A, February 20, 1945.

14 Conner, *Nothing Friendly*, 189–90, 206.

15 Finding of Facts, Opinion, and Recommendation, "Record of Proceedings of a Court of Inquiry Convened on Board the USS *South Dakota,*" 53–56.

16 Reeves, *Lone Flag*, 100.

17 Garrett, *Defences of Macau*, 96, 116; Gunn, *Wartime Macau*, 109; Lopes, "They 'Built' Macau."

18 Reeves, *Lone Flag*, 100.

19 "History of Torpedo Squadron Seven from 30 August 1944 to 15 February 1945," WH, VT-7, CVG-7, *Hancock* (CV-19), 14.

20 "History of Fighting Squadron Seven," VF-7, CVG-7, *Hancock* (CV-19), February 15, 1945, 65.

21 Letter from Fleet Admiral Nimitz to Judge Advocate General, March 29, 1945, "Record of Proceedings of a Court of Inquiry Convened on Board the USS *South Dakota*."

CHAPTER 27

1 Fred Rasmussen, "Baltimore War Hero Rests in Druid Ridge Cemetery," *Baltimore Sun*, May 23, 1998, 2E; individual flight record for Captain David H. Houck, August 1942 to December 1943, NPRC.

2 Bailey, *Bold Venture*, 182–94; FIR 769, 118th TRS, 23rd FG, December 24, 1944; unnumbered FIR, 74th FS, 23rd FG, December 24, 1944, AFHRA, Iris no. 57261; "Soviet Ship Sunk by U.S. Airmen: Chan Lim-Pak Believed Killed" and "2 P-51s Bagged over Hong Kong," December 26, 1944; "Graphic Account of Inhuman Attack on *Reinan Maru*: Rescuers Strafed: Captain Yuasa, Crew Mowed Down" and "Passengers Mowed Down Like Sheep," December 27, 1944; "Lady Passenger of *Reinan Maru* Saved by Junk," December 28, 1944; all from *Hongkong News*, SC HKUL, MF 2521520, reel 6.

3 "Memorial Service Held for Late Mr. Chan Lim-Pak," January 12, 1945, *Hongkong News*, SC HKUL, MF 2521520, reel 6.

4 IDPF for Major David H. Houck, NPRC; United Nations War Crimes Commission, "Case No. 33," 66–67.

5 United Nations War Crimes Commission, "Case No. 33," 67.

6 United Nations War Crimes Commission, "Case No. 33," 66–71.

7 Banham, "Hong Kong's Civilian Fatalities," 34–35.

8 IDPF for Major David H. Houck, NPRC.

9 Interview with Jean F. Balch, October 12, 1996, UNT OHC, number 1353; Scott, *War Below*, 287.

10 IDPF for Lt. (j.g.) Richard L. Hunt, NPRC; Scott, *War Below*, 286–89.

11 Interview with Jean F. Balch, October 12, 1996, UNT OHC, number 1353.

CHAPTER 28

1 Stevens, *Low Level Liberators*, 165–67; Stevens, oral history, 44; WD, VPB-104, FAW-10, February 1945.

2 Stevens, oral history, 28; WD, VPB-104, FAW-10, February 1945.

3 Stevens, *Low Level Liberators*, 70.

4 Rollo, *Guns and Gunners of Hong Kong*, 145–48.

5 Hata, Izawa, and Shores, *Japanese Army Fighter Aces*, 71–72, 125–26; USSBS, *Interrogations of Japanese Officials*, vol. I, 228–29.

6 Stevens, *Low Level Liberators*, 189–90, 207.

7 Stevens, oral history, 38.

8 Stevens, *Low Level Liberators*, 19–20, 41; Stevens, oral history, 26.

9 Stevens, *Low Level Liberators*, 41, 60, 171; Stevens, oral history, 29.

10 Reeves, *Lone Flag*, 28, 75–76, 103–04.

11 Gunn, *Wartime Macau*, 105; Reeves, *Lone Flag*, 28, 103.

12 "Another Raid on Macao," *Hongkong News*, March 1, 1945, HKUL SC, MF 2521521, reel 7; Gunn, *Wartime Macau*, 166–69; Reeves, *Lone Flag*, 103–04.

13 AAR 152, VPB-104, FAW 10, February 25, 1945.

14 WD, VPB-104, FAW-10, February 1945, 11.

15 Gunn, *Wartime Macau*, 168; "Planes Bomb Macao," *Fort Worth Star-Telegram*, February 26, 1945, 3; "Unidentified Planes Raid Portuguese Macao," *Los Angeles Times*, February 26, 1945, 4.

16 Stevens, *Low Level Liberators*, 225–37.

17 In addition to sources already noted, the account of the mission flown by Lt. Paul F. Stevens on February 25, 1945, is based on AAR 152, VPB-104, FAW 10, February 25, 1945; Stevens, *Low Level Liberators*, 193–97; Stevens, oral history, 38–40.

18 See Garrett, *Defences of Macau*, 116; Gunn, *Wartime Macau*, 166–67.

19 AAR 20, VPB-137, FAW 10, April 7, 1945; communication from General Douglas MacArthur to Adjutant General, War Department re. "Attack on Tug Near Macao Harbor, May 7, 1945," May 7, 1945, Iris no. 254593, AFHRA; "Macao Neutrality Again Violated," *Hongkong News*, June 15, 1945, HKUL SC, MF 2521521, reel 7.

CHAPTER 29

1 Anslow, *Tin Hats and Rice*, 219; Jones, wartime diary, March 11, 1945; Stevens, *Low Level Liberators*, 219; WD, VPB-104, FAW-10, March 1945, 7.

2 Stericker, *Tear for the Dragon*, 201.

3 Charter, *First Shall Be Last*, 493–94.

4 Jones, wartime diary, February 15 and 21, 1945.

5 Anslow, *Tin Hats and Rice*, 209, 247; Gittins, *Stanley*, 139; Emerson, *Hong Kong Internment*, 119–20; Endacott, *Hong Kong Eclipse*, 215; Sewell, *Strange Harmony*, 133; Stericker, *Tear for the Dragon*, 202; Wright-Nooth and Adkin, *Prisoner of the Turnip Heads*, 241.

6 "Hongkong Raiders Lose 3 B-24s," *Hongkong News*, April 4, 1945, SC HKUL, MF 2521521, reel 7; Jones, wartime diary, April 2–4, 1945.

7 Jones, wartime diary, April 13, 1945.

8 Bailey, *Bold Venture*, 231, 239; Military History Section, *Imperial Japanese Navy*, appendix A, 251, and appendix B, 261, 274; Williams, "*Amatsukaze*," 183–84.

9 Corrigan and Corrigan, *Hong Kong Diary Revisited*, 326–27; Fisher, *I Will Remember*, 194.

10 Bailey, *Bold Venture*, 217–48; "Blind Bombing," *Hongkong News*, April 5, 1945, and "Bishop Deplores Wanton Bombing of Convent," *Hongkong News*, April 8, 1945, SC HKUL, MF 2521521, reel 7.

11 Anslow, *Tin Hats and Rice*, 243; Jones, wartime diary, May 7 and 24, 1945; Sewell, *Strange Harmony*, 133.

12 Jones, wartime diary, April 25–26 and May 7, 1945.

13 Jones, wartime diary, June 12, 1945.

14 Bailey, *Bold Venture*, 250–52.

15 Jones, wartime diary, June 18–22, 1945.

16 Jones, wartime diary, March 31 and July 18, 1945.

17 Jones, wartime diary, June 5 and July 5, 1945; Stericker, *Tear for the Dragon*, 164.

18 Jones, wartime diary, June 16, July 9 and 13, 1945.

19 USSBS, *Fifth Air Force*, 38.

20 Anslow, *Tin Hats and Rice*, 256–58; Banham, "A Short History," 96–98; Corbin, *Prisoners of the East*, 259–69; Gittins, *Stanley*, 147–48; Jones, wartime diary, July 25–28, 1945; Stericker, *Tear for the Dragon*, 204–05; William J. Carrie, wartime diary, July 29, 1945, https://gwulo.com/node/45875; Wright-Nooth and Adkin, *Prisoner of the Turnip Heads*, 242–43.

21 "Enemy Planes again Bomb Internees," *Hongkong News*, July 26, 1945; "Vivid Account of Stanley Bombing," *Hongkong News*, July 27, 1945; "Internees' Protest against Bombing," *Hongkong News*, July 28, 1945; all documents HKUL SC, MF 2521521, reel 7.

22 Odgers, *Air War against Japan*, 370–72.

23 United States Air Force, *Air-Sea Rescue*, 68–72.

24 "Location of U.S. Naval Aircraft," July 21, 1945 (OP 03 4R, no. 30 45, SC A4 3 0Z), NHHC.

CHAPTER 30

1 Jones, wartime diary, December 21, 1944, February 28 and August 2–7, 1945.

2 Kwong and Tsoi, *Eastern Fortress*, 227; Richard Walding, "Indicator Loops: Royal Navy Harbour Defences – Hong Kong," http://indicatorloops.com/hongkong.htm.

3 Stevens, *Low Level Liberators*, 17; Stevens, oral history, 41.

4 AAR 396, VPB-104, FAW 17, August 14, 1945; Anslow, *Tin Hats and Rice*, 265, 278; Charter, *First Shall Be Last*, 554–55; Emerson, *Hong Kong Internment*, 167; Jones, wartime diary, August 14, 1945; Redwood, *It Was Like This*, 224; Stericker, *Tear for the Dragon*, 205.

CHAPTER 31

1 Corbett, "Shield Force," 36–38; Jones, wartime diary, September 10–11, 1945; Lindsay, *At the Going Down*, 244; "Preparation of Naval Occupation Forces for China Coast," Commander in Chief, British Pacific Fleet, December 6, 1945, ADM199/1478, http://www.naval-history.net/xDKWD-BPF4512Occupati onofChinaCoast1945.htm.

2 Hobbs, *British Pacific Fleet*, 306–16, 385–95; Winton, *Forgotten Fleet*, 360–63, 389–404.

3 Jones, wartime diary, August 29, 1945; Anslow, *Tin Hats and Rice*, 287–88.

4 Hobbs, *British Pacific Fleet*, 310–11.

5 Anslow, *Tin Hats and Rice*, 290; Emerson, *Hong Kong Internment*, 170–73; Jones, wartime diary, August 30, 1945; Lindsay, *At the Going Down*, 231; Stericker, *Tear for the Dragon*, 210–11.

6   Snow, *Fall of Hong Kong*, 262.
7   Hobbs, *British Pacific Fleet*, 314–15; Snow, *Fall of Hong Kong*, 274.
8   Banham, "Hong Kong's Civilian Fatalities," 44–46; Lethbridge, "Hong Kong under Japanese Occupation," 121; Snow, *Fall of Hong Kong*, 221.
9   Hobbs, *British Pacific Fleet*, 312.
10 Jones, wartime diary, September 11, 1945.
11 Jones, wartime diary, September 13, 1945.
12 Jones, wartime diary, September 13–20, 1945; "Preparation of Naval Occupation Forces for China Coast," Commander in Chief, British Pacific Fleet, December 6, 1945, ADM199/1478, http://www.naval-history.net/xDKWD-BPF4512OccupationofChinaCoast1945.htm.
13 Jones, wartime diary, September 19, 22, 26, 1945.
14 Jones, wartime diary, September 27–October 10, 1945.
15 Jones, wartime diary, September 10 to October 27, 1945; Rae Shaw, email to author, January 17, 2021; *Empress of Australia*, merchant shipping movement cards, Registry of Shipping and Seamen: War of 1939–1945, BT 389/12/117, National Archives, Kew, UK.

CHAPTER 32

1   Guy Walker, "My War Years, 1941–45," 1984, https://gwulo.com/node/21942; Reeves, *Lone Flag*, 122–23, 136–37, 167, 169, 172, 174, 196n4–5.
2   Letter from Fleet Admiral Nimitz to Judge Advocate General, March 29, 1945, "Record of Proceedings of a Court of Inquiry Convened on Board the USS *South Dakota*."
3   Toll, *Pacific Crucible*, 165–66.
4   Memorandum from Secretary of the Navy re. Reported Violation of Portuguese Neutrality at Macao on January 16, 1945, by Naval Aircraft, April 21, 1945, "Record of Proceedings of a Court of Inquiry Convened on Board the USS *South Dakota*."
5   Memorandum from Secretary of the Navy to Captain Robert F. Hickey, re. Letter of Admonition, October 23, 1947, "Record of Proceedings of a Court of Inquiry Convened on Board the USS *South Dakota*."
6   Memorandum from Chairman, Board for Correction of Naval Records, to Secretary of the Navy, re. Captain Whitmore S. Butts, USN (62524), Request for Removal of Derogatory Material from His Officer's Record Jacket, April 28, 1949, "Record of Proceedings of a Court of Inquiry Convened on Board the USS *South Dakota*."
7   Memorandum from Lt. Charles E. Golson to Commander in Chief Pacific Fleet re. Statement in Regard to Letter of Reprimand Dated 29 March 1945 from Commander in Chief Pacific Fleet and Pacific Ocean Areas, 28 August 1945; memorandum from Commander John D. Lamade to Commander in Chief Pacific Fleet re. Statement in Regard to Letter of Reprimand Dated 22 March 1945 from Commander in Chief Pacific Fleet and Pacific Ocean Areas,

13 July 1945, "Record of Proceedings of a Court of Inquiry Convened on Board the USS *South Dakota*."

8 Armed Forces of the United States Report of Transfer or Discharge for Capt. John D. Lamade, October 31, 1961, NPRC.

9 "Japanese-Portuguese Relations and the 'Macao Problem,'" February–May 1945, Pacific Strategic Intelligence Section, Commander in Chief United States Fleet and Chief of Naval Operations, May 23, 1945, AFHRA, Iris no. 1039788.

10 Garrett, *Defenses of Macau*, 116; Gunn, *Wartime Macau*, 167; "Macao Neutrality Again Violated," *Hongkong News*, June 15, 1945, HKUL SC, MF 2521521, reel 7; Reeves, *Lone Flag*, xxiv.

11 "Payment of Certain Portuguese Claims," U.S. Senate, 81st Congress, 2nd Session, Calendar 2581, Report 2577, September 20, 1950; "Portugal: Settlement of Certain War Claims," TIAS 2664, October 3, 1947, February 21, May 3, May 20, and August 4, 1949, 3 UST, 4914–21. Several sources claim that the U.S. government paid twenty million dollars to the Portuguese government as compensation for damages incurred during American airstrikes on Macau. However, the actual compensation paid was roughly a quarter million dollars. One possible explanation for the twenty-million-dollar figure is that the State Department lumped the compensation for wartime damage to Macau into a larger payment that included compensation for other incidents in which the U.S. military had killed or injured Portuguese subjects and harmed Portuguese property around the globe during World War II. See Garrett, *Defences of Macau*, 116; Gunn, *Encountering Macau*, 127; Reeves, *Lone Flag*, 194n29.

12 In an entirely separate agreement, the U.S. government agreed to compensate Switzerland, which had been neutral during the war, for losses and damages caused by the U.S. military. Total compensation amounted to sixty-two million Swiss francs or approximately fourteen million U.S. dollars. "Payment of Certain Portuguese Claims," U.S. Senate, 81st Congress, 2nd Session, Calendar 2581, Report 2577, September 20, 1950, 2.

CHAPTER 33

1 Graff, "POWs on the Day."

2 Hornfischer, *Ship of Ghosts*, 197.

3 Adjutant General's Office, War Department, records of World War II prisoners of war, December 7, 1941–November 19, 1946, NARA, record group 389; interview with Jean F. Balch, October 12, 1996, UNT OHC, number 1353; OMPF for ARM2c Jean F. Balch, NPRC; WD, *Ozark* (LSV-2), September 1945.

CHAPTER 34

1 IDPF for Lt. (j.g.) Richard L. Hunt, NPRC.

2 IDPF for Major David H. Houck, NPRC; obituary for Lt. Richard L. Hunt, *Kansas City Times*, December 17, 1948, 9.

3   United Nations War Crimes Commission, "Case No. 33," 66–71; Zhang, "Fall of the Tigers of Hong Kong," 216–24.

4   Beigel, *Buried on the Battlefield*, 6–9, 18, 87; Steere and Boardman, *Final Disposition*, 672–74.

5   Beigel, *Buried on the Battlefield*, 82, 91–93; Steere and Boardman, *Final Disposition*, 532–34, 663–64.

6   IDPF for Major David H. Houck, NPRC; James H. Bready, "Memorial for a Flyer: Major David H.W. Houck Is Honored," *Evening Sun* (Baltimore, MD), May 30, 1950, 18; "Services Planned for Major Houck," *Evening Sun*, October 28, 1947, 18; "Two Japs Sentenced in Houck Death," *Evening Sun*, September 3, 1946, 36.

CHAPTER 35

1   For the full story of this aircraft and its crew, see Bailey, *Bold Venture*.

2   The description of the wreckage of Lieutenant Hunt's TBM-3 is based in part on the author's visit to the wreck site on December 20, 2019.

3   Lethbridge, "Hong Kong under Japanese Occupation," 98.

4   Bailey, *Bold Venture*, 76, 136–38, 153; Endacott and Birch, *Hong Kong Eclipse*, 163; *Hongkong News*, April 20, 1944, 2, SC HKUL, MF 2521519, reel 5; Waichow Intelligence Summary No. 14, December 16, 1942, BAAG, ERC HKHP, EMR–1B–01.

5   Beigel, *Buried on the Battlefield*, 24; Sweeney, "'Representing Canadian Interests,'" 19.

6   AAR 1-A-1-51, VF-81, CVG-81, *Wasp* (CV-18), January 15, 1945; AAR 61, VF-3, CVG-3, *Yorktown* (CV-10), January 15, 1945.

7   Braga, "Rescued from Certain Death," 1–4; Wright-Nooth and Adkin, *Prisoner of the Turnip Heads*, 238.

8   Steere and Boardman, *Final Disposition*, 651, 690.

9   In addition to sources already noted, this chapter is based on the following sources from the NPRC: IDPFs for Maj. David H. Houck; Lt. Daniel S. Kalus; Lt. Billy B. Laughren; Lt. Marvin L. Leedom; Lt. (j.g.) Richard L. Hunt; Lt. (j.g.) Richard A. Kinsella; Lt. (j.g.) John H. Lavender; Lt. (j.g.) Newell O. Maxwell; Lt. (j.g.) Edwin W. McGowan; Lt. (j.g.) Richard C. Scobell; Lt. (j.g.) Donald F. Seiz; Lt. (j.g.) Charles S. Snead; Lt. (j.g.) John E. Tsarnas; Lt. (j.g.) Robert F. Wright; Ensign Erwin G. Nash; Ensign Joseph G. Scordo; Ensign Richard E. Wilson; John F. Gelnaw, AOM1c; Louis W. Gahran, AOM2c; Eugene W. Barrow, ARM3c; and William P. Walton, ARM3c.

EPILOGUE

1   Dudgeon and Corlett, *Ecology and Biodiversity*, 35–36.

2   Wright-Nooth and Adkin, *Prisoner of the Turnip Heads*, 247.

Bibliography

Alderson, Gordon L.D. *History of Royal Air Force Kai Tak*. Hong Kong: Royal Air Force Kai Tak, 1972.

Anslow, Barbara. *Tin Hats and Rice: A Diary of Life as a Hong Kong Prisoner of War, 1941–1945*. Hong Kong: Blacksmith Books, 2018.

Archer, Bernice. *The Internment of Western Civilians Under the Japanese 1941–1945: A Patchwork of Internment*. London: RoutledgeCurzon, 2004.

Archer, Bernice and Kent Fedorowich. "The Women of Stanley: Internment in Hong Kong, 1942–1945." *Women's History Review* 5, no. 3 (1996): 373–99.

Assistant Chief of Air Staff, Intelligence, Historical Division, U.S. Army Air Forces. *The Fourteenth Air Force to 1 October 1943 (AAFRH-9)*. N.p.: Army Air Force Historical Office, Headquarters, Army Air Forces, 1945.

Bailey, Steven K. *Bold Venture: The American Bombing of Japanese-Occupied Hong Kong, 1942–1945*. Lincoln, NB: Potomac, 2019.

———. "The Bombing of Bungalow C: Friendly Fire at the Stanley Civilian Internment Camp." *Journal of the Royal Asiatic Society Hong Kong* 57 (2017): 108–26.

———. "Briefing Failure in Ready Room 4: The Question of Culpability for U.S. Navy Air Strikes on Macau, 16 January 1945." *Journal of the Royal Asiatic Society Hong Kong* 58 (2018): 30–54.

Banham, Tony. "Hong Kong's Civilian Fatalities of the Second World War." *Journal of the Royal Asiatic Society Hong Kong* 59 (2019): 31–50.

———. *Not the Slightest Chance: The Defence of Hong Kong, 1941*. Hong Kong: Hong Kong University Press, 2003.

———. *Reduced to a Symbolic Scale: The Evacuation of British Women and Children from Hong Kong to Australia in 1940*. Hong Kong: Hong Kong University Press, 2017.

———. "A Short History of Bungalow A, St. Stephen's College, Stanley." *Journal of the Royal Asiatic Society Hong Kong* 57 (2017): 88–107.

———. *The Sinking of the* Lisbon Maru: *Britain's Forgotten Wartime Tragedy*. Hong Kong: Hong Kong University Press, 2010.

———. *We Shall Suffer There: Hong Kong's Defenders Imprisoned, 1942–45*. Hong Kong: Hong Kong University Press, 2009.

Beigel, William L. *Buried on the Battlefield: Not My Boy: The Return of the Dead from World War Two*. Redondo, CA: Midnight to 1 AM Publishing, 2019.

Blewett, William E. "A History of the Newport News Shipbuilding and Dry Dock Company." *Journal of the American Society of Naval Engineers* 73, no. 2 (May 1961): 277–86.

Braga, Stuart. "Rescued from Certain Death," *Casa Down Under Newsletter* 23, no. 4 (October 2011): 1–4.

Briggs, Alice. *From Peking to Perth*. Perth: Artlook Books, 1984.

Bruce, Phillip. *Second to None: The Story of the Hong Kong Volunteers*. New York: Oxford University Press, 1991.

Cameron, Nigel. *An Illustrated History of Hong Kong*. Hong Kong: Hong Kong University Press, 1991.

Campbell, Douglas E. *Volume I: U.S. Navy, U.S. Marine Corps, and U.S. Coast Guard Aircraft Lost during World War II – Listed by Ship Attached*. Syneca Research Group, 2011.

———. *Volume II: U.S. Navy, U.S. Marine Corps, and U.S. Coast Guard Aircraft Lost during World War II – Listed by Squadron*. Syneca Research Group, 2011.

———. *Volume III: U.S. Navy, U.S. Marine Corps, and U.S. Coast Guard Aircraft Lost during World War II – Listed by Aircraft Type*. Syneca Research Group, 2011.

Campbell, John. *Naval Weapons of World War Two*. London: Conway Maritime Press, 2002.

Chan Sui-jeung. *East River Column: Hong Kong Guerrillas in the Second World War and After*. Hong Kong: Hong Kong University Press, 2009.

Charter, Anthony Crowley. *The First Shall Be Last: The War Journal of John Charter and Memoirs of Yvonne Charter, Hong Kong 1940–1945 and Stanley Civilian Internment Camp*. Tolworth, Surrey, UK: Grosvenor House Publishing, 2018.

Chennault, Claire Lee. *Way of a Fighter: The Memoirs of Claire Lee Chennault*. Edited by Robert Hotz. New York: G.P. Putnam's Sons, 1949.

China Navigation Company: A Pictorial History, 1872–2012. Hong Kong: The China Navigation Company, 2012.

Chiu, T.N. *The Port of Hong Kong: A Survey of Its Development*. Hong Kong: Hong Kong University Press, 1973.

Coates, Austin. *Whampoa: Ships on the Shore*. Hong Kong: South China Morning Press, 1980.

Commanding General, Army Air Forces and the Chief of the Bureau of Aeronautics, *Pilot's Handbook of Flight Operating Instructions, Navy Model, TBM-3 Airplane (AN 01-190EB-1)*, Washington, D.C., 1945.

Conner, Claude C. *Nothing Friendly in the Vicinity: My Patrols on the Submarine USS Guardfish during WWII*. Annapolis MD: Naval Institute Press, 1999.

Corbett, Brian. "Shield Force: 5358 Wing and the Liberation of Hong Kong." *Royal Air Force Historical Society Journal* 51 (2011): 32–45.

Corbin, Allana. *Prisoners of the East*. Sydney: Macmillan, 2002.

Corrigan, Leonard B. and Gladys Corrigan. *A Hong Kong Diary Revisited*. Baltimore, ON: Frei Press, 2008.

Courtauld, Carol and May Holdsworth. *The Hong Kong Story*. Hong Kong: Oxford University Press, 1997.

Cracknell, Philip. *Battle for Hong Kong: December 1941*. Stroud, UK: Amberley, 2019.

———. *The Occupation of Hong Kong, 1941–45*. Stroud, UK: Amberley, 2022.

Cressman, Robert J. *The Official Chronology of the U.S. Navy in World War II*. Washington D.C.: Contemporary History Branch, Naval Historical Center, 1999.

Day, Colin. "Not Just Refugee Relief." *Journal of the Royal Asiatic Society Hong Kong* 60 (2020): 115–37.

Division of Naval Intelligence, *Standard Classes of Japanese Merchant Ships, Supplement 3 (ONI–208–J Revised)*. Washington D.C.: Office of Naval Intelligence, U.S. Navy, 1945.

Dorr, Robert F. "Bombing in the Beast: Ben Case and the SB2C Helldiver." *Flight Journal* (December 2014): 45–52.

Drea, Edward J. and Hans van de Ven. "An Overview of Major Military Campaigns during the Sino–Japanese War." In *The Battle for China: Essays on the Military History of the Sino–Japanese War of 1937–1945*, edited by Mark Peattie, Edward J. Drea, and Hans van den Ven. Stanford, CA: Stanford University Press, 2011, 27–47.

Dudgeon, David and Richard Corlett. *The Ecology and Biodiversity of Hong Kong*. Hong Kong: Joint Publishing, 2004.

Ebbage, Victor Stanley. *The Hard Way: Surviving Sham Shui Po Camp 1941–45*. Stroud, UK: Spellmount, 2011.

Edgar, Brian. "Myths, Messages and Manoeuvres: Franklin Gimson in August 1945." *Journal of the Royal Asiatic Society Hong Kong* 58 (2018): 7–28.

Emerson, Geoffrey Charles. *Hong Kong Internment, 1942–1945: Life in the Japanese Civilian Camp at Stanley*. Hong Kong: Hong Kong University Press, 2008.

Endacott, George Beer and Alan Birch. *Hong Kong Eclipse*. Hong Kong: Oxford University Press, 1978.

Esposito, Vincent J., ed. *The West Point Atlas of War: World War II: The Pacific*. New York: Tess Press, 1959.

Fisher, Les. *I Will Remember: Recollections and Reflections on Hong Kong 1941 to 1945 – Internment and Freedom*. Totton, Hampshire, UK: Hobbs the Printers, 1996.

Garrett, Richard J. *The Defences of Macau: Forts, Ships and Weapons over 450 Years*. Hong Kong: Hong Kong University Press, 2010.

Gittins, Jean. *Stanley: Behind Barbed Wire*. Hong Kong: Hong Kong University Press, 1982.

Gordon, John. *Fighting for MacArthur: The Navy and Marine Corps' Desperate Defense of the Philippines*. Annapolis, MD: Naval Institute Press, 2011.

Graff, Cory. "POWs on the Day They Learned the War Was Won." *Air & Space Magazine*, August 2020. https://www.smithsonianmag.com/air-space-magazine/candy-food-home-thanx-180975333/

Greenhous, Brereton. *"C" Force to Hong Kong: A Canadian Catastrophe*. Toronto: Dundurn Press, 1997.

Gunn, Geoffrey C. *Encountering Macau: A Portuguese City-State on the Periphery of China, 1557–1999*. Boulder, CO: Westview Press, 1996.

Gunn, Geoffrey C., ed. *Wartime Macau: Under the Japanese Shadow*. Hong Kong: Hong Kong University Press, 2017.

Ha, Louis and Dan Waters. "Hong Kong's Lighthouses and the Men Who Manned Them." *Journal of the Royal Asiatic Society Hong Kong* 41 (2001): 281–320.

Hahn, Emily. *Hong Kong Holiday*. New York: Doubleday, 1946.

Hara, Tameichi, Fred Saito, and Roger Pineau. *Japanese Destroyer Captain: Pearl Harbor, Guadalcanal, Midway – The Great Naval Battles as Seen through Japanese Eyes*. Annapolis, MD: Naval Institute Press, 1967.

Harland, Kathleen. *The Royal Navy in Hong Kong since 1841*. Cornwall, UK: Maritime Books.

Hata, Ikuhiko, Yasuho Izawa, and Christopher Shores. *Japanese Army Fighter Aces, 1931–45*. Mechanicsburg, PA: Stackpole Books, 2012.

Heaver, Stuart. "Remains of U.S. Airmen Killed in 1945 Crash 'Could Still Be on Hong Kong Hillside.'" *South China Morning Post Magazine*, January 11, 2015.

Heywood, Graham. *It Won't Be Long Now: The Diary of a Hong Kong Prisoner of War*. Edited by Geoffrey Charles Emerson. Hong Kong: Blacksmith Books, 2015.

Hobbs, David. *The British Pacific Fleet: The Royal Navy's Most Powerful Strike Force*. Annapolis, MD: Naval Institute Press, 2011.

Holdsworth, May and Christopher Munn, eds. *Dictionary of Hong Kong Biography*. Hong Kong: Hong Kong University Press, 2012.

Hornfischer, James D. *The Fleet at Flood Tide: America at Total War in the Pacific, 1944–1945*. New York: Bantam, 2017.

———. *The Last Stand of the Tin Can Sailors: The Extraordinary World War II Story of the U.S. Navy's Finest Hour*. New York: Bantam, 2004.

———. *Ship of Ghosts: The Story of the USS* Houston, *FDR's Legendary Lost Cruiser, and the Epic Saga of her Survivors*. New York: Bantam, 2006.

Hughes, Thomas Alexander. *Admiral Bill Halsey: A Naval Life*. Cambridge, MA: Harvard University Press, 2016.

Hynes, Samuel. *Flights of Passage: Recollections of a World War II Aviator*. New York: Penguin, 1988.

Irons, Martin. *Phalanx against the Divine Wind: Protecting the Fast Carrier Task Force during World War 2*. Hoosick Falls, NY: Merriam Press, 2017.

Jentschura, Hansgeorg, Dieter Jung, and Peter Mickel. *Warships of the Imperial Japanese Navy, 1869–1945*. Translated by Antony Preston and J.D. Brown. London: Arms and Armour, 1977.

Joint Army–Navy Assessment Committee. *Japanese Naval and Merchant Shipping Losses during World War II by All Causes (NAVEXOS P–468)*. Washington D.C.: Navy Department, 1947.

Kehn, Donald M. *In the Highest Degree Tragic: The Sacrifice of the U.S. Asiatic Fleet in the East Indies during World War II*. Lincoln, NB: Potomac, 2017.

Ko, Tim-keung. "A Review of Development of Cemeteries in Hong Kong: 1841–1950." *Journal of the Royal Asiatic Society Hong Kong* 41 (2001): 241–80.

Ko, Tim-keung and Jason Wordie. *Ruins of War: A Guide to Hong Kong's Battlefields and Wartime Sites*. Hong Kong: Joint Publishing, 1996.

Komamiya, Shinshichiro. *Senji Yuso-sendan-shi (History of Wartime Transport Convoys)*. Tokyo: Kyodo Shuppansha, 1987.

Kush, Linda. *The Rice Paddy Navy: U.S. Sailors Undercover in China: Espionage and Sabotage Behind Japanese Lines during World War II*. Oxford, UK: Osprey, 2012.

Kwong Chi Man. "The Failure of Japanese Land–Sea Cooperation during the Second World War: Hong Kong and the South China Coast as an Example, 1942–1945." *The Journal of Military History* 79 (January 2015): 69–91.

Kwong Chi Man and Tsoi Yiu Lun. *Eastern Fortress: A Military History of Hong Kong, 1840–1970*. Hong Kong: Hong Kong University Press, 2014.

Lai, Benjamin. *Hong Kong, 1941–45: First Strike in the Pacific War*. Oxford, UK: Osprey, 2014.

Lanphier, Frederick A. *WWII Army Air Corps Remembrances of Fred Arthur Lanphier*. Unpublished manuscript, 2002.

Leck, Greg. *Captives of Empire: The Japanese Internment of Allied Civilians in China, 1941–1945*. Bangor, PA: Shandy Press, 2006.

Leiper, Gerald Andrew. *A Yen for My Thoughts: A Memoir of Occupied Hong Kong*. Hong Kong: South China Morning Post, 1982.

Lethbridge, Henry J. "Hong Kong Under Japanese Occupation: Changes in Social Structure." In *Hong Kong: A Society in Transition*, edited by Ian C. Jarvie and Joseph Agassi, 77–127. New York: Frederick A. Praeger, 1969.

Leutze, James. *A Different Kind of Victory: A Biography of Admiral Thomas C. Hart*. Annapolis, MD: Naval Institute Press, 1981.

Lindsay, Oliver. *At the Going Down of the Sun: Hong Kong and South-East Asia, 1941–45*. London: Sphere Books, 1982.

———. *The Battle for Hong Kong, 1941–1945: Hostage to Fortune*. Montreal: McGill–Queen's University Press, 2005.

Lockwood, Charles A. *Sink 'Em All: Submarine Warfare in the Pacific*. New York: E.P. Dutton and Company, 1951.

Lockwood, Charles A. and Hans Christian Adamson. *Zoomies, Subs and Zeroes*. New York: Greenberg, 1956.

Looney, Foster E. and James P. Busha. "Mission into Darkness: Flying the SB2C Helldiver into Probable Suicide." *Flight Journal*, October 2012: 32–40.

Lopes, Gilberto. "They 'Built' Macau." *Macau Magazine*, 1999.

Macri, Franco David. *Clash of Empires in South China: The Allied Nations' Proxy War with Japan, 1935–1941*. Lawrence, KS: University Press of Kansas, 2012.

McCain, Joseph L. and Marlene McCain. "The Story of the Broome Seagull Curtiss SOC-3, BuNo. 1065." *The Blue Bonnet: Newsletter of the USS Houston CA-30 Survivors' Association and Next Generation* 77, no. 2 (August 2019): 8–10.

McGivering, Jill. *Macao Remembers*. Oxford, UK: Oxford University Press, 1999.

McLean, John. *A Mission of Honour: The Royal Navy in the Pacific, 1769–1997*. Derby, UK: Winter Productions, 2010.

McManus, John C. *Deadly Sky: The American Combat Airman in World War II*. New York: NAL Caliber, 2016.

Melson, P.J. *White Ensign, Red Dragon: The History of the Royal Navy in Hong Kong 1841–1997*. Hong Kong: Edinburgh Financial Publishing, 1997.

Military History Section, Special Staff, General HQ, Far East Command. *The Imperial Japanese Navy in World War II: A Graphic Presentation of the Japanese Naval Organization and List of Combatant and Non-Combatant Vessels Lost or Damaged in the War*. Japanese Operational Monograph Series 116. N.p., 1952.

Millman, Nicholas. *Ki-44 Tojo Aces of World War 2*. Oxford, UK: Osprey, 2009.

Mitter, Rana. *Forgotten Ally: China's World War II, 1937–1945*. New York: Houghton Mifflin Harcourt, 2013.

Morison, Samuel Eliot. *History of United States Naval Operations in World War II, Vol. XIII. The Liberation of the Philippines: Luzon, Mindanao, the Visayas, 1944–1945*. Boston: Little, Brown and Company, 1959.

Nolan, Liam. *Small Man of Nanataki: The True Story of a Japanese Who Risked His Life to Provide Comfort for his Enemies*. New York: E.P. Dutton, 1966.

Noles, James L. *Twenty-Three Minutes to Eternity: The Final Voyage of the Escort Carrier USS* Liscome Bay. Tuscaloosa, AL: University of Alabama Press, 2004.

Odgers, George. *Air War against Japan 1943–1945*, vol. 2. In *Australia in the War of 1939–1945*, series 3: Air. Canberra: Australian War Memorial, 1957.

Office of the Assistant Chief of Air Staff, Intelligence. *Air Objective Folder No. 83.4: Canton Area, China*. Washington D.C., 1943.

Office of Naval Records and History, Office of the Chief of Naval Operations, Navy Department, *Glossary of U.S. Naval Abbreviations* (OPNAV 29-P1000), 5th edition, Washington D.C.: Government Printing Office, 1949.

Parillo, Mark P. *The Japanese Merchant Marine in World War II*. Annapolis, MD: Naval Institute Press, 1993.

Redwood, Mabel Winifred. *It Was Like This…* Oxford, UK: ISIS Publishing, 2002.

Reeves, John Pownall. *The Lone Flag: Memoir of the British Consul in Macao during World War II*. Edited by Colin Day and Richard Garrett. Hong Kong: Hong Kong University Press, 2014.

Research and Analysis Section of Combat Intelligence. *Canton–Hong Kong Black Book*. Headquarters United States Forces, China Theater, August 10, 1945.

Reynolds, Clark G. *The Fast Carriers: The Forging of an Air Navy*. Annapolis, MD: Naval Institute Press, 1968.

Ride, Edwin. *British Army Aid Group: Hong Kong Resistance, 1942–1945*. Hong Kong: Oxford University Press, 1981.

Roland, Charles G. *Long Night's Journey into Day: Prisoners of War in Hong Kong and Japan, 1941–1945*. Waterloo, ON: Wilfrid Laurier University Press, 2001.

———. "Massacre and Rape in Hong Kong: Two Case Studies Involving Medical Personnel and Patients." *Journal of Contemporary History* 32, no. 1 (January 1997): 43–61.

Rollo, Dennis. *The Guns and Gunners of Hong Kong*. Hong Kong: Gunners' Roll of Hong Kong, n.d.

Schultz, Duane. *The Last Battle Station: The Story of the USS* Houston. New York: St. Martin's Press, 1985.

Scott, James M. *Rampage: MacArthur, Yamashita, and the Battle of Manila*. New York: W.W. Norton, 2018.

———. *The War Below: The Story of Three Submarines that Battled Japan*. New York: Simon and Schuster, 2013.

Sewell, William G. *Strange Harmony*. London: Edinburgh House Press, 1947.

Sherrod, Robert. *History of Marine Corps Aviation in World War II*. Washington D.C.: Combat Forces Press, 1952.

Smith, Colin. *Singapore Burning: Heroism and Surrender in World War II*. New York: Penguin, 2006.

Snow, Philip. *The Fall of Hong Kong: Britain, China, and the Japanese Occupation*. New Haven, CT: Yale University Press, 2003.

Somers, Paul M. *Lake Michigan's Aircraft Carriers*. Charleston, SC: Arcadia Publishing, 2003.

Stark, Norman P. *A WWII F6F Navy Fighter Pilot's Experiences in the Pacific*. Edited by Sanford Alexandra Stark. Blurb.com self-publishing, 2012.

Steere, Edward and Thayer M. Boardman. *Final Disposition of World War II Dead, 1945–51*. QMC Historical Studies, series II, no. 4. Washington D.C.: Historical Branch, Office of the Quartermaster General, 1957.

Stericker, John. *Captive Colony: The Story of Stanley Camp, Hong Kong*. Unpublished manuscript, September 1945.

———. *A Tear for the Dragon*. London: Arthur Barker, 1958.

Stevens, Paul F. *Low Level Liberators: The Story of Patrol Bombing Squadron 104 in the South Pacific during World War II*. Nashville, TN: Paul F. Stevens, 1997.

Stille, Mark. *Imperial Japanese Navy Antisubmarine Escorts, 1941–45*. Oxford, UK: Osprey, 2017.

Sturma, Michael and Hiroyuki Shindo. "Convoy Hi-72: U.S. Submarines versus Japanese Escorts in the Pacific War." *War in History* 27, no. 2 (2020): 271–85.

Sweeney, Mark. "'Representing Canadian Interests in all Matters Relative to Canadian War Dead': Lt. Col. J.A. Bailie and the Recovery, Concentration and Burial of the 'C' Force Casualties in Japan and Hong Kong." *Canadian Military History* 27, no. 1 (2018): article 14.

Thomas, Evan. *Sea of Thunder: Four Commanders and the Last Great Naval Campaign 1941–1945*. New York: Simon and Schuster, 2006.

Thomas, Gerald W. *Torpedo Squadron Four: A Cockpit View of World War II*. Las Cruces, NM: Rio Grande Historical Collections, New Mexico State University, 1990.

Tillman, Barrett. *Clash of the Carriers: The True Story of the Marianas Turkey Shoot of World War II*. New York: NAL Caliber, 2005.

Tillman, Barrett and Henk van der Lugt. *VF-11/111 "Sundowners" 1942–95*. Oxford, UK: Osprey, 2010.

Tobe Ryōichi. "The Japanese Eleventh Army in Central China, 1938–1941." In *The Battle for China: Essays on the Military History of the Sino-Japanese War of 1937–1945*, edited by Mark Peattie, Edward J. Drea, and Hans van den Ven. Stanford, CA: Stanford University Press, 2011, 207–29.

Toll, Ian. *The Conquering Tide: War in the Pacific Islands, 1942–44*. New York: Norton, 2015.

———. *Pacific Crucible: War at Sea in the Pacific, 1941–1942*. New York: Norton, 2012.

———. *Twilight of the Gods: War in the Western Pacific, 1944–1945*. New York: Norton, 2020.

Trimble, William F. *Admiral John S. McCain and the Triumph of Naval Air Power*. Annapolis, MD: Naval Institute Press, 2019.

Turner, Peggy Seiz and Rolf Turner. *Red Wing to Hong Kong*. Sauk Rapids, MN: Popple Creek AIR, 2012.

United Nations War Crimes Commission. "Case No. 33: Trial of General Tanaka Hisakasu and Five Others, United States Military Commission, Shanghai, 13th August–3rd September, 1946." In *Law Reports of Trials of War Criminals*, vol. 5, 66–81. London: His Majesty's Stationery Office, 1948.

United States Air Force, Historical Division. *Air-Sea Rescue 1941–1952*. U.S. Air Force Historical Study 95. Air University, 1953.

United States Pacific Command, CINCPAC–CINCPOA. *United States Pacific Fleet and Pacific Ocean Areas: Air Target Maps and Photos: China Coast, Ningpo to Canton (A.T.F. No. 152A–44)*. N.p., 1944.

United States Strategic Bombing Survey. *The Fifth Air Force in the War against Japan*. Washington D.C.: Military Analysis Division, 1947.

———. *Interrogations of Japanese Officials*, vols. I and II (OPNAV-P–03-100). Washington D.C.: Government Printing Office, 1946.

———. *The War against Japanese Transportation, 1941–1945*. Washington D.C.: Transportation Division, 1947.

Ward, Robert S. *Hong Kong under Japanese Occupation: A Case Study in the Enemy's Techniques of Control*. Washington D.C.: Department of Commerce, 1943.

Whitfield, Andrew J. *Hong Kong, Empire and the Anglo-American Alliance at War, 1941–1945*. Hong Kong: Hong Kong University Press, 2001.

Williams, Michael. "*Amatsukaze*: A Destroyer's Struggle." In *Warship 2018*, edited by John Jordan and Stephen Dent, 174–89. Oxford, UK: Osprey, 2018.

Winslow, Walter G. *The Fleet the Gods Forgot: The U.S. Asiatic Fleet in World War II*. Annapolis, MD: Naval Institute Press, 1982.

———. *The Ghost that Died at Sunda Strait*. Annapolis, MD: Naval Institute Press, 1984.

Winton, John. *The Forgotten Fleet: The British Navy in the Pacific*. New York: Coward-McCann, 1970.

Wong Suk Har. "Disused Air Raid Precaution Tunnels: Uncovering the Underground History of World War II, Civil Defense Tunnels in Hong Kong." MA thesis, University of Hong Kong, 2010.

Wright-Nooth, George and Mark Adkin. *Prisoner of the Turnip Heads: The Fall of Hong Kong and Imprisonment by the Japanese.* London: Cassell, 1999.

Y'Blood, Willam T. *The Little Giants: U.S. Escort Carriers against Japan.* Annapolis, MD: Naval Institute Press, 1987.

Yenne, Bill. *MacArthur's Air Force: American Airpower over the Pacific and the Far East, 1941–51.* Oxford, UK: Osprey, 2019.

Zhang Tianshu. "The Fall of the Tigers of Hong Kong: Chinese War Crimes Trials of Three Japanese Governors of Hong Kong." In *Historical War Crimes Trials in Asia*, edited by Liu Daqun and Zhang Binxin. Brussels: Torkel Opsahl Academic EPublisher, 2016, 193–230.

Index